The River Scene is a uniquely stimulating guide to the appreciation and preservation of rivers. In this highly illustrated account, S.M. Haslam presents a new scheme for the evaluation of river quality which can be carried out by a wide range of users.

The book presents an overview of river ecology, looking first at the natural environment – river structure, inhabitants, classification and pollution or other damage. This is followed by a discussion of the cultural environment, the importance of which is often overlooked: the history, archaeology, and social and legal contexts of rivers.

Dr Haslam is a leading international authority on rivers and their vegetation. By understanding the natural and cultural environments of rivers and applying the methods she describes, our awareness and appreciation of these beautiful resources can be greatly enhanced, and their conservation for the future aided.

The River Scene

Ecology and cultural heritage

The River Scene

Ecology and Cultural Heritage

S.M. HASLAM M.A., SC.D.

Department of Plant Sciences
University of Cambridge
England

with contributions from
DR J. PURSEGLOVE & DR G.A. WAIT

CAMBRIDGE
UNIVERSITY PRESS

PUBLISHED BY THE PRESS SYNDICATE OF THE UNIVERSITY OF CAMBRIDGE
The Pitt Building, Trumpington Street, Cambridge CB2 1RP, United Kingdom

CAMBRIDGE UNIVERSITY PRESS
The Edinburgh Building, Cambridge CB2 2RU, United Kingdom
40 West 20th Street, New York, NY 10011-4211, USA
10 Stamford Road, Oakleigh, Victoria 3166, Australia

First published 1997

Printed in the United Kingdom at the University Press, Cambridge

Typeset in 11 point Quadraat

A catalogue record for this book is available from the British Library

Library of Congress Cataloguing in Publication data

Haslam, S.M. (Sylvia Mary), 1934–
The river scene : ecology and cultural heritage / S.M. Haslam;
with contributions from J. Purseglove & G.A. Wait.
        p.   cm.
Includes bibliographical references (p.   ) and index.
ISBN 0 521 57410 2 (hc)
1. Stream ecology. 2. Rivers. I. Purseglove, J.W. (John William), 1912–   .
II. Wait, G.A. (Gerald A.) III. Title.
QH541.5.S7H38 1997
574.5'26323–DC20   96–44832 CIP

ISBN 0 521 57410 2 hardback

To

Tina Bone, Desktop Publisher

the quality of whose work for the author over the years is shown by this book,

and

Dr R.G. Sweeting, National Rivers Authority

whose idea it was that I should write it

Contents

Part III The Cultural Environment

Preface

This book is intended to help biologists, naturalists, students, landscape architects and other environmentalists to understand rivers. It aims to give a wide view, and an overview. It is also for specialists in one aspect of rivers who wish to learn, reasonably painlessly, something of other aspects, and for those engaged in high-level surveys who wish to learn more of the background of what they are doing. It is not a Restoration Handbook: readers will be able to say 'this is wrong', but will have to go to elsewhere to learn how to wield the JCB or plant the willow wands. A much greater emphasis than usual is placed on the cultural history of our rivers: they have been used directly and indirectly by people with increasing intensity for over two millennia, and the social or historical ecology is as valid and valuable as the natural ecology.

This book stresses the interpretation and illumination which can be gained solely by looking at rivers, and without the use of specialist equipment. It therefore concentrates on water, structure, vegetation, pollution, birds, artefacts, etc., omitting the equally fascinating fields of invertebrates, fish, chemistry, diatoms, other algae and micro-organisms. Much use is made of pictures, as these can be studied at many levels, and show features from general topography to the effects of drought. Readers interested in the subject should return to these, after the first reading, to acquire more knowledge. The pictures are not solely British: they demonstrate a wider range.

Invertebrates are the main group of organisms used for river study, and are likely to remain so, with the BMWP, TBI, Chandler Score, etc., indices for pollution monitoring, RIVPACS for a more ecological approach, and methods from Watch (Wildlife Trusts), the Field Studies Council, etc., for 'pond (or river) dipping'. There are plenty of standard methods easily available, so they are not repeated here. The use of vegetation for pollution monitoring is government-accepted, but is unlikely to replace the use of invertebrates (if only because of the extent of existing historical data). There are two schemes for classification of vegetation, that by Holmes (1983) and that by Haslam & Wolseley (1981) and Haslam (1987). The former uses species present, using a key, the latter, the communities characteristics of physiographic habitats. Naturally, the two schemes overlap. The schemes can be used by non-zoologists, and as a complementary tool to the use of invertebrates.

There are several high-level river survey classification methods: that from the former National Rivers Authority (river habitat survey) now the Environment Agency; SERCON (system of evaluating rivers for conservation value); that from the Royal Society for the Protection of Birds; and those developed by various County Trusts, etc. Each has been designed for different purposes and has different strengths. That at the end of this book is not intended to compete but to check on the degree of understanding achieved. Readers may use it, or omit it and go straight to one of the others, as wished, for natural ecology. No other method covers cultural ecology.

This book may be read either as a whole, or for one or two subjects at a time. Chapter 6 (pollution monitoring) depends on Chapters 4 (vegetation) and 5 (pollution), but otherwise each chapter can be studied separately.

Dr R.G. Sweeting of the National Rivers Authority asked me to write this book and opened to me a new field of interest in rivers. I hope the finished work interests readers as much, and meets Dr Sweeting's wishes.

Grateful thanks for information, permission to cite, checking or testing go to:

Mrs M. Alvarez, Mrs Y. Bower, Dr J. Cadbury, Miss E. Chapman, Ms E. Cranston, Mr A. Driver, Mrs M.P. Everitt, Dr N. Haycock, Miss J. Hollam, Mrs S.M. Hornsey, Dr J. Purseglove, Dr D. Ward, Mrs P.A. Wolseley, the National Rivers Authority, Reading. Mrs Bower drew most of the figures in Haslam (1990, 1991) and the complex ones new to this book, and Mrs Wolseley, those in Haslam (1978), Haslam & Wolseley (1981), and Haslam (1987). The use of their illustrations is much appreciated, as are Mrs Tina Bone's typing and preparation of script and her new (more straightforward) figures.

Permission to use copyright material was kindly given by Mrs Baird, Belhaven Press (now John Wiley), The Broads Authority, the Syndics of Cambridge University Library, Cambridge University Press, Cambridgeshire Collection, The Master and Fellows of St Catharine's College, Cambridge, Cobden of Cambridge Press, Council of Europe, Field Studies Council, Dr B. Lachat, National River Authority (River Habitat Survey), Oxford Archaeology Unit, Oxford University Press, Mr D. Pannett, Dr J. Purseglove. Crown Copyright is reproduced with the permission of the Controller of HMSO.

Dr G. Wait contributed Chapter 11, and Dr J. Purseglove, the information for Chapter 12: many thanks.

The preparation expenses of this book were paid by the Lankelly Foundation, which has my very sincere gratitude.

1 INTRODUCTION: the river habitat

The river environment

The river environment can be divided into three parts:

Water

It is the presence of water, flowing water, which makes a river.

The water should be of a QUANTITY and QUALITY PROPER TO THE RIVER TYPE. WATER: the ESSENTIAL ELEMENT (Chapter 2).

The Natural Environment

This is around and in the water (or former water area), and is composed of non-living and living features.

1 The river characters, living and non-living, should be PROPER TO THE LOCALITY.

2 DIVERSITY should be HIGH.

3 POLLUTION should be LOW.

The natural environment is here divided into:

RIVER STRUCTURE and its damage (Chapter 3).

RIVER TYPES in relation to vegetation (Chapter 4).

POLLUTION: altering chemical quality (Chapter 5).

ASSESSING the effect of POLLUTION and other interferences, using vegetation (macrophytes) (Chapter 6).

RIVER STRUCTURE FOR LARGER ANIMALS (Chapter 7).

DEVELOPMENT: ENHANCEMENT, IMPROVEMENT AND GEOMORPHOLOGY (Chapter 8).

LAW AND PLANNING (Chapter 9), (for the natural environment).

Cultural Heritage

This can be around and in the water (or former water area).

It is the signs of the use of the river by people from the present back to remote antiquity, water for domestic and industrial supply, power, food, transport, waste disposal, ornament, recreation, healing, and its place in town and village planning and development, and in religion and myth, and recent developments for increased recreation. Aspects of the cultural heritage are:

HISTORIC AND RECENT CULTURAL HERITAGE (Chapter 10).

ARCHAEOLOGICAL HERITAGE (Chapter 11).

RECREATION (Chapter 12).

Finally, the Appendix in this book describes a possible survey and recording method.

FOR THE NATURAL ENVIRONMENT, RIVERS SHOULD BE LIKE THIS:

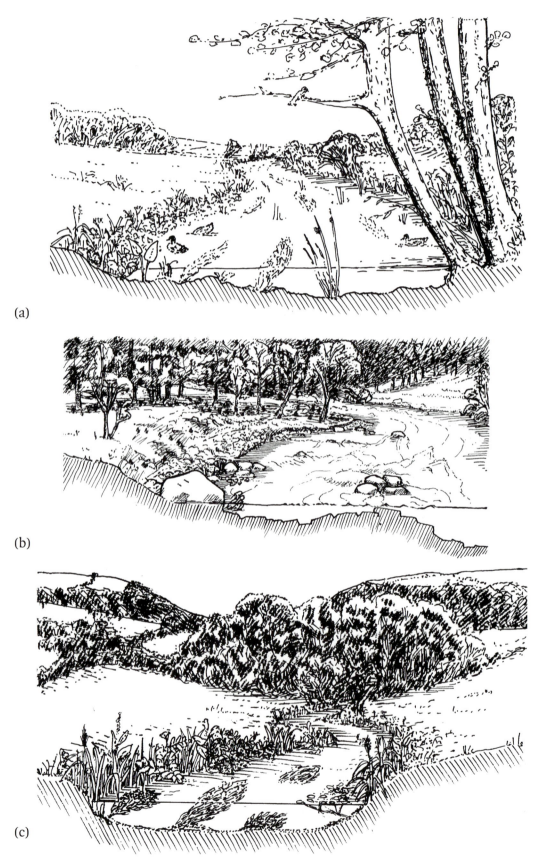

(a)

(b)

(c)

Rivers should have much diversity in their architecture. Architecture is composed of physical structure and vegetation, and either or neither may be the more important ((a), Haslam, 1990; (b), (c), Haslam, 1987).

NOT LIKE THIS:

Rivers should not be over-channelled, over-dried, over-drained, over-dredged or over-disturbed ((a),(e), Haslam, 1990;(c), (d), Haslam, 1991).

FOR THE CULTURAL HERITAGE, RIVERS SHOULD BE LIKE THIS:

Rivers with ancient patterns, developing features, or enhancement. The river remains a focal point ((a)–(e), Haslam, 1991).

NOT LIKE THIS:

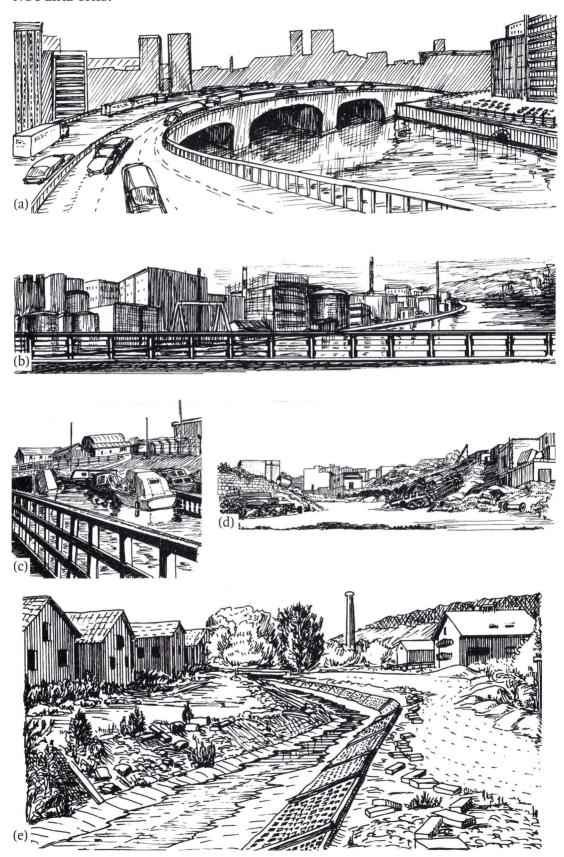

The river and river environment are of little or no interest to inhabitants and planners ((a), (b), Haslam, 1990; (c), (d), (e), Haslam, 1991).

Introduction to the book

There is an increasing wish to have rivers as places of beauty and interest. Many now seek a working knowledge in aspects of river conservation, to understand the streams they see at home, and away, and to foster high-quality, valuable rivers. This book attempts to supply that need. Uses and evaluations conflict: a river can be in a good state simultaneously for cleanliness, otters and wigeon, but not also and at the same site, for moorhen, industrial archaeology, recreational amenity and ornament. Therefore, different elements are assessed separately and the river is finally described in terms of its value for each element. A site may have value for many, one or no features.

A FLEXIBLE MIND IS NEEDED WHEN CONSIDERING RIVER HABITATS. One place may, with safety, convenience and propriety, have an active, mobile stream with no danger or damage to man, beast or property law. In another this may be quite unsuitable, but coverts could be planted for otters. Almost every small reach of river should be of high quality for some facet of river life or cultural heritage.

River systems, waters, banks and the land beside cross and link land habitats. They form corridors with moving water. The water moves in only one direction, downstream, but mobile or bank animals and plants can move up and down stream.

Rivers are a changing system: over years, decades, centuries, they change in position, bank, bed, water and community. That they change is therefore to be expected. The way they change, particularly under human impact, is to be watched with care. The little-managed river has a diverse physical structure, varying on the small scale with flow, water depth, deposition and erosion. These give diversity of flow type, pools and riffles, backwaters and cascades, meanders, silt, sand, gravel and stone, parts stable and unstable, banks and islands. Large-scale variation lies in rocky gorges, flat alluvial plains, cliffs, rolling hills and the many landscape and rock types through which the river flows. Such a physical structure allows diverse communities of plants and animals, from grass swards through nettles and brambles to woods on the edge; and from tall reedy fringes and shallow-water forget-me-nots to water lilies and water-covered hornwort in the channels.

Each species, plant or animal, has its own and distinct habitat requirements, requirements that often partly, but never wholly, overlap with those of other species. Knowing solely a list of the plants or animals present, and knowing the places where each lives, enables the habitat to be known and understood. For example, if a lion and a polar bear are present together, the habitat is a zoo: that is the only place where the habitat ranges of the two overlap. If *Eucalyptus* is found in an (English) oakwood, it has got there somehow from Australia through human activities. The species list of the oakwood is so characteristic that it cannot be found elsewhere. The wood cannot be in Australia: the *Eucalyptus* is the one which does not belong.

River vegetation can be described by (1) **architecture** or pattern, (2) the **number of species present** at any one place, the site diversity, (3) the **amount of channel covered** by the plants (cover in water up to 1 m deep usually), and (4) the **quality of the species**, whether they are typical of nutrient-rich or nutrient-poor places (nutrient status band, 'Colour Band'), whether they are sensitive or tolerant to a given pollution, whether they grow best in swift or still water, etc.

River animal communities can be described similarly but, since animals move, the description is more in terms of number of species, numbers of animals of each species and quality of species. This book is primarily on larger plants, secondarily on birds, for the biota.

Human impact decreases variety (with some exceptions, of e.g. intermittent and mild disturbances). It decreases habitat diversity, and alters chemical quality. It therefore restricts the species which can grow there: the structure, the habitat, for some species is removed (e.g. channelling removes sheltered indentations, and wide gravel bars, from swift hill streams). The species gradually become restricted to those most tolerant of the polluted and uniform channel thus imposed by man. The more habitat-limited, and often rare species may be lost first — most rare species are rare because their habitat requirements are specialised, and occur seldom.

The worst damage to British rivers in the past half-century is:

1 *Loss of water*. Land drainage and abstraction have greatly limited the volume of water available for rivers (and their flood plains). Water has been taken from aquifers (water-bearing rocks) and the land, so less is available to fill the rivers. The rivers have been altered so water speeds quickly to the sea, and less water stays in the rivers.

2 *Loss of physical structure*. Drainage schemes have channelled many lowland, and indeed remarkably many mountain streams, leaving these far too nearly straight, with far too nearly uniform flat beds and uniform 1.5:1 trapezoid banks.

3 *Pollution*. While some of the worst-polluted areas (e.g. the South Wales Coal Streams) have improved since 1965, moderate pollution has spread over the land with the spread of busy roads, new housing, and new industrial estates (bringing pollutants other than sewage to rivers previously receiving only sewage). Fertilisers, biocides and farm spills have compounded the damage.

Rivers are much too unprotected and vulnerable. The loss of water to the nation, and the loss of wildlife and cultural heritage, have become unacceptable. Other river interests, drainage, flood protection, waste disposal, recreation, fisheries have wealthy interests to speak for them – and to cause further damage. River integrity has no one to speak for it: unless the Environment Agency undertakes this difficult, nationally valuable, and life-enhancing task. It is important to know that the CONSERVATION OF RIVER LIFE AND OF LANDSCAPE FEATURES AROUND RIVERS DO NOT NECESSARILY ALTER THE EFFICIENCY OF A DRAINAGE SCHEME.

It is useful to read seventeenth- and eighteenth-century descriptions of river yields, of the thousands upon thousands of fish and birds cropped. Rivers did, and should again, bear such. To support these, invertebrates and plants need to have grown even more abundantly. (Note, plants used to be much-grazed: hence the nuisance caused now, when human impact has removed the grazers.)

Legal and safety note

Modified from Methods for the Examination of Water and Associated Materials *(HMSO series)*.

There may sometimes be legal limitations on going near rivers, but these can usually be complied with if permission is obtained in advance.

The provisions of the Wildlife and Countryside Act 1981, its updates, the Health and Safety at Work ... Act 1979 (with its subsequent Management of Health and Safety at Work Regulations, 1992), the corresponding Scottish and Northern Ireland legislation, all National and Local Safety Regulations, and all laws and regulations with regard to trespass and rights of access must be observed.

Care needs to be taken if plants are removed, not only to comply with the law (which prohibits removal of rooted material) and with local requirements, but also not to cause permanent denudation or erosion of the bed, or to disturb breeding fauna.

A few riverside plants are highly poisonous, such as giant hogweed and hemlock water dropwort. It is wise to know what these few look like and to treat them with care if met.

Care may also be needed in some localities to guard against bacterial and parasitic infection and chemical contamination (THINK BEFORE PUTTING UNGUARDED HANDS IN WATER), pathogenic fungal spores, plants with toxic or vesicant parts and harmful wildlife, nor must it be forgotten that exceedingly dangerous compounds ranging from toxic wastes, to inflammable oils, high explosives and white phosphorous, have been found in both bank and river bed deposits (IF YOU DO NOT KNOW WHAT IT IS, DO NOT TOUCH IT) and that flammable gases such as methane and phosphorines; alkyl mercury and arsenic; and compounds such as chloromethyl sulphonium salts can be synthesised by natural organisms. Proper protective clothing and first aid equipment should be used when necessary.

Polluted river water may give skin rashes, headaches, nausea, vomiting, diarrhoea, fevers short and long (starting anything from a few hours to two weeks after exposure), and other similar ills. Weils Disease (leptospirosis), carried in the urine (mainly but not only) of rats, is of course associated with the presence of rats rather than of sewage treatment works, so can occur in areas of supposedly quite clean water. This is a 'flu' starting three to 19 days after exposure, typically with cramps, especially in the calves. If Weils Disease is suspected, ANTIBIOTIC TREATMENT MUST BE GIVEN BY THE DOCTOR AT ONCE, as this illness is sometimes fatal. Treatment should not wait on the results of tests, if these take over a few hours. (At the time of writing, 1993, a quick test is expected soon.)

The Canoe Club keep their members informed of known trouble, and should be consulted.

2 WATER: the essential element

For water quality see Chapters 5 and 6
(no specialist expertise required)

SUMMARY

For their survival, streams need adequate water. Water shortage is due to drainage, abstraction and drought. Reference water depths, etc. are supplied, and Fig. 2.12 demonstrates standard shallowing patterns of vegetation in smaller streams. Vegetation is very sensitive to, i.e. very dependent on, habitat conditions, so it can be used, for example, to assess these. An outline is given of stream patterning, abstraction and regulation. Many small streams have been lost since 1900.

Introduction

Without water, the river perishes. So do the crops and the people. Until recently, water has been so abundant that the ultimate in extravagance was to spend money like water. Now it is becoming scarce, and so of increasing monetary, as well as other, value. The population is increasing, so more domestic water is required. The water demand per person is also increasing. This increasing demand (e.g. 150 l/day/person) results in increased removal from aquifer, spring and river, a removal greater than the natural replenishment, overall. Water is taken by the increased drainage of the land, lowering ground water level, drying the sponge that hitherto buffered the earth against most droughts, and yet further water is taken to irrigate in the summer the land thus drained. There is no balanced water budget. There is a demand to remove and remove and hope for more rain. This should be rectified.

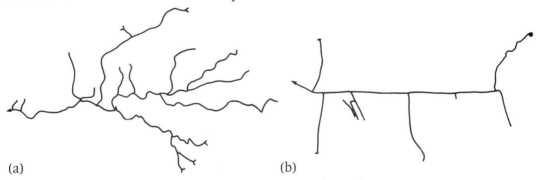

(a) (b)

Fig. 2.1. Drainage, loss of streams. (a) Undrained, (b) drained (Haslam, 1987).

In lowlands, and regrettably increasingly in hills, the upper brooks marked on 1:250 000 maps often carry none but storm water, especially in farmed land. If modern large-scale maps are compared with those drawn pre-1940 (even more, those pre-1900), a staggering number of brooks will be found gone. Streams have perished, to the detriment of both natural and cultural environments, and to the future maintenance of water resources. For long centuries, and rightly, the pressure has been to remove water: to prevent flood, to prevent disease to man and beast, to increase crop yield. The pendulum has now swung too far towards drought, with its even greater potential danger. The danger signs are here in Fig. 2.2. The valley is farmed. Only the distant bridge and the water channel at the side show that here was once a running river.

Fig. 2.2. A dried river in southern Europe (Haslam, 1991).

The river in Fig. 2.3 is still redeemable. There is a bed. It can be re-used if water is returned (the operative phrase – **is returned**). It is only when there is too much human removal of water that minor droughts are major predicaments.

Stream water comes from:

1 *Springs*, where water rises from below to the land surface. Many upper-level springs are now dry, or flow for less time than before. Even lower ones may flow less. Spring water stabilises streams, stabilising discharge (flow type, water depth, scour) and so substrate, and also temperature. Stream habitat alters when this influence is reduced.

2 *Run-off*. Rain falling on the land may be evaporated to the air, or may sink to an aquifer below, but some (and where subsoil and rock are impervious, much) runs off to the river, moving through the soil into which it is absorbed, and, in heavy rain, also running above the earth.

The more that can be stored in the earth, the slower and less violent the effect of

Fig. 2.3. A river, from England, that is redeemable if water is returned (Haslam, 1978).

storms. Flash floods increase with decreased storage: when land is farmed, when it is intensively farmed, when hedges and ditches are lost, when it is built up and covered by tarmac. In built-up areas rain runs straight off, giving a massive, short-lived, high discharge. In wood and bog, much rain is absorbed, release to the river being usually slow and over many days.

The steeper the landscape, the greater the force of the run-off and the stream flow.

The effect of run-off thus varies with rainfall quantity and distribution, with rock, subsoil and soil type, with vegetation type and land use, and with topography.

3 *Effluent from sewage treatment works* (STWs), and from other sources. STW effluents tend to run fairly steadily, and so have, like springs, a stabilising effect on flow parameters, substrate type and temperature. However, while the 'spring effect' is native to the stream, the 'effluent effect' skews it from its proper habitat in these ways, as well as altering the chemical composition of the water (pollution). Most STW effluents enter in middle and lower reaches, returning to the lower river, water which has been prevented from flowing in the upper river. Some rivers, though, now rise and have their beginnings with STW effluent – and that, also, is hardly desirable!

There are other man-made ways of keeping running those rivers which no longer have the ground water to supply them: pumping up water, and lining beds to prevent water draining to the now-distant water table being two of them. Both indicate a deplorable over-use of resources, and it is that over-use which should be remedied, rather than the carrying out of short-term 'Elastoplast' measures.

It is tragic, in the proper sense of it being a doleful or dreadful tale, a disastrous calamity, that Britain's water is being thus lost.

Reference water depths and flow types

Depths less than those given in Table 2.1 should cause concern, as should river systems constantly in the shallower ends of the ranges. Drainage reduces, and is intended to reduce, water quantity. Depths may be increased by storms, controls, narrowing channels (for a given discharge), receiving water transfers and effluents, winding of channels (frequently) and some other alterations. They may be decreased by abstraction and land drainage, including channel straightening, and some other alterations.

Table 2.1. Summer waters. Reference summer water depths and flow types as occurring in the 1970s, when levels were sub-adequate

Stream type[1]		Depth (cm) Stream size[2]				Flow type (not storm)[3] Stream size		
Landscape	Rock, etc.	(i)	(ii)	(iii)	(iv)	(ii)	(iii)	(iv)
Lowland and plain	*Limestone* (soft)	0–10	30–40	30–75	75+	(mod)	mod	mod–slow
	Clay	0–20	20–30	30–75	75+	slow–mod.	slow(+)	slow
	Sandstone, typical	0–20	20–30	30–75	–	mod–slow	slow–mod	–
	New Forest	0–20	20–40	30–100	–	mod–slow	mod–slow	–
	Caithness	30+	40+	50+	deep	slow+	slow–mod	(mod)
	Alluvium	–	50+	50+	deep	slow	slow	slow
	Resistant, bog	(10)	20–30	50–75	deep	slow	mod	swift
	Moor	0–20	20–50	30–75	often deep	(mod)	(mod)	(swift)
	Farmland	10–20	20–40	30–75	–	mod	mod	–
Upland[4]	*Limestone* (hard)	20	20–50	30–75	50+	mod	mod	mod
	Clay	0–20	20–50	30–75	–	mod	(varies)	–
	Coal Measures	10–30	20–40	20–40	50+			
	Sandstone	0–30	20–30	30–75	50+	slow–mod	mod	mod
	Resistant	0–30	20–30	30–60	50+	fast/slow	fast/slow	decrease
Mountain[5]	*Limestone*	10–20	15–30	20–75	50+	rapid and slower		
	Sandstone	10–30	15–40	30–100	75+	rapid and slower		
	Resistant	10–40	20–50	30–100	50+	rapid and slower		
Alpine[6]	*Limestone*	10–20	15–30	20–75	50+	rapid and slower		
	Sandstone	10–30	20 40	30 75|	–	rapid and slower		
	Resistant	20–30	20–40	30–75+	50+	rapid and slower		

[1] See Chapter 4, p. 87, for River Types, Classification A, classed on rock type and landscape categories. Main rock types are shown in italics.

[2] See Table. 4.2, p. 75. Types (i) and (ii) are up to 3 m wide, (ii) being with water-supported species, (iii) 4–8 m, and (iv) 10+ m wide: depth being appropriate.

[3] *Negligible flow*: water hardly moving. *Slow flow*: water obviously moving, water surface calm, trailing plant parts still. *Moderate flow (mod)*: water surface somewhat disturbed, trailing plant parts moving. *Fast flow*: water surface disturbed, trailing plant parts moving vigorously. *Rapid flow/white water (swift)*: water surface broken, much swirling and disturbance. Brackets = probable flows.

[4] Upland rivers are liable to occasional spates washing out vegetation, but in general vegetation is plentiful.

[5] Spate damage frequent, eroding flows, which become slower downstream.

[6] Much fierce flow, turbulent even in indentations at side.

Flow types may be slowed by controls, some channel alterations and, often, drought. They may be made faster by storms, drainage, some channel alterations, and sometimes drought (particularly when the water is very shallow but still running well).

Size (i) and (ii) streams are both up to 3 m wide, (i) being too shallow to bear water-supported species in the given habitat. Drying will therefore reduce a size (ii) to a (i). THEREFORE

SIZE (i) STREAMS SHOULD BE CONSIDERED AS OVER-DRIED SIZE (ii) UNLESS THERE IS EVIDENCE TO THE CONTRARY. Such evidence is that the channel is e.g., a field-ditch, or has very low banks.

Stream patterns

On the map, river systems form patterns, and these patterns differ, one from another. Extremes can be classified as hydrological patterns, as in Fig. 2.4, or on what is typically found in different stream types, as in Fig. 2.5. These can also be partly seen in aerial photographs, which may show some details of the channel (e.g. tributaries too small to be marked on the map, weirs, bank type, tree distribution).

Most rivers have more than one channel, the tributary density varying not just with topography and rock type as shown above, but also with rainfall (in equivalent streams, more tributaries are found in the west than the east coast of Britain), and, very importantly, with land use and drainage.

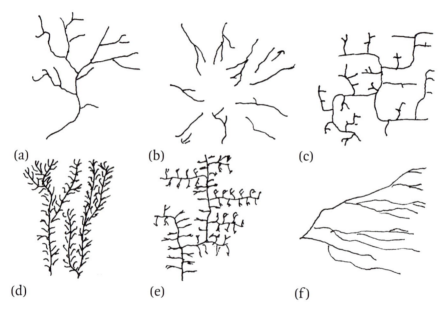

(a)   (b)   (c)

(d)   (e)   (f)

Fig. 2.4. Stream patterns classified hydrologically (re-drawn from Gordon et al., 1992).
(a) Dendritic, (b) radial, (c) rectangular, (d) pinnate, (e) trellis, (f) parallel.

As more tributaries flow into a stream it gets bigger, and streams can be classed on their incoming tributaries, usually as STREAM ORDER (Fig. 2.6). Note that if two of the same order join, the order increases (1+1=2, 2+2=3, 3+3=4), but any number of tributaries of a lower order joining a stream of higher order leave that higher order unchanged (2+1=2, 3+2+2+2=3, 4+3+3+3+3+2+2+2+2+2=4). This is an anomaly, as of course if two of the lesser had joined just before flowing into the main stream, the order would increase (3+2+2+2=3, but if two of the 2 had joined, so 2+2=3, and the whole be 3+3+2, then the final order is 4).

A much worse anomaly, though, has come from land drainage and abstraction. The tributaries to be counted are taken as those shown on a map (1:250 000, 14 or 1:60 000, 1″). This may be fine hydrologically, but is not, ecologically. In the first place in the wetter west and the wetter mountains, the numbers of small rills not shown on the map are vast, in the east and lowlands they are sparse, so the order does not reflect the amount of flowing water habitat. Secondly, once a stream is on the map, it tends to stay there. So in the undrained mountains and moorlands not just marked, but unmarked streams flow all year (except in severe drought), while in the lowlands, many smaller streams are long lost, and the upper reaches of many of those remaining flow only after heavy rain: acting as storm-ditches, in fact. Giving

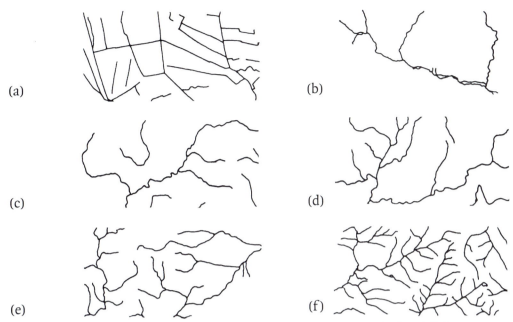

Fig. 2.5. *Stream patterns classified on rock type and topography, modified by land use (all drawn to same scale) (Haslam, 1978). (a) Straight lines, larger dykes and drains in an alluvial plan (fenland). (b) Lowland chalk stream, channels very sparse, some braiding (River Wylye). (c) Lowland (soft) sandstone stream. Denser channels than (b), straightening not excessive (River Tern). (d) Lowland clay stream, denser channels, clay is impervious, and hills are low (River Chelmer). (e) Upland streams, denser again, constricted by hill shape more than by straightening (Welsh Borders). (f) Mountain streams on resistant rock, very dense channels with the high rainfall, steep slopes and impervious rock, close to typical pinnate in Fig. 2.4(d) (Grampian Mountains).*

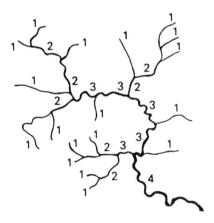

Fig. 2.6. *Stream order (Haslam, 1978).*

stream order – or often, indeed, river pattern – can be misleading in terms of river habitat, and be very misleading if comparing streams from different regions, particularly at the lower levels of stream order and the upstream end of river patterns.

Streams usually get larger as they flow downstream (due to tributaries, to catchment run-off, and incoming effluents), so river length, catchment length or, including tributary area, catchment size and pattern can also be used to describe habitat. These also need care in interpretation, particularly when making comparisons.

Traditionally, water has been held up, ponded, by frequent controls (weirs, dams, sluices, hatches, locks, etc.) in various stream types, particularly in lowland clay rivers, where the ponding was often near-continuous, one weir spilling into the ponded reach of the next. Slow impeded flow is thus now the 'proper' flow for those clay streams, and indeed deeper slower areas in many other types, including chalkstreams, and various hill streams, were traditional habitat for the appropriate plants and animals. Streams without these are therefore skewed from what the conservationist considers the proper water regime.

Rivers 'navigable' for power-boats are now ponded (impounded), with slow deep water (except after heavy storms), and this can also be noted.

The summer water values given in Table 2.1 describe what is actually found. The discharge values recorded by the Environment Agency describe (usually) what is passing through the gauge, gauges being intermittent on larger rivers, and found near the base of some smaller ones. The gauge figures are accurate for the sites of the gauges, and are available over past years and decades, to assess river flows both seasonally and annually. It may be helpful to have and use these when doing intensive river studies. Even if the investigation includes monthly flow type and depth records, it is unlikely to continue for more than a few years, and certainly will not acquire retrospective readings back to 1960!

Water regime depends on: the gradient of the (long) profile of the river from its source to its mouth (the steeper, the greater the erosive power); the rock type, its permeability and the management of the land through which it flows; and the climate, with its variation within the year and between years. Figs. 2.7 and 2.8 show part of this pattern. Since limestone dissolves, rivers on limestone may be particularly concave in the long profile.

Looking up the discharge pattern helps elucidate river ecology. In particular, it is important to know the occurrence of spates, whether from observation or the literature. Spates are fierce storm flows, normally restricted to the hills, increasing in frequency and severity the steeper the landscape (to simplify!).

Intermittent very fierce flows are destructive in a way continuously swift ones are not. Species adapted to frequent spates must re-grow rapidly from fragments – and be able to remain in the habitat as fragments. Species adapted to continuously swift flows are stream-lined in shape, or shelter behind boulders, etc. Some species tolerate both habitats, others one or other (Table 2.2).

Table 2.2 Plant species tolerating fast flow, and those tolerating intermittent spates

Species occurring more often in continuously fast flow:
Ceratophyllum demersum (non–rooted) (pools), *Nuphar lutea, Sagittaria sagittifolia, Sparganium emersum* and Fringing herbs (short bushy emergents, here growing at the sides).

Species occurring more often with intermittent spates:
Elodea canadensis, Lemna minor agg., *Polygonum amphibium, Potamogeton crispus, Ranunculus* spp., *Sparganium erectum, Enteromorpha* sp.

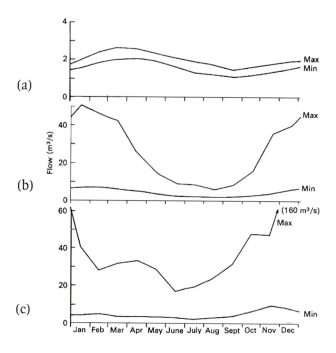

Fig. 2.7. *Seasonal changes in flow patterns (Haslam, 1978). Maximum and minimum mean flow values. (a) Chalk stream. Much spring water, and very porous rock. The summer evapotranspiration and the increased rainfall in winter make only a small difference, as so do (normal) variations in annual rainfall (River Lambourn). (b) Mainly clay lowland stream. No springs and non-porous rock, so the flow depends greatly on summer evapotranspiration and on rainfall and is more variable, and more seasonally variable, than in (a) (River Great Ouse). (c) Mountain river on resistant rock. No springs and impermeable rock, rainfall more unstable and evapotranspiration less than in (b), so flow as variable but less seasonally stable than in (b).*

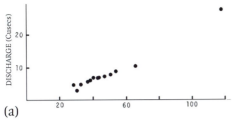

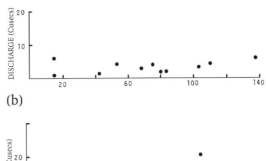

(a)

(b)

Fig. 2.8. *Discharge in relation to rainfall in three British rivers (Haslam, 1987). Each dot represents the figures for one month (for 1966). (a) Lowland hilly resistant rock stream. Discharge directly dependent on rainfall (River Ython). (b) Lowland sandstone stream. Little relationship (River Wey). (c) Lowland chalk stream, mainly spring-fed so discharge largely independent of immediate rainfall (River Kennet).*

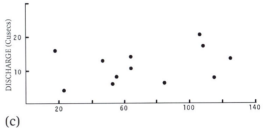

(c)

Abstraction

Water is abstracted from rivers, or from aquifers thus preventing it reaching rivers, over most of lowland and parts of highland Britain. It is abstracted for mains supplies for domestic and industrial use, for farming and directly by some industries, especially mining, and for golf courses. Abstraction from wells for house or farm use is little compared with these. The extent can only be seen when totalling the figures for a region. There is also seasonal variation: most agricultural abstraction is wanted in mid- and late-summer, for instance. Some of the abstraction points may be found in the field or from aerial photographs (Fig. 2.9). Most can be found from official sources. Some abstracted water is returned to the river, as effluent.

(a)

(b)

(d)

(c)

Fig. 2.9. *Abstraction (Haslam, 1991). (a) Abstraction by pump in tractor for sprayer, (b) from borehole, (c) from river by pump in shed, (d) by bucket, (e) from river bed, (f) from borehole, (g) from borehole by pump in house.*

Fig. 2.9 (cont.)

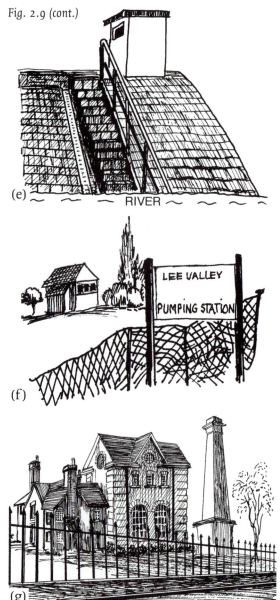

(e)

(f)

(g)

Regulation

Water demand in parts of the country has far exceeded local water supply, and for this reason, and to prevent flooding, many rivers have their flow controlled (Fig. 2.10). In a sense this is true of all British rivers, since all have their flow altered by humans, but it is most particularly in the hill rivers near populated parts that regulation is done, taking control over as much of the flow as possible, lessening peaks of flood flows, and raising depths of drought flow. The effects of this on discharge are straightforward and easy to obtain (Fig. 2.11). Reservoirs have been constructed on many, especially hill rivers. Old-type reservoirs affect flow for some way downstream, new-type ones may be part of the overall regulation of the river.

In addition, water may be moved from one river to another, to enable supplies to reach towns well away from a hill reservoir. These are known as water transfers. The water chemistry of the incoming water differs from that of the indigenous river, though not as much as do STW effluents also reaching each river. Discharge is decreased in the donor river below the transfer point, and increased in the recipient one. The incoming water will flow reasonably steadily, adding to the stability of the recipient, and to the instability of the (lower) donor river.

In the natural river, flow highs and lows depend on the weather, and respond immediately on the hard rocks, but with a delay on the aquifers where the rain feeds the aquifer as well as the river. Consequently, particularly in those large hill rivers where regulation is most common, the effect of high spate flows, and of droughts, is lessened by the regulation. High flash or spate flows have been much increased by human activities. The speed of water running off hills is much faster from concrete, bare soil, slopes not broken by hedges, etc.

Similarly, land drainage has largely removed the 'sink' of water on the land and so increases the effects of drought. Regulation therefore counteracts these extra effects of man on discharge. It is likely to do more, and make the flow more even than it ever was in the past. Over

Fig. 2.10. Reservoirs (Haslam, 1991). (a) Reservoir wall seen from below, (b) drying reservoir seen from above. (Older ones over-spill, newer ones have more control over outflow.)

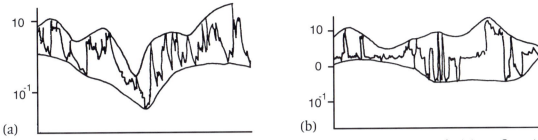

Fig. 2.11. Change in discharge after regulation (River Clwedog) (Haslam, 1987). Maximum and minimum flows. (a) Before regulation, with strong winter peak and summer low, and much variation between maximum and minimum. (b) After regulation. Discharge much more stable.

millennia, plants and animals have adapted to river habitats, and altering flow pattern enough to alter the populations of any given river is causing damage to that river.

Information on flows and regulation best comes from the Environment Agency and its predecessors National Rivers Authority, Water Authority, and the Scottish Environment Protection Agency and its predecessor River Purification Board publications, etc.

Shallowing and vegetation

Whether shallowing is due to drainage, abstraction or drought, the vegetation reacts the same way.

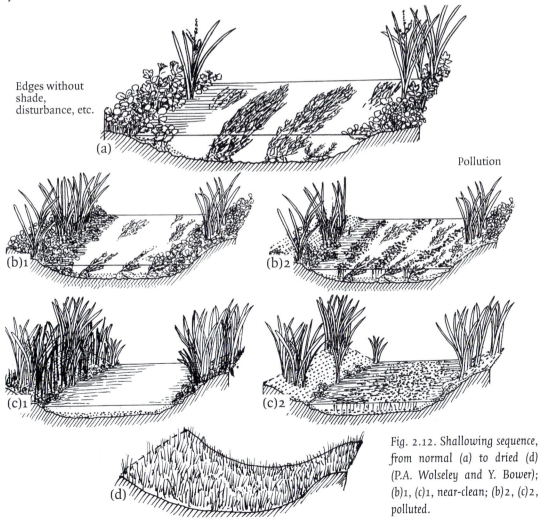

Fig. 2.12. Shallowing sequence, from normal (a) to dried (d) (P.A. Wolseley and Y. Bower); (b)1, (c)1, near-clean; (b)2, (c)2, polluted.

The top part of Fig. 2.12 shows the 'good community' (see also Chapters 3 and 4), represented as with water *c*. 50 cm deep, with vegetation appropriate to that depth in a limestone (or part-limestone) stream. The bottom part of Fig. 2.12 shows the dried stream, grass-covered, but redeemable if water returns – and quickly redeemable if water returns while the water plant propagules in the soil are still alive. The intermediate stages are separated, with clean or near-clean water to the left, more polluted water to the right. The clean-water pattern shows water-supported species disappearing (this happens while the water space is still adequate to house them), and edge species increasing, first short ones like the Fringing herbs, then (habitat permitting) tall ones like the *Sparganium erectum* here depicted. As long as edge species can develop, species diversity will be maintained in the earlier stages: species enter the fringe habitat, and leave the centre. These new species are from the same species assemblage, i.e. species ordinarily found somewhere in a 1 km reach will now all occur in, perhaps, 100 m, in the ordinary way (excluding channel disturbance, etc.).

DIVERSITY AS EXPECTED, (CHEMICAL) QUALITY AS EXPECTED, CHANNEL COVER DOWN EQUALS WATER LOSS (see Chapters 4 and 6 for further explanation).

As the stream dries more, shallowed-damage becomes obvious, and the aquatic species gradually disappear. On the right of Fig. 2.12, blanket weed (long filamentous algae) becomes abundant. Blanket weed is characteristic of pollution (also of mild pollution plus disturbance, and ephemeral habitats in some hill streams). It will probably have been present, but sparser, before shallowing, but the loss of water concentrates the pollution and increases the blanket weed. (The stream here depicted is too shallow for the other pollution-favoured macrophyte, *Potamogeton pectinatus*.) With pollutants building up in soil and water, vegetation will be less than in the cleaner habitat (apart from the blanket weed).

Fig. 2.13. Species movement (Y. Bower). (a) **Stable.** *Plants leave. Plants of same species enter (with suitcases and happy faces). Other species kept out (on bank, sad faces).* (b) **Deepening.** *Plants leave. Plants of same species do not (often) come in. Other species enter.*

In the 1975–76 drought, smaller streams were overwhelmingly in the cleaner (left hand) mode. In the 1990–92 drought, with the spread of rural pollution (from motorways, farm effluents, industrial estates and many more besides), the polluted (right hand) mode was all too frequent. Even without drought, streams in the shallowed state are spreading, and rapidly.

Some stream types, particularly winterbournes, have natural fluctuations between dry and wet (even if the dry periods have increased in recent decades). Here one summer may show a grassed depression (Fig. 2.12, bottom), the next a good stream, able to bear good vegetation (Fig. 2.12, top). When communities have developed over time with such fluctuations, the plants are of strains able to tolerate these, and the complete aquatic community is restored very rapidly. Elsewhere, drying, or even shallowing, is damaging to the plants. Lowland clay stream communities, for instance, took 3–4 years to recover from the 1975–76 drought.

Repeated shallowing may therefore be destructive.

Different species have different depth ranges. All species are constantly (though at different rates) entering and being lost from rivers. In stable conditions, these species are all from the same depth band. When depth changes, the outgoing species are of course those of the original water depth. Incoming species, however, are going to be those that can tolerate the new depth. That is, propagules of many species occur in rivers, and those the river selects for good development are those well adapted to the habitat of that river. The community therefore gradually changes to that wholly appropriate to the new depth. (Some species are likely to be part of both the old and the new community.)

Pollution
(see Chapters 5 and 6)

For water to be suitable, its quality as well as quantity must be suitable. There are a myriad different water types in nature: the chalk spring, the bog stream, the clay river, the alpine cascade, etc., all varying with the local habitat conditions.

To maintain these different water types, all chemically different in both macro- and microsolutes, inorganic and organic; pollution, the human alteration of water type, should be prevented. More realistically, it should be minimised! Pollution comes from domestic, industrial and farm effluents, and from changing land use, whether for farming, motorways or anything else.

Pollution is described in Chapter 5, its assessment by vegetation in Chapter 6 (using the river types from Chapter 4).

Other changes and vegetation

These include

1 On similar hills, higher rainfall leads to fewer large macrophytes (and more prominent mosses); as in streams of south-west versus north-east England.

2 Decreasing spate and drought flows, by regulation, has the opposite result.

3 Channelization (usually) gives shallower, more scouring flows and (in shallow streams) less vegetation and fewer slow-flow species.

4 Weirs slow and deepen water near the obstructions, with effects varying with the habitat produced.

These need assessing, with the complicating factors of topography, rock type, pollution, etc. For example, on similar hills sandstone bears more vegetation than resistant rock; on similar hills and with similar flow, Fringing herbs wash out on resistant rock in less pollution; built-up land and intensive farming increase flash flows; and reservoir effects differ with overspill and regulation, and are greater in hills. In well-drained land with less water, effects are magnified.

3 RIVER STRUCTURE
and its damage

**Also see Chapter 2 for water quantity, Chapter 7 for the structures required for the larger fauna and Chapter 8 for geomorphology and structural enhancements
(no specialist expertise required)**

SUMMARY

A stream in ecologically good condition is varied. It has a varied bank, a varied bed and, in consequence, a varied vegetation (except where torrential mountain flow prevents this last) and varied invertebrates, and usually it has a winding pattern. This diverse architecture is too often reduced by human impacts to a straight uniform channel, near-devoid of larger plants and animals. Ecologically satisfactory and unsatisfactory patterns are demonstrated in this chapter, as is vegetation for bank protection. Land drainage lowers water level (raising the height of stream banks) and speeds flow (through straightening and smoothing channels). It therefore leads to uniformity of channel (unless environmental expertise is used). Different management techniques and disturbances are described. The possibility of legacy areas is introduced. These are stretches of river with good structure (and fairly good water quality) where flora and fauna can grow well, and spread out to the rest of the river. Buffer strips are advocated – strips of unpolluted vegetation beside streams, providing buffered habitat enhancing and protecting the stream itself. The importance of organic carbon, from trees above as well as from instream vegetation, is noted.

Streams in settlements are assessed using ornamental (and aesthetic) as well as conservation criteria, and their relation to human welfare and civic pride is stressed.

Introduction

In the USA, the legal definition of pollution includes both chemical quality (as understood in Britain) and physical structure. Damage to stream structure can therefore be pollution and unlawful. This is excellent. Too many take legal requirements for chemicals seriously, but forget the structural damage, which can be as bad for the river environment.

Structure is the physical habitat, the patterning in, on and among which live the plants and animals. For vegetation, the structure is mainly the inorganic parts, the bed, bank, etc., which are mainly made by inorganic means – discharge, erosion, sedimentation and the like – but partly by trampling livestock, burrowing water rats, grazing swans, etc., and indeed by the vegetation itself. (Human impacts alter this structure in varying degrees.) For fish, the vegetation is as much part of the river structure as is the gravel in the bed. The identity of 'structure' therefore depends on the organisms using it.

Loss of structure therefore means the loss of diversity and complexity of the architecture, the architecture both of the vegetation, and of the bank and bed.

Natural structure varies with river type. An Alpine torrent derives its patterning mainly from rocks and trees, while in a chalk stream vegetation structure is of high importance for the animal life.

Fig. 3.1. This river has good structure. Except for the over-high banks, no-one would guess it had shortly before been subjected to a land-drainage scheme. Existing trees along one side have been retained and a few more planted on the opposite bank (River Alne, Warwickshire) (Purseglove, 1989).

Natural streams move. They wind (meander), undercutting and eroding concave banks, and building new land on the inside of bends, so the stream channel moves across the flood plain. Natural streams form shoals, sometimes with dramatic results as when, in the late thirteenth century, the outfall of the Great Ouse was altered from via Wisbech to via Denver. Massive shoaling had occurred, and it was easier for a great flood to find a new course than to break through the shoals. Minor shoaling is constant, causing obvious human inconvenience. Shoals occupy water space and hinder flow, leading to floods, which alter courses and so alter boundaries. Floods are increased – or made – by things obstructing flow, such as bends, shoals, debris, etc., and by controls on flow, such as weirs, dams and sluices.

Therefore, river structure is managed. The early European management was firstly for navigable channels, then for protecting settlements from flood, then for valley drainage. All of these are most commendable. Then came arterial drainage, and now, field, bog and moor drainage. Speed the flow, grow the crops – but lose the nation's water supply? Lose the heritage of rivers and river life? Lose all the wetland, wood and permanent pasture surrounding, and forming part of the habitat of the river? Human welfare rightly comes above that of the river, but placing greed and wastefulness above the welfare of the river, as now, is surely unjustified.

To keep rivers in their existing channels, intermittent removal of shoals is needed where silt accumulates (not needed in swift mountain streams, rarely in upper chalk ones), and when this silt is not moved in ordinary winter storms (as it is, in many upland streams). Recovery from silt removal takes *c.* 3 months to 2 years. Recovery from excavation-dredging and straightening may take decades.

Banks are traditionally dredged in a 1.5:1 slope in a smooth trapezoid channel. Contrast Fig. 3.1 and (a) on p. 3! With drainage, bed levels are made lower, so banks get higher. Some rivers, particularly those flowing swiftly through soft substrates, develop high banks (at least in low flows). Otherwise, though, the height of the bank shows the degree of drainage, natural rivers flooding frequently. In theory, drained banks still form corridors of wildlife, plants and animals, but their value is much reduced when they are made uniformly smooth (without diversity and complexity of structure), are frequently sprayed, mown and dredged, or are planted with alien grasses.

When a river bed has been lowered, this also affects all streams and ditches flowing into it. They are, at best, likely to erode, and at worst, to be themselves drained or even lost, with the loss of the major length of the aquatic habitat.

Good – and bad – structure is described below. As in all ecology, if the good is not known, it cannot be achieved. That which has not been thought of, only rarely comes from planning. As C.E. Warren (1971) says, 'we cannot depend upon chance to bring about desirable events'.

Much can be done! Trees and thickets can be fostered, ponds can be made parallel to the river, loops can be maintained, wide margins can be given, reedswamp fringes can be present, bank structure can be diverse. Grazing can be to the water's edge, drinkers (drinking bays) can

Fig. 3.2. *Do not turn this (a), into this (b) (the same river!) (Purseglove, 1989).*

be constructed, or river banks may be fenced, with tall herbs on steeper slopes. Many options are available. However, since many invertebrates require particular habitats, do not move far, and cannot survive a waiting period for the habitat to develop, their needs should be considered during the planning: see Dr P. Kirby's (1992) book on habitat management.

As J. Purseglove (1989) writes, 'rivers can be supremely life-enhancing. Engineers who have destroyed for five decades can become creators. Machines can, at trifling expense and no sacrifice to drainage efficiency, create habitats for rare plants, dragonflies, crayfish, otters and much more. And by so doing, add to human happiness. Young and old, public and specialists, all benefit from rivers of good structure. While beautiful rivers do not pay the National Rivers Authority much directly (although they do purify, and bear fish: for fishing licences), they attract visitors, and so benefit the local economy.' UGLY AND DESTROYED RIVERS ARE UNNECESSARY.

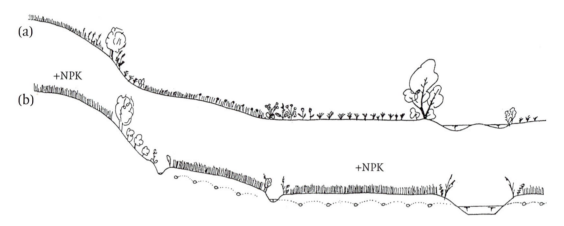

Fig. 3.3. Results of draining (modified from Kohler et al., 1989). NPK = nitrogen, phosphorus and potassium. (a) Undrained, (b) drained.

River structure

Bank structure

Examine the height, slope, texture, nature and diversity (variety) of the banks in each of the following figures, and note how they provide different habitats for flora and fauna.

Fig. 3.4. Banks in a nearly pristine state.

Table 3.1. Environmental implications of channel modifications in flood alleviation and land-drainage schemes and their subsequent maintenance

Factor	Physical or chemical environmental effects	Potential ecological consequences	Probable severity	Remedial or ameliorative action[1]	Comments
1 Enlargement of channel to provide increased flow capacity	Change in physical dimensions of habitat to give (i) reduced depth under dry weather flow (ii) greater channel width (iii) change in water velocity for given discharge	Removal of biota from existing channel by reconstruction work: high, temporary, turbidity reducing plant photosynthesis, blanketing substrate down stream and affecting macroinvertebrates and possibly feeding of fish	Often very variable, but of short duration	Reinstatement by reintroduction: working from downstream to upstream work: little can be done to avoid this but working short distances at any one time helps to reduce severity	Recolonisation occurs by drift from upstream: high turbidity and suspended solids are 'natural' phenomena associated with floods but duration may be longer during engineering operations
2 Modification of channel shape, both in profile, plan and cross-section	Reduction in habitat diversity (i) smooth profile removes variation in depth (pool:riffle configuration with tendency towards uniform substrate material	Loss of many microhabitats and their associated flora and fauna: reduction in overall community diversity	Severe	Dig out deeper pools below level of designed profile	Fortunately, tendency for channel to return to natural configuration unless constrained by massive structures (e.g. concrete channel or piling etc.)
	(ii) trapezoidal cross-section destroys habitat diversity, especially shallower margins	Loss of habitat diversity; marginal plants unable to establish foothold; loss of (some) macroinvertebrates and larger fauna	Severe	Construct with an irregular channel cross-section and especially with marginal ledges ('berms') to allow reinstatement of marginal plants. If flood channel must be straight, encourage dry weather channel to meander within its confines	Not an ideal solution but will encourage some habitat diversity
	(iii) straight channel removes meanders having deep fast water on outside and shallow on inside of bends; modifies velocity and suspended solid carrying capacity	As above; channel length reduced and even with increased width, habitat area may be lost	Severe		
3 Channels lost or put underground	Habitat loss	Habitat loss	Severe	Restore	
4 Channels made smaller and lower (banks steeper)	Less waterspace, shallower, over-steep banks, shading banks	Habitat change and usually loss	Moderate to severe	Widen, improve banks	
5 Bank modifications	(i) Removal of trees to provide access (mainly for machines) and reduce obstruction of flood plain	Loss of shading so that increased light reaching water encourages algal and macrophyte growth; loss of detrital input during leaf-fall and aerial insects for fish food	Variable, usually moderate to severe	Consider the bank-retaining capacity of trees before action. Remove only from one (preferably north) bank. Plant trees parallel with flow to reduce risk of flood loss	Tree loss is slow to recover but other vegetation may return within one to four seasons
	(ii) removal of bankside vegetation by mechanical means or herbicides	As above. Herbicide spray drift may affect other plants	Moderate	Restrict control to part of bank each season	
	(iii) construction of raised or flood-banks	Increased carrying capacity of channel may modify habitat	Significant for species restricted to e.g. earth cliffs		
6 Maintenance of channels	(i) Removal of deposited sediment and vegetation by mechanical means	Loss of habitat for larger fauna	Mild to moderate	Restrict to partial treatment in any one season	Avoid breaking hard bed during maintenance work (restrict to drainage schemes)
	(ii) removal of hard bed	Habitat modification, removal of benthic fauna, loss of flora and fauna associated with it	Moderate to severe	Avoid drift on backing from spraying the land beside	
	(iii) removal or control of vegetation by means of herbicides	Loss of plants and associated animals; invasion of more resistant species leading to community changes	Variable, usually mild to moderate		

[1] Bring in landscape architect and ecologist at the planning stage, and avoid habitat becoming severely damaged in the first instance

Modified from Hellawell (1986).

Fig. 3.5. Traditional grazed edge (pre-drainage) (old woodcut).

Fig. 3.6. Modern grazed edge, made lower more by dredging than by long-term compaction (Haslam, 1991).

Fig. 3.7. Worn and eroding edge – worn at a rate depending on the type of original bank material, its compaction and the use of the bank (Master and Fellows, St Catharine's College, Cambridge).

Fig. 3.8. A modern worn edge – a much-managed stream (Haslam, 1991).

Fig. 3.9. A nineteenth century edge – after the first main drainage (Haslam, 1990).

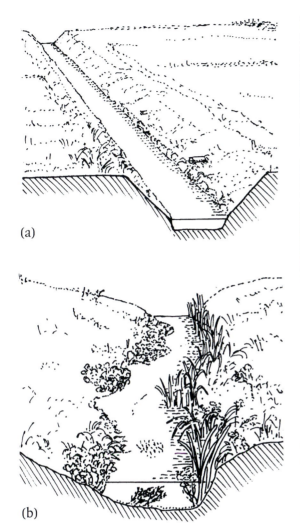

Fig. 3.10. *After dredging. The river tries to escape from the straightened form imposed. (a) This escape has been resisted, the stream being stoned, (b) slight escape, (c) water level falling with water use ((a), (b) Haslam, 1987, (c) Haslam, 1991).*

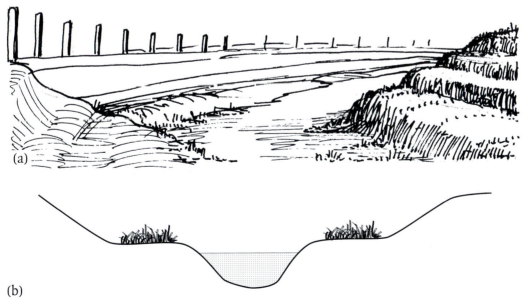

Fig. 3.11. *The two-stage (double trapezoid) and multi-stage channel. (a) Banks close (Haslam, 1991), (b) banks separated – more possibility of good-quality habitat.*

Fig. 3.12. Piped and 'lost' tributary (Haslam, 1991).

Fig. 3.13. Low banks where streams do not flood. (a) Spring, (b) water-supply channel, (c) discharge controlled by reservoir above (Haslam, 1991).

Fig. 3.14. Low natural bank, flooding irrelevant (Haslam, 1991).

Fig. 3.15. High natural bank (Haslam, 1991).

3.16. Active, moving stream (Haslam, 1991).

Fig. 3.17. Recently-drained peat, newly developing and active channel (Haslam, 1991).

Fig. 3.18. Built-up edges (Haslam, 1991).

Fig. 3.19. Local protection (Haslam, 1991).

(a) Channellisation is not in accordance with hydraulic parameters and is expensive to maintain.

(b) Stone blocks (rip-rap), for protection of convex bank. The zone of deposition is unnecessary and useless. There is no habitat for edge vegetation but some for invertebrates.

(c) New bank of stones and wire netting. These are wrongly placed hydraulically, and falling apart. The ugliness was not even successful!

Fig. 3.20. Rural banks like this are unsatisfactory ecologically, and often hydraulically ((a), (b), Lachat, 1988; (c), (d), (e), Purseglove, 1989).

Fig. 3.20 (cont.)

(d) Here, the ugly stoned bank is successful in engineering terms, it being stronger than the water force exerted by these very small streams.

(d)

(e) Eight years after traditional river engineering, this little river looks as sterile as ever. Black Brook, Leicestershire.

(e)

Bank protection *(other than that on the previous pages!)*

River banks can be protected by trees (see Fig. 3.21) (for other functions of riverside trees, see below, pp. 52–7, and Chapters 4, 5, 7 and 8).

Smaller plants are also bank protectors. Brambles are effective in preventing erosion (and are good animal habitat). Fescue swards are also valuable. The roots are narrow and tolerate drought, and are unlikely to crack the bank. The even sward makes erosion difficult. Growth is fairly slow, especially where nutrients are, or have been made, low, so maintenance is cheap. For conservation, a wildflower grassland may be developed. The results can be spectacular. (Expert advice should be sought, since the purpose is to restore the community native to that area. Self-regeneration is best, if impossible, locally collected seed is desirable, and 'wildflower grassland seed' packets of unknown provenance should NEVER be used, since they are

Fig. 3.21. *The bank held by trees (Haslam, 1978). This is stabilising and purifying.*

likely to contain seed of species not just from other parts of Britain, but also from foreign countries.) Invertebrate needs should be considered too.

The final community is likely to be better if an old grassland can be restored (propagules survive for many years). Two-stage channels (Fig. 3.11) and large flood banks can well bear wildflower grasslands, and be an oasis in an arable desert. Tall fast-growing grasses should NOT be planted on banks. Such swards need frequent cutting, or spraying with growth retardants, and both are expensive. The roots are large and long, and the bank may crack in drought. Tussocky species (like cocksfoot) are caught in flow and encourage erosion.

By the water's edge, tall monocotyledons (reedswamp species) are very effective in bank maintenance. Their removal, in eroding streams, can rapidly lead to bank fall. (Recommended species are on pp. 86, 224–5.)

If really necessary, banks may be re-inforced with local stone, and if vandalism is likely, this can be covered with soil and planted, with, e.g. fescue or brambles. Living mats are FAR preferable to mats of wire, steel, concrete, car tyres – and even cars – lining the banks.

Excellent structure can be found, even within towns, with proper care, or with suitable non-interference, e.g. Figs. 3.75, 3.78.

Channel and bank (whole)

Substrate types vary from entirely mud and silt, to entirely rock and boulder, and many patterns can occur.

Consolidated and unconsolidated substrates form very different habitats for invertebrates and micro-organisms, when much unconsolidated material is present, and also affect rooted vegetation. Particle size can be crucial, e.g. a 2 cm deposit of silt destroys a gravel spawning ground. Different plant species grow in different substrate types (Fig. 3.24).

The substrate should be that proper to the river type (see below and Chapter 4), e.g. loose sand beds can properly occur, sparsely, in easily erodable sandstone streams. Abundant sand

Fig. 3.22 Supporting and protecting the bank with trees (Lachat, 1991). (a) Branches of various local varieties are woven into a geotextile covering, in due course rooting and so stabilising the bank. (b) A year after planting, despite large floods growth has been rapid, and banks are established.

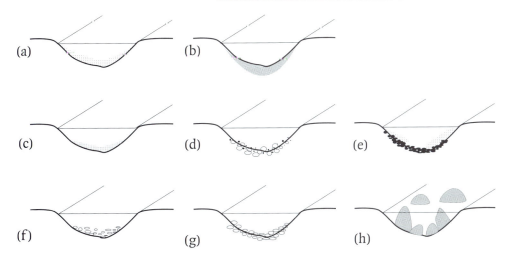

Fig. 3.23. Some patterns of substrate textures. (a) Silt shoals, (b) consolidated clay, (c) unconsolidated sand, (d) soft consolidated mix, (e) consolidated gravel, loose silt at sides, (f) coarse unconsolidated, (g) coarse, consolidated stony, (h) bouldery.

beds are due to disturbance. Typically, substrate type varies across the river, and along the river. Across the river, the edges are usually the most sheltered, and the most likely to bear finer particles. Flow is generally quieter at the edge. Along the river, there is, particularly in hills and in little-dredged streams, a typical alternation of pools with deeper slower water, and riffles with shallower swifter water. The size of the pattern varies with river type, the sequence extending from perhaps 10 m to well over 100 m, typically being 5–7 times the width of the stream. Riffles tend to have consolidated, stable substrates. Whether they are mix–gravel, stone or boulder depends on the landscape and rock type. Riffles usually have eroding flows, and no sediment deposition in the centre. The Substrate in the pools tends to have finer particles, the upper band being consolidated or

---

Consolidation of bed material

1. **Very hard**
   Mixed particle sizes tightly packed and overlapping particles. Difficult to dislodge with foot.

2. **Firm**
   Mixed particle sizes overlapping particles. Some can be dislodged by foot.

3. **Medium, semi-consolidated**

4. **Rather loose, slightly consolidated**
   Some packing of particles. Can be dislodged by foot.

5. **Loose, unconsolidated**
   Loose, no packing. Easily moved by foot.

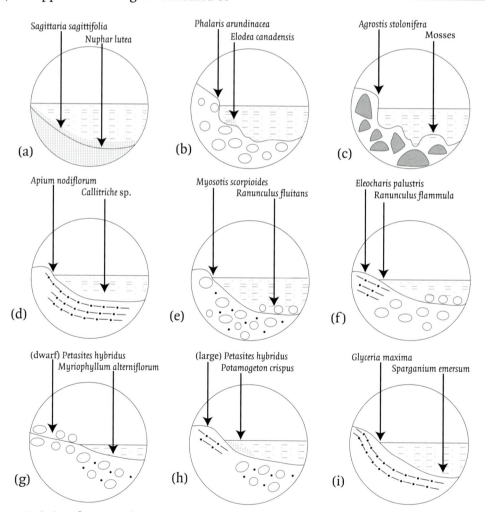

Fig. 3.24. *Variation of species with substrate. The diagrams show a variety of substrates, from large boulders (circles) to silt (dots) (dash plus dot is 'soil', mixed substrate), with typical species for each texture. The central line is that of the hard, or consolidated bed, with loose material lying above it. Nutrient status varies ((a), (i), high; (f), (g), low; the rest, medium).*

unconsolidated, and being made of any material or mix depending on the circumstances. Vegetation is different in pools and riffles, in pattern, and usually species, but the difference varies with local circumstances, including bed stability (for anchorage), depth (for species tolerating different water depths), degree of scour in the riffle (for preferred or tolerated flow type, and degree of scour tolerated), and substrate type (which may vary from being firm silt, mix, gravel, stone or bare rock to being unconsolidated, whether silt, sand or a deep pile of loose stones in the pools, which move in every spate, and are near-impossible for plant roots to survive in). In addition, in intermediate chemical states, the fact that silt holds more nutrients (and pollutants) than coarser material may mean that pools bear more nutrient-rich (or polluted) communities than riffles. Riffles may be too shallow or scoured for much vegetation, so that pools bear more vegetation; or pools may be too deep, so that riffles bear more. Yet again, both types may bear much (though different) vegetation, or both may bear negligible vegetation. Invertebrate communities vary with these habitats likewise.

Lowland streams

These are usually without large stones or boulders (except on some resistant rock). Structure is largely due to vegetation, though without some complexity of bed and bank, vegetation is unlikely to be complex.

Patterns are most easily shown by drawings (Figs. 3.25–3.34). The beds should be looked at first, noting shape, depth and the variations in both, then the shoals or other unconsolidated material. Next, the bank should be examined, as before, for slope and variety. Study of vegetation and channel position should be omitted on the first reading.

(Lowland clay stream, size (iv), Britain) Species include *Nuphar lutea*, *Sagittaria sagittifolia*, *Scirpus lacustris*, *Sparganium emersum*, *Elodea canadensis*, *Lemna minor* agg., *Rorippa amphibia*, *Sparganium erectum* and blanket weed.

Fig. 3.25. *Clay, gentle low underwater bank, uneven silt shoals at side. Bank dredged but not recently (Haslam, 1987)*

(Lowland clay, size (i), Britain) Dominated by *Sparganium erectum*.

Fig. 3.26. *Clay, common dredged-stream type, with tall herbs on bank, which is common in arable land, or where fenced from grazing (Haslam, 1991).*

(Eutrophic moraine stream, size (iii), Germany) Species include *Nuphar lutea, Phalaris arundinacea, Acorus calamus, Potamogeton crispus, Sparganium emersum* and *Lemna minor* agg.

Fig. 3.27. Steeper below-water banks, uneven shoaling (Haslam, 1987).

(Rolling lowland sandstone stream, size (iii), Germany) Species include *Sparganium erectum, Sp. emersum, Phalaris arundinacea, Callitriche* spp., *Potamogeton crispus, Nuphar lutea* and *Butomus umbellatus.*

Fig. 3.28. Low banks and uneven shoaling (Haslam, 1987).

(Lowland sandstone stream, size (iii), Britain) Species include *Callitriche* spp., *Ranunculus* spp., *Sparganium emersum, Elodea canadensis, Nasturtium officinale* agg. and *Phalaris arundinacea.*

Fig. 3.29. Lop-sided bed, a natural shape. Rivers left alone swing from side to side, eroding the concave, depositing on the convex side. Dredging makes all flat (Haslam, 1987).

(Stream flowing down from the Ardennes hills, size (iv), Belgium) Species include *Ranunculus fluitans*, *Phalaris arundinacea*, *Sparganium emersum* and *Elodea canadensis*.

Fig. 3.30. More lop-sided. Bank diverse and complex, gentle and cliff; a natural shape. Depth and silting vary. GOOD FOR DIVERSITY OF PLANT AND ANIMAL LIFE *(Haslam, 1987).*

(Moraine sand stream, size (ii), Denmark) Species include *Sparganium emersum*, *Sp. erectum*, *Glyceria maxima*, *Ranunculus peltatus*, *Elodea canadensis* and *Myosotis scorpioides*.

Fig. 3.31. The same pattern as the last, largely man-made (Haslam, 1987).

(Lowland (chalk) limestone stream, size (ii), France) Species include *Apium nodiflorum*, *Callitriche* spp., *Sparganium erectum*, *Phalaris arundinacea* and *Iris pseudacorus*.

Fig. 3.32. Much-managed, polluted with effluent and agrochemicals, frequently dredged, straightened, constricted (Haslam, 1987).

(Lowland (Jurassic) limestone stream, size (iii), France) Species include *Ranunculus* spp., *Sparganium emersum*, *Sp. erectum*, *Iris pseudacorus*, *Myosotis scorpioides*, *Callitriche* spp. and *Mentha aquatica*.

Fig. 3.33. This differs from the last only in human impact. It is FAR, FAR BETTER for river life, though it does occupy more space (Haslam, 1987).

(Lowland limestone stream, size (iv), Ireland) Species include *Scirpus lacustris*, *Ranunculus* spp., *Glyceria maxima*, *Juncus effusus*, *Iris pseudacorus*, *Oenanthe crocata*, *Sparganium erectum*, *Phalaris arundinacea* and *Alisma plantago-aquatica*.

Fig. 3.34. Another excellent stream. Note variation in inorganic and living structure, and that flooding would do little harm, as the fields slope (Haslam, 1987).

Highland streams

With increasing steepness of hills, structure tends to be increasingly due to physical complexity, and decreasingly due to vegetation. A boulder, for instance, may have a dipper perched on it, lichens on the top, mosses in the splash zone, mosses and algae below water, many small animals under and near it, and larger plants and fish in its shelter: the boulder controlling the river life. With less dredging, more channels are lop-sided, and banks are more variable.

(Upland limestone stream, size (iv), Britain) Species include *Ranunculus* spp., *Mentha aquatica*, *Myosotis scorpioides* and *Nasturtium officinale* agg.

Fig. 3.35. *Variable, no boulders, restricted in valley (Haslam, 1987).*

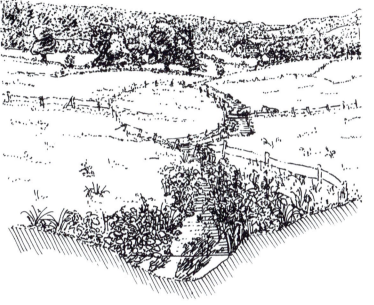

(Stream on top of the Ardennes hills, size (ii), Belgium) Species include *Nasturtium officinale* agg. *Ranunculus* spp. and *Phalaris arundinacea.*

Fig. 3.36. *Lop-sided, from natural causes (Haslam, 1987).*

(Upland resistant rock stream, size (iii), Britain) Species include *Sparganium erectum, Elodea canadensis, Phalaris arundinacea* and *Polygonum amphibium.*

Fig. 3.37. *Variation in depth and substrate type (rock to silt) (Haslam, 1987).*

(Mountain resistant rock stream, size (ii), Germany) Species include *Petasites hybridus* and mosses.

Fig. 3.38. Increasing bed structure (mountain landscape, unlike the above), but channel formerly dredged. Note the uniform steep banks (with large Petasites hybridus) (Haslam, 1987).

Fig. 3.39. Mountain stream in resistant rock again, eroding to stones, but undredged, with natural gravel bars. (Petasites hybridus, if present, will be dwarf), Scotland (T. Bone).

(Hill limestone stream of the south (Hérault), size (iii), France) Species include *Ranunculus* spp. and mosses.

Fig. 3.40. It may be easier for large plants to grow in limestone with its more stable substrates. Note bed and bank structure, including trees (Haslam, 1987).

(Resistant rock (Alpine) stream, size (iv), Pyrenees, France). Species include *Phalaris arundinacea* and mosses.

Fig. 3.41. *Alpine stream with surprisingly low structure. Note restriction by hills (Haslam, 1987).*

(Alpine resistant rock stream, size (iii), Corsica) Species include *Osmunda regalis* and mosses.

Fig. 3.42. *Alpine stream with excellent structure (Haslam, 1987).*

(Southern Apennines stream, hard rock, size (iii), Italy) Macrophytes absent.

Fig. 3.43. Unstable unconsolidated stone and gravel. Banks all right (though over-uniform, left side loose stones, right side overhanging trees), bed good visually, but bad for river life (Haslam, 1987).

Alluvial dykes and streams

Alluvial streams are those rising outside the plain, bringing a flow of outside water. In many cases, the channel position is, within limits, a result of human choice; dredging and maintenance are frequent. Dykes are entirely man-made and so need much maintenance (see appendix).

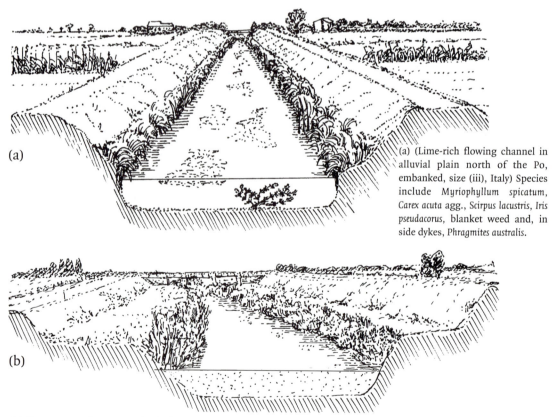

(a)

(a) (Lime-rich flowing channel in alluvial plain north of the Po, embanked, size (iii), Italy) Species include *Myriophyllum spicatum, Carex acuta agg., Scirpus lacustris, Iris pseudacorus*, blanket weed and, in side dykes, *Phragmites australis*.

(b)

(b) (Eastern coastal stream, embanked, size (iii), Italy) Species include *Typha latifolia* and *Phragmites australis*.

Fig. 3.44. Alluvial streams embanked against flood (Haslam, 1987).

(Channels in new polder, showing large (size (iii), foreground) plus small channel pattern (middle) near Dronten, The Netherlands. The water is probably brackish. Species include *Potamogeton pectinatus* and *Phragmites australis*.

Fig. 3.45. *Alluvial stream or dyke in foreground, small dyke behind. (Haslam, 1987)*

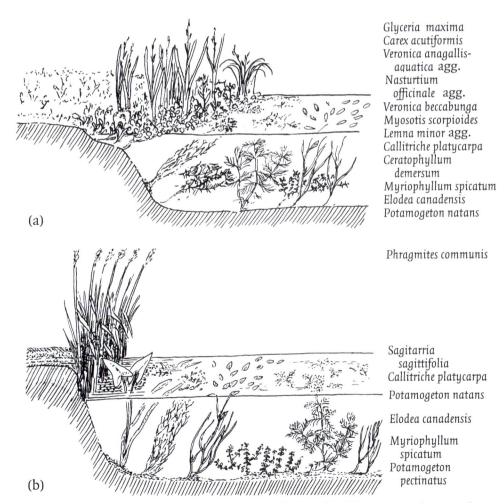

Glyceria maxima
Carex acutiformis
Veronica anagallis-
    aquatica agg.
Nasturtium
    officinale agg.
Veronica beccabunga
Myosotis scorpioides
Lemna minor agg.
Callitriche platycarpa
Ceratophyllum
    demersum
Myriophyllum spicatum
Elodea canadensis
Potamogeton natans

Phragmites communis

Sagitarria
    sagittifolia
Callitriche platycarpa
Potamogeton natans

Elodea canadensis

Myriophyllum
    spicatum
Potamogeton
    pectinatus

Fig. 3.46. *Alluvial dykes with dredged channels (Haslam & Wolseley, 1981). (a) Good edge habitat, good vegetation, emergents on edge, water-supported species on bed (lime-influenced), (b) more silt, over-steep banks, good water-supported vegetation, poor emergents*

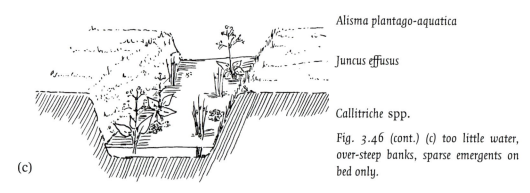

(c)

Alisma plantago-aquatica

Juncus effusus

Callitriche spp.

Fig. 3.46 (cont.) (c) too little water, over-steep banks, sparse emergents on bed only.

A typical pattern of river destruction (loss of structure)

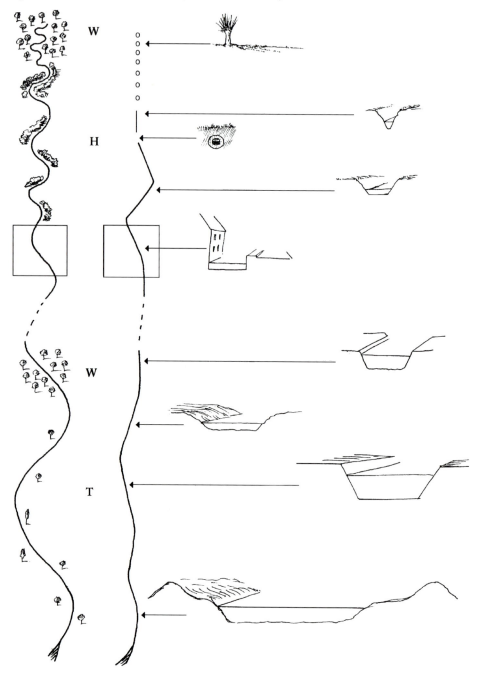

Fig. 3.47. *Altering of channel shape and position with intensive management (Haslam, 1990). W, wood; H, Hedge; T, isolated tree. Left, traditional stream; centre, altered one; right, sections through altered channel.*

The stream in Fig. 3.47 has been drained, put underground upstream, been straightened, and channelled into a smooth, uniform trapezoid shape. Downstream, the channel has been embanked. Most of the trees and bushes have been removed.

Architecture of river vegetation

This, again, is easier to illustrate in pictures than in words. For good architecture there must be first, **adequate vegetation (on edge, bed or both),** and secondly there must be a **variety of shape and pattern, whether in one spot, across a section, or along a reach.**

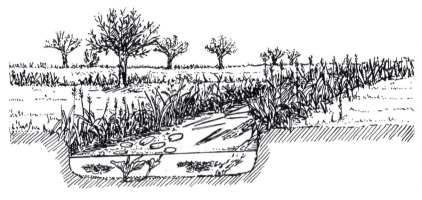

(Alluvial stream, size (iii), Britain) Stream rising in lowlands, but traversing alluvial plain for much of its length. Species include *Nuphar lutea, Ceratophyllum demersum, Lemna minor* agg., *Sparganium emersum, Sp. erectum* and *Enteromorpha* sp.

Fig. 3.48. *Good variety in cross-section. Bank and bed uniformity decrease the potential (Haslam, 1987).*

(Lowland clay stream, size (iv), Britain) Species include *Nuphar lutea, Sagittaria sagittifolia, Scirpus lacustris, Sparganium emersum, Elodea canadensis, Lemna minor* agg., *Rorippa amphibia, Sparganium erectum* and blanket weed.

Fig. 3.49. *Vegetation similar but more confined to sides. Clumps in water good for duck (Haslam, 1987).*

(Lowland sandstone stream, size (iii), Britain) Species include *Callitriche* spp., *Ranunculus* spp., *Sparganium emersum, Elodea canadensis, Nasturtium officinale* agg. and *Phalaris arundinacea.*

Fig. 3.50. *Diversity of bed and, with bends, bank, gives adequate architecture (Haslam, 1987).*

(Moorland resistant rock stream, size (iii), Britain) Species include *Scirpus fluitans, Glyceria fluitans* (long-leaved form), *Phragmites australis, Sparganium erectum* and *Myosotis scorpioides.*

Fig. 3.51. *High-quality architecture (Haslam, 1987).* (Also see Fig. 3.34.)

(Lowland limestone stream, size (iv), Ireland) Species include *Scirpus lacustris, Ranunculus* spp., *Glyceria maxima, Juncus effusus, Iris pseudacorus, Oenanthe crocata, Sparganium erectum, Phalaris arundinacea* and *Alisma plantago-aquatica.*

Fig. 3.52. *High-quality architecture (Haslam, 1987).*

(Lowland (Jurassic) limestone stream, size (iii), France) Species include *Ranunculus* spp., *Sparganium emersum, Sp. erectum, Iris pseudacorus, Myosotis scorpioides, Callitriche* spp. and *Mentha aquatica.*

Fig. 3.53. *Architecture still good (Haslam, 1987).*

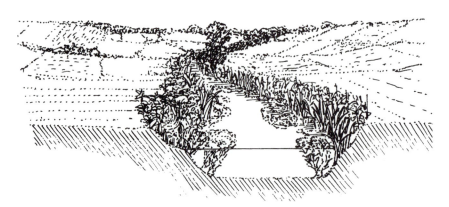

(Lowland (chalk) limestone stream, size (ii), France) Species include *Apium nodiflorum, Callitriche* spp., *Sparganium erectum, Phalaris arundinacea* and *Iris pseudacorus.*

Fig. 3.54. *Much-managed but otherwise similar stream. Note decline: loss of tree, of bank diversity, of bed variety and vegetation (Haslam, 1987).*

(Upland limestone stream, size (iv), Britain). Species include *Ranunculus* spp., *Mentha aquatica*, *Myosotis scorpioides* and *Nasturtium officinale* agg.

Fig. 3.55. Not very good (too uniform, low species diversity and bank pattern) but improved by intermittent trees. (Haslam, 1987).

(Clay stream, size (ii), Belgium) Species include *Apium nodiflorum*, *Callitriche* spp., *Glyceria maxima*, *Lemna minor* agg., *Agrostis stolonifera* and *Phalaris arundinacea*. However, the pollution in this area is such that no species-rich streams were recorded.

Fig. 3.56. Perhaps better than expected in a lowland arable landscape, but highly constricted (Haslam, 1987).

Fig. 3.57. Architecture good in quantity, poor in diversity (mostly Sparganium erectum) (Haslam, 1990).

Fig. 3.58. Architecture poor in quantity, good in diversity (Haslam, 1987).

(Dyke, size (ii), Ost Friesland, Germany)
Species include *Glyceria maxima*.

Fig. 3.59. *Architecture limited in both quantity and diversity (Haslam, 1987).*

Fig. 3.60. *Negligible vegetation, but bed and bank shape permit recovery if disturbance is prevented (Haslam, 1990).*

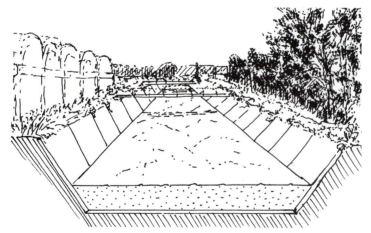

(Lime-rich flowing channel in alluvial plain north of the Po, size (iii), Italy)
Irrigation channel with fast-flowing water derived from turbid river. Macrophytes
absent.

Fig. 3.61. *Negligible vegetation, and no recovery prospects without change to bed and bank (Haslam, 1987).*

Stability

(see Chapter 8)

Rivers move, they have a flow of running water, so there is necessarily scour and deposition; to some extent all the time, but increased by many hundreds-fold in the greatest of floods. Rivers change, but they change within definable limits, and in a semi-cyclical way. They are, in effect, in a state of changeless change. Excluding human impacts, a river eats away one portion of land, and builds up another in exchange. In terms of millions, and often even thousands of years, though, there is overall change, land masses being worn away, eroded away, by their rivers.

For human convenience, rivers should be static, never changing course, never flooding, never shoaling. The activity of rivers is therefore inconvenient to us, and stability becomes a concern.

While all rivers are unstable, instability is greatest when:

- soil, subsoil and rock are easily eroded;
- banks and beds are constantly disturbed (whether by dredging, boats or cattle, etc.), and have no chance to become compacted under use;
- floods are of high discharge, and flash-floods increase;
- engineering is not hydraulically successful, e.g. scour has been increased beyond the tolerance of the banks;
- intensive farming, or poor-quality effluents or run-off, provide much sediment to the river;
- bank surface is particularly susceptible to scour (e.g. poorly-anchored bushy plants sticking out).

Flood safety, the protection of settlements from flooding, is paramount, and planning for this safety includes the assessment of river stability. Conversely, conservationists must not be surprised if a beautifully created refuge is suddenly not there any more!

Channel position

The natural river, unless constricted by topography (Fig. 3.62) or human impacts (Fig. 3.63), winds and is sited on the valley floor.

The stream may show more than one wave pattern (Fig. 3.67). Fig. 3.10 shows the stream starting to wind after straight dredging – unless further constrained.

The slope, and to a large extent the width of a stream, unlike the water speed, depth, etc., remain constant from day to day and nearly so from year to year. Most of the flow, substrate, sedimentation and depth characters of a stream are summarised in, and can partly be deduced from, the width–slope pattern (slope being measured on the 1″ OS map, of the reach above the site recorded).

Topography affects the fierceness of flow, and so the distribution of plants and animals. In the high mountains, the steeper and narrower streams have no large plants, but almost all upland and lowland streams can potentially contain vegetation. Luxuriant vegetation, however, is confined to certain parts of the width–slope pattern, its distribution depending on rock type and topography. Different plant species are found on different width–slope patterns, and their distributions can usually be interpreted in terms of the habit of the plant.

THE STRUCTURE OF THE RIVERSCAPE INCLUDES THE POSITION OF THE RIVER. GOOD STRUCTURE IS THE RIVER IN THE RIGHT PLACE, at the bottom of the valley, winding unless constricted by topography (e.g. as in Figs. 3.41, 3.62).

Fig. 3.62. River in steep valley, flowing nearly straight.

Fig. 3.63. Semi-straightened channel on valley floor. Main water flow in straight channel on hillside (Haslam, 1990).

(a)

(b)

Fig. 3.64. The natural winding channel in streams of different sizes. (a) In sands, influenced by grazing. Note positions of erosion and deposition, (b) in easily-eroded sandstone, managed. (c) in harder sandstone, little-managed.

Fig. 3.64 (cont.)

(c)

NEWLY CUT WINDING
RIVER COURSE

OLD CUT STANKED OFF AND
ALLOWED TO SILT UP

OLD STRAIGHT CHANNEL

Is this – putting the loops back and sealing off the straightened channel which was cut through by earlier engineers – the future face of land drainage? This drawing was taken from a scheme carried out on the River Wandse in Hamburg-Rahlstedt in Germany in 1982.

Fig. 3.65. *Stream straightened by over-drainage, and restored to its former course. The straight one was not cost-effective. The old channel still showed as a depression, with some marsh plants. (Purseglove, 1989).*

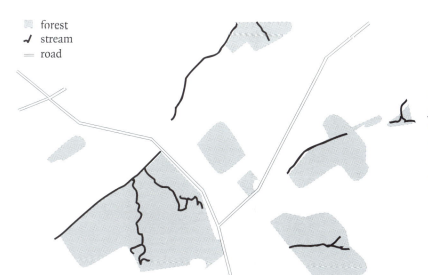

forest
stream
road

Fig. 3.66. *These streams in farmland are mostly lost, those in forest (which is less intensively managed) are much denser (re-drawn from Lachat, 1991).*

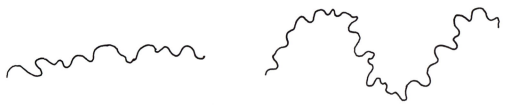

Fig. 3.67. Streams with one (a) and two (b) wave patterns in their winding.

Trees and shade
(also see pp. 57, 223–6)

Before men cut them down, forests covered much of Britain, and so surrounded streams, in the absence of marsh or mountain, etc. In natural woodland (where trees have fallen), glades are frequent, and streams in these, and other sunlit parts, would have had abundant vegetation. This must have been so, because of the known abundance of fauna which depend, directly or indirectly, on river plants. Certainly, invertebrates, leaves and wood fall from trees, adding to river productivity, but these cannot substitute for vegetation in the river itself.

Shade is thus a natural part of the river. However, it is also a man-made damage factor, since shade reduces vegetation. Hedges cast heavy shade on narrow widths, and can quite prevent macrophyte development in smaller brooks. Wider streams can have satisfactory weed control with a line of trees on the south bank. Banks may shade and reduce vegetation, usually in much-drained land where brooks are narrow and banks high. Tall herb vegetation can do the same. Within the stream, shade may be provided by the river plants themselves: tall emergents shade short ones, all emergents shade water-supported species, plants higher in the water shade those lower. Finally, light reduction is provided by the water itself. Water carrying much silt reduces submerged vegetation, and other turbidities and colourings act the same. (Coloured and turbid water may be polluted, and damage plants for this reason, also.) Different species differ in their tolerance to low light (Table 3.2).

Trees can be good habitats for invertebrates with aquatic larvae and flying adult stages, such as dragonflies, and, even more, for feeble flyers that require shelter, e.g. mayflies. Sponge flies spend much time here. Some insects lay their eggs on leaves or branches overhanging water. The cool shade favours some species, canopy breaks, especially south-facing, favour others. Both leaves and (particularly dead) wood are valuable as food in the river, and removing these for no better reason than tidiness should be avoided. (However, open as well as shaded habitats are needed for invertebrate protection.)

turbid water

Fig. 3.68. Different forms of shading.

Table 3.2. Tolerance of different plant species to shade, and to turbid water (Haslam, 1978)

Species are divided into groups, with the most tolerant species in Group 1, and tolerance lessening in the subsequent groups.

a) Shade tolerance

1. Shade-tolerant species
   Sparganium emersum

2. *Callitriche* spp.
   Phragmites australis (probably)
   Sparganium erectum

3. *Alisma plantago-aquatica*
   Ceratophyllum demersum (probably)
   Elodea canadensis
   Myosotis scorpioides

4. *Apium nodiflorum*
   Berula erecta
   Glyceria maxima (probably)
   Nuphar lutea
   Potamogeton crispus
   Sagittaria sagittifolia

5. *Nasturtium officinale* agg.
   Veronica anagallis-aquatica agg. (probably)
   Zannichellia palustris (probably)

6. Light-requiring species
   Ranunculus spp.
   Veronica beccabunga

b) Tolerance to turbid water

1. Most tolerant of turbid water
   Ceratophyllum demersum
   Lemna minor agg.
   Nuphar lutea
   Polygonum amphibium
   Scirpus lacustris

2. Intermediate
   Callitriche spp.
   Myriophyllum spicatum
   Potamogeton natans
   Potamogeton pectinatus
   Sparganium emersum
   Sparganium erectum

3. Least tolerant of turbid water
   Elodea canadensis
   Potamogeton perfoliatis
   Ranunculus spp.
   Mosses

Group 1 species occur often in medium continuous shade, and are common in medium discontinuous shade. They occasionally occur in heavy discontinuous or dapple shade. Group 6 species are sparse in medium dapple shade and in light continuous shade.

Shade types are defined as the percentage of full sunlight reaching 1–2 m above water level, between mid-June and mid-September, i.e.
   • Heavy shade   10–40% full sunlight
   • Medium shade 45–65% full sunlight
   • Light shade   70–80% full sunlight

Since shading affects the whole plant whereas turbidity affects only those parts in the water, there are differences between the two lists above. The plants most tolerant to turbidity either have parts above the water surface, or are characteristic of deep water (*Ceratophyllum demersum*) or both (e.g. *Nuphar lutea*). The species least tolerant of turbidity all grow submerged, the mosses and *Elodea canadensis* usually growing close to the substrate so that they receive the least of the light entering the water. *Ranunculus* spp. are also the least tolerant of shading.

Tree removal damages the river habitat. Channelling including tree removal can mean the loss of three-quarters of the fish, and more of the waterfowl. It may also widen the river since trees stabilise banks. For a given discharge of bankful floodwater, the watercourse with 50% cover of trees and shrubs, on both banks, may be only half the width of the channelled one. Dredged banks are not necessarily stable! Trees are a basic tool to stabilise banks and to decrease flood hazard. Any one tree may be a nuisance – but may be felled and a replacement one planted elsewhere.

Pollards, once polled above the browsing level of cattle, need re-polling every seven to ten years. This is a likely interval for maintenance dredging (silt removal), so the two can be done together provided only short stretches of willows are pollarded at any one time. They form excellent invertebrate habitat, particularly when old, so total habitat must not be removed. Polls can, in winter, be hammered into the banks, giving free, fast-growing, native new trees, keeping local varieties. (They may need fencing against grazing when young.) NB stands of mature trees need re-inforcing by young ones (which may again need fencing).

Trees form good wildlife habitat (see Chapter 8). In moderate quantities, they add to the fishing revenue from the streams. Clumps often form a better habitat than lines, though shade over small rills can make them safe for otters to travel. Native species of tree generally have a better invertebrate fauna. Dead trees are valuable habitats, and should be retained wherever safe.

Mixed sunlight and dappled shade give a good diverse aquatic system, open areas being warm and light, and shaded areas, being cool. Coniferous riverside trees increase soil erosion. Litter from birch, willow, hazel and rowan (trees with lighter shade) decomposes faster than that from oak, beech and most conifers (which cast heavier shade) and is especially important for invertebrates. Trees are also an economic (see p. 149 and Chapter 4) as well as a wildlife and river management asset.

Buffer strips
(also see Chapters 5 and 8)

Buffer strips or zones are names given to strips of land beside rivers left untreated (unpoisoned) by agrochemicals, not built up, and not with bare soil liable to erode into the river. Properly speaking they should be covered with vegetation, not used for footpath, etc. Their primary economic function is to (partly) purify polluted water flowing to the river from cultivated fields, roads, etc. This is also, of course, useful to conservation, as is anything lessening pollution.

Buffer strips are also valuable for structure and architecture, since at worst there may be only little management on the river bank, and at best, there is diverse vegetation on the strips, some tree clumps, some scrub, some tall and some short herbaceous vegetation, of value in itself, and for its direct and indirect (little bank management) influence on the river.

Buffer strips are a new concept – as a water treatment measure – and their optimum width (maximum cleansing for minimum land use) is not yet established. (This is discussed further in Chapters 5 and 8.) For structure, the wider the better, with the proviso that 1 m is very much better than nothing, and that over the length of a river, a variety of vegetation types, woody and herbaceous, should be allowed to develop. Wet grassland, woodland, etc. are also valuable as invertebrate and waterfowl habitat.

(a)

(b)

Fig. 3.69. *Buffer strips beside streams (intentional or otherwise). ((a)–(g) Haslam, 1987; (h), (i) Haslam 1991)*
(a) Wide: grassland. (b) Narrow: tall herbaceous vegetation.

Fig. 3.69 (cont.) (c) Trees on the left. (d) Narrow: mixed herbaceous types. (e) Mixed damp herbaceous vegetation, right-hand side only. Note the better fringe vegetation on the right of the river.

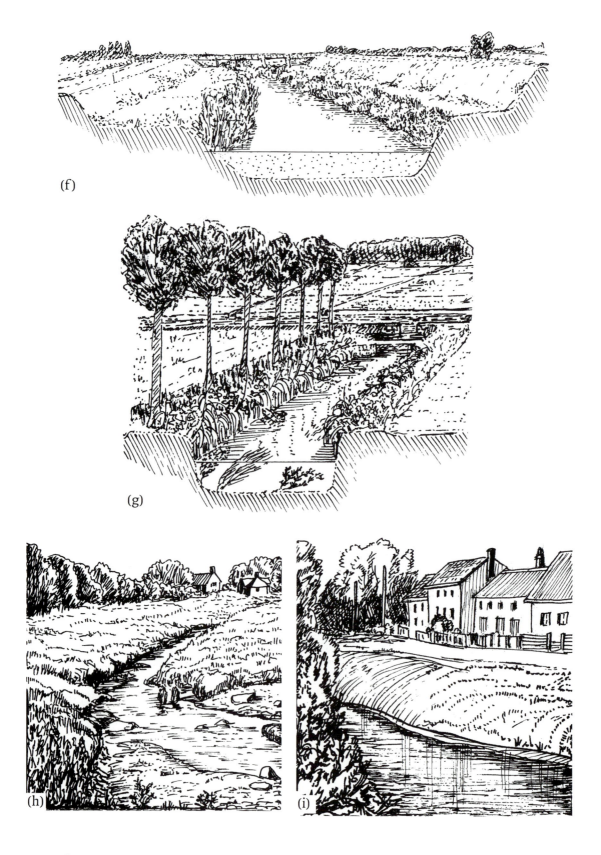

Fig. 3.69 (contd). (f) Two-stage channel used as a buffer strip. Short herbaceous vegetation. (g) Very narrow, but with trees on left. (h) Formerly canalised river has been 'downgraded' to a narrow stream, and the land formerly used for the canal, etc. is now a grassed buffer strip. (i) 'Unused' land between road and river, grassed and, in effect a buffer strip.

Organic carbon and debris dams
(see Chapter 8 for further detail)

The significance of organic carbon, and plenty of it, in the river system is only now being recognised. It is needed, of course, as food for herbivorous and detritus-feeding animals, and in carbon-low substrates (e.g. loose sands). Where debris (leaves, twigs, branches) accumulates there can also live invertebrates: and only partly because of the shelter; mostly because of the debris. Debris dams are where something, usually a fallen branch or tree, falls across the stream, and accumulates smaller debris as it is deposited where flow is checked. In lowland Britain some post-1945 floods have been caused by fallen trees swept into, and blocking, rivers. Each reach should be treated on its merits. Where not flood hazards, dead wood should be allowed in the river.

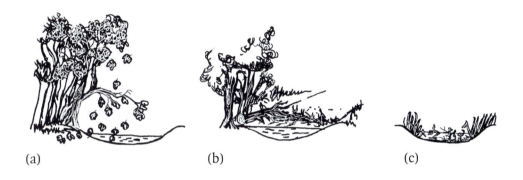

(a)   (b)   (c)

Fig. 3.70. *Sources of organic carbon. (a) Leaves (invertebrates), (b) fallen branch and debris dam, (c) river vegetation (and dead animals).*

Most of river organic matter (mainly decaying plants) is humic and fulvic acids, together comprising humic substances. These were once thought almost structureless and inert, but are now known to have highly specific (though unusual) structure, and be extremely active chemically. They interact with other soil chemicals, through many and varied processes. (These are – and non-experts may disregard this list! – ion exchange, hydrogen bonding, charge transfer, covalent bonding, hydrophobic sorption and partitioning, non-equilibrium sorption and transport; and they influence transport, photolysis, hydrolysis, bio-availability and volatilisation.) Consequently **they are most important for water purification**, being able to remove part or all of many pollutants (including heavy metals, organic pollutants and fertilisers) from the water, either converting them to harmless substances, or removing them (permanently, or reversibly) from the river supply. Organic matter plays an important role in stabilising basic chemical processes, adding activity, resilience and buffering. It is possible to have too much organic matter, as from dead cattle (animals do not form humus) or cut thick, living vegetation. It is far more common to have too little for the efficient functioning of the ecosystem.

Sediment
*(see Chapter 5 for its polluting effect,
and Chapter 7 for some faunal requirements)*

Deposited sediment, usually silt, influences river structure (see 'River structure', above). When silt is deposited, structure is damaged. Unless wash-out occurs (as in the highlands), structure can be restored only by a second structural damage, a maintenance dredge. Silting has been vastly increased by human impacts: fields are left bare, many protective hedges and ditches are being lost, peatland is being drained, effluents and urban run-off bring sediment, and so do coal and clay mines. All this extra sediment has to pass through the river.

Fish gills, and filter-feeding invertebrates, can be suffocated by silting. Small non-mobile organisms may be smothered. Even vegetation may be either smothered with much silting, or rendered easily washed out in storms by growing up into the silt and losing anchorage in the firm bed.

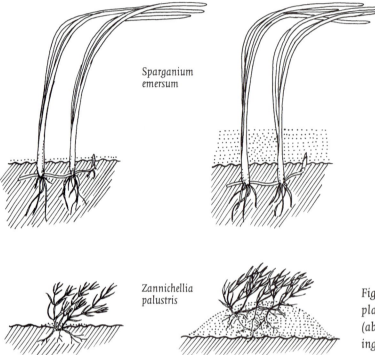

Sparganium emersum

Zannichellia palustris

Fig. 3.71. *Effect of sedimentation on plants of constant rooting level (above) and plants with variable rooting level (below) (Haslam, 1978).*

Legacy areas

Legacy areas (refugia) are reaches where vegetation, and its associated animals and micro-organisms, can survive, hold out against bad conditions elsewhere, and when these bad conditions pass, colonise the rest of the river. The legacy of the past can restore the habitats of the future. Legacy areas require clean(ish) water as well as good structure: and necessarily such water right along the river. Polluted rivers may have clean tributaries, though, which can form legacy areas.

Legacy areas must be long enough to contain: stable, self-perpetuating communities of vegetation, perhaps a minimum length of 100 m in lowlands, 200 m in highlands; breeding populations of the smaller animals, perhaps the same size; and home habitats for the larger animals, which may be much longer (e.g. up to 30 km for otters, though good structure need cover only 10% of this; see Chapter 7). Good, i.e. diverse and complex, structure must be present over the relevant length, and disturbance must be minimal. (Maintenance dredging, taking great care not to break the hard bed, and tree care, etc., may be occasionally needed and acceptable.)

Selection should be made of a variety of habitats appropriate to the relevant river type (e.g. in forest and grazed land, with riffle and pool). The land beside the selected sites (see Chapter 5) must be either helpful, or at least neutral (not harmful), to the conservation and well-being of the habitat: avoiding agrochemicals and farm effluents, for instance.

Some habitats may instead be chosen for the preservation of a single species, e.g. earth cliffs for kingfishers. Or they may be small local habitats, like a dead tree, doing no harm to human needs, but providing a habitat for many plants and animals for maybe a decade or more.

Could part of the EA money allocatable for conservation be used to create legacy areas? Or to protect areas already suitable (like parts of riverine Sites of Special Scientific Interest)?

Grazing, trampling, cutting and biocides
(also see Chapter 8 for further information)

Banks and beds of streams are grazed, by domestic and wild animals, both large animals and small ones. In the wild, where human impact is low, grazing is very heavy, productive rivers supporting a diverse and numerous higher fauna (see Chapter 7).

Bank grazing leads to, and maintains, grassy swards. It selectively encourages the spread of species whose growing points are out of reach of being eaten, like the sward grasses with growing points at ground level. Hence, fescue and such-like increase in the land habitat, and *Agrostis stolonifera* and short *Glyceria* spp. near the water's edge. By this edge, tall reedswamp species, and unpalatable ones like *Iris*, grow in ungrazed, and open places. Sheep are the most effective, but horses may provide the greatest floral diversity. Vegetation structure may be crucial: grass tussocks may harbour invertebrates for breeding, resting or both, and a change in grazing leading to a flat sward removes this habitat.

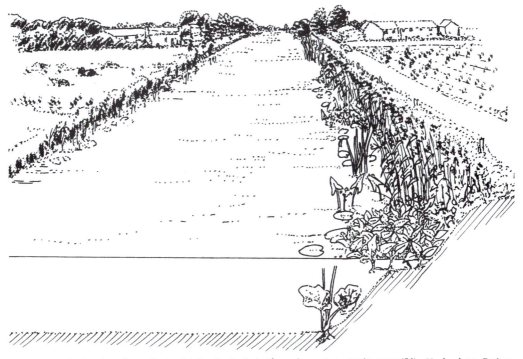

(Clay channel, size (iv), The Netherlands) Species include *Phragmites australis, Typha angustifolia, Nuphar lutea, Rorippa amphibia* and *Sagittaria sagittifolia.*

Fig. 3.72. *Left bank grazed, few emergents, mostly short. Right bank ungrazed, tall and short aquatics, diversity high (Haslam, 1987).*

Channel vegetation may, like grass, also grow quickly, this is particularly so, at present, for *Ranunculus* spp. In both, quick growth is an adaptation to grazing. Bed vegetation is grazed by invertebrates, herbivorous fish, crayfish, swans and other herbivorous waterfowl, and water rats. Formerly, there were beaver and now there may be domestic livestock in shallower parts. The enormous animal yield of the past means the plant yield must also have been enormous. Now invertebrates are fewer, and larger fauna very sparse indeed. Hence, even though the quantity of vegetation is also down, if there are no checks, quick-growing plants can be a flood hazard and a nuisance. Spates remove the surplus in the highlands, but in lowlands other steps are often needed.

Grazing is therefore a natural, an accidental, and an intentional management tool for banks and their vegetation.

In the past, vegetation seldom seems to have been a nuisance. In addition to grazing, there was disturbance by boats in larger rivers, by boats, carts and domestic animals in smaller (lowland) ones, and by swans and other waterfowl in both.

Grazing involves trampling by the animals doing the grazing, which is significant with the larger herbivores, particularly with cows, horses (and pigs, formerly more abundant). Where light trampling slowly firms the bank soil, it may well confirm the vegetation. Where it disrupts the soil, erosion increases and vegetation decreases. This is the usual modern pattern (dredging, etc., removing any centuries-old firmed soil). Cattle primarily eat emergents, but the bed as well as the bank may be damaged by their trampling (Table 3.3). Stock come to rivers for water more than for food. Non-erosive trampling is good: providing habitat niches for some invertebrates and indeed for plants.

In the absence of sufficient checks to vegetation, it may reach nuisance levels for anglers or boats, or hazard levels for floods. Vegetation is relevant only in tiny floods, floods where the water level is raised, by the presence of vegetation, high enough to cause waterlogging (or flooding) of crops. Major floods sweep majestically over the land, and a few plants in the bottom of the stream are neither here nor there.

Overall, about a quarter of Main River in England and Wales is cut (including channels now administered by the Environment Agency, but formerly so by Internal Drainage Boards). Cutting, dredging and herbicides as management tools become traditional and self-perpetuating in different regions. Twenty per cent of Main River is hand-worked.

Fig. 3.73. *Grazing and trampling. (a) Trampled drinking bay, (b), (c) bank grazing (Haslam, 1991).*

Handwork, though best for conservation (see Appendix, this chapter), is being replaced as mechanisation spreads.

Banks are cut, to keep them smooth (see above!) to prevent erosion as well as to remove bulk that might aid floods. (In small streams tall bank vegetation may occupy a significant amount of channel space.) Cutting prevents woody growth developing. Bank cutting is usually done in autumn.

Channels are cut to prevent flood hazard, and sometimes to encourage spawning grounds. Cuts vary from several times a summer to once in two years, or even less, depending on plant growth. Cutting in late autumn decreases next year's growth of *Ranunculus*. Cutting in early summer increases the nuisance growth of this plant.

Table 3.3. Effect of cattle on brook vegetation

a Comparison of stable and unstable beds in otherwise similar brooks
typical loss of vegetation cover:

	Stable	Unstable
Cattle alone	30%	50%
Cattle plus shade	20%	All
Cattle plus pollution (moderate)	70%	All

b Species distribution in otherwise-similar brooks, with unstable substrates (% occurrence)

Without cattle	Tall emergents, *Phalaris arundinacea* (25%), *Iris pseudacorus* (11%), *Sparganium erectum* (11%)
	Short emergent, *Mentha aquatica* (11%)
With cattle	Tall emergent, unpalatable, *Iris pseudacorus* (15%)
	Short grass, *Glyceria fluitans* (30%)
	Within-water, *Callitriche* spp. (16%), *Ranunculus* spp. (8%)

When beds are cut, a 100% total cut may be unnecessary. It is worth considering whether, for free water movement, an 80% or 60% cut is as good. (Just because 100% was needed before a drainage scheme does not mean 100% was needed after it, when water levels are so much lower.) Also, problem species can be cut, leaving rare and non-invasive ones to provide the vegetative environment. Cuts need not be straight. Wavy bands, and erratic ones (clearing the problem species) can be quite as good for water movement, and much better for conservation. (Central cutting is best for water movement.)

Two instances deserve special mention. Firstly, the (Thames) Lea requires little maintenance, BECAUSE THE ENGINEERING WAS PLANNED TO HAVE THIS RESULT. Secondly, the (Hants) Test and Itchen have ANGLERS WILLING TO PAY for river maintenance. Consequently, river structure is good or indeed excellent, and neither the valley nor the people are drowned. WITH THOUGHT AND MONEY, CONSERVATION IS COMPATIBLE with other considerations. Cutting is the main tool. Surely EA need not be outdone by private enterprise? Could not River Conservation Trusts be encouraged, and pay the difference between ecological and non-ecological management?

Herbicides may be used on the bank, to keep them smooth and plants short. Ecological management for this is preferable, where possible. Tall reedswamp plants may be sprayed when they grow well into the channel (and are not removed by spates) and so even may thick channel vegetation. Herbicides are used in the water, particularly in wetland dykes (see Appendix to this chapter) but also in rivers, usually for anglers. Such rivers usually – unlike the Test and Itchen – have no tradition of the anglers paying for good management by cutting. So the anglers are prepared to poison the river, affecting animals as well as plants. (Atrazine and simazine cannot now be used non-agriculturally, as on railway banks or Local Authority land.)

Management possibilities are numerous, and good river structure can, with imagination, result. Diversity and complexity of structure can be created – safely! It is uniform lack of structure which is awful.

Boats

Boats disturb and disrupt vegetation. Over-much vegetation hampers boat movement, over-little leads to eroding banks and much expense in piling or otherwise protecting them. Therefore, to maintain vegetation is an economic as well as a conservation objective.

Tall monocots (reedswamp species) are particularly good at protecting the bank, preventing erosion. Significant species include *Acorus calamus* (sweet flag), *Phragmites australis* (reed), *Sparganium erectum* (bur-reed) and *Typha* spp. (bulrush, reed mace).

Table 3.4. Canal vegetation in relation to boats

Boat movements per hectare per week	Result
(a) Water-supported vegetation in the channel	
2000	Satisfactory
4000	Little and at the sides, may be lost
(b) Reed swamp fringe	
1000	Good, may be too thick for anglers on the bank
4000	About as much disturbance as tolerable to maintain an effective fringe
5000	Fringe too little, and being lost

From Murphy & Eaton (1983).

Fig. 3.74. Boats in country and town ((b), (c), Haslam, 1991).

River structure in settlements

(also see Chapter 10, which covers the subject in more detail)

In towns and villages, there are the same criteria for good structure as in the country, but there are extra constraints and values. The development of structure may be constrained by existing buildings, channel positions, flood safety, disturbance and general patterns of the past. Secondly, aesthetic value, beauty, is properly a criterion for city streams. There is a beauty of the natural, there is also a beauty of the ornamental. The beauty of the natural river is often impossible to achieve in the necessary constraints of the town, so the beauty of the ornamental need not be in conflict.

Human environment shapes human behaviour (this has been proven often enough in mammalian studies – and on a group level applies likewise in humans). Where the river environment in settlements can be enhanced, the health, happiness and honesty of those in that environment are surely also enhanced. This is a high aim and achievement for those managing rivers!

Fig. 3.75. Urban streams from the same town, (a) (b), wanted stream, (c) unwanted and neglected.

The streams in Fig. 3.75 are from the same town, that in (a) and (b) is a thing of beauty enhancing the town, that in (c) is of similar size, shape and vegetation, and is not. Why? This deserves careful study. The answer is not stream vegetation quality: in all three it is polluted. (c) Is trying to re-develop a winding structure, and also has the better habitat for emerged aquatics. (a) Has stoned sides and has been cut shorter and more often. This is a small part of the difference.

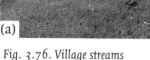

Fig. 3.76. *Village streams*

(a)

(b)

(c)

(d)

The main difference is that in (a) and (b) the people are happy and proud to house the stream in their midst, and in (c) they are indifferent, and have left it to the impersonal, indifferent care of the local authority. This is the crucial factor: the attitude and care by those in charge.

In Fig. 3.76 (a) and (b), the stream is cared for, and enhances village beauty. In (c), the stream itself is just a nuisance – but, fortunately, the fence, trees and bridges compensate. (d) Has both a beautiful and well-cared-for stream, and beautiful houses behind. Contrast this with (a) and (b) where the stream has to compensate for the houses. Not that all new development need be, or is, ugly (see Fig. 3.79).

Streams such as those in Fig. 3.77, however, whether in village or town, have nothing to recommend them. All natural beauty is removed, no ornamental beauty is added.

Both the rivers in Fig. 3.78 are things of beauty, one new, one old. The planning makes use of the water to enhance beauty, as also in Fig. 3.79.

The *good river* in a settlement comes from a proper appreciation of how water and buildings can enhance each other, plus the care of that water. This means that initial planning should preserve wildlife as far as feasible, and increase and maintain the water's natural beauty. Sometimes this is possible through leaving WELL alone. The stream in Fig. 3.80 runs through the centre of a town, but has a belt of trees around, and natural beauty is maintained. No ornamental beauty need be added.

Fig. 3.82 shows two opposite faults. In (a), the living (natural) structure of the river is good, but beauty is lost by not considering and planning the human structures and the bank around it. In (b) much thought has gone into the river itself as a source of pleasure, but the natural environment has been lost, and the overall scene is remarkably unpleasing. The river is not a planned part of a beautiful townscape, but a local leisure facility, of no concern to the rest. On the natural side, there is no provision for vegetation, therefore none for the animals depending on vegetation.

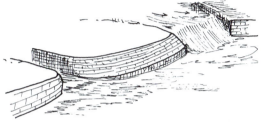

Fig. 3.77. Over-lined streams (Haslam, 1991, 1990).

(a)

(b)

Fig. 3.78. Town rivers. ((a), Haslam, 1991).

Fig. 3.79. A country house (R.M. Haslam).

Fig. 3.80. Stream in middle of town – EXCELLENT structure.

Fig. 3.81. River at edge of town. River with both natural and ornamental beauty.

Fig. 3.82. *Rivers showing lack of planning for the total environment (Haslam, 1990).*

Fig. 3.83. *The river ignored (Haslam, 1990).*

Finally, the river in Figure 3.83 has nothing to recommend it. It is detrimental to the human and the natural environment. No one's development, health or happiness is anything but lowered. Pollution hinders river life, so do the sides, steep and deep. There is no room for emergents, for invertebrates needing to crawl up for their adult stage, for duck nesting, for otters, for ... A truly awful scene.

Appendix: Wetland dyke (ditch) management: recommendations for conservation
(mainly adapted from Wolseley et al., 1984)

Wetland drainage channels are entirely human-controlled. The water level and water movement must be appropriate for the relevant crop. In Britain, the water is usually 1.3 m below ground in summer for arable, 0.3 m for permanent pasture. On clay, winter water level is lower than on peat.

Although management primarily affects structure, water and soil quality is also influenced. MANAGEMENT CAN POLLUTE. Disturbing the bed pollutes the dyke from chemicals released from bed to water, altering oxygen status (Biological Oxygen Demand rising from e.g. 4.5 to 6.8), nitrogen (ammonium-nitrogen rising to e.g. 0.56 ppm, nitrate-nitrogen from 0.09 to 1.10 ppm). Lowering water level on peat can increase sulphate and therefore acidification.

Cleaning

1. Channels should never all be cleaned at the same time throughout an area, as this destroys much of the potential for colonisation as well as the diversity of seral stages. Some overgrown non-arterial channels should be retained to provide diversity of habitat for other species.

2. Use cleaning methods that favour good ditch communities. Machine cleaning is not necessarily inimical to conservation requirements. If the channel bottom is not disturbed and the banks are not scraped, good aquatic communities can develop. However, at present, hand cleaning always provides less disturbance to aquatic communities while much machine cleaning is destructive because the bottom is removed and the banks are scraped. Given this situation it is worth encouraging hand cleaning where possible.

3. Avoid using any sort of chemical weed control, as this decreases diversity, particularly of the more sensitive species, and it does not appear significantly to reduce vegetation cover of weed species in the following season and may provide problems of removing dead plant material.

4. Cleaning intervals should be as varied as possible throughout an area as some species flourish in regularly cleaned channels and other (perennial) species favour less disturbance. However, high species diversity in all layers is most often associated with field channels that are managed on a three- to five-year interval.

5. Where arterial and through flow drainage channels are of exceptional wildlife interest, collaboration with bodies concerned in the management of these channels is essential. In order to do this effectively, monitoring of the aquatic flora of these channels, throughout the cleaning cycle, would provide the basic information for future maintenance of diversity. Although dredging of the channels temporarily destroys the habitat, if this is done in sections, colonisation can occur from upstream sites.

Water levels and quality

6. Ensure that penned summer levels are maintained at a high level in channels of conservation interest, and that winter levels do not allow ditches with a good submerged and floating community to become dry for long periods, especially in cold weather.

7. As yet we have little evidence concerning the particular effects of changes in management, but the combined effect of improved pasture with its attendant increased fertiliser application, bank fencing, and ditch deepening create a species-poor habitat with low structural diversity.

8. Most arterial channels carry water from other areas, and this can quickly downgrade good ditches. Therefore, all channels of conservation interest must have sluices on them to prevent this water entering the channel. This has become a major source of damage to good ditches.

9. Man-made channels were created either for arterial drainage or as field boundaries. In the latter situation they were created with the major constraint of using as little land space as possible while providing an efficient stock-proof boundary. In order to avoid the expense of regular maintenance that is essential for the requirements of a good submerged aquatic community, conservation bodies should consider increasing the width of some field channels on one side (so as not to destroy both marginal habitats) to create a larger area for the development of a submerged community, and to slow down the rate at which the channel will become shaded by tall monocot vegetation.

Fig. 3.84 (see next page) deserves careful study. In the centre are four characteristics of a good ditch: vegetation (composition and architecture), bank type, management regime, and land use beside the ditch. Going out from the centre are habitat variables resulting in different vegetational and structural features. These include over-little and over-much management (**NB both** directions unsatisfactory), altering land use beside the channel, altering stock access, pollution, and changing channel characters of size and flow. Each arrow should be followed through, to see the fascinating balance between habitat factors and vegetation – and the sensitivity of vegetation to all such habitat factors.

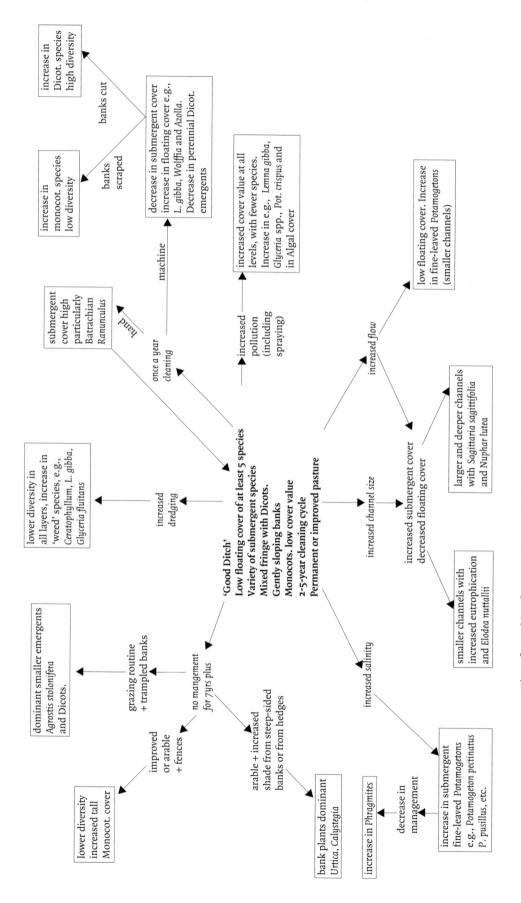

increase in
Dicot. species
high diversity

increase in
monocot. species
low diversity

banks cut

banks scraped

decrease in submergent cover
increase in floating cover e.g.,
L. gibba, Wolffia and Azolla.
Decrease in perennial Dicot.
emergents

machine

increased cover value at all
levels, with fewer species.
Increase in e.g., Lemna gibba,
Glyceria spp., Pot. crispus and
in Algal cover

submergent
cover high
particularly
Batrachian
Ranunculus

hand

once a year
cleaning

increased
pollution
(including
spraying)

low floating cover. Increase
in fine-leaved Potamogetons
(smaller channels)

increased flow

lower diversity in
all layers, increase in
'weed' species, e.g.,
Ceratophyllum, L. gibba,
Glyceria fluitans

increased
dredging

larger and deeper channels
with Sagittaria sagittifolia
and Nuphar lutea

'Good Ditch'
Low floating cover of at least 5 species
Variety of submergent species
Mixed fringe with Dicots.
Gently sloping banks
Monocots. low cover value
2–5-year cleaning cycle
Permanent or improved pasture

increased channel size

increased submergent cover
decreased floating cover

dominant smaller emergents
Agrostis stolonifera
and Dicots.

grazing routine
+ trampled banks

no mangement
for 7yrs plus

increased salinity

smaller channels with
increased eutrophication
and Elodea nuttallii

improved
or arable
+ fences

arable + increased
shade from steep-sided
banks or from hedges

lower diversity
increased tall
Monocot. cover

bank plants dominant
Urtica, Calystegia

increase in Phragmites

decrease in
management

increase in submergent
fine-leaved Potamogetons
e.g., Potamogeton pectinatus
P. pusillus, etc.

Fig. 3.84. Habitat factors and vegetation in dykes, Somerset Levels, England (after Wolseley, 1986).

4 RIVER TYPES
in relation to vegetation

(no expertise required for start; some, which can be gained from text
and by working in the field, needed for: identification of plants, River Classification A,
identification of fragile watercourses, causes of change, and survey method;
expert knowledge of plants needed for River Classification C)

SUMMARY

The vegetation of streams is determined by: rock type, water force (here assessed by topography), stream size, and human impact. Aids are given for the identification of species and of stream types and on the use of macrophytes to interpret habitat conditions. One classification is described in detail. Each main stream type is described by channel cross-section, the minimum diversity, cover and nutrient status band expected in an undamaged channel, the expected species assemblage, and notes on frequency, distribution, etc. For the Holmes classification, where only an outline is given, identification is through a species key. Fragile water-courses are introduced: habitat types – and so vegetation – are very easily destroyed by small human-caused changes, e.g. change of land use, minor pollutions. Finally, an introduction is given to the way river vegetation changes, both the 'changeless change' within stable rivers and the shift in vegetation with habitat alteration.

Summary identification

Look carefully at the streams, surroundings and vegetation in Figs. 4.1 and 4.2, then return to them after reading the text. It may take practice, but the figures can in due course be used as summary-aids to stream identification. This classification can then be checked in Classification A on p. 87. Figs. 4.1 and 4.2 contain much information on landscapes, land use, stream patterns, stream features and vegetation.

Introduction

River types are determined by:

Water force

Water force is the integrated physical effect of water on a plant (or other object), aggregated over time. This is controlled by the shape, size and height of hills; the size and shape of the catchment area, the land use (vegetation type, whether built-up) of that area, the precipitation, its total, seasonal and daily distribution, and the rock type. Rock type determines rock porosity, and so the amount of water being absorbed and not available as run-off to the river. Aquiferous rocks stabilise flow, non-porous ones make discharge more variable. Different rock types weather differently, so giving different types of stream banks and, more importantly, stream beds, affecting particle size, shape and pattern.

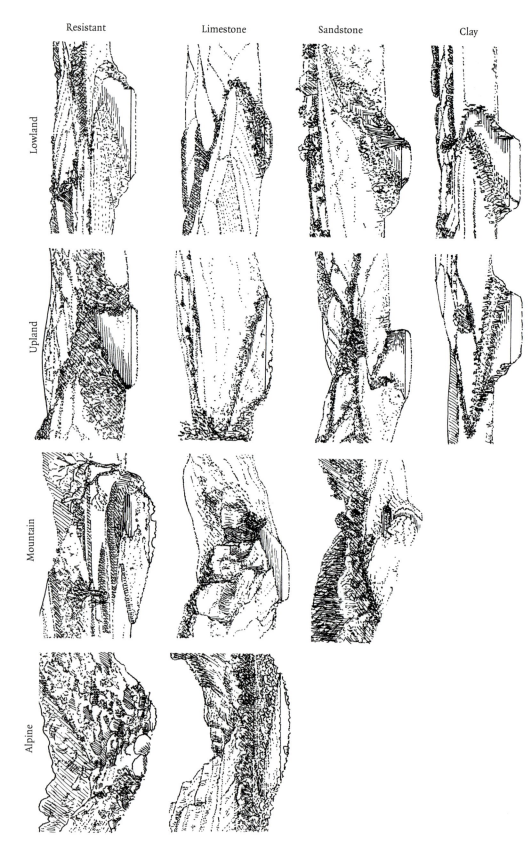

Fig. 4.1. River types in relation to landscape and rock type. Note the differences in channel position, outline, bank, water and substrate, and in the vegetation diversity and cover (Haslam, 1987).

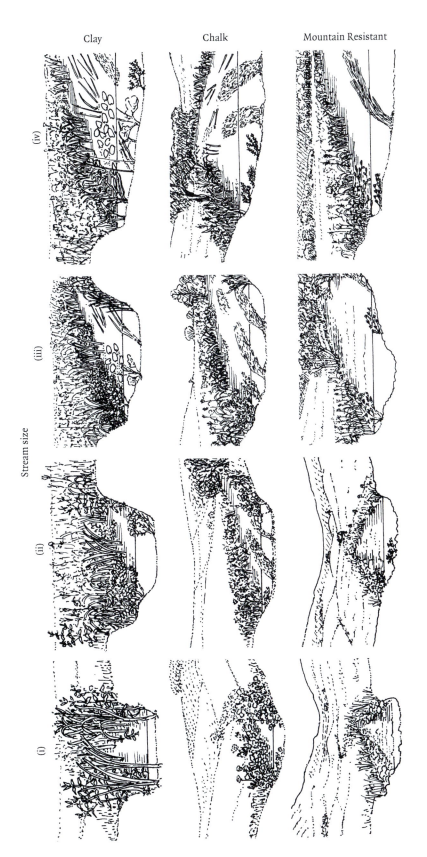

Clay　　　　Chalk　　　Mountain Resistant

Stream size

(i)　(ii)　(iii)　(iv)

Fig. 4.2. River type in relation to stream size and rock type. Note the differences in channel outline, bank, water depth and flow, and in the vegetation type, diversity and cover. (Sizes in Table 4.2, p. 75.)

For a given discharge, the water force is controlled by the channel features: width, depth, slope, vegetation patterns, etc. In the most Alpine streams, upper reaches are devoid of macrophytes. With some lessening of water force, mosses occur sparsely in the splash zone of boulders, and in very sheltered spots in the stream. With yet lower water force, mosses increase, and spread to the now-stable parts of the beds, and flowering plants come in and increase as the water becomes quieter.

Within Britain, steepness can be used to predict water force, as shown in Table 4.1.

Table 4.1. Landscape classification

	Hill height (usual) (m)	Fall from hill top to stream channel in upper reaches (usual) (m)	Slope of channel of upper streams (from one-inch map) (usual)	Liability to spate
Plain	—	—	—	—
Lowland	Up to 245m	Up to 60	Less than 1:100	Negligible
Upland	245–365m	90–150	1:40 to 1:80	Some
Mountain	610+	185+	Greater than 1:40	Much
Alpine	610+	305+ or rainfall very high	Greater than 1:40	Great

Notes:

Where data are inconsistent, the fall from hill to channel should be used.

A mountain-rising stream will remain mountainous in flow characters for some way into an alluvial plain.

Rainfall is higher in the west than the east, meaning a higher water force in the west for a given landscape type.

Soft limestones and sandstones are always classed as lowland, clay hills over 215m are upland.

(Note: contour lines are in feet on maps, hence the unusual metric numbers.)

Europe-wide, however, hill shape, rock porosity, and precipitation in relation to landscape vary too much, and no one factor can be used to integrate the others.

Rock type

Rock type is the second in importance as it is usually clear cut and easily determined (e.g. a catchment is, or is not wholly on chalk). Rock type influences topography and hill shape (e.g. chalk versus slate), and, as mentioned above, water force is influenced by catchment and channel slope, and these in turn vary with rock erodability. Rock type influences water force, and stability of discharge (through porosity, and spring formation).

Rock type affects river substrate. Resistant rock may break down to large particles, giving stone or gravel beds of varying thickness and stability. Alluvial deposits may provide fine particles for their watercourses. Sandstone erodes easily, and, of course, often to sand as well as to other particle sizes. Limestones, in contrast, dissolve easily, leaving fewer particles on the bed. (This is particularly noticeable in the highlands.) The combined stability of bed and flow influence vegetation. In near-still waters there is little difference, but in swifter ones, even on low hills, an unstable resistant rock stream may bear much less vegetation than an otherwise-similar sandstone one (and in mixed areas, like east Wales and north-east Scotland, sandstone patches may be located in this way).

The primary effect of rock type is, though, the CHEMICAL one: rock type gives the basic chemical, nutrient environment of the river. Subsoil and soil type, and human impacts (including land use) modify this.

Stream size (upstream–downstream variation)

<table>
<tr><td colspan="2" align="center">Table 4.2. Stream size classification</td></tr>
<tr><td>Size (i)</td><td>Small streams (brooks or ditches) without water-supported species, up to 3 m wide. Emerged aquatics present or absent.</td></tr>
<tr><td>Size (ii)</td><td>Small streams (brooks) with water-supported species (usually with deeper water than i), up to 3 m wide. Water-supported species present, emergents present or absent.</td></tr>
<tr><td>Size (iii)</td><td>Medium streams (small rivers), 4–8 m wide. Any type of vegetation or empty.</td></tr>
<tr><td>Size (iv)</td><td>Large streams (medium and large rivers), 10+ m wide. Any type of vegetation or empty. (Usually 10–30 m.)</td></tr>
</table>

(Channels with negligible flow, e.g. wetland dykes and drains, are graded similarly.)

The stream is a continuum, reaching from its source right down to its mouth in the sea, a distance of maybe only a kilometre or two, maybe many hundreds of kilometres. Vegetation varies along this length. For convenience, categories must be used to describe portions of river which have something in common. A classification is a man-made grid, imposed on a non-man-made, non-grid system, so intermediates will occur. For vegetation, the system shown in Table 4.2 works. Different grades have been used for animal habitats, e.g. stream widths of 0–2, 2–25, 25+ m.

Width is easier to measure than depth, so is the primary factor used. Depth, though, is more important as a vegetation-controlling factor, and when summer depth is outside that expected from the width (see River Classification A, and Chapter 2), then the site should be re-classified by depth, an unusually deep size (ii) being classed as (iii), etc.

Human impact

(See Chapters 2, 3, 5, (6), 7–12, Appendix.) Water force, type, channel size, and other river features can be, and in lowland and most highland British rivers have been, much altered by human impact. It affects every aspect of rivers and their ecology.

The rivers described in this chapter, by both Classifications A and C, are ones altered by human impact. No unaltered British rivers are known or suspected. The degree of impact, however, varies. The rivers described by Classification A are those with low impact for the region (Chapter 6 describes the high impacts and how to assess them).

Species identification, habit and habitat banding

Identification books

Spencer-Jones, D. & Wade, M. (1986). *Aquatic plants: a guide to recognition.* (Common species, colour photographs.)

Haslam, S.M., Sinker, C.A., & Wolseley, P.A. (1982). *British Water Plants.* (Complete, fully illustrated in black and white. The key below is modified from this.)

Clapham, A.R., Tutin, T.G., & Moore, D.M. (1987). *Flora of the British Isles.* Third Edition. (Total flora, definitive, no illustrations.)

Key to commoner species of (lowland) rivers

(modified from Haslam et al., 1982).

Specimens should be carefully compared with good illustrations as rare species may be locally abundant.

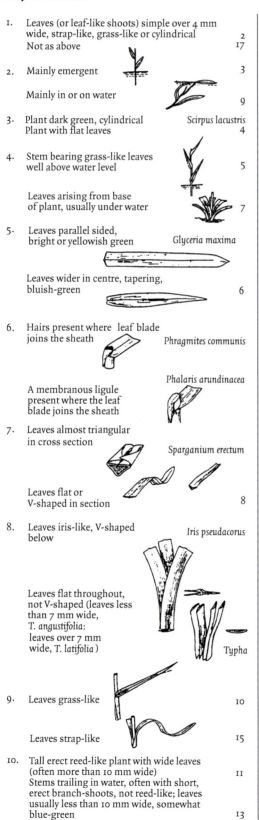

1. Leaves (or leaf-like shoots) simple over 4 mm wide, strap-like, grass-like or cylindrical — 2
   Not as above — 17

2. Mainly emergent — 3
   Mainly in or on water — 9

3. Plant dark green, cylindrical — *Scirpus lacustris*
   Plant with flat leaves — 4

4. Stem bearing grass-like leaves well above water level — 5
   Leaves arising from base of plant, usually under water — 7

5. Leaves parallel sided, bright or yellowish green — *Glyceria maxima*
   Leaves wider in centre, tapering, bluish-green — 6

6. Hairs present where leaf blade joins the sheath — *Phragmites communis*
   A membranous ligule present where the leaf blade joins the sheath — *Phalaris arundinacea*

7. Leaves almost triangular in cross section — *Sparganium erectum*
   Leaves flat or V-shaped in section — 8

8. Leaves iris-like, V-shaped below — *Iris pseudacorus*
   Leaves flat throughout, not V-shaped (leaves less than 7 mm wide, T. angustifolia: leaves over 7 mm wide, T. latifolia) — *Typha*

9. Leaves grass-like — 10
   Leaves strap-like — 15

10. Tall erect reed-like plant with wide leaves (often more than 10 mm wide) — 11
    Stems trailing in water, often with short, erect branch-shoots, not reed-like; leaves usually less than 10 mm wide, somewhat blue-green — 13

11. Ligule (at base of blade, on upper surface) a dense eyelash-like fringe of hairs, leaves bluish-green — *Phragmites communis*
    Ligule membranous, conspicuous — 12

12. Leaves flat, tapering above, blue-green; leaf sheaths without keel; ligule over 6 mm long — *Phalaris arundinacea*
    Leaves channelled, parallel-sided for much of their length, bright green; leaf sheaths keeled on the back; ligule less than 6 mm long — *Glyceria maxima*

13. Youngest leaf rolled in shoot, which is thus cylindrical — *Agrostis stolonifera*
    Youngest leaf folded in shoot, which is thus laterally compressed — 14

14. Leaf blades tapering for much of length, up to 8 mm wide (submerged leaves may be parallel-sided) — *Catabrosa aquatica*
    Leaf blades parallel-sided nearly to tip usually above 5 mm wide — *Glyceria fluitans*

15. Leaves long-tapering, bending in current from junction of blade and sheath — *Scirpus lacustris*
    Leaves parallel-sided almost to the tip, bending in current from the base — 16

16. Leaves usually over 1 cm wide, separated; veins at the leaf-tip few, well separated — *Sagittaria sagittifolia*
    Leaves usually under 1 cm wide, grouped into shoots; veins at the leaf-tip many, crowded — *Sparganium emersum*

17. Plant 2–3 mm wide, floating — *Lemna minor*
    Plant composed of stems and leaves, rooted — 13

18. Plant submerged and leaves thread-like — 19
    Leaves not submerged, or leaves not thread-like — 23

19. Leaves opposite or alternate — 15
    Leaves whorled — 22

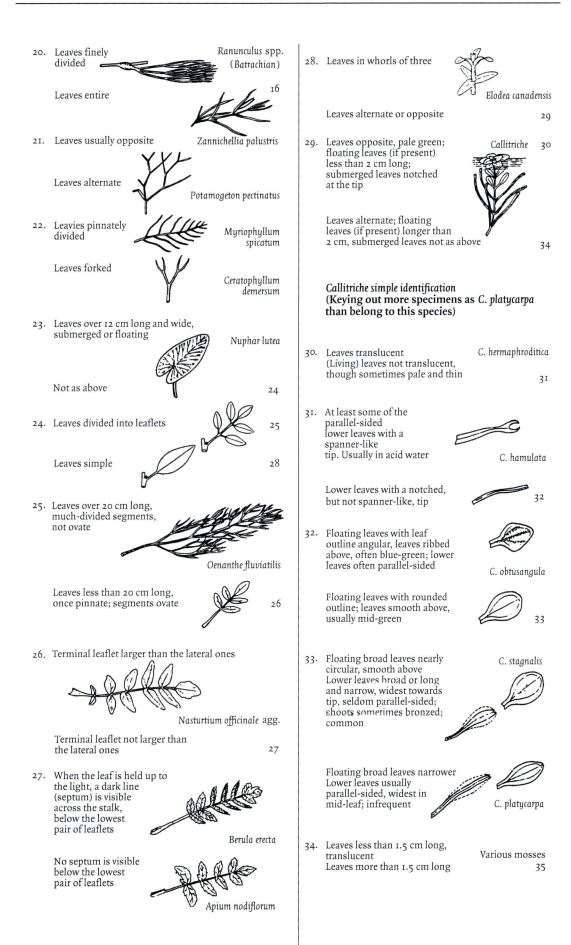

20. Leaves finely divided — Ranunculus spp. (Batrachian) 16

Leaves entire

21. Leaves usually opposite — Zannichellia palustris

Leaves alternate — Potamogeton pectinatus

22. Leavies pinnately divided — Myriophyllum spicatum

Leaves forked — Ceratophyllum demersum

23. Leaves over 12 cm long and wide, submerged or floating — Nuphar lutea

Not as above 24

24. Leaves divided into leaflets 25

Leaves simple 28

25. Leaves over 20 cm long, much-divided segments, not ovate — Oenanthe fluviatilis

Leaves less than 20 cm long, once pinnate; segments ovate 26

26. Terminal leaflet larger than the lateral ones — Nasturtium officinale agg.

Terminal leaflet not larger than the lateral ones 27

27. When the leaf is held up to the light, a dark line (septum) is visible across the stalk, below the lowest pair of leaflets — Berula erecta

No septum is visible below the lowest pair of leaflets — Apium nodiflorum

28. Leaves in whorls of three — Elodea canadensis

Leaves alternate or opposite 29

29. Leaves opposite, pale green; floating leaves (if present) less than 2 cm long; submerged leaves notched at the tip — Callitriche 30

Leaves alternate; floating leaves (if present) longer than 2 cm, submerged leaves not as above 34

Callitriche simple identification
(Keying out more specimens as C. platycarpa than belong to this species)

30. Leaves translucent — C. hermaphroditica
(Living) leaves not translucent, though sometimes pale and thin 31

31. At least some of the parallel-sided lower leaves with a spanner-like tip. Usually in acid water — C. hamulata

Lower leaves with a notched, but not spanner-like, tip 32

32. Floating leaves with leaf outline angular, leaves ribbed above, often blue-green; lower leaves often parallel-sided — C. obtusangula

Floating leaves with rounded outline; leaves smooth above, usually mid-green 33

33. Floating broad leaves nearly circular, smooth above — C. stagnalis
Lower leaves broad or long and narrow, widest towards tip, seldom parallel-sided; shoots sometimes bronzed; common

Floating broad leaves narrower — C. platycarpa
Lower leaves usually parallel-sided, widest in mid-leaf; infrequent

34. Leaves less than 1.5 cm long, translucent — Various mosses
Leaves more than 1.5 cm long 35

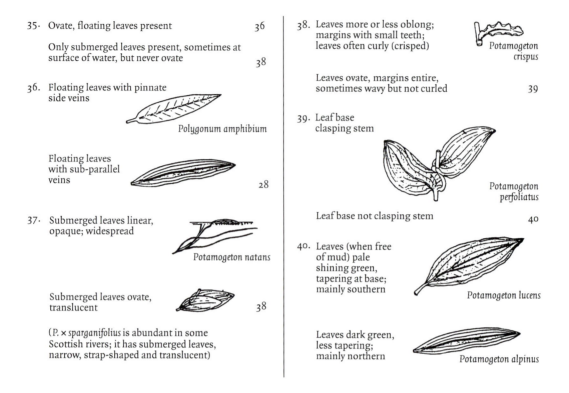

35. Ovate, floating leaves present   36

    Only submerged leaves present, sometimes at
    surface of water, but never ovate   38

36. Floating leaves with pinnate
    side veins

    Polygonum amphibium

    Floating leaves
    with sub-parallel
    veins   28

37. Submerged leaves linear,
    opaque; widespread

    Potamogeton natans

    Submerged leaves ovate,
    translucent   38

    (P. × *sparganifolius* is abundant in some
    Scottish rivers; it has submerged leaves,
    narrow, strap-shaped and translucent)

38. Leaves more or less oblong;
    margins with small teeth;
    leaves often curly (crisped)
    Potamogeton crispus

    Leaves ovate, margins entire,
    sometimes wavy but not curled   39

39. Leaf base
    clasping stem

    Potamogeton perfoliatus

    Leaf base not clasping stem   40

40. Leaves (when free
    of mud) pale
    shining green,
    tapering at base;
    mainly southern
    Potamogeton lucens

    Leaves dark green,
    less tapering;
    mainly northern   *Potamogeton alpinus*

Fig. 4.3 *Some common or ecologically useful watercourse species (Haslam, 1978). Alphabetical list:*

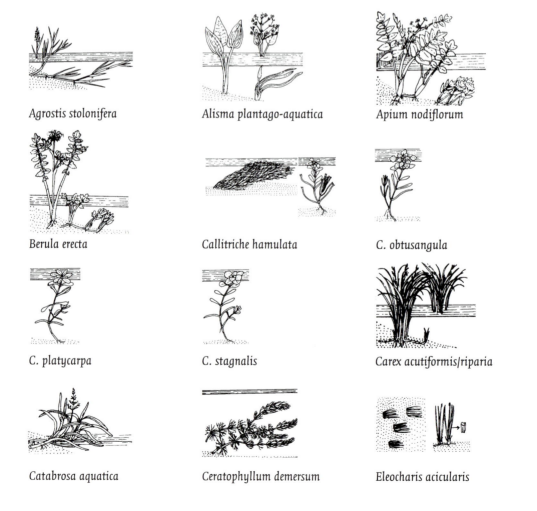

Agrostis stolonifera

Alisma plantago-aquatica

Apium nodiflorum

Berula erecta

Callitriche hamulata

C. obtusangula

C. platycarpa

C. stagnalis

Carex acutiformis/riparia

Catabrosa aquatica

Ceratophyllum demersum

Eleocharis acicularis

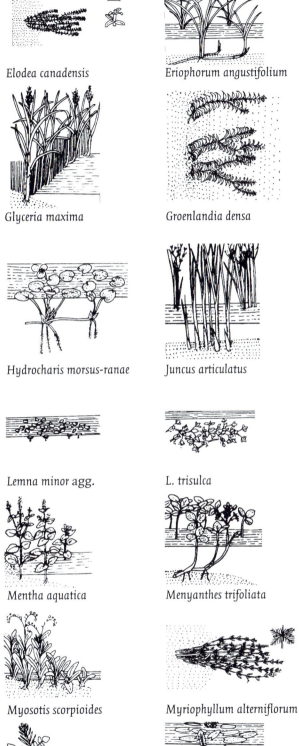

Scirpus fluitans

Elodea canadensis

Eriophorum angustifolium

G. fluitans (and without the floating leaves, *G. pedicillata, G. declinata*)

Glyceria maxima

Groenlandia densa

Hottonia palustris

Hydrocharis morsus-ranae

Juncus articulatus

J. bulbosus

Lemna minor agg.

L. trisulca

Littorella uniflora

Mentha aquatica

Menyanthes trifoliata

Mimulus guttatus

Myosotis scorpioides

Myriophyllum alterniflorum

M. spicatum

Nasturtium officinale agg.

Nuphar lutea

Oenanthe crocata

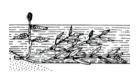

O. fluviatilis

Phalaris arundinacea

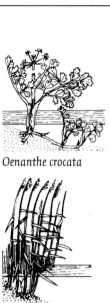

Phragmites australis

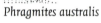
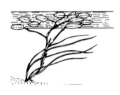

Polygonum amphibium

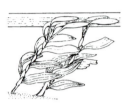

Potamogeton alpinus

P. crispus

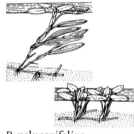

P. natans

P. pectinatus

P. perfoliatus

P. polygonifolius

P. × sparganifolius

Ranunculus aquatilis/peltatus

R. calcareous

R. penicillatus

R. circinatus

R. flammula

R. fluitans

R. trichophyllus

Rorippa amphibia

Sagittaria sagittifolia

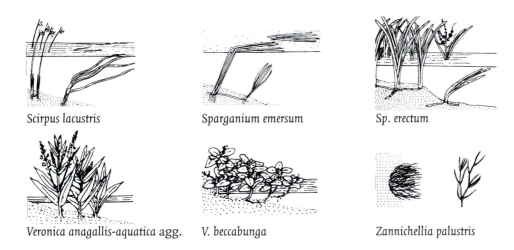

Scirpus lacustris   Sparganium emersum   Sp. erectum

Veronica anagallis-aquatica agg.   V. beccabunga   Zannichellia palustris

Fig. 4.4. Species typically tolerant and semi-tolerant to Sewage Treatment Works and similar effluents (includes species from the alphabetical list above).

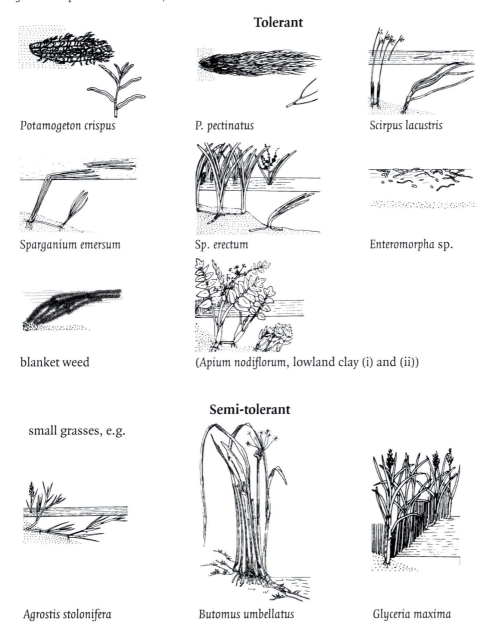

Tolerant

Potamogeton crispus   P. pectinatus   Scirpus lacustris

Sparganium emersum   Sp. erectum   Enteromorpha sp.

blanket weed   (Apium nodiflorum, lowland clay (i) and (ii))

Semi-tolerant

small grasses, e.g.

Agrostis stolonifera   Butomus umbellatus   Glyceria maxima

Lemna minor agg.

Nuphar lutea

Rorippa amphibia

(Phalaris arundinacea, highlands)

The fringing herbs comprise short, bushy dicotyledenous herbs frequently fringing streams, especially on lowland and chalk sandstone.

Apium nodiflorum

Mimulus guttatus

Veronica anagallis-aquatica agg.

Berula erecta

Nasturtium officinale agg.

Veronica beccabunga

Mentha aquatica

Nutrient status order

Different species occur in habitats of different nutrient status. By studying river habitats, it is possible to list species in order from those occurring in the most nutrient-deficient (dystrophic) to the most nutrient-rich (eutrophic) streams (defined here by the study of river habitats). The list (Table 4.3) is based on many thousands of sites, but other researchers, with different sites, may produce rather different orders – no doubt equally valid within their parameters.

The nutrient status, or Colour Band for any site is determined by:
1 locating each species present on Table 4.3;
2 ignoring unbanded species; and
3 deciding which band or bands best represents these species, weighting abundant species as more important than sparse ones.

If 5+ 'coloured' species are present, the band can normally be assigned with certainty (e.g. Blue with *Agrostis stolonifera, Mimulus guttatus, Myosotis scorpioides, Nasturtium officinale, Ranunculus* sp., *Solanum dulcamara.*)

If 3–4 'coloured' species are present, and present in the same band, the band can again be assigned easily (e.g. Purple: *Elodea canadensis, Potamogeton perfoliatus, Glyceria maxima*).

Table 4.3 Colour (nutrient status) Banding.
Species listed from nutrient-deficient to nutrient-rich

Sphagnum spp.
Drosera rotundifolia
D. anglica
Narthecium ossifragum
Eriophorum angustifolium
Littorella uniflora
Menyanthes trifoliata
Potamogeton polygonifolius
Carex rostrata
Ranunculus flammula
Sparganium angustifolium

Brown
(dystrophic)

Caltha palustris
Ranunculus hederaceus
R. omiophyllus
Oenanthe crocata (channel, not bank)
Myriophyllum alterniflorum
Callitriche hamulata
Juncus articulatus
Eleocharis acicularis
Scirpus fluitans
Juncus bulbosus
Nymphaea alba (not planted)
(*Nuphar lutea* local, with others from here)
Eleocharis palustris

Orange

Glyceria fluitans (with long floating leaves)
Potamogeton gramineus

P. × *sparganifolius*
Carex acuta (hill)
Potamogeton alpinus
Phalaris arundinacea
Iris pseudacorus (highland)
Mosses (hill)
(*Carex acutiformis* with others from here)
Blanket weed sparse, hills
Petasites hybridus

Yellow
(oligotrophic)

Mimulus guttatus
Lemna trisulca
Veronica beccabunga
Berula erecta
Mentha aquatica
Ranunculus (short leaved, Batrachian)
Callitriche spp. (not *C. hamulata*)
Mosses, lowlands
Nasturtium officinale agg.
Ranunculus (medium leaved, Batrachian)
Solanum dulcamara
Apium nodiflorum
Myosotis scorpioides
(*Oenanthe crocata,* banks)
Veronica anagallis-aquatica agg.
Potamogeton natans
Hippuris vulgaris
Ranunculus trichophyllus
Sparganium erectum

Blue
(mesotrophic, limestone and other rocks)

Elodea canadensis
Carex acutiformis agg.
Phragmites australis
Potamogeton perfoliatus
Ranunculus penicillatus, long-leaved
Polygonum amphibium
Blanket weed
Groenlandia densa
Zannichellia palustris
Oenanthe fluviatilis
Ranunculus fluitans
Glyceria maxima
Alisma plantago-aquatica
(*Nymphaea alba* former clay stream position)
Potamogeton lucens
Myriophyllum spicatum
Acorus calamus (introduced)
Potamogeton crispus
Phalaris arundinacea
Iris pseudacorus (lowland)

Purple
(semi-eutrophic

Epilobium hirsutum
(*Caltha palustris,* just on bank (often planted))
Enteromorpha sp.
Ceratophyllum demersum
Rumex hydrolapathum
Sparganium emersum
Sagittaria sagittifolia
Butomus umbellatus
Potamogeton pectinatus
Rorippa amphibia
Scirpus lacustris
Nuphar lutea

Red
(eutrophic)

Non-banded include:

Agrostis stolonifera and other small grasses not listed above
Lemna minor agg.
Other and rare aquatics (many of which can be banded by detailed study in their habitats).
Land species

If, though, one or two 'coloured' species are present in one Colour Band, or three or four spread among several Colour Bands, the band assigned is doubtful. With fewer species, and more of them unbanded, assignment becomes impossible (e.g. Blue–Purple? *Nasturtium offici-nale*, *Elodea canadensis*, *Phalaris arundinacea*). Doubtful Colour Bands, though, if occurring repeatedly in different sites along a stream (e.g. *Yellow–Blue* in a mountain stream), may be considered certain.

Each species is placed by its median habitat. Some species have very narrow ranges (e.g. *Sphagnum* spp.), others are wider but do not overlap with species far from their listed place (e.g. *Potamogeton alpinus*, *Rorippa amphibia*). In contrast, *Sparganium erectum* is one of the widest-ranging species, occurring with most of the listed species, though being most frequent where it is here placed. Species listed twice are *Nuphar lutea* and *Iris pseudacorus*, near-absent in the middle part between the two mentions, and *Phalaris arundinacea*, stretching between the two. *Nymphaea alba* was wide-ranging earlier, but is now rarely present in more nutrient-rich streams unless planted.

The validity of banding streams by nutrient status, by relating it to absolute nutrient status as given by rock type, is shown in Tables 4.4, 4.5 (those not statistically minded can ignore this!).

Table 4.4.
The correlation of nutrient status banding of species, with stream size and rock type (Germany).
Nutrient regimes are described by the Colour Band system
The table gives the probability of random distribution with respect to stream size type. The values mean that e.g. the probability of *Orange* Band species occurring randomly in all stream sizes is 0.05 in size (i) streams, etc.

| | Stream size | | | |
| | Brooks and ditches | | Rivers | |
Colour Band	**(i)**	**(ii)**	**(iii)**	**(iv)**
Orange (nutrient-poor)	0.05	<0.001	<0.001	0.001
Turquoise (nutrient-medium)	0.3	<<0.001	<0.001	0.01
Purple (nutrient-rich)	—	0.01	<0.001	0.3[1]

[1] Probability higher because of the frequent occurrence of pollution-tolerant species which happen also to belong to the *Purple* Colour Band.
Probabilities of e.g. <0.001 indicate that the group tends towards non-random distributions on different rock types.
Probabilities of e.g. 0.3 indicate that the group tends towards random distribution in different rock types.

Table 4.5. The correlation of nutrient status banding
of species with stream size (Germany)
The table gives the probability of random distribution with respect to stream size (stream sizes are eliminated separately). The values mean that the probability of *Orange* Band species occurring randomly in all stream sizes is 0.01 in limestone streams, etc.

Colour Band	Limestone, etc.	Muschel-kalk	Eutrophic moraine	Sandstone	Alluvium	Diluvium, peat, loess, etc.	Resistant rock
Orange (nutrient-poor)	0.01	0.5	—	0.5	0.7	—	0.001
Turquoise (nutrient-medium)	0.01	0.01	0.3	<<0.001	0.2	—	0.01
Purple (nutrient-rich)	<0.001	0.01	0.01	0.05	0.05	0.3	0.5
Overall effect in stream sizes (i)–(iv)	<<0.001						
Overall effect in stream sizes (ii)–(iv)	<0.001						

Probabilities of e.g. <0.001 indicate that the group tends towards non-random distributions in different stream sizes.
Probabilities of e.g. 0.7 indicate that the group tends towards random distribution in different rock types.

Determination of cover

Some people can assess cover by eye and with no difficulty. Those without that gift may find the following figures a useful guide. The cover used for these definitions is that in water up to 1 m deep, or in side bands if all water is deep.

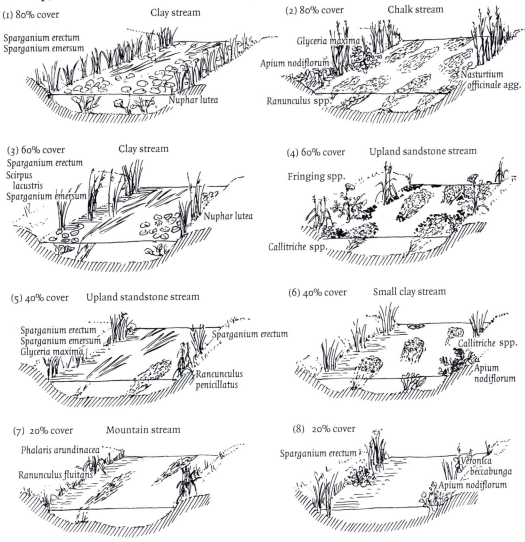

Fig. 4.5. Cover (Haslam & Wolseley, 1981).

Tall monocotyledons

Tall monocots grow in shallow non-scouring habitats: they are emerged species (except for the submerged form of *Scirpus lacustris*) so need shallow water, and as large stiff plants they are susceptible to scouring flow and erosion. Conversely, being tall and dense-leaved, where they can grow, they can shade out all shorter species. Therefore, the characteristic habitat is fringing the banks of larger streams, and covering the bed of small ones with slow flow or negligible water (though not dry). When plentiful, they hinder flow, and so may be cut, dredged or sprayed. In watercourses they are usually restricted to water up to 1 m deep. Weed control to prevent them dominating deeper channels is unnecessary.

Tall monocot distribution is thus controlled by a combination of:

1 **Depth of water and availability of substrate** suitable for anchorage and nutrition (reasonably soft but firm, and (except for *Carex rostrata*) not nutrient poor).

2 **Water flow.** Swift flow, whether continuous (e.g. highland or larger chalk streams) or intermittent (frequent storm flows) prohibits tall monocot clumps (in its path of full force).

3 **Management practices.** Rivers shoal, and shoal especially where abundant silt comes from the rock type (e.g. clay) or the land use (e.g. intensive farming). The shoaling occupies water space, so increases flood hazard. On shoals, fringing tall monocots can grow down into the water – if there are good substrate and (necessarily) lack of scour. This adds to the flood hazard.

4 **Pollution.** Pollution, of course, restricts or prevents development.

When water depth is reduced, by over-abstraction, land drainage or drought; water depth; and force of flow are reduced, and tall monocots can spread. They can therefore be used to monitor water force. Typical quantities of tall monocots are shown in Fig. 4.6. Larger amounts are suspect.

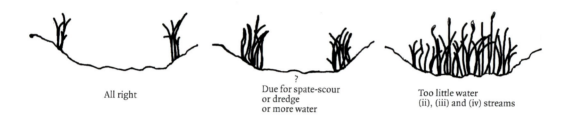

All right   Due for spate-scour   Too little water
                                  or dredge   (ii), (iii) and (iv) streams
                                  or more water

Fig. 4.6 Patterns of tall monocotyledons.

The most important tall monocotyledons in British watercourses are:

Acorus calamus	*Phalaris arundinacea*
Carex spp. (particularly *C. acuta*, *C. acutiformis*,	*Phragmites australis*
C. pseudocyperus, *C. riparia*, *C. rostrata* (high-	*Scirpus lacustris*
land))	*Sparganium erectum*
Glyceria maxima	*Typha* spp.
Iris pseudacorus	

Of these, *Sparganium erectum* is the most widespread, and is, in fact, the most frequent British river aquatic. Although each species has, of course, its own habitat range, they can also be treated as a group.

Phalaris arundinacea occurs the furthest into the highlands, growing even on rocky shores and 'islets' in hill rivers. In lowland rivers it is usually further up the bank, sometimes not even reaching to the water. It can tolerate nutrient-poor conditions. It seldom dominates stream beds.

Sparganium erectum is the most frequent, and often comes in next downstream after *Phalaris arundinacea* in hill rivers. Unlike the latter it does not grow far up banks, and mostly grows around water level. It spreads very rapidly when conditions become favourable – it will spread across stream beds. Outside dykes and ditches, such spread is due to water shortage, since in 'proper streams', (size (ii) and above), water depth and force prevent this.

Glyceria maxima most often occurs with high silt (downstream reaches, silt wetlands, etc.), and in water regime lies in between *Phalaris arundinacea* and *Sparganium erectum*.

Scirpus (*Schoenoplectus*) *lacustris* grows in deeper water. It is not a typical or usual bank-edge species, and only doubtfully belongs on this list. Its rhizome can anchor in a flowing-water river bed. With greater flow and depth, and earlier in the summer, *Scirpus lacustris* bears a sward of submerged leaves. The emerged shoots develop more with less water and in late summer. Although mid-river clumps of this species do not necessarily indicate water shortage, obviously they are commoner with water shortage.

Phragmites communis is infrequent in rivers, occurring mostly in brackish-water reaches. In wetland dykes and drains, though, it is common, thriving under moderate interferences and dominating shallow channels if unchecked. *Acorus calamus* is introduced, and its distribution is restricted. Its habitat resembles that of *Sparganium erectum. Carex* spp. and *Typha* spp. occur rather similarly to but sparser than *Sparganium erectum. Iris pseudacorus* is both sparse (except in north west Scotland) and rarely occurs in quantity.

River classification A: Haslam and Wolseley Method
(modified from Haslam & Wolseley, 1981)

In this system, rivers are classified according rock type, landscape and stream size. Plant communities listed are those characteristic of the main stream habitats of Britain. Naturally, intermediates of communities and habitats occur, and where these are suspected both alternative habitats should be consulted. Not all sites will have the exact vegetation listed here. If undamaged, however, the vegetation should have the same diversity, Colour Band and percentage cover.

Each section, divided according to rock type, is headed by a description applicable to all streams on that rock type. Where more than one landscape type occurs on a given rock type the next subdivision is by landscape. Finally, each size of stream found in that landscape and rock type is described and defined, and its typical vegetation is listed. When the species list is divided into abundant and associate species, all species occurring in the lists of abundants can be deemed to occur also in the list of associates.

Standard information given, for each type, includes:
- **Rock type**
- **Landscape type**
- **Stream size**
- **Colour Band**
- **Species diversity number:** *minimum* number of species expected in an undamaged (low-impact site, see Appendix for survey method).
- **Percentage cover:** *minimum* percentage cover expected in an undamaged site in water up to 1 m deep (or at sides, if all of river deeper or too turbid to see depth).
- Cross-section **illustration:** this shows the typical appearance of the stream and its banks. The banks at the site being examined should be carefully compared with those in the illustration, since unusually steep slopes around water level decrease emergent vegetation, and unusually gentle ones increase it. These factors should be considered before damage is assessed (Chapter 6). Any extreme drainage and channelling, greatest in smaller lowland streams, is clearly shown.

The 'probable species' and Colour Bands given should remain stable if habitats do so too. Cover should remain stable in the lowlands, and is noted as variable in hill streams anyway.

The diversity data in this chapter come from records made from 1970 to 1980 (and to 1990). It is likely that, over the lifetime of this method, diversity and perhaps cover will alter. Changes will be observed by experienced and long-term workers and the script can be appropriately corrected. Changes will be less easily detected by beginners, and assessments of pollution depend on accurate expectations of diversity (Chapter 6). If a change is suspected, and no long-term workers are available for consultation, studies should be made of reaches of rivers whose history for the past eight years is known, and which are not much suffering from pollution or water shortage, and have representative 'low' management for the region. These survey records can be used as the standards.

Water depths also may alter with land drainage, abstraction, rainfall and other factors. Water quality may alter with changes in land use, pollution, and other factors.

Limestone streams

Chalk – Lowland

Chalk is very pure soft limestone, normally forming rolling lowland hills up to c. 250 m high. Much of the brook water comes from springs, giving fairly swift stable flows of sparkling clear water over gravelly beds with – for lowlands – little silt. (Abstraction has often reduced surface water, and pumping or bottom-sealing may be used to obtain water. Since chalk is aquiferous, it is particularly badly affected, but other rock types also have lowered water levels from abstraction and most types have lowered levels from land drainage.) Clean rivers are mesotrophic, with a high hardness ratio (calcium plus magnesium divided by sodium plus potassium) and particularly low levels of magnesium, phosphate-phosphorus, chloride and sulphate-sulphur.

Chalk streams occur from Dorset to Kent, and from Hampshire to Yorkshire. Many streams which are 'chalk streams' in terms of fisheries or geography, e.g. River Dorset (Avon), have outcrops of other rocks in the catchment, which influence the vegetation.

Small streams without water-supported species (type (i))

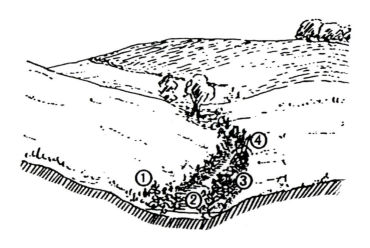

| *Blue* | 3 spp. | 20% cover |

Local, dry for most of the summer or for most or all of the year.

Probable species:	*Mentha aquatica* ①	*Veronica beccabunga* ③
	Myosotis scorpioides ②	Small grasses
	Phalaris arundinacea ④	Land spp.
	Veronica anagallis-aquatica agg.	
If wetter:	*Apium nodiflorum*	
If wetter again:	*Nasturtium officinale* agg.	

CHALK

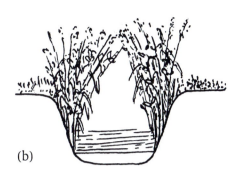

(a)

(b)

Variants: (a) dried grazed channels, (b) dug ditches

Small streams with water-supported species (ii)

Blue   6 species   75% cover

Common, c. 30–40 cm deep, perennial flow or dried in late summer. Gravelly. *Apium nodiflorum* and *Berula erecta* frequently submerged. Fringing herbs in carpets, short bands or short small clumps (the carpets typically submerged, and even the clumps often partly submerged).

Often abundant:	*Apium nodiflorum*	*Nasturtium officinale* agg. ③
	Berula erecta ②	*Ranunculus* spp. (short-leaved) ①
	Callitriche spp.	
Often associated:	*Catabrosa aquatica* ④	*Phalaris arundinacea*
	(*Hippuris vulgaris*)	*Sparganium erectum*
	Lemna minor agg.	*Veronica anagallis-aquatica* agg.
	Mentha aquatica	*Veronica beccabunga*
	Mimulus guttatus	Small grasses
	Myosotis scorpioides	Mosses

Variant:
(a) *Potamogeton lucens* in flatter areas with some alluvium.

Medium streams (iii)

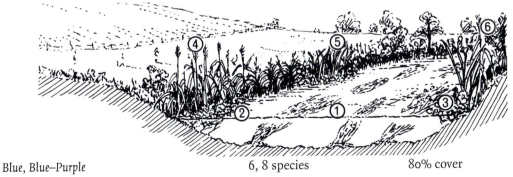

Blue, Blue–Purple   6, 8 species   80% cover

Common, c. 30–75 cm deep. Flow usually moderate. Gravelly, little silt. Fringing herbs as above.

CHALK/OOLITE

Often abundant:	*Ranunculus* spp. (medium-leaved)①	
Smaller or shallower:	*Berula erecta* *Callitriche* spp. ②	*Nasturtium officinale* agg. ③
Often associated:	*Apium nodiflorum* *Carex acutiformis* agg. ⑥ *Catabrosa aquatica* *Mentha aquatica* *Myosotis scorpioides* *Phalaris arundinacea* ④	*Sparganium erectum* ⑤ *Veronica anagallis-aquatica* agg. *Veronica beccabunga* Small grasses Mosses
And in deeper, slower, siltier reaches, one to three of:	*Elodea canadensis* *Glyceria maxima* *Groenlandia densa* *Oenanthe fluviatilis*	*Scirpus lacustris* (*Sparganium emersum*) Blanket weed

Note. In swifter parts the species in the last list indicate eutrophication.

Large streams (iv)

Blue–Purple, Purple	9 species	80% cover

Infrequent, 75 cm or more deep. Flow usually moderate to slow. Some silting. Fringing herbs usually in wisps or small short clumps.

Often abundant:	*Ranunculus* spp. (long–medium-leaved) ①	
Very shallow:	*Berula erecta*	
Very silty:	*Scirpus lacustris* ②	
Often associated:	*Apium nodiflorum* *Callitriche* spp. *Carex acutiformis* agg. ③ *Elodea canadensis* ④ *Glyceria maxima* ⑤ *Mentha aquatica* *Nasturtium officinale* agg. *Oenanthe fluviatilis* ⑥	(*Potamogeton crispus*) (*Rumex hydrolapathum*) *Sparganium emersum* ⑦ *Sparganium erectum* ⑧ *Veronica anagallis-aquatica* agg. *Zannichellia palustris* ⑨ Small grasses

Oolite – Lowland

Oolite is a soft limestone, less pure than chalk, normally forming rolling hills up to *c.* 120–245 m. Oolite usually outcrops on ridges, with clay (solid or boulder) in the valleys between and sometimes also on the ridge. Oolite streams therefore soon flow on to clay, and there are no large and few medium streams solely on oolite. Brook flows vary from chalk-like (swift stable flows of sparkling clear water over gravelly beds) to slower, less clear, and more silty streams. As on chalk, the substrate is mesotrophic with a high hardness ratio and low nutrient levels. Many are polluted as well as shallowed.

Lowland oolite streams occur from Somerset to Lincolnshire, being most in the Cotswolds, Northamptonshire Wolds, and the ridges projecting north from these into Lincolnshire.

Small streams without water-supported species (i)
Local, dry for most of the summer.

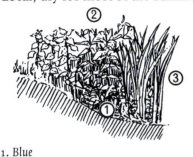

Probable species:	*Apium nodiflorum* ①
	Epilobium hirsutum ②
	Nasturtium officinale agg.
	Phalaris arundinacea
	Sparganium erectum ③
	Veronica beccabunga
	Grasses
	Land spp.

Variant:
(a) Dried grazed channels (see Fig. on p. 88).

1. *Blue*   3+ species   40+% cover

Local, dry for most of the year. Often sunk with steep banks.

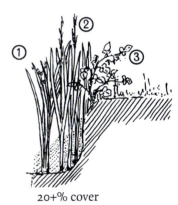

Probable species:	*Sparganium erectum* ①
Often associated:	*Epilobium hirsutum*
	Glyceria maxima ②
	Phalaris arundinacea
	Solanum dulcamara ③
	Land grasses
	Land spp.

2. *Purple*, with tall emergents only   1+ species   20+% cover

Small streams with water-supported species (ii)

Blue   6+ species   50+% cover

Frequent, usually 20–30 cm deep. Moderate flow. Silty and gravelly. Species like chalk streams, but a little more *Purple* in Colour Band.

OOLITE/HARD LIMESTONE

Often abundant:	Apium nodiflorum①	Sparganium erectum②
	Ranunculus spp.	Blanket weed
	(short- and medium-leaved)③	
Often associated:	Berula erecta	Sparganium emersum
	Callitriche spp.	Enteromorpha sp.
	Phalaris arundinacea	and one to three others from the
		Blue or Purple bands

Variants:
(a) Brooks indistinguishable from chalk (e.g. upper River Thames).
(b) Brooks like chalk–clay ones (see below).
(Note: with variant (b) eutrophication as a result of human activities can be diagnosed only if there is, in the vicinity, an otherwise similar stream (or a reach of the same stream) with a species assemblage from a Bluer band. Then, the difference between the two indicates the degree of eutrophication.)

Medium streams (iii)

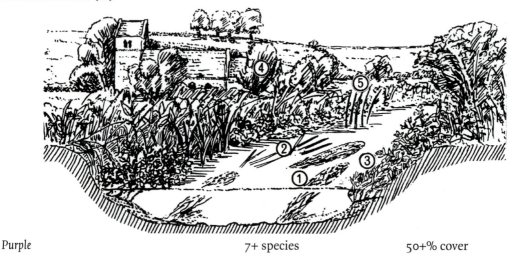

Purple   7+ species   50+% cover

Infrequent, c. 30–75 cm deep. Flow usually moderate. Some silt.
Species like those in chalk streams, but less Blue and more Red in Colour Band.

Often abundant:	Ranunculus spp.	Sparganium emersum
	(short- or medium-leaved)①	Blanket weed
Often associated:	Apium nodiflorum②	Enteromorpha sp.
	Schoenoplectus lacustris③	Often other, usually Purple, spp.
	Sparganium erectum④	

Hard limestone

Most hard limestone streams are mountainous. Even though the hills are often well below 610 m, the fall from hilltop to stream channel is over 180 m, giving high force to the water. Silting, as on soft limestone, is low, and so the steeper channels contain negligible silt. There is an unusually great difference between the mountain vegetation, which is very sparse indeed, and the upland vegetation, which is abundant and often similar to that of chalk. Unless a stream is clearly upland, therefore, absence of plants (in a site whose former vegetation is unknown), cannot be assumed to be due to damage. In some parts acid peat can cover hard limestone, and this peat can be deposited in small slow channels, bringing in *Orange* or even *Brown* species. If the streams are influenced solely by the peat, their vegetation will be that of resistant rock streams with peat. With increasing limestone influence vegetation will be transitional between this and that of pure limestone. In nutrient status, the (non-peaty) silt is close to that of soft sandstone (with higher sodium) and is richer than that of chalk. However, where swift flow leads to coarse substrates, stream nutrient status can be low. Water level is often much lowered in more populated parts. Also see the general notes on topography and damage assessment in the section on resistant rocks.

Fringing herbs are usually emerged, not very large, and can be abundant and diverse in small brooks. Mosses are nearly as frequent as on resistant rocks (and much more so than on hard sandstone). On moorland, etc., dry (or shallow) small channels with *Juncus effusus* are very characteristic.

Hard limestone streams are most common in the Pennines, with smaller areas in e.g. the Mendips, and south and north Scotland.

Hard limestone – Upland, and Lowland

The land use is typically good grassland in the valleys, perhaps with moorland on the hills. As always in the hills, local variations in topography can lead to streams or reaches with greater scour and thus fewer plants. Substrates are mixed-grained, with much gravel. Lowered water levels may sharply decrease vegetation quantity and quality.

Small streams without water-supported species (i)

1. *Yellow to Blue* (with *Red Epilobium hirsutum*)   1+ species   10+% vegetation

Infrequent, often *c.* 20 cm deep

HARD LIMESTONE

Probable species:	*Mimulus guttatus* ①	*Veronica beccabunga* ②
	Nasturtium officinale agg.	Small grasses

Variants:
(a) In lowlands   *Sparganium erectum* is frequent
(b) Ditch-like, lowland or *Epilobium hirsutum*   *Sparganium erectum*
low upland, often with: *Phalaris arundinacea*   Small grasses
(c) Peaty, also with   *Caltha palustris*   *Juncus articulatus*
perhaps: *Eleocharis palustris*   *Iris pseudacorus*

(d) Peaty dry channels, with *Juncus effusus* dominant or with other species.

(e) Empty channels, often dry but with scouring storm flows, and with stony or peaty substrates.

(f) Small dry shallow grassy channels.

(g) Magnesian limestone. This outcrops in a narrow band along the eastern edge of the Pennines, and in a patch north of Teesside, in lowland or nearly-lowland country. Land use is arable and grassland. Undamaged vegetation is uncertain as the only large river on the rock is seriously polluted, and the other streams tend to be either small and shaded, etc., or large but on the rock for too short a distance to be affected by it.

2. Blue   3 species?   30% cover

Shallow (e.g. 20 cm) to summer-dry. Slow flow, usually silty. Vegetation often damaged.

Probable species:	*Apium nodiflorum*	*Solanum dulcamara*
	Epilobium hirsutum	*Sparganium erectum*
	Glyceria maxima	

Small streams with water-supported species (ii)

(*Orange to*) Blue   5+ species   50+% cover

Probable species:	*Mimulus guttatus* ①	*Veronica beccabunga*
	Myosotis scorpioides	Small grasses
	Nasturtium officinale agg. ②	Mosses
	(*Sparganium erectum*)	Blanket weed ③

Variants:
(a) Peaty, also with   *Caltha palustris*   *Phalaris arundinacea*
perhaps: *Juncus articulatus*   *Ranunculus flammula*

(b) More water force and/or a mixture of peaty and limestone substrate produces little vegetation, with mosses the commonest species.

(c) In a low-rainfall area without spate there may be 5+ species and 80+% cover.

Often abundant: *Ranunculus* spp.
Often associated: *Apium nodiflorum*   Mosses
                      Callitriche spp.   Blanket weed
                      Nasturtium officinale agg.

HARD LIMESTONE

Medium streams (iii)

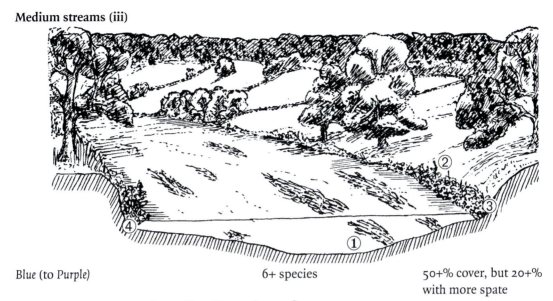

Blue (to *Purple*)	6+ species	50+% cover, but 20+% with more spate

Frequent, *c*. 30–75 cm deep. Usually moderate flow.

Often abundant: *Ranunculus* spp. ①
Often associated: (*Groenlandia densa*)   *Veronica beccabunga*
                       Mentha aquatica ②   Small grasses
                       Myosotis scorpioides ③   Mosses
                       Nasturtium officinale agg. ④

Variants:
(a) Downstream, deeper reaches also have *Purple* (and *Red*) species: 7+ species in all. These may include: *Elodea canadensis*   *Zannichellia palustris*
                       Myriophyllum spicatum   *Enteromorpha* sp.

(b) When there is slow flow, but high rainfall and some sedimentation, there may only be 2+ species in all.
Often abundant: *Potamogeton natans*   *Sp. erectum*
                       Sparganium emersum
Often associated: *Callitriche* spp.   Mosses
                       Small grasses

(c) Peaty streams without high water force may have 2+ species in all.
In addition perhaps: *Carex* spp.   *Phalaris arundinacea*
                       Juncus articulatus

(d) With more water force and/or a mixture of peaty and limestone substrate, mosses are the most frequent species, and small grasses and blanket weed are not rare.

Large streams (iv)

Blue to *Blue–Purple*   7+ species   40% cover

Rare, 0.5 m and deeper. Typically with moderate flow. Species list probably similar to type (iii).

Hard limestone – Mountain, and Alpine

Before the forests were cut down, flow would have been less swift and fierce, the forests acting as a 'sponge'. Scrub, bog, peaty soil, etc. behave similarly but to varying extents. The destruction of these, and the addition of all that increases flash scouring flows – like construction, agriculture and large roads – decrease potential vegetation. This decrease is most on steeper slopes where soil and silt are least. This catchment impact applies to all British rivers but most to those where water force has been greatly increased (on other rock types also).

Land use is often good grassland in the valleys, with poor grassland and mountain or moorland vegetation above. The fall from hilltop to stream channel must be carefully checked, as mountain limestone streams (i.e. those with falls of at least 185 m from hilltop to stream) can occur with hills only *c*. 300 m high, even if these are found only at the head of the catchment. Local variations in topography can lead to upland tributaries in flatter areas (or very mountainous ones in steeper areas, etc.). Intermediates occur between mountain and upland streams. Exposed rock (or boulders) is common on the bed, where the swift flow and fierce spates combine with the unsuitable substrate to make the habitat unfavourable for vegetation. Alternating stretches of swifter shallower (often rapid) water and slower deeper water are common.

Small streams (i) and (ii)

(Yellow to Blue)   0+ species   0+% cover

Frequent, *c.* 10–30 cm deep. Most channels empty. Channels with plants usually have mosses, whether with or without emergents.

Probable species	(*Petasites hybridus*)	Mosses
	(*Veronica beccabunga*)	(Blanket weed)
	(Small grasses)	

Variants:

(a) Peaty, perhaps with *Juncus articulatus* or *Eleocharis palustris*.
(b) Peaty dry channels, with *Juncus effusus* dominant or with other species.
(c) Small dry shallow grassy channels (and grading to upland).

Damage ratings must be calculated against a locally determined standard, and are unlikely to be detailed.

Medium streams (iii)

(Yellow to Blue–Purple)   0+ species   0+% cover

HARD LIMESTONE/CLAY

Frequent, usually 20–75 cm deep. Many channels empty.

| Probable species | (*Petasites hybridus*) ① | Mosses |
| | (Small grasses) | (Blanket weed) |

Variant:

(a) In lower reaches, or other stretches with lower water force, the following are infrequently found:

Carex acutiformis	*Ranunculus* spp. (short-leaved)
Elodea canadensis ③	*Sparganium erectum*
Nasturtium officinale agg.	*Zannichellia palustris*
Phalaris arundinacea ②	

Large streams (iv)

Yellow (to Blue–Purple)   (0+), 1+ species   0+% cover

Infrequent, *c.* 30 cm – 2 m deep. Many channels empty.

Probable species	(*Elodea canadensis*)	(Small grasses)
	(*Phalaris arundinacea*)	Mosses
	(*Ranunculus* spp. (short- to	Blanket weed
	medium-leaved)	

Variant:

(a) Slower parts may have more vegetation, and perhaps also:

Eleocharis palustris	*Potamogeton pectinatus*
Mimulus guttatus	*Sparganium erectum*
Myriophyllum spicatum	*Veronica beccabunga*

Clay

Clay is the commonest rock of lowland Britain. It strongly influences river vegetation, and clay communities also occur where thick boulder clay overlies other rock types and when small outcrops of other rocks occur in a mainly clay catchment. Brook water comes from run-off, and so is unstable, depending on rainfall. The non-porous land surface increases the instability of flow, and leads to there being many brooks in a given area. Much silt is washed off the land onto the stream bed and this, coupled with the unstable flow, leads to substrates which are silty and, especially in river centres, unstable. The water is usually somewhat turbid. The substrate is eutrophic, both because much silt is present and because the silt is nutrient-rich, with the highest levels of calcium, magnesium, sodium, phosphate-phosphorus, chloride and sulphate-sulphur found in any stream type, with a medium hardness ratio. Much-drained in recent decades, this is perhaps the stream type most widely polluted.

Lowland

The landscape varies from nearly flat to low hills up to *c.* 180 m. The low topography leads to slow flows and much silting. Lowland clay is the commonest habitat in southern and eastern England, and (as thick boulder clay) is locally important elsewhere (e.g. Anglesey).

CLAY

Small streams without water-supported species (i)

1. With tall emergents only.

Blue–Purple   1+ species   30+% cover

Frequent, dry for part of the year (or shallow with very slow flow). Often dug *c.* 2 m below ground level, with steep banks, the tall plants of which may partly shade the channels. Substrate usually silty. Often shaded with little or no vegetation.

Often abundant:	*Epilobium hirsutum* ①
	Land grasses
wetter:	*Sparganium erectum* ②
drier:	*Urtica dioica*
	Land spp.
Often associated:	*Glyceria maxima* ③

Phalaris arundinacea

Variant:
(a) Grade into ditches.

2. With short emergents.

Blue with *Epilobium hirsutum*   3+ species   10+% cover

Frequent, shallow (e.g. 5–20 cm), sometimes dry for part of the summer. Slow to moderate flow. Silty to gravelly. With more scour than (1), sometimes less deeply sunk, and often somewhat further downstream. Fringing herbs often tall, sometimes in large clumps. Many shaded, with little or no vegetation.

Often abundant:	*Apium nodiflorum*	*Sparganium erectum* ①
Often associated:	*Epilobium hirsutum*	*Phalaris arundinacea* ③
	Myosotis scorpioides	*Veronica beccabunga*
	Nasturtium officinale agg. ②	Small grasses

Variants:
(a) Dry with much grass, sometimes grazed
(b) Swift flow with coarse substrate and little vegetation.

CLAY

Small streams with water-supported species (ii)

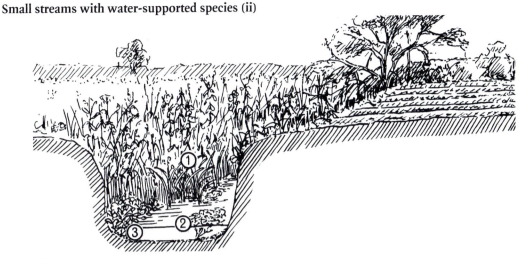

1. Smaller.

Blue   2+ species   20+% cover

Common, shallow (*c.* 10–30 cm), sometimes dry for part of the summer. Moderate to slow flow. Silty to gravelly. Often sunk 1–3 m below ground level and partly shaded by tall plants on these high banks. Fringing herbs often tall, sometimes in large clumps, always emerged. Many shaded, with little or no vegetation.

  Often abundant: *Apium nodiflorum*   *Sparganium erectum*①
                     Callitriche spp.②   *Veronica beccabunga*③
                     Nasturtium officinale agg.

If vegetation is less than expected, this is as likely to be due to drainage as to pollution.

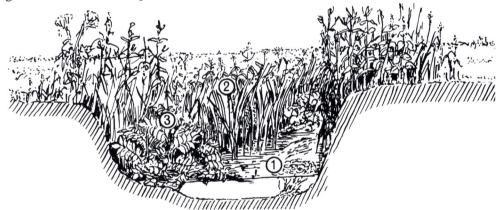

2. Larger.

Blue to Purple   6+ species (4+ if Blue or cover high)   50+% cover

Common, usually 20–30 cm deep, sometimes to *c.* 50 cm. Flow perennial, usually slow to moderate. Silty (to gravelly). Fringing herbs always emerged, usually tall, typically in (large) semi-circular clumps extending from the banks.

  Often abundant: *Callitriche* spp.①   *Sparganium erectum*②
  Often associated: (*Alisma plantago-aquatica*)   *Veronica beccabunga*
                      *Apium nodiflorum*③   Small grasses
                      Myosotis scorpioides   *Nasturtium officinale* agg.
                      Phalaris arundinacea   *Purple* species also occur

Potamogeton natans and *Ranunculus* spp. (e.g. *R. penicillatus* long-leaved; *R. trichophyllus*) usually indicate cleaner streams.

Variants:

(a) Swift flow with coarse substrate and little vegetation.

(b) In the west, e.g. South Wales, where the clay is harder and equally low-lying, vegetation is closer to that of limestone, with e.g. *Berula erecta, Solanum dulcamara, Veronica anagallis-aquatica* agg.

CLAY

Medium streams (iii)

Purple, Purple (–Red) (with *Blue*)   8+ species   60+% cover

Common, *c.* 30–75 cm deep, rarely more. Typically slow (to moderate) flow, with considerable silt. Fringing herbs emerged, usually tall, often in (large) semi-circular clumps growing out from the banks, particularly from gently sloping banks and during drought flows; fringing herbs also often in wispy small clumps.

Often abundant:	(*Elodea canadensis*)	(*Sagittaria sagittifolia*)
	*Nuphar lutea*②	*Sparganium emersum*①
Often associated:	(*Apium nodiflorum*)	*Phalaris arundinacea*
	Callitriche spp.	*Rorippa amphibia*⑥
	Lemna minor agg. ⑤	*Scirpus lacustris*④
	Myosotis scorpioides	*Sparganium erectum*
	Nasturtium officinale agg.③	Small grasses

Ranunculus (usually long-leaved *R. penicillatus*) or *Blue* species usually indicate cleaner streams. Eutrophication increases *Purple* and *Red* species.

Variants:

(a) Undercut or vertical banks decrease emergents.

(b) Swift flow with coarse substrates, and a depth of *c.* 30 cm leads to very little vegetation.

Typical species:	(*Potamogeton crispus*)	*Zannichellia palustris*
	Sparganium erectum	Small grasses

(c) In the west, e.g. South Wales, with harder and equally low-lying clay, vegetation is closer to that of limestone: *Blue–Purple*.

Often abundant:	*Berula erecta*	*Nasturtium officinale* agg.
	Callitriche spp.	*Sparganium erectum*
Often associated:	*Apium nodiflorum*	*Ranunculus* e.g.
	Elodea canadensis	*penicillatus*
	Potamogeton crispus	Mosses

Large streams (iv)

Purple–Red, Red (with *Blue*)   9+ species   60+% cover

UPLAND CLAY

Very frequent, sides usually at least 75 cm deep, centre often deeper and without vegetation. Flow usually slow, water somewhat turbid. Silt beds frequent (or bed of clay). Fringing herbs, when present, usually wispy, always emerged.

Often abundant:	*Nuphar lutea*①	*Scirpus lacustris* ③
	*Saggittaria sagittifolia*②	*Sparganium emersum* ④
Often associated:	*Butomus umbellatus*	*Sparganium erectum*⑤
	*Elodea canadensis*⑥	and a range of *Purple* and *Blue*
	Lemna minor agg. ⑦	species
	*Rorippa amphibia*⑧	

A high proportion of *Blue* and *Purple* species usually indicate clean streams (though the converse need not apply). Eutrophication increases the proportion of *Red* species.

Upland, and Mountain

Landscape with hills *c.* 345 m; the streams consequently have swifter flow. The silting and instability of flow associated with clay mean that on these higher hills (unlike those of chalk and soft sandstone) the streams form a different habitat. There is less silt, swifter flow, and a lower trophic status than in lowland streams of equivalent size. For equivalent impacts, the effects are greater, and vegetation is often much reduced. Upland clay areas are small, and there are no large rivers.

The main upland clay areas are to the north of the Mendips and the Wessex peninsula. The main mountain areas are on the Welsh Marches.

In e.g. north-west England, near-lowland streams on hard clay (and clay-mix) have upland–mountain vegetation and are classed here.

Small streams without water-supported species (i)

Blue?   1+ species, southern and upland   0+ species, the rest.

Rare, shallow and sometimes summer-dry. Little vegetation.

Probable species: *Sparganium erectum*
Small grasses

Upland and southern – small and medium streams with water-supported species (i) and (ii)

Blue, Blue–Purple (Purple)   4+ species in upper reaches
                                          6+ in lower ones   20+% cover

Infrequent, *c*. 30–75 cm deep. Flow usually moderate. Substrate mixed-grained. Fringing herbs usually shorter than in the lowlands, but emerged, and typically clumped (not in bands).

Probable species: (*Alisma plantago-aquatica*)   *Potamogeton crispus*
                         Apium nodiflorum   *Ranunculus* spp. (medium-
                         Callitriche spp.   leaved
                         Elodea canadensis   *Sparganium emersum*
                         Lemna minor agg.   *Sp. erectum*
                         Nasturtium officinale agg.   Mosses
                         Phalaris arundinacea

Ranunculus, Purple and *Red* species, enter in lower reaches.

Variants:
(a) If the flow is checked (e.g. by gates) species characteristic of lower reaches enter further upstream
(b) Steeper landscapes have less vegetation, approaching that listed below for northern and upland regions.

Mountain and upland, north-west England, etc. – small and medium streams with water-supported species (ii) and (iii)

0+ species

Infrequent, *c*. 20–75 cm deep. Flow usually fast (to moderate). Substrate mixed-grained (too coarse).

Probable species: Mosses.

Hard-clay lowland, north-west England, etc. – small streams with water-supported species (ii)

Blue (–Purple)   3+ species   20+% cover?

Local, 20–30 cm deep. Flow usually slow. Substrate mixed-grained.

Often abundant: *Callitriche* spp.
Often associated   *Alisma plantago-aquatica*   *P. natans*
                         Nasturtium officinale agg.   *Sparganium erectum*
                         Phalaris arundinacea   Small grasses
                         Potamogeton crispus

Medium streams (iii)

Purple (with Blue)   5+ species   50+% cover?

Local, *c*. 50 cm deep. Flow slow to fast. Substrate mixed.

Often abundant: *Elodea canadensis*   *Phalaris arundinacea* (as a fringe,
                         Myriophyllum spicatum   not as a channel dominant)
Often associated: *Myosotis scorpioides*   *Zannichellia palustris*
                         Petasites hybridus   Small grasses
                         Sparganium emersum   Mosses
                         Sp. erectum

Alluvial streams

These streams rise on the higher ground, usually clay, outside the plain, and when in the plain the vegetation gradually changes from that of clay (see above) to being somewhat like that of dykes and drains. As the watercourses still carry silt and water from the high ground, particularly during storm flows, the vegetation does not become that of an undamaged drain (when on silt or peat); because of the extra silting, it is more eutrophic. As the stream leaves the higher ground the flow becomes slow, the channel dyke-like in section and the substrate fine-grained. The larger streams, particularly in the Fenland, are much-managed, bearing only vegetation tolerant of this. These streams are necessarily confined to the larger alluvial plains.

Streams largely on clay, even in the alluvial plain

See Table 4.5 and clay, above.

Streams largely on peat or silt – smaller channels (i) and (ii)

Blue–Red	8+ species	80+% cover

Local, usually at least 50 cm deep. Little water movement except in storms.

Probable species:

*Ceratophyllum demersum*①   *Sagittaria sagittifolia*
Lemna minor agg.③   *Sparganium emersum*②
*Nuphar lutea*①   *Sp. erectum*④
*Phalaris arundinacea*⑦   *Enteromorpha* sp.⑥

Variants:
(a) Further from the high ground there is an increase in species which are in the dykes and drains (see table 4.6 and cross-sections pp. 130–2).
(b) The more the peat, the higher the proportion of non-eutrophic species.
(c) The more the silt, the higher the proportion of *Red* species (though a *Red* Colour Band indicates damage). CARE. Side channels to alluvial streams, sited solely in the plains, count as dykes, not streams: they have different habitat and ecology.

Coal measures streams

The landscape is upland or mountain (where coal measures outcrop in lowland areas, as in parts of the English Midlands, they are classed as clay). The substrate is often fairly coarse, because of the high water force in steeper areas. The nutrient status of the silt is high, fairly close to that of clay, so the streams are nutrient rich where low water force permits silt to accumulate. Peaty moorland may overlie the rock in some parts, and influence the vegetation. Coal

COAL MEASURES

Measures streams are usually polluted from mine and industrial effluents, so the undamaged vegetation is difficult to ascertain, and that described here may be incomplete. Also see the general notes on topography in the section on resistant rocks. Coal measures streams are most common in South Wales and the southern Pennines, but also occur elsewhere, e.g. southern Scotland.

Upland and lowland small streams (i) and (ii)

Blue to Purple (with Blue)   4+ species   20+% cover

Infrequent, c. 10–40 cm deep. Usually have slow flow and little spate.

Probable species:

	Alisma plantago-aquatica	*Sparganium emersum*
	Callitriche spp.	*Sp. erectum*
	Elodea canadensis	*Veronica beccabunga*
	Lemna minor agg.	Small grasses
	Potamogeton crispus	
	P. natans	

Variants:

(a) Swifter flow, less vegetation.

(b) Lowland streams with less water force have 4+ species, 40+% cover.

(c) Ditch-type variants have tall emergents and may be summer-dry, with e.g. *Epilobium hirsutum, Sparganium erectum.*

(d) Dry shallow grassy channels.

Mountain, and swifter upland small streams (i) and (ii)

(Yellow)   0, 2+ species   0+% cover

Infrequent, c. 20–40 cm deep. Channels often empty.

Probable species: *Myosotis scorpioides*   Mosses
                    (Small grasses)

and other species from (i + ii) above.

Variant:

(a) More peaty. Probable species, as well as the above, include:

	Eleocharis palustris	*Petasites hybridus*
	Juncus articulatus	*Phalaris arundinacea*

Medium and large streams (iii) and (iv)

Yellow to Blue–Purple   3+ (mountain)
                              8+ (upland) species   10+%, 25+% cover

Frequent, depth from 30 cm to deep. Clean vegetation dubious. Less, and Yellower vegetation in swifter streams; more, and more Purple vegetation in slower ones.

Probable species:

	Alisma plantago-aquatica	(*Ranunculus* spp.)
	Callitriche spp.	*Sparganium emersum*
	Lemna minor agg.	*Sp. erectum*
	Mimulus guttatus	Small grasses
	Phalaris arundinacea	Mosses
	Potamogeton natans	*Enteromorpha* sp.[1]
	Potamogeton pectinatus[1]	

[1] Only in polluted streams.

Sandstone streams

Soft (fertile) sandstone and sands – lowland

Soft sandstone country varies from nearly flat to hills occasionally reaching *c.* 345 m high. Intermittent patches of boulder clay are often frequent, and the vegetation described here may perhaps be slightly influenced by these. Brook water comes from springs and run-off. In flow, bed stability, silting, and water clarity, sandstone streams are intermediate between chalk and clay ones. Sand is common on the beds, and in swifter reaches may cause unstable substrates and sparse vegetation. The substrate is mesotrophic, but differs from that of the equally mesotrophic chalk in having more silt on the beds, higher concentrations of nutrients (particularly calcium, nitrogen, sodium and phosphate-phosphorus) in the silt and a lower hardness ratio. Water levels are threatened.

Soft sandstone mainly outcrops in southern England, the Cheshire–Shropshire region, and East Anglia. Large streams are few, and mainly too polluted to determine their undamaged vegetation.

Small streams without water-supported species (i)

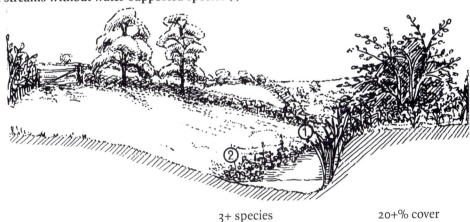

Blue　　　　　　　　　　　3+ species　　　　　　　20+% cover

Infrequent, usually dry for part or all of the summer. If wet, then shallow and flow usually slow. Substrate may be sandy.

Probable species:　　*Apium nodiflorum*　　　　　　*Sparganium erectum*①
　　　　　　　　　　Epilobium hirsutum　　　　　　*Veronica beccabunga*
　　　　　　　　　　*Myosotis scorpioides*②　　　　Small grasses

Variant:
(a) Grade into dug ditches.

LOWLAND SANDSTONE

Small streams with water-supported species (ii)

Blue (Blue–Purple)   6+ species   50+% cover

Frequent, usually not over 30 cm deep. Usually with moderate or slow perennial flow and a mixed-grained substrate. Fringing herbs are short, as in chalk streams, but are emerged, not forming submerged carpets, and more often in clumps than bands.

Often abundant:	*Apium nodiflorum*	*Callitriche* spp.
Often associated:	*Lemna minor* agg.	*Sparganium erectum*
	Myosotis scorpioides	*Veronica beccabunga*
Variants:	*Nasturtium officinale* agg.	Small grasses

(a) In slower, more silty flows *Potamogeton natans* and more eutrophic species may occur.

(b) Smaller streams, particularly if nearly or quite dry for part of the summer, have 4+ species,
probably: *Apium nodiflorum*   *Nasturtium officinale* agg.
             Callitriche spp.   *Sparganium erectum*

(c) Steep or undercut banks may sharply decrease fringing herbs.

Medium (and to large) streams (iii) (to (iv))

Blue to Purple   8+ species(6+ if without *Purple*)   60+% cover

Frequent, *c.* 30–75 cm deep, sometimes deeper. Flow slow and moderate. Fringing herbs are short, as in chalk streams, but are emerged, not forming submerged carpets, and more often in clumps than bands.

Often abundant:	*Callitriche* spp.①	*Sparganium emersum*②
	Ranunculus spp.③	
Often associated:	*Apium nodiflorum*	*Phalaris arundinacea*⑥
	*Elodea canadensis*④	(*Rorippa amphibia*)
	(*Glyceria maxima*)	*Sparganium erectum*
	Lemna minor agg.	*Veronica beccabunga*
	Myosotis scorpioides	Small grasses
	Nasturtium officinale agg.⑤	

Variants:

(a) Slow streams are without *Ranunculus* and may have, or be dominated by, *Potamogeton natans*.

(b) Streams in less fertile regions may have vegetation approaching that on New Forest acid sands (see below).

(c) Undercut or very steep banks decrease emergents.

New Forest sands streams – lowland

These streams rise on very infertile land, but downstream eutrophication is unusually great, as the silt from the sandstone accumulates in the lower reaches; the change from *Orange* to *Purple* can be rapid. Intermediates occur, of course, between the nutrient-poor and nutrient-rich variants described below. See also the description above of soft sandstone streams. The streams are found in and near the New Forest, Hampshire.

NEW FOREST SANDS

Small streams with water-supported species (ii)

1. *Orange* (with *Blue*) 4+ species 50+% cover

Local, shallow, may dry in summer. Sandy.

Probable species: *Eleocharis palustris* *Myriophyllum alterniflorum*
 Scirpus fluitans (wetter)
 Juncus articulatus *Oenanthe crocata*
 Juncus bulbosus *Potamogeton natans* (wetter)
 Myosotis scorpioides *P. polygonifolius*
 Small grasses

2. *Blue* 1+ species 10+% cover

Infrequent, 20–40 cm deep. With perennial flow and humus-stained water. Mostly shaded, with Callitriche spp. the most frequent in such streams.

Probable species: *Callitriche* spp. *R. omiophyllus*
 Catabrosa aquatica *Sparganium emersum*
 Ranunculus aquatilis *Veronica beccabunga*

Medium streams (iii) (to (iv))

1. *Blue* 6+ species 60+% cover

Local, mostly less than 50 cm deep. Usually with moderate flow and humus-stained water. Sandy.

Probable species: *Apium nodiflorum* *Phalaris arundinacea*
 Callitriche hamulata *Potamogeton natans*
 Callitriche spp. *Ranunculus peltatus*
 Mentha aquatica *Sparganium emersum*
 Nasturtium officinale agg. *Sp. erectum*
 Oenanthe crocata

2. *Purple* 7+ species 60+% cover

Local, wider and downstream of (1), mostly 50 cm–1 m deep. With slow flow and somewhat turbid water. Silty.

Probable species: *Alisma plantago-aquatica* *Nuphar lutea*
 Callitriche spp. *Phalaris arundinacea*
 Elodea canadensis *Sparganium emersum*
 Lemna minor agg. *Sp. erectum*
 Myosotis scorpioides

Hard sandstone (not Caithness)

Hard sandstone country is mostly upland, though there are some mountain areas and, in central Scotland, lowland and very mountainous topography. In the steeper parts, flow is as unstable and fierce as on resistant rocks, and as sandstone is more erodable, and also produces more silt, the upper streams with the fiercest flows are emptier than those on comparable resistant rock topography. In the uplands, though, where silt can accumulate, a species-rich, high-cover vegetation often occurs. Compared with lowland soft sandstone streams, however, the silt is washed downstream more, which means *Purple* and *Red* species occur more in lower reaches, and less in upper ones, than they do in soft sandstone streams. Sand or (in steeper streams) exposed sandstone are common, and both decrease bed stability. The alternating stretches of shallow swift and deep slow water so characteristic of resistant rock streams are less common on hard sandstone. The variation in possible flow regimes means that, except in clearly defined upland regions (and in Caithness), it can be difficult to identify stream type, so the description fitting the site most closely, from the several possibilities, should be used. The nutrient status (nutrient concentrations and hardness ratio) is close to that of chalk. Also see general notes on topography and damage assessment in the section on resistant rocks.

Fringing herbs in upland brooks are like those of chalk in that they are abundant, sometimes in carpets, often in bands and long clumps, and are short. However, because the flows are more eroding than on chalk, submerged carpets are absent. Mosses are less frequent than on any other hard rock (because of the unstable substrates).

Hard sandstone occurs mainly in the Welsh mountains (east), west and north-west England, and central and eastern Scotland.

Hard sandstone – upland, and lowland

The land use is typically grassland, arable or orchard, etc. The combination of high silting and fairly low water force means that vegetation can be dense throughout the streams. As always in the hills, however, local variations in topography can lead to areas of more or of less scour, and so to more or less vegetation.

Small streams without water-supported species (i)

Blue   3+ species   10+% cover

UPLAND SANDSTONE

Infrequent, summer-dry or with perennial shallow (c. 10–30 cm) flow. A little silting. Low banks. Similar to chalk brooks of equivalent size, but with fewer species.

Probable species: *Apium nodiflorum*①   *Phalaris arundinacea*
                    Myosotis scorpioides   *Veronica beccabunga*
                    Nasturtium officinale agg.② Small grasses

Variants:

(a) Dry shallow grassed channels.

(b) Sunk ditches, shaded or with tall species such as *Epilobium hirsutum, Sparganium erectum.*

(c) In less-fertile ground, dry channels with *Juncus effusus* and perhaps grasses, often with 100% cover.

Small streams with water-supported species (ii)

Blue   5+ species   40+% cover

Frequent, usually less than 30 cm deep. Slow or moderate flow. Silting at sides and in plant clumps. Banks usually low. Water sometimes peat-stained. Similar to chalk brooks of equivalent size, but without submerged carpets of fringing herbs, and normally without Ranunculus.

Often abundant: *Callitriche* spp. ①

Often associated: *Apium nodiflorum*   *Sparganium erectum*
                    Mimulus guttatus   *Veronica anagallis-aquatica*
                    *Myosotis scorpioides*②   agg.
                    Nasturtium officinale agg.④ *V. beccabunga* ③
                    Phalaris arundinacea   Small grasses
Variants: Mosses

(a) In nearly lowland areas, *Elodea canadensis, Potamogeton natans,* perhaps *Sparganium emersum* and a selection from the above list are found.

(b) In swifter streams there is less diversity and lower cover.

(c) High steep banks with tall plants lead to sparse stream vegetation.

Medium streams (iii)

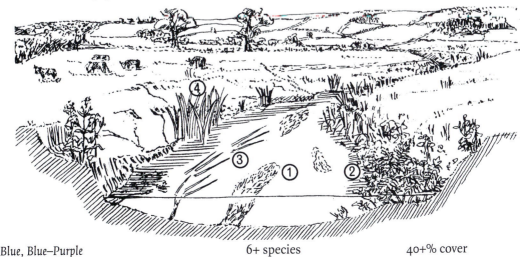

Blue, Blue–Purple   6+ species   40+% cover

UPLAND STREAMS

Frequent, usually 30–75 cm deep. Usually with moderate flow, a mixed-grain substrate, and some silting. Water sometimes peat-stained. Not unlike equivalent chalk streams, but recognisably different. Fringing herbs can be fairly large.

Often abundant: *Ranunculus* spp. (particularly medium-leaved spp.)①

Often associated:

Apium nodiflorum ②
Callitriche spp.
Myosotis scorpioides
Nasturtium officinale agg.
Phalaris arundinacea
Sparganium emersum ③

Sp. erectum ④
Veronica beccabunga
Small grasses
Mosses
Probably one or two *Purple*
    or *Red* species

Variants:

(a) Nearly lowland streams have less *Ranunculus,* and more *Callitriche* spp., *Elodea canadensis, Glyceria maxima, Potamogeton natans* and *Sparganium emersum.*

(b) Lower or slower (and therefore siltier) reaches have more *purple* and *red* species, especially:
Elodea canadensis
Myriophyllum spicatum
Potamogeton crispus

(c) Swifter streams have lower diversity and cover, and fewer *Purple* and *Red* species.

Large streams (iv)

Blue–Purple, Purple   7+ species   25+% cover

Infrequent, *c.* 0.5–1+ m deep. Silting occurs. Usually without vegetation in the centre.

Probable species:

*Myriophyllum spicatum*①
*Nuphar lutea*③
*Potamogeton pectinatus*④

Ranunculus spp. (medium-
    to long-leaved spp.)②
*Sparganium emersum*⑤
Sp. erectum ⑥

There is a wide variety of other possible species. The *Ranunculus* species are sometimes dominant.

Variants:

(a) In swifter flows there are 5+ species, and *Ranunculus* is usually *R. fluitans.*

(b) In slow flows, mainly in long lowland stretches near the river mouth, there are more *Purple* and *Red* species:

Elodea canadensis
Myriophyllum spicatum
Nuphar lutea

Potamogeton crispus
Potamogeton perfoliatus
Scirpus lacustris

and also: *Polygonum amphibium*

Hard sandstone – mountain

The land use is, typically, poor grazing. Spatey swift flows, erodable bedrock and incoming silt lead to unstable habitats (particularly in upper reaches) and sparse vegetation throughout. Damage ratings must be calculated against a locally determined standard, and may not be detailed.

Such streams are few, and are mainly in South Wales and central Scotland.

Small streams without water-supported species (i)

(Blue)	o(+) species	o(+)% cover

Local, *c.* 10–30 cm deep. Most channels empty.

Probable species:	*Myosotis scorpioides*	*Veronica beccabunga*
	Petasites hybridus	Small grasses

(The grasses (mainly *Agrostis stolonifera*) are found both reaching into the water from the banks, and as temporary patches in the centre of the channel washed down from upstream.)

Small streams with water-supported species (ii)

(Yellow to Blue)	o(+) species	o(+)% cover

Local, *c.* 15–40 cm deep. Most channels empty.

Probable species:	*Mimulus guttatus*	Small grasses
	Petasites hybridus	Mosses
	Veronica beccabunga	

(The small grasses are as in (i) above.)

Variant:

(a) *Myriophyllum alterniflorum* in less fertile landscapes.

Medium streams (iii)

(Yellow) to Blue	o(+), 2+ species	o+% cover

Infrequent, usually 30–100 cm deep. Channels often empty.

Probable species:	*Mimulus guttatus*	Mosses
	Sparganium erectum	Small grasses
	Veronica beccabunga	
Rarer water-supported species include:	*Sparganium emersum*	
	Enteromorpha sp.	

Large streams (iv)

Blue, Blue–Purple	o+, 5+ species	o+%, 20+% cover

Infrequent, often over 75 cm deep.

Probable species:

Elodea canadensis	*Sparganium erectum*
Phalaris arundinacea	Small grasses
Ranunculus spp. (mainly *R. fluitans*)	Mosses
	Enteromorpha sp.

Hard sandstone – Alpine

The very fierce flow and unstable substrate keep most channels empty. Damage ratings must be calculated against a locally determined standard, and are unlikely to be detailed.

They are local, mainly in east-central Scotland and South Wales.

Small streams (i) and (ii)

(*Yellow, Blue*)   o(+) species   o(+)% cover

Local, with shallow very eroding flows.

Least-rare species:	*Veronica beccabunga*	Mosses
	Small grasses	

Medium streams (iii)

(*Yellow, Blue*)   o(+) species   o(+)% cover

Local, 30–75+ cm deep, with eroding flows.

Least-rare species:	*Callitriche* spp.	Small grasses
	Phalaris arundinacea	Mosses
	Ranunculus spp. (short-leaved)	

Caithness sandstone

CAITHNESS SANDSTONE

In Caithness, the far north of Scotland, there is lowland topography with a peaty, high-rainfall (mountainous) character to the vegetation.

Small streams without water-supported species (i)

Yellow, Blue   1+ species   1+% cover

Usually over 30 cm deep, slow flow.

Probable species:	*Carex* spp.	*Sparganium erectum*
	Juncus articulatus	Small grasses
	Phalaris arundinacea	

Small streams with water-supported species (ii)

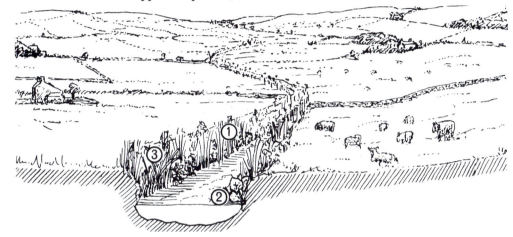

Yellow to Blue   4+ species   25+% cover

Usually at least 40 cm deep, slow to moderate flow.

More probable species:	Small grasses	Mosses
Less probable species:	*Callitriche* spp.	*J. effusus* ①
	Caltha palustris ②	*Mentha aquatica*
	Iris pseudacorus	*Mimulus guttatus*
	Juncus articulatus	*Sparganium erectum* ③

Medium streams (iii)

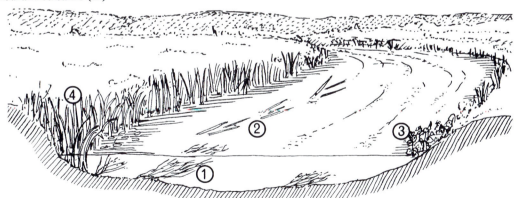

Blue, Blue–Purple   5+ species   25%+ cover

Probable species:	*Callitriche* spp.	*P. pectinatus* ①
	Caltha palustris	*Sparganium emersum* ②
	Mimulus guttatus ③	*Sp. erectum* ④
	Myosotis scorpioides	Small grasses
	Potamogeton natans	Mosses

Large streams (iv)

Blue–Purple   7+ species   25%+ cover

Rare. Deep, varying flow type. Species generally similar to those of type (iii).

Calciferous and fell sandstone, sandstone with limestone bands

The vegetation of these streams is intermediate between those on hard sandstone and those on hard limestone. The landscape is usually upland, but is lowland in parts. Because of the combination of lower water force (upland–lowland, not mountain), high silting (sandstone) and high rock fertility (lime), the vegetation is more slanted towards *Purple* than in the sandstone or limestone streams. Silt and sand are common on the bed.

In some parts, however, particularly uplands, peaty moor overlies the landscape. This greatly reduces the fertility of the streams, and the vegetation, and slants the plant community towards *Yellow*.

The North Yorkshire Moors have both sandstone and limestone outcrops, and the streams are mountain streams, but the less-calcareous ones can best be classified here, as species-poor members of the peaty variants below.

Calcareous sandstone streams occur in north-east England and south-east Scotland.

Small streams (i) and (ii)

Blue   4+ species   25+% cover

Frequent, usually 20–50 cm deep.

Probable species:	*Callitriche* spp.	*Sparganium erectum*
	Elodea canadensis	*Veronica anagallis-aquatica*
	Myosotis scorpioides	agg.
	Nasturtium officinale agg.	*Veronica beccabunga*
		Mosses

Variant:
(a) Dry shallow channels.

Peaty variants:
(a) Dry or shallow-water channels with abundant *Juncus effusus* and perhaps other species.

(b) Empty channels, often dry, stony or with swift flow.

(c) Locally frequent channels, 20–30 cm deep, with fast flow, peat-stained water and stony substrate.

Probable species:	(*Mimulus guttatus*)	(Small grasses)
	(*Petasites hybridus*)	Mosses
	(*Phalaris arundinacea*)	

Other *Yellow* or *Orange* species may be present.

Medium (to large) streams (i) (and (iv))

Blue–Purple   7+ species   25+% cover

Frequent, usually 30 cm to 1 m or more deep.

Probable species:	*Elodea canadensis*	*Scirpus lacustris*
	Myosotis scorpioides	*Sparganium emersum*
	Phalaris arundinacea	*Sp. erectum*
	Polygonum amphibium	*Veronica beccabunga*
	Potamogeton natans	Mosses
	Ranunculus spp.	*Enteromorpha* sp.

Peaty variants:
(a) locally frequent, usually 25–60+ cm deep, with fairly swift flow and peat-stained water, substrate stony or mixed-grained. Diversity variable but usually low; cover low.

Probable species:	*Carex acutiformis*	*Ranunculus* spp.
	Eleocharis palustris	*Sparganium erectum*
	(*Epilobium hirsutum*)	Small grasses
	Myosotis scorpioides	Mosses
	Phalaris arundinacea	

(b) Local, with less peat than above (sometimes downstream of the above) and intermediate in habitat and vegetation. (*Yellow–*)*Blue*, 5+ species and 40+% cover.

Probable species:	*Epilobium hirsutum*	*Phalaris arundinacea*
	Mimulus guttatus	*Sparganium erectum*
	Myosotis scorpioides	Small grasses
	Petasites hybridus	*Enteromorpha* sp.

Resistant rock streams

Resistant rock landscapes vary from almost flat to steeply mountainous. Brook water comes from run-off which, in the hillier regions with high rainfalls, leads to unstable flows of great water force. The streams vary greatly, and many intermediates occur between the vegetation types listed here. The descriptions of several possible types should be consulted if the identification is doubtful. Because of the variation with small changes in topography, etc., when pollution or other damage needs to be assessed, the reference vegetation usually must be determined first on low-impact, but otherwise-similar reaches. In steeper slopes (with potential vegetation) a three-point instead of an eight-point scale may be needed. The topographical type of a stream depends on the water force it receives from run-off, etc., and is determined primarily by the hilliest topography in the catchment and secondarily by the proportion of the stream to be found in each landscape type. Where acid peat (from the land around, or from the subsoil) occurs on the channel bed, the streams are the most nutrient poor of any found in Britain. The inorganic silt has the lowest nutrient status in Britain, being particularly low in calcium, phosphate-phosphorus, chloride and sulphate-sulphur, and the hardness ratio is as low as on soft sandstone. In swift streams, with stony and bouldery substrates and very little silt, nutrient status is again very low, though higher than in streams where acid peat occurs on the bed.

Fringing herbs in shallow streams without excessive water force are short, emerged, well-anchored, and more in clumps than bands. Emerged carpets can occur where several species are co-dominant. In larger streams the plants become more wispy and are confined to the sides. They are washed out more easily than on other rock types.

Resistant rock streams occur over most of highland Britain, which covers the north and west, from Sutherland to Cornwall.

Bog streams, blanket bog, bog plains – lowland

Bog streams occur in blanket bogs in almost flat catchments, particularly in the Scottish Highlands. The substrate is acid peat (e.g. *Sphagnum*). Water movement is little, except after rain, so water force is low and fierce spate flows are absent. The water is peat-stained.

Bog streams are found mostly in the Scottish Highlands, but also occur in wet peaty places elsewhere.

Small streams without water-supported species (i)

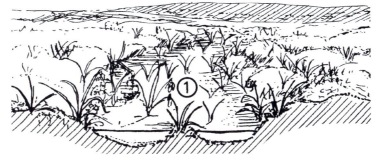

BOG STREAMS/RIVERS

Brown   1+ species   25+% cover

Rare, but may be locally frequent, often c. 10 cm deep.

    Probable species: (*Carex* spp.)   (*Menyanthes trifoliata*)
                                    *Eriophorum angustifolium*①   (*Sphagnum* spp.)
                                    (*Juncus* spp.)

Small streams with water-supported species (ii)

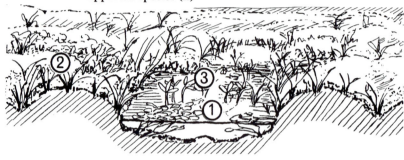

Brown (Brown–Orange)   4+ species   40+% cover

Rare, but may be locally frequent, often 20–30 cm deep.

    Probable species: *Carex* spp.   *Potamogeton polygonifolius*①
                                  Drosera anglica   *Ranunculus flammula*
                                  *Eriophorum angustifolium*② Mosses
                                  *Menyanthes trifoliata*③

    Note. In this habitat, count the mosses as *Brown* not *Yellow*.

Rivers with much blanket bog

These rivers have fine peaty soil in sheltered parts (edges, etc.), and vegetation is mostly confined to these peaty places. The main flow is usually swift, the spates are of considerable force, and the substrate is normally coarse, often bouldery. The water is peat-stained and of variable depth. These rivers may arise from, and be downstream of, blanket bogs, or they may start in hills, and flow into boggy areas below.

The habitat depends on the joint effect of (a) the amount of erodable blanket bog and similar acid peat in the catchment, which determines the amount of peat being washed into the stream, and (b) the flow regime, as over-swift flows prevent any of this peat being deposited on the stream bed. As there are many possible variations in these two factors, the absence or impoverishment of the community is as likely to be because the flow is too swift or the bog too small than because the site is damaged by drainage, pollution, etc. Note that the division between stream sizes (iii) and (iv) is here given on vegetation rather than on width, i.e. on a flow (plus substrate) character. Currently, peatland drainage is bringing much more peat into the streams, acidifying them (NB this is NOT the same as acid rain!). Once peat is lost from the land, it and its effects will be lost from the streams.

These streams occur mainly in the north of the Scottish Highlands.

Medium streams (iii)

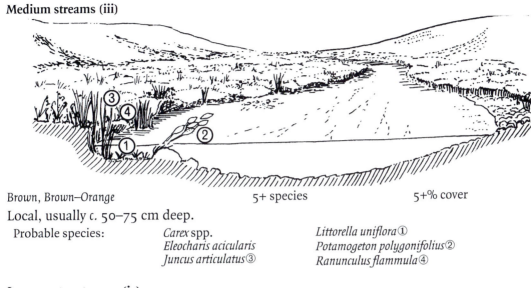

Brown, Brown–Orange   5+ species   5+% cover

Local, usually *c.* 50–75 cm deep.

Probable species: *Carex* spp.   *Littorella uniflora*①
                              Eleocharis acicularis   *Potamogeton polygonifolius*②
                              *Juncus articulatus*③   *Ranunculus flammula*④

Large spatey streams (iv)

Orange   6+ species   1+% cover

Local, deep.

Probable species: *Callitriche hamulata*①   *Myriophyllum alterniflorum*②
                              Callitriche spp. (other than *C.*   *Ranunculus flammula*
                              hamulata)   *Ranunculus* spp. (short-
                              *Eleocharis acicularis*③   leaved, e.g. *R. aquatilis*)
                              *Juncus articulatus*④   Mosses

Moorland

These streams occur in nearly flat, peaty areas, where the peat entering the streams is less, and more mineralised, than in the blanket bog types above. The spate force is low, flow usually moderate to fast, substrate mixed-grained to rather coarse (but rarely bouldery), and the

RESISTANT MOORLAND

water is hardly peat-stained. There are few large rivers, since if the streams are long enough to become large they usually flow into steeper topography and are described below. A slight variation in the fertility of the land will, by bringing more inorganic silt, or more acid peat, into the stream, move the Colour Band towards *Blue* or *Orange* respectively. Accurate diagnoses can be made from changes in Colour Band, cover or diversity over a period of years, or by using good local reference communities.

The two largest areas in which these streams are found are in south-west England (Bodmin Moor, Dartmoor, etc.) and in the Solway peninsula prior to much impact.

Small streams without water-supported species (i)

Orange to Blue   1+ species   5+% cover

Rare, often dry in late summer. Often shaded.

     Probable species: *Apium nodiflorum*   *Oenanthe crocata*
                              Myosotis scorpioides   *Ranunculus omiophyllus*

Small streams with water-supported species (ii)

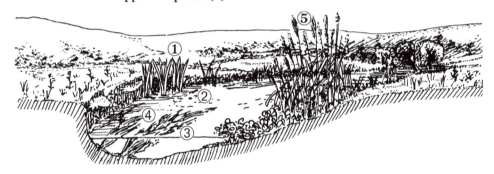

Orange, Yellow, with Blue   5+ species (2+ if less than 2 m wide)   40+% cover

Infrequent, usually 20–50 cm deep.

     Probable species:

Widespread:	*Callitriche* spp.	*Sparganium erectum*①
	*Potamogeton natans*②	
If northern:	*Eleocharis acicularis*	*Phalaris arundinacea*
	Juncus articulatus	*Sparganium emersum*
	Mentha aquatica	
If southern:	*Scirpus fluitans*③	*Myosotis scorpioides*
	Glyceria fluitans (with long floating leaves)④	*Phragmites communis*⑤
	Juncus bulbosus	*Ranunculus omiophyllus*

     Variants:

(a) Narrow channels with little water in summer are likely to bear *Callitriche* spp. with one or two species from (i) above.

(b) With more acid peat, *Littorella uniflora* and perhaps other *Brown* species will be present.

Medium streams (iii)

Yellow (Orange–Blue)   7+ species   40+% vegetation

Not common, usually 30–75 cm deep.

Probable species:

Widespread:	*Callitriche* spp.	*Sparganium erectum*①	
	*Potamogeton natans*②	Mosses	
If northern:	*Callitriche hamulata*	*Nuphar lutea*③	
	*Eleocharis acicularis*④	*Nymphaea alba*⑤	
	*Equisetum palustris*⑥	*Sparganium emersum*⑦	
If southern:	*Scirpus fluitans*	*Myosotis scorpioides*	
	Glyceria fluitans (with long floating leaves)	*Oenanthe crocata*	

Variants:

(a) Swifter streams with coarser substrates are species poor with vegetation confined to local sheltered areas.

(b) With more acid peat, *Littorella uniflora* and perhaps other *Brown* species will be present.

Large streams (iv)

Orange–Yellow   4+ species   5+% cover

Rare, often deep. Vegetation sparse and confined to local sheltered areas. Species as for type (iii) above.

Farmland, lowland-rising streams

These are small streams rising in the lowlands (either in lowland areas, as in parts of Cornwall, or on the fringes of hills). The soil is more fertile than in the peaty types described above, but it varies with the details of landscape and land use, and the vegetation is usually sparse, presumably due to excessive impact on what is, by nature, a sensitive habitat. Narrow streams are often shaded or with eroding flows, and silty flood plain rivers have this silty sub-strate disturbed during spates. The water is not peat-stained.

Lowland farmland can be arable and fertile, even where tributaries arise. Most rivers of this type are in north-east Scotland (particularly the Aberdeenshire area), where the upper tributaries rise in the uplands (the vegetation of the tributaries is described below).

It is also possible to have slower-flowing minor tributaries in alluvial valleys, flood plains, etc. Their vegetation varies with the local habitat factors, but can be related to types described in this book.

Small streams without water-supported species (i)

Yellow to Purple   1+ species   1+% vegetation

Local, shallow. Usually slow to moderate flow. Fine- to coarse-grained substrates.

Probable species:	*Apium nodiflorum*	*Petasites hybridus*①	
	Epilobium hirsutum	*Phalaris arundinacea*②	
	*Oenanthe crocata*③	Grasses	

Variants:

(a) Grading at one extreme almost to ditches with tall emergents dominant.

(b) At the other extreme there are almost-empty hill streams (see upland and mountain below).

Small (to medium) streams with water-supported species (ii) (and (iii))

Yellow to Blue   2+ species   5+% cover

Local, *c.* 20–40 cm deep. Usually moderate flow. Mixed to coarse substrates. The wider streams come from the less-fertile catchments.

    Probable species:

Apium nodiflorum	*Oenanthe crocata*
Callitriche spp.	*Ranunculus* (short-leaved,
Myosotis scorpioides	e.g. *R. aquatilis*)
(*Myriophyllum alterniflorum*)	*Veronica beccabunga*
Nasturtium officinale agg.	Mosses

Medium streams (iii)

Blue to Blue–Purple   7+ species   20+% cover

Rare, with usually moderate flow and mixed grain substrates. (See the section on small to medium streams above for streams of this width on the less-fertile catchments.)

    Probabale species:

Epilobium hirsutum	*Sparganium eectum*
Myosotis scorpioides	*Veronica beccabunga*
Nasturtium officinale agg.	Mosses
Ranunculus spp. (shortish leaves)	

Farmland, lowland streams rising in the hills

Small (to medium) streams (i) and (ii) (and (iii))

Yellow–Blue to Blue–Purple

These are streams rising in the hills but flowing into lowlands or small flood plains for long enough for their vegetation to be affected by this flatter ground (which may be on resistant rock, alluvium or other substrate).

The vegetation of these streams varies greatly with the steepness of the hills on which they rise, the comparative length of the stretches on hills and on flatter ground, and the nature of the flatter ground (more silt, and therefore e.g. *Glyceria maxima*, in a small alluvial plain, more mixed-grained substrates, and therefore e.g. *Elodea canadensis* (slower) and *Ranunculus* spp. (faster), on resistant rock). Consult the descriptions of streams rising in the lowlands, also those on upland and mountain streams, and those on streams in alluvial plains. Catchment impact reduces potential vegetation.

Large streams (iv)

Blue to Purple   4+ species   5+% cover
(when far into the flatter ground)   (50+% in favourable habitats)
Local, deep. With slow flow and with some to much silt.

UPLAND RESISTANT

When a hill river first enters a flood plain it keeps the vegetation of the hill river. In the longer flood plains or lowlands, the vegetation changes slowly. The species of faster flow listed below occur more towards the hills, and those of slower flow towards the mouth. In very long flood plains on fertile rocks (e.g. rivers flowing from the Pennines to the Plain of York), the vegetation may approach that of clay streams.

Probable species:

*Phalaris arundinacea*①   *Sparganium emersum*②
*Polygonum amphibium*③   *Sp. erectum*
Ranunculus fluitans   Small grasses
*Rorippa amphibia*④

Upland resistant rock streams

The land use in upland areas is mostly grassland, with arable (and orchards, etc.) below, and perhaps more rough pasture on the hilltops. Upland streams may also occur within mountainous regions, when streams are so sited as to receive little run-off. The reverse also applies: mountain streams can occur in upland regions. Spates are frequent, but their force is low (though on the rare occasions when a really fierce spate does occur there is long-term damage to the vegetation). Flow is fairly swift, and there are frequently alternating stretches of swift shallow coarse channels, and slow deeper siltier ones. The substrates are usually basically mixed-grained and often coarse (but hardly ever bouldery). (Swifter normal flows and fiercer spates convert upland rivers to mountain rivers.) Drainage schemes are common.

As mentioned in the section on lowland farmland above, there are also fertile, mainly arable regions, with richer vegetation – particularly in north-east Scotland – where the upper tributaries rise in uplands but much of the catchment is lowland. Stream vegetation is often similar to that of hard sandstone in a rather steeper landscape. Also placed in this category are the lower reaches of larger rivers which rose in the mountains and flowed through flatter landscapes (not flood plains) for many miles.

Usual type
Small streams without water-supported species (i)

1. Narrow (*c.* 0.5–1 m) summer-dry channels on wide (flat) hilltops with rough pasture. Locally very frequent. Often 100% cover. The characteristic, and usually the only species: *Juncus effusus*①

2. Other channels

Orange to Blue　　　　　　　　　　　(1–)2+ species　　　　　　　　10+% cover

Infrequent, usually 10–30 cm deep. Perennial eroding flows.

Probable species:

Apium nodiflorum	*Oenanthe crocata*
*Juncus articulatus*①	*Petasites hybridus*
*Mentha aquatica*③	*Veronica beccabunga*
Nasturtium officinale agg.②	Small grasses

3. Channels with low run-off at the higher altitudes may have emerged short carpets of fringing herbs, Colour Band *Blue*, with 4+ species and 60+% vegetation, with much silt.

4. Grazed (grassy) channels also occur.

Small streams with water-supported species (ii)

Blue　　　　　　　　　　　　　　4+ species　　　　　　　　20+% cover

Frequent, usually 20–30 cm deep. Usually with eroding flows.

Probable species:

Callitriche spp.①	*Sparganium erectum*②
*Mimulus guttatus*③	*Veronica beccabunga*
Myosotis scorpioides	Small grasses
Phalaris arundinacea	Mosses

Variant:
(a) As in type (i) and (ii) above, but also with *Callitriche* spp., mosses.

Medium streams (iii)

| *Blue* (with *Orange* to *Red*) | 2+,6+ species | 10+%, 40+% cover |

Frequent, usually 30–60 cm deep. Wash-out during storm flows more likely than for types (i) and (ii).

Probable species:

Callitriche spp.
*Elodea canadensis*②
Mimulus guttatus (northern)
Myosotis scorpioides
*Phalaris arundinacea*③

Ranunculus spp.
  (particularly short-
  leaved spp.)④
*Sparganium erectum*①
Veronica beccabunga
Mosses

Large streams (iv)

| *Blue* | 1+ species | 5+% cover |
| | (may be much higher) | (may be much higher) |

Infrequent, usually 50 cm or more deep. Wash-out in storms more damaging than for type (iii).

Probable species:

Apium nodiflorum
Callitriche spp.
  (*Epilobium hirsutum*)
  (*Myosotis scorpioides*)
  (*Petasites hybridus*)

Phalaris arundinacea
Ranunculus spp. (short-
  to medium-leaved)
Sparganium erectum

Variant:

(a) With decreased spates (e.g. from reservoir sited upstream), either greater diversity or high cover of *Ranunculus* spp., with or without high diversity.

More fertile landscapes, north-east Scotland, etc.

Small streams without water-supported species (i)

| *Blue* (–*Yellow*) | 2+ species | 20+% cover, often 75+% |

Locally frequent, usually 10–30 cm deep. Moderate to fast flow. Mixed substrate.

Often abundant:

Mimulus guttatus
Nasturtium officinale agg.

Phalaris arundinacea

Often associated:

Myosotis scorpioides

Small grasses

Variants:

(a) More oligotrophic upper tributaries, with the above vegetation and one or more of:

Caltha palustris
(*Mentha aquatica*)

Petasites hybridus

(b) Dry grassy channels.

(c) Swifter streams with sparse grass or other vegetation.

Small streams with water-supported species (ii)

| *Blue* (–*Yellow*) | 5+ species | 50+% cover (less with higher water force) |

Locally frequent, usually 10–30 cm deep. Typically with alternating zones of fast and slow clear water. Stony or mixed substrates. Water sometimes peat-stained.

Often abundant: *Callitriche* spp.   *Mimulus guttatus*
                    (*Callitriche hamulata*)

Often associated: *Myosotis scorpioides*   *Sparganium erectum*
                    (*Myriophyllum alterniflorum*)   Small grasses (including *Glyceria*
                    Nasturtium officinale agg.   *fluitans* with long floating leaves)
                    Phalaris arundinacea   Mosses

Variants:
(a) More water force, and a selection of:
                    Phalaris arundinacea   Mosses
                    Small grasses

(b) Channels with much-grazed banks have more fringing herbs.

(c) Channels with ungrazed banks have fewer fringing herbs and more *Phalaris arundinacea*.

Medium streams (iii)

Blue (with *Orange* to *Purple*)   8+ species   50+% cover

Local, usually 30–75 cm deep. Alternating zones of moderate and faster or slower flow. Mixed or (firm) stony substrates. Water often peat-stained.

Probable species: *Callitriche* spp.   *Potamogeton crispus*
                    Callitriche hamulata   *Ranunculus aquatilis/peltatus*
                    Glyceria maxima   *Sparganium erectum*
                    Iris pseudacorus   Small grasses
                    Mimulus guttatus   Mosses
                    Myosotis scorpioides   (other *Orange* and *Yellow* species
                    Nasturtium officinale agg.   may also occur)
                    Phalaris arundinacea

Large streams (iv)

Blue–Purple   9+ species   60+% cover

Local, 0.5+ m and deep. Flow slow or intermittently fast. Substrate mixed-grained.

Often abundant: *Ranunculus* spp.

Often associated: *Caltha palustris*
                    Elodea canadensis   *Potamogeton crispus*
                    Glyceria maxima   *Potamogeton natans* hybrids
                    Iris pseudacorus   *Sparganium erectum*
                    Phalaris arundinacea   Small grasses

Mountain resistant rock streams

Mountain landscapes comprise the greater part of the resistant rock areas. Land use is predominantly grassland below, and mountain and moorland vegetation on the hilltops. Locally, upland or very mountainous (alpine) streams may occur in mountain regions, where local topographical variations lead to unusually low, or unusually high, water force respectively, and similarly, mountain streams can occur in upland regions (with unduly high water force for the area) or very mountainous ones (with unduly low water force). Fierce spates are frequent, and this and the characteristically swift normal flow usually prevent much bulk of vegetation developing except in wide and long lower reaches where water force has diminished. Alternating reaches of swifter coarser shallower channels, and of slower finer-particled deeper ones, are common. The swifter reaches frequently have rapid flow, with the water broken by boulders or large stones, and the slow reaches are only rarely silty (more often gravelly or stony). Drainage-altered channels are all too common.

Small streams without water-supported species (i)

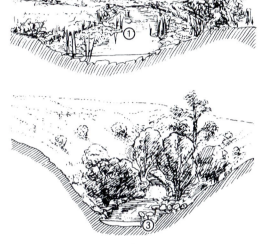

Blue (Orange)   0+, 2+ species   0+% cover

Frequent, c. 10–40 cm deep. Perennial eroding flow. Where flow is less fierce, fine particles are deposited at the sides, and plants can grow well there.

Probable species:

Caltha palustris
*Juncus articulatus*①
*Mimulus guttatus*②
*Petasites hybridus*③

Phalaris arundinacea
Ranunculus flammula
Veronica beccabunga
Small grasses

The small grasses (mainly *Agrostis stolonifera*) are found both reaching into the water from the banks and as temporary patches in the centre of the channel that have been washed down from upstream.

Variants:

(a) Fringing *Juncus articulatus* is common, and frequently the sole species, in streams with gently sloping banks on areas of open peaty moorland. It is lost after drainage.

(b) Fringing herbs increase on banks of drained (channelled) streams.

(c) *Petasites hybridus* is often found in rather shaded streams with medium-sloping banks.

(d) Dry channels with *Juncus effusus* (and sometimes other species).

(e) Damp grassy channels.

Small streams with water-supported species (ii)

Yellow to Blue   1+ species   1+% cover

Common, c. 20–50 cm deep. Eroding flow but less scour in the channel centre than is typical of type (i).

Probable species:

Callitriche spp.
Caltha palustris
Mimulus guttatus
Myosotis scorpioides
Petasites hybridus

Phalaris arundinacea
Veronica beccabunga
Small grasses
Mosses

The small grasses found are as in type (i).

Variants:

(a) *Juncus articulatus* type as in type (i), but also with mosses (or *Callitriche*).

(b) Increased fringing herbs as in type (i).

(c) *Petasites hybridus* type as in type (i).

(d) *Orange* species in more peaty landscapes.

Medium streams (iii)

Yellow to Blue (Blue–Purple)   1+, 3+ species   1+%, 25+% cover

Common, *c.* 30 cm–1 m deep, often varying within one reach. May have 75% cover in some flood plain areas.

Probable species:	*Callitriche* spp.	*Phalaris arundinacea*③
	Juncus articulatus	*Ranunculus* spp. (short-
	Mimulus guttatus	leaved) ①
	*Myriophyllum alterniflorum*②	*Sparganium erectum*
	Petasites hybridus	Small grasses
		Mosses

Variants:

(a) In more peaty landscapes:	*Callitriche hamulata*	*Juncus articulatus*
	Eleocharis palustris	*Oenanthe crocata*
(b) With more inorganic silt and shelter:	*Elodea canadensis*	*Potamogeton crispus*
	Myriophyllum spicatum	

(c) In parts of central Scotland, important species include *Potamogeton natans* hybrids, e.g. *Potamogeton* × *sparganifolius*.

Large rivers (iv)

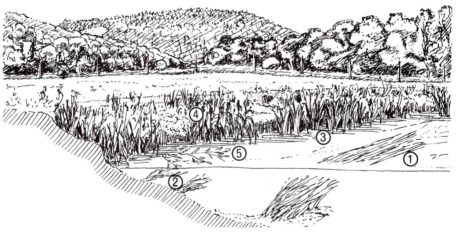

Yellow to Blue–Purple   0+, 4+ species   0+%, 25+% cover

Common, *c.* 0.5–2 m deep usually, often varying within one reach.

Probable species:	*Callitriche* spp.	*Ranunculus fluitans* (shorter-
	Elodea canadensis	leaved species infrequent) ①
	*Myriophyllum alterniflorum*②	*Sparganium erectum*③
	M. spicatum	Small grasses
	*Phalaris arundinacea*④	Mosses
	*Polygonum amphibium*⑤	

Variants:

(a) *Myriophyllum alterniflorum* and *Myriophyllum spicatum* rarely occur together: *M. alterniflorum* is found in upper reaches, *M. spicatum* in lower reaches.

(b) If there are two or more *Ranunculus* spp., *R. fluitans* occurs in the more downstream reaches and, if both are found at the same site, *R. fluitans* grows in the deeper water.

(c) In slower reaches, *Polygonum amphibium* is characteristic.

(d) In silty (but not too disturbed) reaches, *Sparganium emersum* is characteristic.

(e) In parts of central Scotland important species include *Potamogeton natans* hybrids, e.g. *Potamogeton × sparganifolius.*

Alpine

'Alpine' landscapes occur particularly in Snowdonia, the Lake District and parts of the Scottish Highlands (including much of the far north, where the very high rainfall increases water force in the same way as does the steeper topography further south). Land use is predominantly mountain to moorland vegetation, with rough pasture below. Within the regions, mountain streams may locally occur where water force is less (but the substrate is mineral), bog streams may occur on local blanket bogs, and bog rivers where there is both much bog in the catchment and flat-enough topography to allow the deposition of enough peat in the channel. The water is sometimes peat stained. The very swift normal flow, extremely fierce spate flows, and the consequent bouldery or coarse and unstable substrate, usually prevent even mosses from growing well. If macrophytes are present at all they are sparse and few, and most sites have none.

Small streams (i) and (ii)

ALPINE RESISTANT

(Yellow)   o(+) species   o(+)% cover
Local to frequent, *c.* 20–40 cm deep. Perennial flow.

    Probable species: *Juncus articulatus*①
                              Mosses
    Variant:
    (a) Dry channels with loose scree and no aquatic species.

Medium streams (iii)

(Orange–Yellow)   o(+) species   o(+)% cover
Local to frequent, 30–75+ cm deep. More nearly dystrophic (nutrient-poor) than types (i) and
(ii) as acid peat can, in more downstream and peaty conditions, occur at the sides. Most channels are empty, as in types (i) and (ii), and most of those with plants have solely mosses.

    Probable species: (*Callitriche* spp.)   (*Potamogeton polygonifolius*)
                             (*Glyceria fluitans* with long floating   (Small grasses)
                             leaves)   Mosses
    (The small grasses (mainly *Agrostis stolonifera*) are found both reaching into the water from
    the banks and as temporary patches in the centre of the channel washed down from
    upstream.)

Large streams (iv)

(Yellow)   o(+) species   o(+)% cover
Local to frequent, depth from 0.5 m to deep. Most channels are empty, but the proportion containing vegetation is higher than for type (iii).

    Probable species: *Callitriche* spp.   *Ranunculus* spp.
                             Carex acuta   *Sparganium emersum*
                               Juncus articulatus   Small grasses
                               Myriophyllum alterniflorum Mosses
                             Phalaris arundinacea
    (Small grasses are found as for type (iii) above.)
    Variants:
    (a) With lower water force there can be *c.* 6 species present, the vegetation approaching that
    of mountain streams.
    (b) With more bog peat, more *Orange* species are present.
    (c) With more inorganic silt, more *Purple* or *Red* species are present.

Streams on mixed catchments

A mixed catchment is one which, upstream of the site recorded, consists of two or more rock types. Vegetation usually reflects the proportion of each, subject to the following:

1 Rocks near the headwaters are the most important, and those at the side near the mouth the least so.

2 When the proportions of the different rock types are equal, the rock around the site is the more important.

3 (Soft) limestone and clay have a stronger influence than (soft) sandstone.

4 Hard sandstone has a stronger influence than hard limestone, which in turn has a stronger influence than resistant rocks or coal measures.

5 When sandstone and limestone are either or both of the rock types concerned, or in any habitat of mixed nutrient status (e.g., mesotrophic/eutrophic), deeper slower flows, allowing silting, lead to markedly more eutrophic vegetation, and swifter shallower flows lead to markedly less eutrophic vegetation.

6 Drift (boulder clay, etc.) is important only when thickly covering large proportions of the catchment, as in the boulder clay of Anglesey.

7 The change in plant community after crossing a rock boundary occurs much sooner if tributaries enter which rise on the new rock type, or if the new rock type is substantially more fertile.

8 River plants are very sensitive to rock type, and when vegetation does not fit that expected from the rock type map, and does not show a characteristic damage pattern (see Chapters 5 and 6), a larger-scale geological map should be consulted. There will probably be a small patch of, say, limestone in a clay area.

9 As streams on hard rocks have lower species diversity and less total vegetation than those on soft rocks, the effects of changes in rock are less, and are less easy to detect. The vegetation of streams on hard rocks also alters greatly with topography. Within resistant rock areas, for instance, granite and basalt form flatter landscapes, and their streams consequently contain more *Callitriche* species and *Glyceria maxima*.

Necessarily, most streams flowing on two rock types are quite large. The few small ones occur where there is a mosaic of rock types (e.g. hard sandstone and resistant rock), or where boulder clay is thick enough to influence the river plants but not so thick as to obscure the effect of the solid rock below. Examples of streams influenced by extra factors follow.

Soft limestone–clay

Extra:

1 In streams of type (iii) – and also of types (ii) and (iv) – species occurring more frequently on mixed catchments than on clay or limestone alone are:

Groenlandia densa	*Potamogeton crispus*
Myriophyllum spicatum	*Potamogeton perfoliatus*
Oenanthe fluviatilis	*Zannichellia palustris*

2 In streams of types (iii) and (iv) – and rarely of type (ii) – with catchments with different proportions of the two rocks, the main change on passing from limestone to clay, and increase of *Nuphar lutea* and *Sparganium emersum*, occurs when the clay influence starts, which is when there is little clay in the catchment.

3 Similarly, the main increase of *Sparganium erectum*, in all sizes of streams on passing from full limestone to full clay, is when the catchment is half limestone, half clay.

4 Boulder clay may lend instability to the bed of a limestone stream, and decrease the vegetation.

Soft limestone–sandstone

Extra:

1 Streams rising in fertile sandstone but with most of their length on chalk have some eutrophic influence (*Purple* or *Red* species) throughout.

Table 4.6. Common wetland dyke species

INFREQUENT SPECIES (in order of increasing nutrient status on peat)

FREQUENT SPECIES

The three main habitats tend to have rather different species groupings

Habitat lists (alphabetical)
(i) Peat
Carex acutiformis agg.
Ceratophyllum demersum agg.
Glyceria maxima
Lemna minor agg.
Nuphar lutea
Phragmites australis
Sagittaria sagittifolia
Sparganium erectum
(ii) Silt
Alisma plantago-aquatica agg.
(*Apium nodiflorum*)
Carex acutiformis agg.
Ceratophyllum demersum agg.
Glyceria maxima
Lemna minor agg.
(*Nasturtium officinale* near lowland)
Phalaris arundinacea
Phragmites australis
Potamogeton pectinatus
(*Potamogeton perfoliatus* agg.
near lowland)
Sagittaria sagittifolia
Sparganium erectum
(iii) Clay
Apium nodiflorum
Carex acutiformis
Glyceria maxima
Lemna minor agg.
Nasturtium officinale
Phalaris arundinacea
Phragmites australis
Potamogeton natans
Potamogeton pectinatus

Yellow (semi-oligotrophic)
Potamogeton alpinus
Eleocharis acicularis
Scirpus fluitans
Glyceria fluitans,
with long floating leaves
Utricularia vulgaris
Stratiotes aloides (Broads)

Turquoise (mesotrophic)
Lemna trisulca
Hydrocharis morsus-ranae
Lemna polyrhiza
Azolla filiculoides (Western)
Zannichellia palustris
Rumex hydrolapathum†
Sagittaria sagittifolia
(larger channels)
Equisetum palustre
Potamogeton grass-leaved spp.
Ranunculus spp. (Batrachian)
Typha spp.
Mentha aquatica
Myosotis scorpioides
Nasturtium officinale
Apium nodiflorum
Rorippa amphibia
Myriophyllum verticillatum
Butomus umbellatus

Purple (semi-eutrophic)
Nymphoides peltatus†
Groenlandia densa
Myriophyllum spicatum
Hippuris vulgaris
Polygonum amphibium
Potamogeton crispus††
Scirpus maritimus
(not far inland; also see
group 1)
Nuphar lutea
Sparganium emersum
(larger channels)
Potamogeton pectinatus
Scirpus lacustris
(larger channels)

} Species common on little-managed and non-eutrophicated sites

Peat of increasing nutrient status
† Commoner on peat than other substrates
†† Rare on peat than other substrates

Silt of increasing nutrient status
Myriophyllum verticillatum
Potamogeton crispus
Ranunculus spp.
} commoner than on peat
Ranunculus sceleratus locally frequent on little-managed areas
Fringing herbs locally frequent, at edge of lowland or on higher ground

Clay of increasing nutrient status
Myriophyllum spicatum
Myriophyllum verticillatum
Fringing herbs
} commoner than on peat or silt
Potamogeton crispus commoner than on peat

TOLERANT SPECIES

Species found in habitats with much impact
Agrostis stolonifera and other small grasses
Callitriche spp.
(particularly
C. platycarpa)
Enteromorpha sp.
Blanket weed

If near coast:
Potamogeton pectinatus
Scirpus maritimus

Dominating drier dykes or on banks of the above
Phragmites australis
Glyceria maxima

Less commonly:
Carex spp.
Sparganium erectum
Phalaris arundinacea

If additional species are present, the stream Colour Band usually applies

2 Small proportions of infertile sandstone in the catchment may have no influence on the limestone reaches.

Hard sandstone–resistant rock

Extra:

1 Streams on mixed catchments have more *Elodea canadensis*, *Potamogeton natans* and *Sparganium emersum* than streams solely on one of the rock types.

2 When catchments have different proportions of the two rocks:

(a) in streams rising on resistant rock and flowing on to sandstone, the following decrease with decreasing sandstone: *Callitriche* spp., *Potamogeton crispus* and *Sparganium erectum*.

(b) in (the fewer) streams which rise on sandstone and flow on to resistant rock, with decreasing sandstone there is an additional decrease in *Nasturtium officinale* agg.

(c) Mosses increase with decreasing proportions of hard sandstone.

Hard limestone–resistant rock streams

Extra:

In catchments with different proportions of the two rocks, mosses decrease with decreasing proportions of resistant rock.

Wetland dykes

Alluvial plains with wetland dykes occur in the Fenland, the Somerset Levels, Romney Marsh, the Pevensey Levels, the Trent plain, south-east Wales, and to a smaller extent elsewhere. Subsoil is usually peat (not bog), silt or clay. The peat tends to be nutrient-medium, the silt is richer, and clay is richer again. (See Chapter 3 Appendix for variation and habitat factors.)

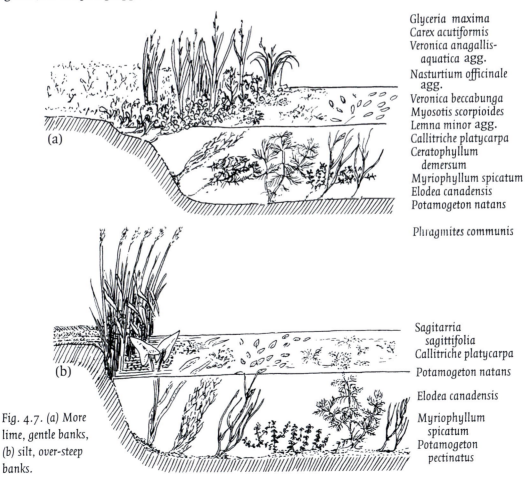

Glyceria maxima
Carex acutiformis
Veronica anagallis-aquatica agg.
Nasturtium officinale agg.
Veronica beccabunga
Myosotis scorpioides
Lemna minor agg.
Callitriche platycarpa
Ceratophyllum demersum
Myriophyllum spicatum
Elodea canadensis
Potamogeton natans

Phragmites communis

Sagitarria sagittifolia
Callitriche platycarpa
Potamogeton natans
Elodea canadensis
Myriophyllum spicatum
Potamogeton pectinatus

Fig. 4.7. (a) More lime, gentle banks, (b) silt, over-steep banks.

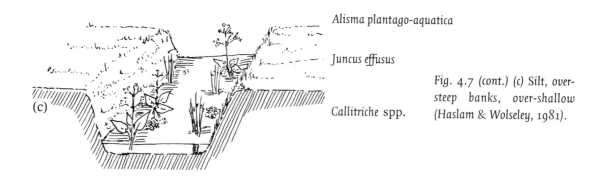

Alisma plantago-aquatica

Juncus effusus

Fig. 4.7 (cont.) (c) Silt, over-steep banks, over-shallow (Haslam & Wolseley, 1981).

Callitriche spp.

River classification B: Small-scale interpretation of differences

The picture and classification scheme used above is for large-scale differences between rock types, landscape types and stream sizes.

However, once the overall community type has been determined in this way, a much more detailed pattern can be interpreted. Minor differences can be interpreted in terms of, e.g. proportion of water coming from the ground and from run-off, proportion of ground water coming from different sources (lime-rich, and nutrient-poor), proportion of ground water coming from polluted water seeping through the ground and from clean water welling up. Small-scale patterns occur with incoming tiny effluents, such as run-off from non-major roads, or from one or two houses, or an incoming clean spring run. Mosaics of substrate type, within the same reach, can each bear different communities, see Chapter 3. Variations of land use beside the river can also be detected. Plant communities are extraordinarily sensitive to such changes, and once one researcher has determined the pattern, all others can use the plant pattern as diagnostic of the particular river type.

An example of the multiple physical and chemical factors which alter dyke vegetation in small but identifying ways is described in Chapter 3 Appendix. Another example comes from the Rhine valley, where the flowing-water channels in the alluvial plain reflect the amount of polluted water coming to them from the Rhine. Each community represents a different degree of pollution.

Table 4.7. Rhine plain communities.

Without further knowledge, sites A and E would be considered different, but A–D, or B–E could be variants of a community as described above. With detailed study, all are different, A clean, E polluted – but E still has a good community. It has been **skewed** from what it should be, but the damage is not enough to **reduce** it from what it should be.

Species	Community					Species	Community				
	A	B	C	D	E		A	B	C	D	E
Potamogeton coloratus	✓					*Potamogeton friesii*			✓		✓
Juncus subnodulosus	✓					*Sparganium emersum*			✓		✓
Mentha aquatica	✓	✓				*Elodea nuttallii*				✓	
Berula erecta	✓	✓	✓	✓	✓	*Nuphar lutea*				✓	
Chara hispida	✓					*Zannichellia palustris*				✓	
Agrostis stolonifera	✓	✓				*Ranunculus fluitans*					✓
Phalaris arundinacea		✓				*Potamogeton crispus*					✓
Callitriche obtusangula			✓	✓	✓	*Hippuris vulgaris*					✓
Veronica anagallis-aquatica			✓	✓							

From Carbiener & Ortschiet, 1987.

RIVER VEGETATION IS EXTREMELY SENSITIVE TO HABITAT AND SO CAN BE USED TO UNDERSTAND, DIAGNOSE AND INTERPRET THAT HABITAT once a basic understanding of river ecology is achieved.

River classification C: Holmes method, typing rivers according to their flora
(Holmes 1983, modified Holmes, 1993)

In Method A, physiographic variables (landscape, etc.) are used to classify rivers on the broad scale. In Method B (which can be used alone or after Method A), small differences in plant pattern and behaviour are analysed for the small habitat differences they interpret. Method C returns nearer to the large scale, and uses the plants present to identify the river type, and so the physiographic variables come into the result, rather than being used at the beginning.

The Holmes method is not described here in full, as the surveyor must be able to identify over 200 species, including mosses, liverworts and algae, so more taxonomic expertise is needed than can be given in this book.

The plants recorded are those growing on the lower bank as well as those within the water. This second habitat expands the community interpretation. There is no gain without some loss, as usual, and as pollution assessment is necessarily based on the plants affected by (potentially) polluted water, this method cannot measure pollution with any accuracy. The plants are also surveyed more intensively, along a length of 100 m to 1 km of the bank being usual. This brings longer species lists, and locates far more rare species, which is particularly necessary in assessments of conservation status. (But it misses the variation in frequency shown in short sites which is necessary for interpretation of quality.)

In other words, C is used for detailed assessment of plants, A plus B for interpretation of habitat. Those working on River Corridor Surveys are most likely to use C. (Readers using C, for instance the Environment Agency, may find it helpful to study the principles for A and B – principles being the same for all methods).

For C, surveyors should have a checklist of all the species used so that each species is looked for. A small plant is more likely to be missed if the surveyor is saying 'What plants are here?' than if the question is: 'Is *Amblystegium fluviatile* here? Is *Anthoxanthum odoratum* here?', and the full 200+ species are checked for, individually.

The community identification is set out like a key in a Flora. Each clause is numbered, and, when calculated, fits one of the two alternative scores given at the right. This number leads to the next appropriate couplet, and, finally, to the name and description of the river type surveyed. Here just the outline is presented – Holmes' book should be consulted for use.

I Lowland rivers with minimal gradients, predominantly in south and east England, but may occur wherever substrates are soft and chemistry increased.

II Rivers flowing in catchments dominated by clay.

III Rivers flowing in catchments dominated by soft limestone such as chalk and oolite.

IV Rivers with impoverished ditch floras, usually confined to lowlands and mainly in England.

V Rivers of sandstone, mudstone and hard limestone catchments in England and Wales, with similar features to those of type VI.

VI Rivers predominantly in Scotland and northern England in catchments dominated by sandstone, mudstone and hard limestone; substrate usually mixed coarse gravels, sands and silts mixed with cobbles and boulders.

VII Mesotrophic rivers where bedrock, boulders and cobbles are the most common components of the substrate; usually downstream of type VIII.

VIII Oligo-mesotrophic, predominantly hill rivers where boulders are an important component of the substrate; intermediate, and often between types IX and VII.

IX Oligotrophic rivers of mountains and moorlands where nutrient and base levels are low, and bedrock, boulders and coarse substrates dominate.

X Ultra-oligotrophic rivers in mountains, or streams flowing off acid sands; substrates similar to type IV but often more bedrock.

Fragile watercourses: their identification and protection

Fragile streams are those easily destroyed by human impact. They succumb, and their character is lost, with pollution, change in land use or whatever that is so little that a more robust stream type, with greater resilience, would tolerate it – not necessarily remaining unharmed, but remaining recognisable. No doubt many fragile stream types are lost, and beyond recall. Those that remain should be preserved. Risks can be from any aspect of human impact.

Threatened by altered chemistry

Most of our present fragile streams are threatened by more and/or different chemicals reaching the stream. These streams are low in inorganic solutes, and low in nutrients. This means that the whole nature of their water quality can be changed by quite low inputs, inputs undetectable in, say, a large clay river. Such streams include:

1 Chalk springs and seepages, low in all solutes except lime. These have low-nutrient species such as *Parnassia palustris* and *Pinguicula vulgaris*, and more typically chalk species, like *Mentha aquatica*, may be discoloured (often purple), and the more nutrient-rich chalk species (the lower part of the *Blue* Colour Band on p. 83) are absent or rare.

2 Acid sands streams, e.g. New Forest ones. These have *Yellow*- or *Orange*-banded species (p. 83), e.g. *Ranunculus omiophyllus, R. flammula, Myriophyllum alterniflorum*, and are without more nutrient-rich species (those of the *Purple* and *Red* Colour Bands).

3 Streams acid from blanket bog, moorland peat and acid-leaf forest (birch or conifer). These are still locally common, but at the present rate of drainage and conversion to farmland must be considered as in danger. *Brown*- to *Yellow*-banded species are present (though mesotrophic, *Blue*, ones may also be there, except in bogs).

4 Wetland dykes of the lowest nutrient status, those without outside (polluted) water, without intensive management, and in permanent pasture. These are identified by habitat, and by a diverse water-supported and non-nutrient-rich community, including, e.g. *Hydrocharis morsus-ranae, Utricularia vulgaris*, and rare *Potamogeton* spp.

For their protection, land beside the streams must have traditional management, and no agrochemicals or further drainage.

Threatened by water loss and change of pattern

These are streams whose water may be taken away, and whose shape and outline may be altered, where this destroys either the total habitat, or its conservation value, i.e. STREAMS THREATENED WITH STRUCTURAL DAMAGE.

The two streams shown in Fig. 4.8 are comparable in rock type and landscape and size. The upper one is in a forest, and is in excellent condition. In the lower one the forest has been removed and the land converted to good-quality grassland. This – if agrochemicals are low – can still support good streams (though not those of forest type). But here the land has been much drained, the streams made so narrow that the bottoms are shaded by the banks, although the shading tree lines are preventing plants growing below them anyway. Finally, the water is shallow and with scouring flow, the channels having been straightened, and water table much lowered. Protective measures do not need listing!

(a)

(b)

Fig. 4.8. *Effect of land use (Haslam, 1987). (a) Oligotrophic forest stream, with little management, resistant rock, south Norway, species include* Potamogeton polygonifolius, Glyceria fluitans *(long-leaved form),* Sparganium emersum, Alisma plantago-aquatica, Sparganium erectum, Ranunculus flammula *and* Luzula sylvatica. *(b) Small, narrow, steep-sided streams in grassland, often within tree-bands. Resistant rock, south Norway, macrophytes absent.*

Threatened by disturbance

Streams threatened by disturbance properly classed here are *either* in areas where most streams are destroyed, and the habitat is in danger of loss if any of the remainder are much disturbed, those unusually susceptible, or those destroyed by very mild disturbance, e.g. peat streams whose very soft substrates are easily disrupted by mild cattle trampling.

Rivers change: the changing vegetation of rivers

Stable rivers are in a state of changeless change (Chapter 3). (Although, all too often rivers are now in a state of overall change, i.e. decline, with deteriorating chemical quality and physical structure (Chapters 3, 5, 6).) Plants and animals grow, mature and die. Vegetation is washed out when dying, when weakened by pollution, disturbance, sedimentation or other harm, and, in fierce flow, is also washed out when growing well. New plants enter and grow: plants and propagules are washed from upstream, blown by wind, carried on birds' feet, carried by man (usually accidentally).

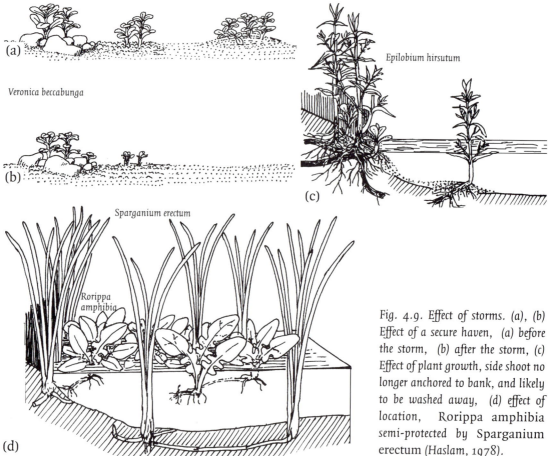

Fig. 4.9. *Effect of storms. (a), (b) Effect of a secure haven, (a) before the storm, (b) after the storm, (c) Effect of plant growth, side shoot no longer anchored to bank, and likely to be washed away, (d) effect of location, Rorippa amphibia semi-protected by Sparganium erectum (Haslam, 1978).*

The changeless change is demonstrated in Fig. 4.10. Species formerly of the river are being washed out, to the right. In the centre are other plants of the same species assemblage happily settling in to their new home. On the left, are species requiring deeper and (for two) more nutrient-rich conditions, and these are ruefully realising this 'home' is not for them.

Of the species that stay put, some grow into new areas, some lose older and dead portions, some have parts torn or eaten away, etc. A plant, particularly if large, collects silt and alters the flow round it because of that silt, so altering habitat and changing its own habitat and that for incoming species. The species most likely to remain are those most typical of the habitat (nec-

deeper water spp.   shallower water spp.

Fig. 4.10. *Changeless change.*

essarily!). They are among the species best adapted to those conditions. The species finding the habitat sub-optimal or unsuitable in depth, flow, chemistry, structure, disturbance, etc., are those most likely to be easily washed away.

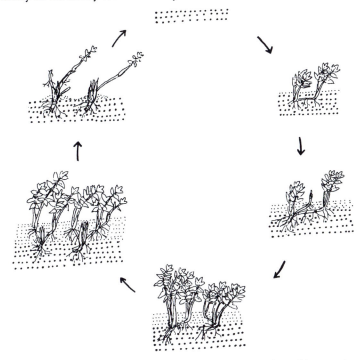

Fig. 4.11. *Cyclic change (Haslam, 1978). Bare soil is colonised by Berula erecta. Plants grow larger, become bushy, and are washed off in storms. Silt is accumulated in the clump, and is washed off with it.*

Unchanging rivers (Table 4.7) grade imperceptibility to changing ones. The two surveys of the Tyne in Fig. 4.12 are significantly different. In the five years between the surveys, the water force of this mountain river has decreased, so more plants of more species have been able to colonise, and grow well. This is shown by a glance at the river maps, while the differences within the stable Avon (Table 4.7) take careful study to appreciate. As in the Avon, the Tyne shows no change in quality: in both pictures the species are from the same assemblage, the same community. It is just that there are more. The differences are due to (1) the 1975–6 drought, which lessened water force and scour over the whole catchment – this effect would, in due course, pass, and (2) building a reservoir on the main river, which makes the water downstream of it more stable and habitable for the macrophytes – this effect is long term. Both changes have the same effect, the first being natural, the second, man-made.

Table 4.7. Site species lists with changeless change (River Dorset, Avon)

(a) = abundant. Sites are representative, and show no overall change in diversity, cover, nutrient status band or pollution-tolerance (e.g. change from *Potamogeton crispus* to *Myriophyllum spicatum*).

1972	1979
1) *Callitriche* sp. *Carex acutiformis*, *Myosotis scorpioides*, *Nasturtium officianle*, *Potamogeton pectinatus*(a) *Sparganium emersum*, mosses, blanket weed.	*Apium nodiflorum*, *Callitriche* sp., *Myosotis scorpioides* *Myriophyllum spicatum*, *Nasturtium officinale* agg., *Oenanthe fluviatilis*, *Potamogeton pectinatus*(a), *Ranunculus* sp., *Zannichellia palustris*, blanket weed.
2) *Myosotis scorpioides*, *Nasturtium officinale* agg., *Ranunculus* sp.(a) blanket weed.	*Callitriche* sp., *Elodea canadensis*, *Ranunculus* sp.(a), *Sparganium erectum*, Moss.
3) *Apium nodiflorum*, *Butomus umbellatus*, *Lemna minor*, *Myriophyllum spicatum*, *Potamogeton crispus*, *Ranunculus* sp., *Zannichellia palustris* (a), *Veronica anagallis-aquatica* agg., grass.	*Glyceria maxima*, *Myriophyllum spicatum*, *Nasturtium officinale* agg., *Ranunculus* sp., *Sparganium erectum*, *Veronica anagallis-aquatica* agg.
4) *Apium nodiflorum*, *Mentha aquatica*, *Nasturtium officinale* agg., *Ranunculus* sp., *Sparganium erectum*.	*Apium nodiflorum*, *Mentha aquatica*, *Myosotis scorpioides*, grass.
5) *Apium nodiflorum*, *Berula erecta*, *Callitriche* sp., *Nasturtium officinale* agg., *Ranunculus* sp., moss.	*Apium nodiflorum*, *Callitriche* sp., *Carex acutiformis*, *Myosotis scorpioides*, *Ranunculus* sp.

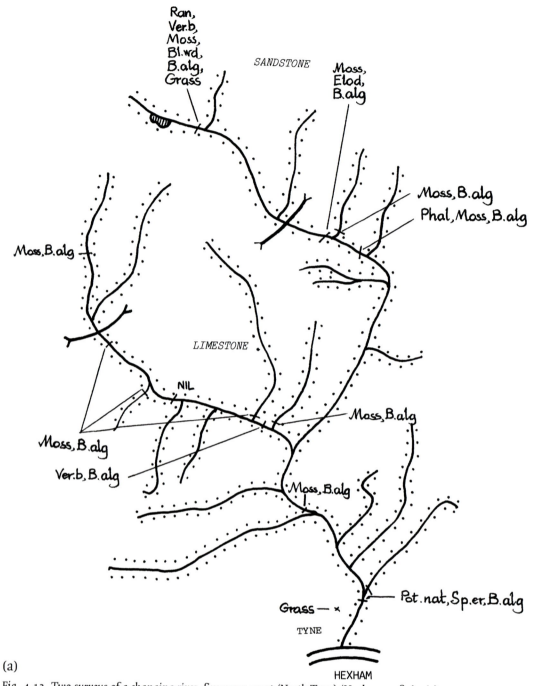

(a)

Fig. 4.12. *Two surveys of a changing river, five years apart (North Tyne) (Haslam, 1987). (a) 1973.*

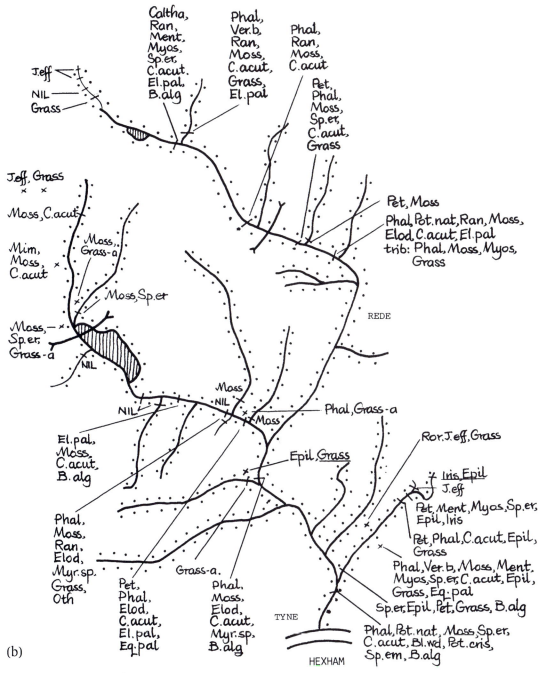

(b)

Fig. 4.12 (cont.) (b) 1978.

Causes of change in stable river vegetation

(For further understanding: omit when first reading. Also see Chapter 3)

In the nature of the plant

Species with rhizomes, stolons, etc., grow, and old parts die. This changes plant positions. Short-lived species die, vacating their portion of channel. Propagules are washed in and out. Plants grow up, and shade those below – the potentially taller species shade the most (shading order: trees, tall herbs and reedswamp species, short emergents, floating-leaved species, taller and shorter submerged species). Propagules, rhizomes, etc. may remain dormant, and shoots may be up prominently only in some years, when some factors, e.g. shade, silt, are suitable.

Due to the water

Depositing and eroding, slower and swifter, shallower and deeper flows lead to different communities. The flow 'selects' appropriate species from among those whose propagules are available.

The effect of wash-out varies with both flow (both normal and storm), and species (floating *Lemna minor* more easily washed out than deep-rooted *Nuphar lutea*; bushy poorly-anchored *Apium nodiflorum* more easily than streamlined, well-anchored *Ranunculus* spp., etc.). Flows vary with landscape and precipitation, with seasonal variations in that rainfall, and with human impact: drainage, abstraction, controls, dams, etc. If a thick (e.g. *Sparganium erectum*) fringe is decreased by spates in the highlands – or management in the lowlands – shorter emergents can grow instead. If bare banks are left, erosion may follow. Overall stream scour keeps stream centres free of tall plants, allowing water-supported communities to develop. At the sides, where flow (except in alpine flows) is less, emergents can develop, often in water which is too shallow for water-supported plants (but emergents, if present, shade out lower plants). Flow is a natural controller and determinant of vegetation patterns.

Due to the substrate

As with flow, so with substrate: it 'selects' appropriate species from those available. Substrate material, consolidation, and pattern of distribution influence vegetation – and hence the fauna living in or dependent on that vegetation.

Silt banks form, and are washed away. The process may be with or without the aid of plant clumps. Silt banks growing high enough will bear land plants and form new land. Substrate, and so vegetation, can be deliberately altered. Dredging may simply remove accumulated silt (which in a natural river would be both less in quantity, and more likely to be dealt with by wash out or new channel), with underground flora and fauna remaining in place. If the hard bed is broken in a deeper dredge, recovery is slower, years instead of months. After full excavation dredging it takes years, or even decades, for the flora and fauna to recover – it is not just substrate, but structure which is lost. Small changes are also made, e.g. for fords or recreation.

Due to disturbance (and see above)

After disturbance, whether due to storm, animal or human impacts, habitats may open, allowing invasion, and then close. Ephemeral as well as indigenous species may enter. (Over-little disturbance has less effect, over-much may prevent vegetation in the long term.

Trampling may alter bank shape and bank vegetation, and alter beds directly or via the bank effects. Boats damage bank and bed. Grazing and cutting, by stock, birds, fish, etc. can change bank and channel vegetation, and change it differently from season to season, and from year to year. Grazing encourages even swards, primarily of grasses. In the absence of disturbance, where woody plants are able to grow they will do so. The scrub/tree layer regenerates naturally.

Due to pollution (see Chapters 5, 6)

Effluents, their presence, intensity and type, change vegetation and animals, changes being anything from slight to total destruction. Minor changes include skewing communities, as well as loss. Changes may be rapid, and often drastic, as after spills – where recovery may be speedy, particularly if the affected reach is short. Change may be gradual, with gradually increasing pollution load (e.g. from sewage treatment works serving villages to which are slowly added new roads, new housing estates, a new industrial estates, or new pig and cow units).

Herbicides used to manage banks or channels are also pollution. There is also run-off from the land and it is often forgotten that run-off from intensive farming, peat drainage, busy roads and built-up areas may cause severe pollution. Buffer strips, and diversion to STWs, are proper evading measures.

Protected plants

Watercourse (or watercourse bank) plants protected under British law are:

Most of these are unlikely to be met by investigators, but some may be locally abundant, e.g. *Luronium natans*. It is ironic that *Hydrilla verticillata* is an explosive pest species in the southern USA!

Alisma gramineum

Carex recta

Chara canescens

Damasonium alisma (also in *Red Data Book*)

Elatine hydropiper

Eleocharis austriaca

Equisetum ramosissimum

Eriocaulon aquaticum

Euphorbia hyberna

E. rivularis

Galium debile

Hydrilla verticillata

Iris versicolor

Leersia arizoides

Luronium natans

Najas flexilis

N. marina

Potamogeton nodosus

Riccia bifurca

Rorippa austriaca

Sagina normaniana

Sagittaria rigida

Scirpus triquetrus

Senecio congestus (presumed extinct)

S. paludosus

Teucrium scordum

Introduced plants

Several species of watercourses and their banks are introduced:

Acorus calamus

Azolla filiculoides

Calla palustris

Crassula helmsii[1]

Egeria densa

Elodea callitrichoides

E. canadensis[2]

E. nuttallii (common form)[1]

Fallopia japonica[1]

Heracleum montegazzianum[3]

Impatiens capensis

I. glandulifera[1]

Iris versicolor

Lagarosiphon major

Lemna minuta[1]

Lysichoton americanus

Myriophyllum heterophyllum

M. verrucosum

Reynoutria japonica

Sagittaria rigida

Vallisneria spiralis

---

[1] Spreading, causing concern. [2] Explosive in nineteenth century. [3] Poisonous.

5 POLLUTION:
altering chemical quality

(no specialist expertise required}

SUMMARY

Pollution is human altering of chemical status enough to alter the structure or nature of plant or animal communities. Rivers purify, and management should increase, and not decrease, this ability. Land use influences run-off composition and hence stream composition. Nutrient-poor influences include bog peat and conifers, nutrient-rich ones, ploughing and fertilising land. River silting and flash floods are increased by intensive farming, large fields and built-up areas. Other pollution sources include: 1 Agrochemicals (fertilisers and biocides) (to improve this, change usage, and put buffer strips along streams). 2 Run-off from roads and built-up areas (to improve this, connect to sewage treatment works (STW) or put settling ponds and vegetated ditches). 3 Small effluents, rubbish dumps (to improve these, where possible, stop at source; where not, connect to STW or put settling ponds and vegetated ditches). 4 STW and other large effluents (improve standards ('consents') and see these are kept). 5 Seepage from contaminated land (to improve this, stop it).

Introduction

The chemicals in the river water and substrate come partly from the surroundings of the stream, the soil, subsoil and rock, and partly from outside the stream. Both may be altered, contaminated, or skewed, by human interference. Soil may be farmed, moved, built-over or otherwise changed. Water may have added or altered chemicals. The stream therefore may be, and in Europe ordinarily is, chemically different to what it would be if people were absent. Since the original stream quality can only be guessed at, the reference taken as 'clean' is that of streams on traditionally managed land with minimum entry of effluents or other pollutants.

What then is pollution? It can best be defined by its effects. These effects always give rise to changes, varying according to the type and intensity of the pollution, in the structure or nature of the plant or animal community. Pollution is shown by the effects of substances added or removed by people. (This is *ecologically* valid.) Other definitions multiply, e.g. in British law, pollutants are 'substances capable of causing harm to... any... living organisms supported by the environment.' Changing land use alters stream life, and is thus pollution. Substances entering streams enter a restricted environment. Pollutants may move downstream with the water, or be deposited on the bed, accumulating particularly in silt, and only later being washed down. In the stream they may be chemically altered (broken down, precipitated, etc.), and if this is to less-harmful substances, this is self-purification (cleaning) in and by the river. The usual way out of the river is to the sea, though some pollutants may be dredged out. They may go down through the bed to the ground water table or aquifer, or some may diffuse out to the air. Poisons from towns, factories, farms, fields, mines, etc. may accumulate and become concentrated in streams, polluting them and any large river into which they flow. Within the river, chemical (e.g. oxidation) and biological (e.g. microbial) processes may render the pollutants harmless, but some substances are resistant to such processes even when in very low concentrations. Other substances are decomposing slowly, so downstream purification is ineffective if concentrations are high or if further impurities are constantly added downstream, e.g. from a series of sewage works.

THE RIVER, like a sewage treatment works (STW) is AN EFFECTIVE PURIFYING AGENT. Like an STW it can be overloaded (and it is overloaded at a fairly low level) and it can remain polluted not just close to a pollution entry, but also far downstream of it. A meandering channel, being longer than a straight one and so with more river surface areas, cleans better than a straight one. A third of run-off nitrate can be reduced in a stream at maximum cleaning efficiency (see pp. 145–6).

RIVER (CHEMICAL) QUALITY DEPENDS ON LAND USE AND EFFLUENTS ENTERING as well as on the natural chemical nature of the rock, etc.

Pollution damages plants and animals to an extent determined by the type and extent of the pollution, and the habitat of the river. Behaviour and presence are affected, both animals and plants growing badly in pollutions not poisonous enough to kill them. Species sensitive to a pollution are eliminated first, with pollution-favoured species (if any) entering in moderate pollution. No larger plants and animals can live in gross pollution (though e.g. birds may pass through areas too polluted for them to live long-term). Both vegetation, and fish, birds, etc., influence habitat as well as being influenced by it, and therefore a severely polluted river will develop differently to a clean one in its physical structure and functioning.

This chapter describes pollutants. For pollution assessment methods, see Chapter 6. The relative harm done by e.g. a motorway and a STW has to be estimated in the field for the sites concerned.

Water entering with pollutants

1 **Rainwater.** Rainwater brings with it pollutants from the air, such as nitrogen and sulphur acid and non-acid compounds, heavy metals, organics, etc. Such polluted precipitation is often known as 'acid rain'. The content of these pollutants is so low that, to influence the river, other sources of solutes must be very low.

2 **Run-off.** Rainfall falls on the catchment and runs off to the land (below or above ground), collecting chemicals from the land over and through which it flows. This water is an important component of all streams, and is the most important water source when springs are absent and few, and effluent intake, low. ALL the relevant land contributes: moorland, pasture, woodland, arable, roads, towns, etc. ALL have run-off very different in composition, so stream quality is much influenced by human use of the land.

3 **Water rising from underground**, springs, etc. This water may well up from aquifers near or far from ground surface, being of recent origin or up to 100 000 or more years old. It may be run-off moving very slowly. It may form most of the stream water (as in chalk spring-runs) or but a small part. It contains chemicals from the rock or the substrate in which it has been stored, plus those that have percolated down from the land above, regrettably including everything from that land above – agrochemicals such as biocides and fertilisers, the mixed bag of poisons in the Rhine and other such rivers, etc.

4 **Effluents.** These are waters that have been removed from the aquifer and stream system, and, after use, return to the stream. Necessarily, all have been changed – polluted – by humans, most often seriously changed. The largest supply comes from sewage treatment works. It is never like river water, and is usually damagingly polluting over greater or lesser stream lengths. STW effluent sometimes comprises most of the water of a river. Locally, cooling water from power stations, etc. can enter in large quantities. This is chemically changed (e.g. with added disinfectant, metals, various washing or polluting effluents), but is usually much cleaner than STW effluents, though the rise in temperature may be significant. Then there are efflu-

ents from factories, mines, septic tanks, farms and goodness knows what, all important around the country.

Different rivers have different proportions of ground water, run-off, and effluent. In fact the plant communities may accurately reflect, and be used to assess, the varying proportions of ground water, and indeed of different types of ground water, in a stream system.

Streams depending largely on spring water are very easily harmed by abstraction from aquifers. Such damage is now common, but it was also the cause of some of the earliest river-shallowing damage.

Effluents may be little in a few highland catchments (though as the solutes are low in streams from such catchments, pollution has a disproportionately great effect). The other extreme is rivers whose water is more from effluents than any other source.

The purifying power of the river

The greater the purifying power, the more, obviously, a river can clean incoming pollution. The first step in river cleanliness is therefore TO ENHANCE, OR AT ANY RATE NOT FURTHER DIMINISH the river's own purifying ability. Self-purification is, after all, free, as well as being good for river health! Purifying power is increased by LIGHT, OXYGEN, and GOOD VEGETATION, the last both as providing microbial habitat, and as providing organic carbon. Excellent cascades can compensate for poor vegetation, and vice versa. If there are lakes on the river, these much aid purification, and trap moving sediment.

Light

Light increases oxidation, so controls and speeds many breakdown processes. LIGHT CAN BE IMPROVED BY:

1 Returning streams in underground pipes to surface flow.

2 Widening narrow brooks to prevent bank shade.

3 Adding open glades at intervals to channels heavily-shaded by woods or hedges.

Oxygen

Oxidation is necessary and aids many breakdown processes. OXIDATION IS IMPROVED BY:

1 Removing hindrances to access to air, returning water flowing underground to the surface.

2 Increasing oxygen absorption from the air by making water more turbulent and flowing, with weirs, bridge piers, white-water rapids, cascades, etc.

3 Increasing vegetation. Plants make oxygen by day (and though they use it by night, it is only in special circumstances that damaging deoxygenation occurs during the night, usually when putrefying matter is present also).

Reduction

Note that some breakdown processes work better in reducing (reduction is the opposite of oxidation) conditions (e.g. sulphate decomposition) or with both oxidising and reducing ones (e.g. nitrate). However, organic pollutions so easily lead to reducing conditions, and organic-rich muds are so often oxygen-deficient that, at present, steps are taken only to increase oxidation, not reduction, in the river.

Vegetation

Most purification is by micro-organisms, and such micro-organisms occur in all (normal) rivers, though they are greatly increased in the presence of larger plants. These provide surface area and shelter for physical habitat, and chemical exudations. Species therefore differ in purifying ability, both in degree, in rate of decomposition around them, and in kind – some pollutants breaking down faster in the presence of the chemicals exuded from one species, others with those from another.

Vegetation quantity can be high, provided oxidation throughflow is good or tall monocots are abundant. Many invertebrates eat dying or dead plant or animal material, rendering it more fit for microbial decay. Vegetation provides habitat for these, as for the micro-organisms.

A variety of plant species is therefore desirable. The micro-organisms vary with the incident chemicals as well as with macrophyte species, those feeding well on (i.e. degrading) a certain substance increasing with the presence of that substance (the micro-organisms take about three weeks to adapt in a *Phragmites* root zone purification bed).

VEGETATION AND ORGANIC CARBON ARE IMPROVED BY:

1 Providing water and structure of good quality (see Chapters 2, 3, 6). (Giving instream plant life.)

2 Providing overhanging trees and shrubs (but not much shading). (Giving input from, and good vegetation architecture.)

3 Refraining from draining any remaining peaty soil around the river (so humus continues to enter river) (also see buffer strips, below).

Pollutants entering the river

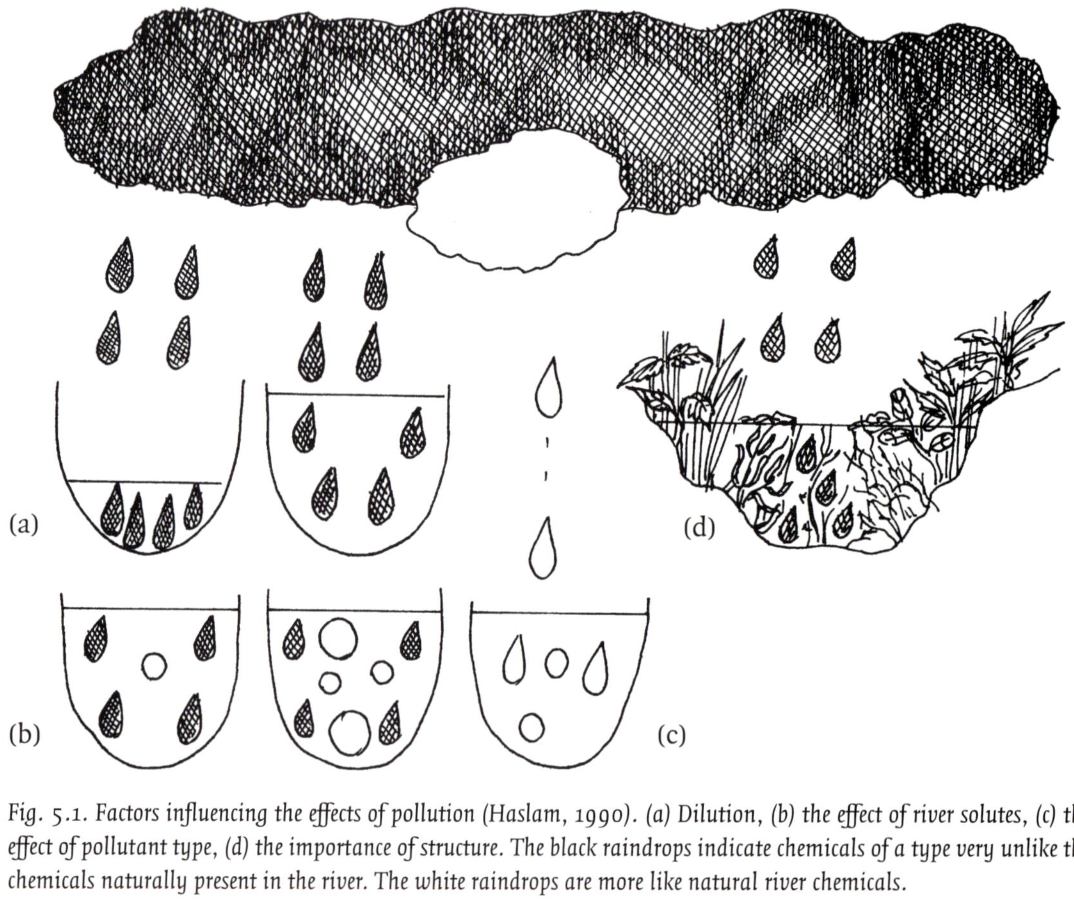

Fig. 5.1. *Factors influencing the effects of pollution (Haslam, 1990). (a) Dilution, (b) the effect of river solutes, (c) the effect of pollutant type, (d) the importance of structure. The black raindrops indicate chemicals of a type very unlike the chemicals naturally present in the river. The white raindrops are more like natural river chemicals.*

The less the pollution entering, the less the effect, of course. Fig. 5.1 shows that the effect also varies with both river conditions and pollutant type. The more pollutants are diluted (Fig. 5.1(a)), the less the ecological effect on the river (NB the same quantity reaches the sea, whatever the dilution!). If river solutes are concentrated (abundant) then the river has a considerable buffering, and it is less easy to change its quality (Fig. 5.1(b)). The closer the pollutant is to natural river chemicals, the less the effect (Fig. 5.1(c)). Structure is also important in purifying: the better the structure, the greater the purifying power AND the greater the resilience (Fig. 5.1(d)).

Pollutions have traditionally been divided into point-source and diffuse. Point-source is an effluent from an identifiable place, a sewage treatment works, a mine, etc. Diffuse pollution is that which comes in over a length of river, like agrochemicals from all the riverside edge of an arable field. The distinction is now breaking down with so many intermediate types, e.g. a road parallel to a river with frequent run-off entries.

Pollutants are numerous, but most fall into four groups.

Agrochemicals

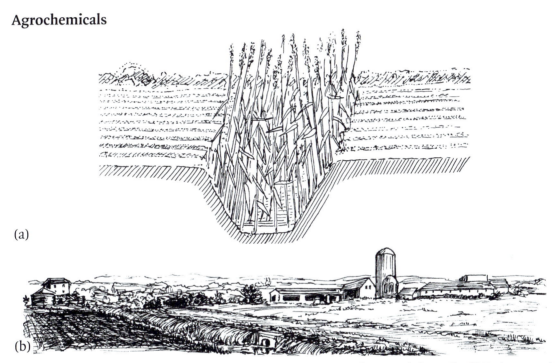

(a)

(b)

Fig. 5.2. (a) *Agrochemical pollution,* (b) *the same and farm effluent ((a) Haslam & Wolseley, 1981; (b) Haslam, 1990).*

Agrochemicals (Fig. 5.2) are those put on fields – fertiliser (including slurry, manure and sewage sludge where used) and biocide. They run off, they leach out, they may be sprayed directly on the watercourse. They also enter through under-drains (the small drains collecting water from fields). Although ordinarily fertiliser leaks out as a chronic pollution, severe storms can give the same results as a large spill – sudden, short lived, high concentrations, actually causing kills (e.g. a one-in-220-year flood carried the equivalent of 90 kg/ha/day of nitrate-nitrogen in one day – the normal stream load being 35 kg/ha/year). Another flood carried the equivalent of 30 years run-off of phosphorus in one day.

Agrochemicals are also put on gardens (Fig. 5.3). Since there are fewer guidelines and often less knowledge, the agrochemical pollution from a suburb can be worse than that from a similar-sized area of farmland. This is highly deplorable. Much can be done, in the small area of a garden, to reduce, or better, eliminate, the use of fertilisers and synthetic biocides. Urban and transport land (e.g. railway banks) also have pesticides in their run-off.

Small brooks have small volumes of water, so low dilution. A 20 m length receives the same, whether the channel is 1 m or 20 m wide. So they are MORE polluted by the arable land beside them than are larger rivers (something often forgotten) (Fig. 5.4).

Fig. 5.3. *Potential bad agrochemical pollution from (a) gardens, (b) under-drains (Haslam, 1991).*

Fig. 5.4. *Small brook (top, left) more polluted than the main stream (right) from agrochemicals.*

AGRICULTURAL POLLUTION IN THE RIVER CAN BE DECREASED by:

1 Applying the chemicals in concentrations and ways that lessen leaching to the river.

2 Having little-managed land, such as wetland, woodland, moorland, or traditionally-managed grassland near the river (including riverine Set-Aside and Water Fringe areas).

3 Introducing specific BUFFER STRIPS (zones) (Fig. 5.5), leaving unpoisoned land in a band along the watercourse.

4 Making BANKS wide, with diverse and large vegetation.

Fig. 5.5. *(a) With buffer strip.*

Fig. 5.5 (cont.) (b) Adjoining reach with severe agrochemical pollution.

If the buffer strip is rich in humus or organic carbon, and wet at least in winter, like a peaty marsh, swampy woodland or grassland waterlogged in winter with 'hot spots' of organic carbon, then a 5 m strip produces a surprising degree of purification. Because solutes move in it vertically as well as horizontally, and flow in the buffer strip is downstream as well as down and across to the river, giving a spiralling or confused path, a buffer strip of only 15 m wide can give maybe 150–200 m of flow path, allowing much chemical processing to take place before the water reaches the river. In farmland, 10–20 m of buffer strip may be adequate, but 50–100+ m is better. For catching chemicals from the root zone and incorporating them into vegetation (where they are in temporary storage, and in a suitable form for later breakdown), the wider the strip, and the larger the plants, the better. Only a narrow zone is needed to clean nitrates from water, and the nitrogen eventually goes into the air. Reduction of nitrogen by 70–100% in strips 20–30 m wide is quite common for subsurface flow.

Phosphate is more difficult. Since phosphorus, unlike nitrogen, is not lost to the air, it stays in the soil (except for any washed on further). It may be taken out of the soil solution and rendered unavailable, but the soil gradually becomes saturated with phosphate. One estimate is that a c. 1 m band becomes saturated in about 5–6 years or so. It is, though, considered that a suitably wide strip bearing suitably varied vegetation would remove phosphate indefinitely, by sustainable processes and, hopefully, guidelines will soon be available. In a buffer strip, sediment is trapped before reaching the river, and the concentration of a whole range of other chemicals (including nutrients and biocides) are reduced substantially, the substances being degraded, precipitated or adsorbed. In Sweden, comparing the costs of buffer strip purification with those of sewage treatment works, has shown that 10 m buffer strips pay for themselves in only 2–3 years!

Vegetation diversity and high organic carbon improve purifying ability, and give greater resilience to the purifying habitat (for instance, for nitrogen, poplar wood is better than grassland). Alder fixes nitrogen in its root nodules (one estimate is 70 kg/ha/year), so increases nitrogen in nitrogen-poor areas. Poplars and willows are better choices for strips intended to reduce nitrogen.

'Wild' buffer strips need not be economically worthless. Apart from pasture and meadow, possibilities include:
- Osier or withy beds for baskets, other craftwork, fences, spiling, etc. Also willows for cricket bats, etc.
- *Phragmites* reed beds for thatching.
- Alder beds for clogs (tourist), alder or aspen for pulp for good-quality paper.
- Rushes for chair seats, and other craft.
- *Phalaris arundinacea* (reedgrass) beds for hay.
- Hazel copse, for coppicing (fences, etc.).

• Mixed soft vegetation for farm litter, horticultural insulation.
• Any bushy or woody vegetation as cover for shooting.
These are also uses valuable for conservation, as are linear ponds beside streams.

Under-drains direct to the river by-pass buffer strips, of course, and so should be checked to see if it is feasible to stop the drains at the entrance to the buffer strip. Two options are possible. The under-drain can just be stopped at the start of the strip, leaving the water to filter through the soil, with considerable cleaning. Or, a small pond can be dug out, a 'horseshoe' wetland, as it is called (Fig. 5.6). These can each reduce nitrogen as much as 4 kg a year.

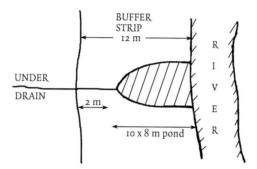

Fig. 5.6. Horseshoe wetland (recommended size for a 12 m buffer strip).

Banks of course purify in the same way, and the wider the bank, and the more diverse and large its vegetation types, the more effective the purification. Even a stoned bank may do some purification, provided run-off seeps through earth under the stones.

Run-off from roads and built-up areas

(a)

(b)

Fig. 5.7. Run-off: (a), (b), roads and built-up areas.

Fig. 5.7 (cont.) (c) Pollution by motorway, Seabrook, England. The drainage ditch of the minor road bears middle-nutrient species with colouring/contraction indicating nutrient deficiency. Tolerant species in lagoon with motorway run-off. Recovery slow and stream to left (Saltwood) shows good vegetation, in habitat similar except for pollution (Haslam, 1990).

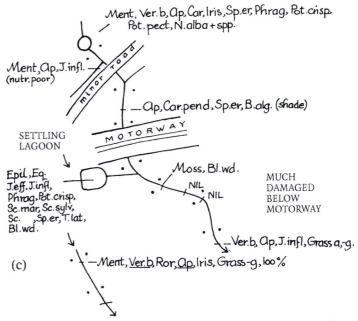

(c)

Run-off from roads and built-up areas flowing to the river, not to the STW, may come from the river, or from some way away (Fig. 5.7). It consists of a poisonous cocktail of petrol, tyre spread, hydrocarbons and other organic products of these, heavy metals, etc. It is highly poisonous. Too often 'muck' on roads is thought of as good clean soil – but how does soil get on to a motorway or other busy road? THIS IS BAD POLLUTION.

Run-off from a motorway, even when passed through a settling lagoon, can ruin the vegetation of a fragile (solute-low) stream type (Chapter 4 and Fig. 5.7c above). It is well known that in a town unpurified surface run-off is more poisonous than the effluent from a (good) STW. The effect of busy rural roads, and of town extensions with surface run-off not connected to the STW, is often forgotten. It is to spread a toxic pollution, not easily biodegradable, throughout Britain, wherever busy roads go. (NB Oil must, by statute, be intercepted.)

RUN-OFF POLLUTION IN THE RIVER CAN BE DECREASED (Fig. 5.8) BY:

1 Connecting the flow to a STW, or if not possible, then

2 Using settling ponds, with as long a retention time as possible, then letting the water run slowly through a ditch dominated by tall monocotyledons, or, less good, other vegetation types. (The first patent for a design using submerged plants was granted in 1992 in the US.)

3 Using buffer strips, horseshoe wetlands and opened drains (as described for agrochemical pollution, above).

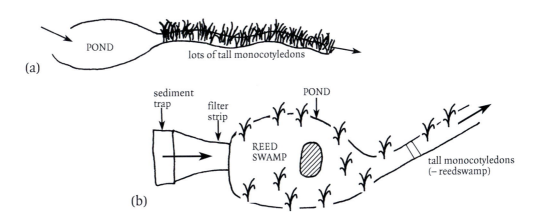

Fig. 5.8. Run-off amelioration, (a) simple, (b) complex (and more effective).

Small effluents

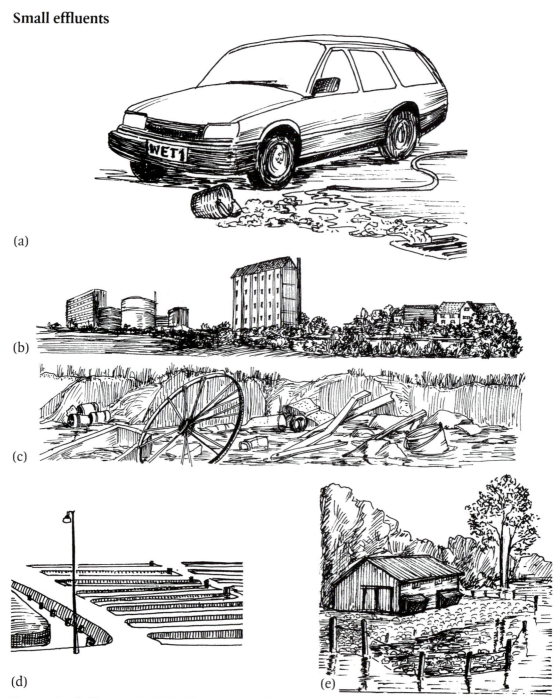

Fig. 5.9. *Small effluents and rubbish (also see Fig. 5.2(b)). (a) Run-off from car washing, (b) factory, (c) rubbish, (d) fish farm, (e) duck farm ((a), (b), (c) Haslam 1990, (d), (e) Haslam, 1991).*

Small effluents and rubbish enter from the water's edge or in pipes or ditches (Fig. 5.9). These come from many sources, including septic tanks, garages, car-washing, farms (slurry, silage, etc.), fish-farms, factories, spills of all sorts. These, with increased run-off pollution, are now collectively a serious hazard. Individually, most are tolerable by rivers and larger streams. By the score or the hundred, though, as now, they are not acceptable. Often the perpetrators do not know there is an effluent, or that it is poisonous.

SMALL EFFLUENTS, FOR IMPROVEMENT, need:

1 In the first place, identification. The river bank should be walked, and each source of effluent or nasty run-off should be located. The Environment Agency (in Scotland the Scottish Environment Protection Agency) has probably listed some, but not all sources.

2 Once they have been found, the effluents may be, as appropriate, diverted to the STW, treated as described for run-off above, or, best, prevented from arising.

3 Buffer strips, horseshoe wetlands and opened drains, as described for agrochemical pollution above, may be used.

Although well-run fish farms have, individually, effluents with minor (or moderate) pollution, harm to the river can come either from badly-run farms, or, and more often, from the cumulate effects of many fish farms on the same river. Pollution comes from wastes from fish, surplus food fed to the fish, and the biocides and hormones the fish are treated with. Investigations are desirable (including the species of fish farmed – relevant if they escape to the river).

Large effluents

Fig. 5.10. Large effluent (Haslam, 1990).

Large effluents are those from STWs, larger factories (and mines) (Fig. 5.10). All these (except some small mines) now receive treatment, though the discharged effluents vary widely in quality. The best possible, the declared aim of the Dutch Government for all effluents, is that they should have no detectable effect on the river fauna and flora. The Environment Agency (in Scotland the Scottish Environment Protection Agency) will have lists of all major effluents. TO IMPROVE, put suitable advice and pressure on the Sewage Treatment Works.

Summary

The larger effluent sources are necessarily sparse. Over the past century the worst have improved; but with the increase of population, large STWs now occur more widely. With the spread of village and small-town industrial estates, industrial pollution is also spreading far more widely: moderate pollution has spread across Britain.

Domestic and industrial sources are far the worst polluters in Europe, far outstripping agro-pollution. They include run-off, small effluents, and large effluents. The enormous increase in number, spread, and toxicity has come from the vast increase in the smaller sources (run-off and small effluents). Rivers hitherto clean, with no STW, but with new roads, intensive farming, housing and industrial estates, may now be moderately or even severely polluted.

Effect of land use

Nearly everywhere in Britain, people have chosen the land use. It may have stayed the same for centuries, giving 'traditional' land-use influence on the streams, or it may have changed recently, and indeed changed repeatedly. Agrochemicals, effluents and run-off are described above. This section is concerned with land-use practices. Land use determines the land chemicals, and so the type of run-off to the stream. This is true on the large scale – the water running off blanket bog is different to that running off barley fields – and on the small scale – the run-off from recently deep-ploughed soil differs (contains more nutrients) to that from shallow-ploughed; and run-off from permanent pasture differs to that from ley. Land use influences run-off and so influences rivers.

Rivers whose nature is altered by changes in land use deserve as much attention as those altered by more direct pollution. **In particular, many now-rare and fragile river types (see Chapter 4) are so because they are low in inorganic solutes, and consequently easily destroyed by substituting a land use which has a solute-richer run-off (e.g. changing permanent pasture to arable, moor to fertilised grassland).** Where it is not practical to preserve traditional land use, buffer strips (see above) – and wide ones, on dry land! – should be created around the streams.

Land use affects the pattern, as well as the composition, of the run-off (Fig. 5.11). Run-off is easier (faster) when soil is covered with a short sward rather than tall woody-mix vegetation, and is even more so when the soil is bare. Similarly, it is faster the fewer cross-ditches and cross-hedges there are to slow the water movement.

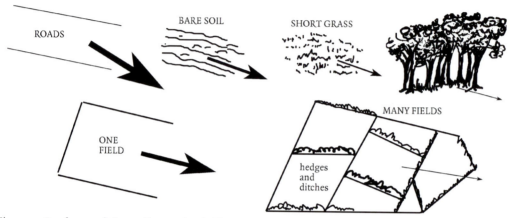

Fig. 5.11. *Land use and river sedimentation (wider arrows, more material carried to the stream).*

Instead of rain sinking into the earth and the ground water table, as into a sponge, increasing intensity of farming leads to quicker run-off, therefore to high short-term floods, called flash-floods (rather than slowly developing floods of lower peak flows). These flashier floods erode far more silt, so taking this to the river. These floods are also more liable to flood land downstream, since the peak discharge is so much greater. Therefore, the streams are likely to be more unstable, unstable in flow, and with unstable silt on the bed (see Chapter 3). Flash floods are still more extreme on built-up land, where rain cannot get into the soil at all.

Draining land leads to the loss of brooks, inadequate water in streams and river, less purification of agrochemicals, and less water stored in the land. Drainage exacerbates the bare-soil effect of intensive farming, further increasing river silting. The silt causes shoaling, unstable beds, smothering of plants and animals, and increases river nutrient status (in intermediate nutrient bands, see Chapter 4). The silt comes from the top soil, so it is the soil most fertile for farming, which is thus removed. Drainage means dredging. When a river bed is disturbed (dredging and on the small-scale trampling, etc.) bound chemicals, nutrients and pollutants, are released into the water.

Nutrient-poor, acid, oligo- and dystrophic influences

The influences leading to these types of stream are primarily:

1 acid peat and humus as in bog, moor, heath;

2 acid-leaf forest, birch, (most) conifers;

3 nutrient-poor rock, as in most resistant rock (slate, gneiss, etc.) and acid sands (e.g. New Forest Sands);

4 acid rain.

Low-nutrient rock is just that: few nutrients move into the river. 'Acid' organic material, though, is both nutrient-low, and organic-high, containing a lot of organic substances derived from *Sphagnum* etc., and this also affects the stream (this type of stream is referred to as 'dystrophic').

Fig. 5.12. Nutrient-poor stream.

Much acid peat is now being drained. This means peat erosion. While large quantities of peat are draining through the river, the river will be acidified where more of this peat is deposited, or where it is more concentrated in the water. (The streams near the source may be unaffected, as these have always had much peat, but further downstream peat is arriving in greater quantities, and acidification occurs.) Once peat has been lost from the catchment, though, the river will be less dystrophic, as peat no longer enters the river. Many mountain and moorland rivers are being altered in this way, their traditional vegetation (and so fauna) being lost. Otters may not be able to live permanently in some acidified headwaters.

Particles are deposited in quieter sequences of rivers. If acid peat accumulates, the habitat is more acid, approaching that of blanket bog. If mineral silt – even low-nutrient silt – accumulates, the habitat is more nutrient-rich. Therefore, the relative nutrient status of these quieter reaches, as opposed to swifter, non-depositing ones, depends on the material deposited.

WHEN ASSESSING, the following should be noted:

- presence of nutrient-poor influences, proportion of catchment covered;
- type of nutrient-poor influence, wood (type), acid peat (type), rock;
- changes taking place, peat drainage, afforestation, deforestation (short-term, both these last are nutrient-rich due to soil disturbance);
- overgrazing of peaty land, which can cause erosion; and also
- the presence of fragile stream types, those dependent on the continuance of traditional management for their existence.

Nutrient-rich, fertile, eutrophic influences

Fig. 5.13. Cultivated landscape, intensively farmed (Haslam, 1990).

Cropping land removes nutrients (and organic carbon) with the crops, and the soil becomes deficient unless nutrients are replaced. When this was difficult and expensive (using manure, rabbit legs, pigeon dung, etc.) the land did not become over-rich, but with cheap powder fertilisers, the run-off, and so the rivers and the ground water, contain unused fertilisers.

These are primarily:
- farming   )
- fertiliser, manure   ) Agricultural
- ploughing – deep, first-time, and intermittent) practices
    ploughing release the most nutrients   )
- (ash from burnt stubble)   )
- very fertile marshes, woods, etc.
- nutrient-rich rock, e.g., clay, marl, some fertile sandstones and alluvium,
- effluents such as farm slurry, effluents from STW, septic tanks and fish farms.

Disturbing soil releases a rush of nutrients. Both afforestation and deforestation, over large areas, may lead to much sediment run-off, from soil disturbance. This means a short-term increase in nutrients (except from peat) as well as silting.

'Neutral' influences include woods, marshes, rough pasture, unfertilised grassland, etc. This will increase nutrient status in a nutrient-deficient catchment, and decrease it in a nutrient-rich one.

Each step from 'wild' land, through unimproved pasture, improved grassland, orchard, temporary grassland, arable and intensive arable farming increases the nutrient run-off to, and so the influence on, the river. This run-off increases the downstream eutrophication which, in a lesser degree, is native to the river.

6 ASSESSING the effect of pollution and other interference using vegetation (macrophytes)

(introduction, and cover–diversity number require no special expertise; damage rating
needs the ability to determine the reference vegetation for the relevant river type,
using Classification A (Haslam & Wolseley method) in Chapter 4,
and to name some species at the site in question)

SUMMARY

Vegetation is sensitive to changes in chemical status, so plant communities vary with the intensity and type of pollution, and can be used to assess these. Vegetation monitoring assesses the habitat for vegetation. This method of assessing pollution is valuable when large lengths need surveying rapidly, since 40+ sites can be recorded in one day and written up in the next. Otherwise it is complementary to other methods, whether invertebrate, diatom, or pesticide levels, estimating, as does each method, a rather different aspect of pollution. The plant community of a site is recorded, and the difference between this and the 'reference vegetation' for that habitat forms the damage rating. That part of the damage due to pollution is the pollution index. Vegetation is sensitive to all habitat changes, physical as well as chemical, and the 'cover–diversity' number, a very simple measure, can be used to estimate vegetation well being, and so, in lowlands etc., the total impact of human activities.

Introduction

Vegetation is the simplest, quickest and – in one botanist's opinion – most reliable tool for assessing stream pollution in summer (mid-June to mid-September), and in lowlands, plains, and those hills where vegetation is plentiful and predictable. A graded damage rating can be used, though there is also a much simpler overall tool to gauge total impact, the cover–diversity number. About 40 sites a day (over say 150 miles) can be recorded. Sites are usually undamaged by the survey. For any one catchment type, the ability to name 35 species will permit pollution assessment (naming 80 will be adequate for the whole British Isles). No naming is needed for the cover–diversity number.

Since, ultimately, animal life depends on plant life, it is likely that if the river plants are right, the river animals also are right (given lack of disturbance, the appropriate vegetation structure, and suitable land habitat, where appropriate).

Vegetation assessments are for soil as well as water, since plant roots grow in soil. As silt holds more solutes than water, plants may be more affected by soil than by water chemistry. The soil is more stable in composition. Large plants stay put, so if a plant clump has been in place for say five years, then for that five years conditions have been tolerable for that plant species.

The Standing Committee of Analysts recommends methods for examining waters, and waste materials. It recommends the use of macrophytes and diatoms as well as invertebrates and chemicals, although the two former are, as yet, seldom used.

When both vegetation and invertebrate indices are calculated for the same river, the difference in the organism's response to oxygen depletion is important. In moderate organic pollution, the poorest invertebrate community is where oxygen is least, as found perhaps 1–2 km downstream of the effluent entry. Since plants make their own oxygen, they are unaffected by moderate depletions, and it is the toxicity of the pollution which harms them. Consequently, the vegetation index is worst by the effluent entry itself. Index comparisons must therefore be of worst point with worst point, not with specific distances below entry. Vegetation is the tool of first choice for locating minor (non-visible) effluents, and assessing minor, particularly organic effluents, which have little effect on river oxygen. Invertebrates are the tool of first choice for assessing minor heavy metal pollutions, however. Vegetation is, in general terms, useful when time is short or river lengths great, since 40+ sites can be surveyed in a day, and the result can be analysed the next (within the habitat limits above). Trouble spots can be located for detailed invertebrate and chemical investigation.

How vegetation responds to pollution

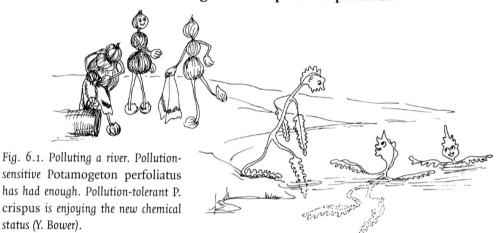

Fig. 6.1. *Polluting a river. Pollution-sensitive Potamogeton perfoliatus has had enough. Pollution-tolerant P. crispus is enjoying the new chemical status (Y. Bower).*

Fig. 6.2 depicts the effect of typical sewage treatment works (STW) and equivalent pollutions on a well-vegetated stream (see Chapter 4 for river types). Fig. 6.2(a) shows a clean stream, with 10 species in a short reach, and plants covering 80% of the bed; the stream shown in Fig. 6.2(b) has mild STW pollution. There are still eight species in the reach, but the cover is less, and in comparison with the stream in (a), the site looks rather blighted. Some species present in both are sensitive to pollution, others are tolerant. (NB pollution-tolerant species do grow in clean streams.) However, in (a), three of the ten species, that is 30%, are pollution tolerant, whilst in (b), four of the eight are, i.e. 50%. This is a suspiciously high number, and, when coupled with another bad indicator, means pollution.

In the damage rating described in Table 6.2, the top 'a' grade means 'all right', not 'clean or excellent'. Few streams these days merit either a clean or an excellent grading. The best have something or things mildly wrong, and are 'all right'.

In Fig. 6.2(b), two pollution-sensitive species present in (a) have gone. As conditions get more difficult, whether from pollution, fierce flow, uniform banks or anything else, survival becomes more difficult, and plants weakened by these difficulties are more likely to be washed out. Instead of having say 20 clumps of a species in 100 m of river, where there will be a clump visible from almost any bridge or vantage point, there may be only say two clumps, and most views will not contain one. In the habitat depicted in Fig. 6.2, it is chance as to whether it is *Apium nodiflorum* or *Myosotis scorpioides* that is seen. What matters is that sensitive species have decreased. Plants in the fringing herb group (see Chapter 4) are bushy and short-rooted, so are easily caught in flow and washed away. In pollution, the root system is weaker, so the clumps are yet more vulnerable. (Clumps anchor worst on, so are most easily washed away, from resistant rock streams – see Chapter 4).

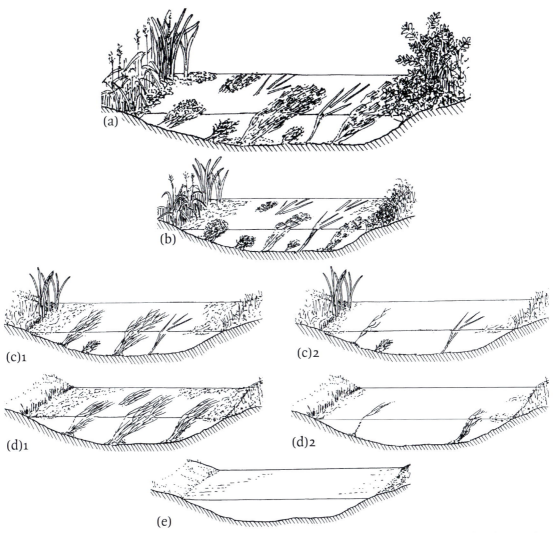

Fig. 6.2 (below and right). A typical effect of increasing pollution on plant community. (a) clean, (b)–(e) increasing pollution. Species present: (a) Ranunculus sp. (abundant), Apium nodiflorum, Callitriche sp., Myosotis scorpioides, Phalaris arundinacea, Potamogeton crispus, Nasturtium officinale, Sparganium emersum, Sp. erectum, Veronica beccabunga, (b) Callitriche sp., Myosotis scorpioides, (Phalaris arundinacea, Potamogeton crispus, Ranunculus sp., Sparganium emersum, Sp. erectum, blanket weed (long trailing filamentous algae), (c) Potamogeton crispus, P. pectinatus, Sparganium emersum, Sp. erectum, blanket weed, (d) Potamogeton pectinatus (abundant), blanket weed, (e) no large (macrophytic) plants (P.A. Wolseley & Y. Bower).

Also, in Fig. 6.2(b) pollution has reduced Ranunculus from dominant to sparse. Three pollution-tolerants are retained, one, Sparganium emersum, has actually increased. Blanket weed (long trailing algae, mostly Cladophora sp.) has entered. In lowland streams like this one, blanket weed is favoured by pollution.

Moving down to Fig. 6.2(c), all pollution-sensitive species have gone. Two alternatives are given (the left probably has lower anions, differences in other pollutants being unknown). On the left, blanket weed has expanded, and the other European pollution-favoured species, Potamogeton pectinatus, has come in and become common. (The clean-water occurrences of this species are in brackish or some peaty waters.) P. pectinatus usually means pollution and its presence, plus blanket weed, is an almost infallible indicator, except near the coast (and in Caithness). P. pectinatus does not grow in very shallow water, blanket weed does. Blanket weed also increases in ephemeral habitats in hill streams, and with disturbance, particularly where there is also some pollution.

In general, pollution may cause LOSS (as in (c) 2 and (d) 2) or it may cause SKEWING (as in (c) 1 and (d) 1), altering rather than reducing vegetation. Bad enough pollution causes total loss anyway, as in Fig. 6.2(e). When less bad, the course the pattern takes depends on the type of pollution, and the habitat.

In Fig. 6.2(c), only diversity has been halved. All, 100%, of the species are pollution tolerant. In (c)1 the cover is good, but is made up of pollution-favoured species; in (c) 2 the cover is bad. Cover is reduced by pollution – and also by grazing, cutting, disturbance, etc. Only nutrient-rich species remain (except for the wide-ranging *Sparganium erectum*) (see Chapter 4). STW effluent is rich in nutrients as well as in poisons!

Dividing species into those tolerant, semi-tolerant and sensitive to pollution as in Table 6.3 is convenient but naive (species neither tolerant nor semi-tolerant are deemed sensitive). Not only do all variations in species response exist, but there are innumerable pollutants, which may act singly, cumulatively and synergistically. Species vary in tolerance geographically, and with their habitat. Using simple groups is thus a convenient starting point, but for detailed work study should be made in the individual site, to determine local responses: and then to use these to interpret and assess habitats (see pp. 17, 34, 131, 137).

In Fig. 6.2(c), therefore, diversity is down, pollution tolerance is up, pollution-favoured species are in, and cover has altered. In Fig. 6.2(d), *P. pectinatus* and blanket weed are alone present: depicted as either dominant, with 80% cover, or sparse, just wisps. (This depends on pollution type, as well as, e.g., water force.) The banks are now without emerged aquatics, and there may be a 'toxic line', a yellowing of bank plants near the water, with normal green vegetation above the usual flood level. A toxic line is more common with industrial than with domestic effluents. A different type of plant yellowing is characteristic of many organic pollutions. This other yellowing is found most in shoots furthest into the water, on unconsolidated silt (i.e. where pollutants are most concentrated). In the same conditions other species may be flaccid or over-lush.

Finally, Fig. 6.2(e) shows a stream too grossly polluted for any vegetation to develop. Regrettably, this is less diagnostic of pollution than are (c) and (d). Sites devoid of vegetation may indeed be grossly polluted, but they may also be heavily shaded, be just dredged, or have many plant-eating fish, etc. Evidence is needed on the cause of the emptiness. The look or smell of the water may (or may not!) be evidence.

It has, though, been shown that POLLUTION AFFECTS VEGETATION, AND ITS EFFECTS CAN BE ASSESSED AND INTERPRETED. In a stream of the type given in Fig. 6.2, vegetation should be as in (a) – in, say, a

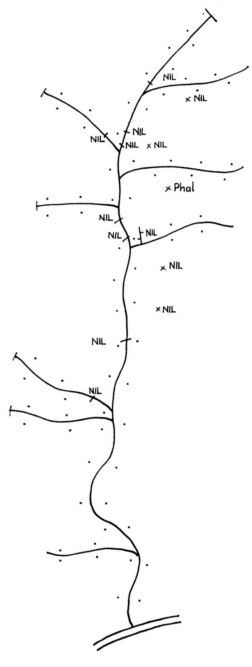

Fig. 6.3. Gross pollution (sparse dots beside stream = lowland; denser dots, increasingly hilly); crosses indicate small tributaries). River Neckar, Germany (Haslam, 1987).

Welsh hillstream, or the lower Great Ouse, the expected vegetation type will be different (see Chapter 4). The best available vegetation can be listed, and that is the reference vegetation for the stream type. From place to place even along one reach this 'best available' will vary. In diversity, cover, Colour Band and species assemblage it will, in stable conditions, be effectively stable, but *Berula erecta* may be present in one site, *Veronica beccabunga* in another, *Potamogeton perfoliatus* here, *Elodea canadensis* there. The species are drawn from the same assemblage. When the vegetation is damaged, and so reduced from e.g. that in Fig. 6.2(a), something is wrong. This 'wrong' can be defined, giving the overall damage, and the overall reduction and skewing. Finally, that part of the reduction due to pollution (rather than, say, cattle) is assessed.

Fig. 6.3 shows a poor river, grossly polluted with no vegetation. (Damage ratings (see Table 6.2) are all at the lowest value, h for horrible.) Fig. 6.4 is of an unusually good river – for present-day lowland Europe. (England has nothing as good). Here, several sites have 'a' (for all right) as their damage rating.

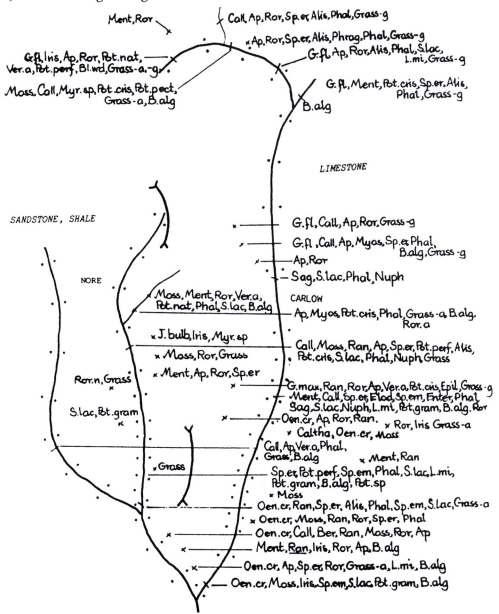

Fig. 6.4 *A satisfactorily good, clean river (underlined names mean the species is abundant; for full species names for this and subsequent figures see the list of plant names at the end of the book). River Barrow, Ireland (Haslam, 1987). Note long species lists per site, and blanket weed and Potamogeton pectinatus rare. (In Europe it is unreasonable to expect an entire river in excellent condition.)*

Fig. 6.5 is of a river as bad as it can be while still having plenty of vegetation. *Potamogeton pectinatus* is abundant. Fig. 6.6 is slightly better. The river is still immediately diagnosable as severely polluted, but the species lists are longer. As well as there being an industrial complex near the source, this river has additional bad effluents entering intermittently. Each cuts the diversity, species other than *Potamogeton pectinatus* and blanket weed tending to disappear, until downstream self-purification permits their re-entry.

Fig. 6.7 is also of a badly polluted river, though pollution is less than in Fig. 6.5. This river pattern is more like the (c) 2, (d) 2 of Fig. 6.2, the vegetation being reduced from, rather than skewed from, what it should be. This may be because the bed is unstable, making anchorage there difficult (the type of pollution is perhaps different also).

Fig. 6.8 shows a variety of damage in an upper chalk stream. Structure is poor, in that there is much too little water. Pollution comes from domestic and farm effluents (also from silt and agrochemicals, which are not discussed here). The vegetation is at the blanket weed-plus-poor-'proper'-community stage . (Water is too shallow for *Potamogeton pectinatus*.) Entering the river are ① a good chalk stream, from a spring, clean (except for passing through watercress beds). *Ranunculus* is abundant, bright green, well-grown, and there are enough other species to show the water is clean. Another channel, ②, had initially similar water, but the effluent from six cottages and a cow unit has altered it. *Callitriche* is dominant, as it also is in ③, where it is fish farm effluent that has been added to, and dominates, the chalk water. *Ranunculus* is the typical dominant of chalk streams. Small sandstone streams, which both contain more nutrients and have a different nutrient balance, often have much *Callitriche*, which is also often tolerant to

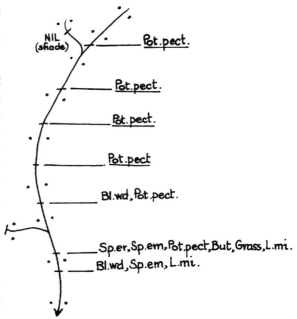

Fig. 6.5. *River in the stage shown in Fig. 6.2(d), improving with the downstream entry of a cleaner branch. River Trent, England (Haslam, 1987).*

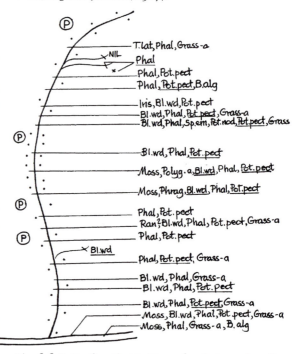

Fig. 6.6. *Better than that in Figure 6.5, but severely polluted – at the Fig. 6.2 (c) 1 and (d) 1 level. (P = pollution entering; note decreased diversity). River Alzette, Luxembourg (Haslam, 1987).*

some organic pollutions (see below). There is no difference in ①, ② and ③, for diversity and cover; all are mesotrophic (middle-nutrient, Blue Colour Band), all score *a*. Illumination comes from the deeper knowledge that abundant *Callitriche* (without abundant *Ranunculus*) is 'wrong' here, it shows a skewed community, one skewed from chalk, into resembling sandstone. More skewed still are channels ④, recently cut, and ⑤, with fish-farm effluent alone. None of these little tributaries has a strong enough chemical influence to alter the already polluted community in the main river.

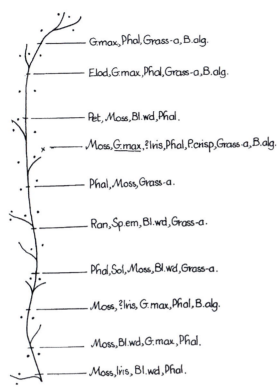

G.max,Phal,Grass-a,B.alg.

Elod,G.max,Phal,Grass-a,B.alg.

Pet,Moss,Bl.wd,Phal.

Moss,G.max,?Iris,Phal,P.crisp,Grass-a,B.alg.

Phal,Moss,Grass-a.

Ran,Sp.em,Bl.wd,Grass-a.

Phal,Sol,Moss,Bl.wd,Grass-a.

Moss,?Iris, G.max,Phal,B.alg.

Moss,Bl.wd,G.max,Phal.

Moss,Iris,Bl.wd,Phal.

Fig. 6.7. *Another polluted river, but vegetation more reduced than skewed (unstable substrate). See Fig. 6.2 (c)2. River Attert, Luxembourg (Haslam, 1987).*

Fig. 6.9 shows a slow and slight improvement in a severely polluted river over six years. The change between any consecutive two figures is too small to be a proven improvement. That between the first and last, is certain.

Lastly, Fig. 6.10 shows a striking improvement over time (10 years) in the main river Tame, both upstream and downstream, and temporary improvement in the Cole tributary, which was cleaned up, and then again overloaded. Pollution status changes, and vegetation can monitor this change.

Table 6.1 shows changes over time in the Aberdeen River Don. The upper section (above Mossat) has a stable bed vegetation, but the edges have become more nutrient rich. The streams have been channelled, and the fringe plants are no longer on nutrient-poor gravel banks, but on nutrient-medium earth banks. The middle section (Mossat to Inverurie) has been acidified. The mountain peat is being drained, and more peat is reaching this middle section than before (see land use, Chapter 5).

Downstream, in the period of study, urban pollution first decreased (major effluents improved) then increased (multiple small sources became of overriding importance).

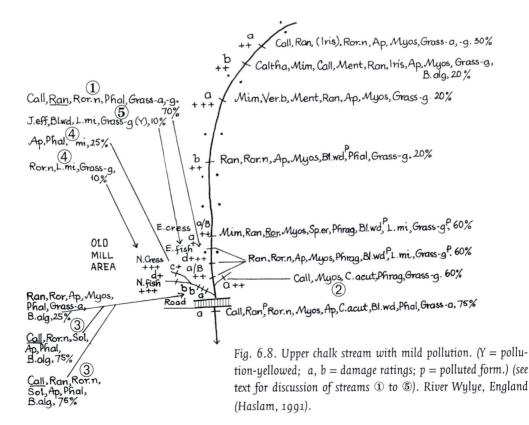

Fig. 6.8. *Upper chalk stream with mild pollution. (Y = pollution-yellowed; a, b = damage ratings; p = polluted form.) (see text for discussion of streams ① to ⑤). River Wylye, England (Haslam, 1991).*

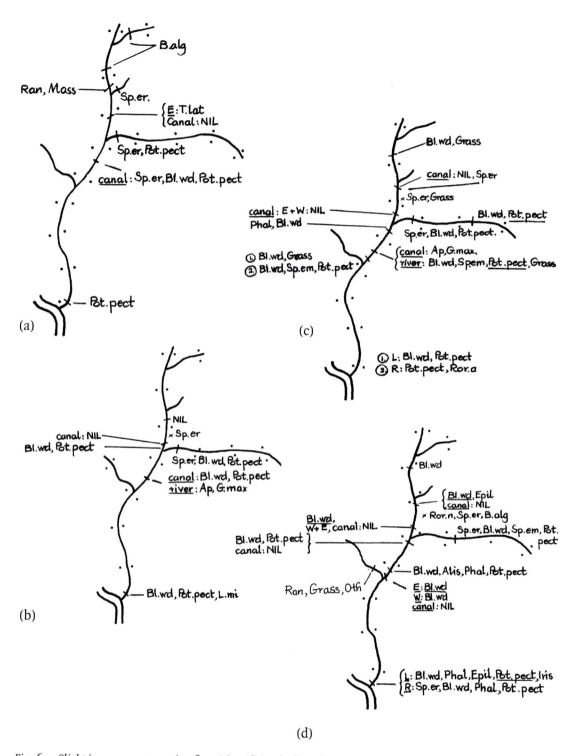

Fig. 6.9. *Slight improvement over time from (a) to (d) in a badly polluted river. River (Severn) Stour, England (Haslam, 1987).*

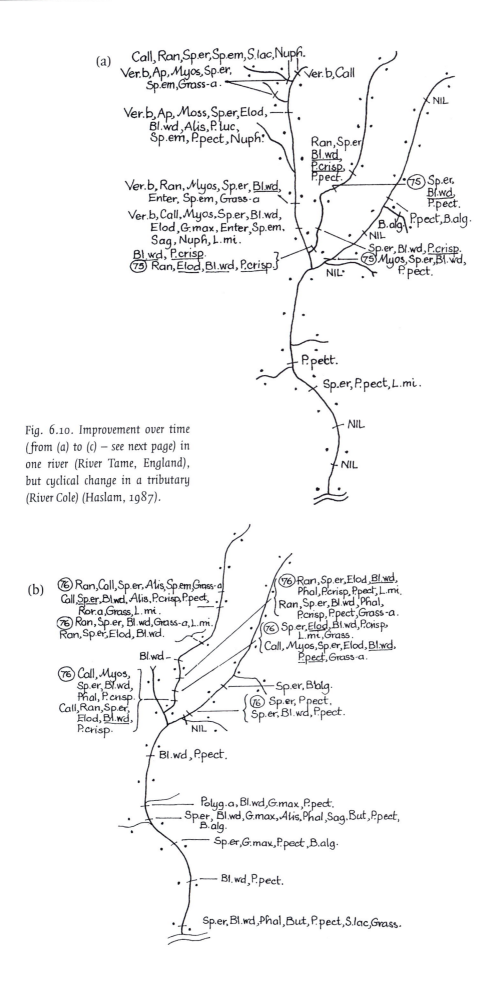

(a)

Call, Ran, Sp.er, Sp.em, S.lac, Nuph.
Ver.b, Ap, Myos, Sp.er, Sp.em, Grass-a .
Ver.b, Call

NIL

Ver.b, Ap, Moss, Sp.er, Elod, Bl.wd, Alis, P.luc, Sp.em, P.pect, Nuph.

Ran, Sp.er, Bl.wd, P.crisp, P.pect.

75 Sp.er, Bl.wd, P.pect.

Ver.b, Ran, Myos, Sp.er, Bl.wd, Enter, Sp.em, Grass-a
Ver.b, Call, Myos, Sp.er, Bl.wd, Elod, G.max, Enter, Sp.em, Sag, Nuph, L.mi.
Bl.wd, P.crisp.
75 Ran, Elod, Bl.wd, P.crisp.

P.pect, B.alg.

B.alg.
NIL
Sp.er, Bl.wd, P.crisp.
75 Myos, Sp.er, Bl.wd, P.pect.

NIL.

P.pect.

Sp.er, P.pect, L.mi.

NIL

NIL

Fig. 6.10. *Improvement over time (from (a) to (c) — see next page) in one river (River Tame, England), but cyclical change in a tributary (River Cole) (Haslam, 1987).*

(b)

76 Ran, Call, Sp.er, Alis, Sp.em, Grass-a
Call, Sp.er, Bl.wd, Alis, P.crisp, P.pect, Ror.a, Grass, L.mi.
76 Ran, Sp.er, Bl.wd, Grass-a, L.mi.
Ran, Sp.er, Elod, Bl.wd.

Bl.wd

76 Call, Myos, Sp.er, Bl.wd, Phal, P.crisp.
Call, Ran, Sp.er, Elod, Bl.wd, P.crisp.

NIL

76 Ran, Sp.er, Elod, Bl.wd, Phal, P.crisp, P.pect, L.mi.
Ran, Sp.er, Bl.wd, Phal, P.crisp, P.pect, Grass-a.
76 Sp.er, Elod, Bl.wd, P.crisp, L.mi, Grass.
Call, Myos, Sp.er, Elod, Bl.wd, P.pect, Grass-a.

Sp.er, B.alg.
76 Sp.er, P.pect.
Sp.er, Bl.wd, P.pect.

Bl.wd, P.pect.

Polyg.a, Bl.wd, G.max, P.pect.
Sp.er, Bl.wd, G.max, Alis, Phal, Sag, But, P.pect, B.alg.
Sp.er, G.max, P.pect, B.alg.

Bl.wd, P.pect.

Sp.er, Bl.wd, Phal, But, P.pect, S.lac, Grass.

Fig. 6.10 (cont.)

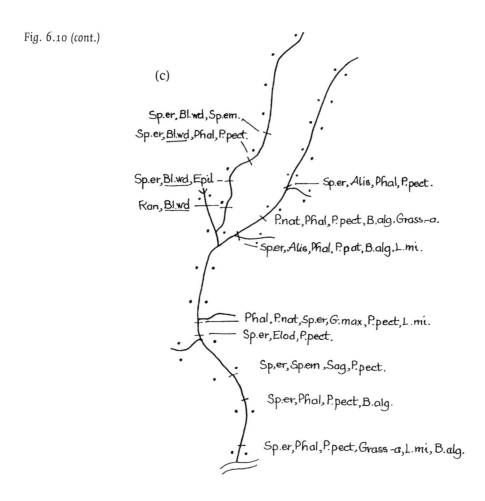

(c)

Benthic algae, blanket weed, sewage fungus and 'sewage algae'

Small algae, fungi and bacteria grow in all rivers. It is only when their growths are large enough to be easily seen from above the water that they come within the scope of Chapters 4 and 6 of this evaluation scheme. These larger growths may be:

Benthic algae

Algae may grow on the bottom (on the substrate) plentifully enough to be seen as a green covering. Benthic algae are widespread in many river types, particularly on stable larger particles not recently scoured, and in pollution. They are ignored in this scheme.

Blanket weed

When algae grow out from the bottom to trail in the water and be a part of the macrophytic vegetation of the river, they form blanket weed. Most commonly this is *Cladophora* sp. in flowing waters, also *Vaucheria* sp. or *Spirogyra* sp. in stiller ones (other genera occur also). Blanket weed (even if solely *Cladophora*) should not be described as '*Cladophora* sp.', since *Cladophora* is fairly ubiquitous, but the large growths of blanket weed are not. Alternative terms are e.g. 'large trailing masses of *Cladophora* sp.'.

Table 6.1 Changes in nutrient status in River Don as estimated from vegetation

(a) Distribution of nutrient-poor indicators
(in particular, *Callitriche hamulata, Caltha palustris, Eleocharis palustris, Glyceria fluitans* (long-leaved), *Juncus articulatus, J. bulbosus, Myriophyllum alterniflorum, Petasites hybridus* (dwarf), *Ranunculus flammula*)

	Records of nutrient-poor species as % total species records							
	1978	1983	1986	1987	1988	1989	1990	1991
Don, upstream of Mossat	23	27	20	—	—	—	20	—
Don, Mossat to Inverurie	4	8	6	—	—	—	44	—
Don, Inverurie to upper paper mill effluent	0[1]	11	12	18	11	9	4	3
Don, to mouth	0[1]	0.5	2	4[2]	3	4[3]	1	3
Urie	4	8	7	—	—	—	8	—

[1]   Few records in all. 1969, two records, both 0.
[2]   Mainly *Callitriche hamulata.*
[3]   Mainly *Myriophyllum alterniflorum.*

(b) Distribution of nutrient-rich indicators
(*Glyceria maxima, Myriophyllum spicatum, Potamogeton crispus, P. sparganifolius, Sparganium emersum, Sp. erectum*, blanket weed and (long) sewage algae)

	Records of nutrient-rich species as % total species records							
	1978	1983	1986	1987	1988	1989	1990	1991
Don, upstream of Mossat	0	0	0.5	—	—	—	0	—
Don, Mossat to Inverurie	30	25	18	—	—	—	14	—
Don, Inverurie to upper paper mill effluent	36	22	38	29	26	36	34	44
Don, to mouth	44	40	41	26	34	47	50	55
Urie	9	9	5	—	—	—	7	—

Blanket weed is encouraged by pollution, particularly of organic and nutrient-rich materials. Given mild or moderate pollution, blanket weed often grows better with disturbance, such as dredging, or swifter water, as on weirs. In highland streams, blanket weed may develop during low flows. Smothering blanket weed is always due to pollution. Growths in polluted and fairly clean water look different, and can be distinguished by experienced observers.

Sewage fungus

This is a mix of bacteria, fungi and algae, usually also with ciliates, etc. It forms growths attached to the bottoms, sides or vegetation of rivers, which, like blanket weed, may be sparse or may quite smother the river. Sewage fungus is typically pale to mid-brown, but can be a variety of colours – though not green and stringy like blanket weed.

Sewage fungus is typical of highly organic pollutions with little breakdown: sewage, paper-mill effluent, etc. With untreated sewage effluent, sewage fungus is the first 'macrophyte' to appear downstream. It is followed by blanket weed further down when considerable breakdown has occurred. Other pollutions may have no or little sewage fungus, and have blanket weed as the first macrophyte. This does NOT mean they are less contaminating, merely that they have either inadequate raw organic matter or over-toxic components for sewage fungus.

'Sewage algae'

This is not an official term, but is a convenient description for growths intermediate between blanket weed and true sewage fungus. They indicate pollution.

Damage rating

THE DAMAGE RATING ASSESSES ALL TYPES OF DAMAGE, CHEMICAL AND PHYSICAL, IN RELATION TO THE REFERENCE (OPTIMAL) VEGETATION FOR THAT RIVER TYPE. THE POLLUTION INDEX IS THAT PART OF THE DAMAGE RATING WHICH IS DUE TO CHEMICAL DAMAGE, POLLUTION.

In lowlands, and often lower hills, an eight-point damage rating can be calculated. As water force increases towards mountains, the grades become less precise, but even in mountains a three-point scale is often possible (good–fair–bad), when there is a comparable undamaged reach where a reference community can be recorded.

An index is a way of giving complex data to busy decision makers. It is a way of bringing important points to the notice of the investigator. Once it has been calculated, though, the investigator should return to the real vegetation for study (any calculation is artificial).

NO METHOD IS BETTER THAN ITS FIELD DATA. Mis-identify the species, misprint the cover, and the interpretation is wrong. Sophisticated computer programs based on wrong or inadequate field data can bamboozle everyone – but action taken on them will not have the desired effect on the river, as the river does not comply with false values.

Streams, general

Recording the vegetation

To calculate the rating, the site vegetation is first recorded as described in Chapter 4, Classification A. Beginners should not use size (i) streams (up to 3 m wide, no water-supported species), or any mountain streams. A three- or five-point rating can often be given to both, but only by experienced observers. Small channels may have monodominant tall monocotyledons in both clean and badly (but not grossly) polluted habitats, and this must be recognised.

Table 6.2. Damage rating and pollution index.
Calculation of stream damage rating for British streams

Site length: view from raised point site (see Appendix)

1 Species diversity allowance:

Number of species present[1]	0	1–2	3–4	5–6	7–8	9+
Assign figure of:	5	4	3	2	1	0

2 Decrease in diversity: difference between expected and actual number of species[2]

3 Percentage decrease in percentage vegetation cover

% loss in cover in water up to 1 m deep[3]	100	80–95	60–75	40–55	20–35	0–15
Assign figure of:		5	4	3	2	1	0

4 Change in Colour Band

Change	Over one band	One, or change to uncertain or nil	Half	Dubious	No change
Assign figure of:	4	3	2	1	0

5 Percentage of pollution-tolerant species: add score of 1 for each tolerant species (and 1 if one or more land species are rooted in streams of sizes (iii) and (iv)), a half for each semi-tolerant species

% tolerant spp.	nil spp.	100	75–95	50–70	30–45	15–25	0–10
Assign figure of:	5	5	4	3	2	1	0

Assign 4 if only sensitive spp. are present but the number present is not over one-sixth of those expected, and 3 if one-quarter of those expected are present.

6 Weighting for special species

	Much *Potamogeton pectinatus*	Sparse *P. pectinatus* the only species	Much blanket weed
Assign figure of:	4 (2 if intermediate)	1	2

7 Britain only: weighting for clay, etc. in lower reaches and lowlands

Clay, size (iv)   } Subtract 2   Clay, size (iii), slower
Clay (mix), size (iv)   Flatter sandstone, size (iii)–(iv)   } Subtract 1
                                              Clay-mix, size (iv), and size (iii) if flat

Table 6.2 (cont.)

Add the numbers for criteria 1–7. The damage rating is then:

Total	0–4	5–7	8–10	11–13	14–16	17–18	19–21	22+
Damage rating	a	b	c	d	e	f	g	h (*g* if channel has over 15% cover)

1 Use aggregates for *Ranunculus* spp., *Callitriche platycarpa/obtusangula/stagnalis* and mosses. Mosses restricted to man-made structures (bridge piers, concrete slopes, etc.) should be disregarded.

2 A negative number is recorded as 0.

3 Or in bands at side if water all deep or turbid.

Convert to pollution index of A–H if no physical damage present. If physical damage eliminates vegetation, irrespective of pollution, site is unclassable, U. If physical damage mild, a rating of *d* will have an index of C, B, or A, i.e. C+. Sites with *a* rating but yellow or flaccid species (below) are B.

Pollution may alter plant habit

1 Particularly with organic pollution (including oil):

Yellow leaves: *Agrostis stolonifera, Apium nodiflorum, Callitriche* spp.*, Catabrosa aquatica, Glyceria maxima, G.* spp., short-leaved, *Myosotis scorpioides, Phalaris arundinacea.*

Flaccid or over-lush species: *Agrostis stolonifera, Apium nodiflorum, Glyceria maxima, G.* spp., short-leaved, *Phalaris arundinacea, Potamogeton crispus, Sparganium erectum.*

2 With heavy metal pollution:

Shorter internodes and fewer shoots are found on at least some submerged and semi-submerged species. For detection, plants from cleaner but otherwise similar habitats are needed for comparison.

Table 6.3.
Species tolerant to pollution from sewage treatment works and similar effluents, Britain

Tolerant		**Semi-tolerant**	
Potamogeton crispus	blanket weed	*Agrostis stolonifera*	*Lemna minor* agg.
P. pectinatus	(*Apium nodiflorum*	small *Glyceria* spp.	*Nuphar lutea*
Scirpus lacustris	small clay lowland	(short leaves)	*Rorippa amphibia*
Sparganium emersum	*Mimulus guttatus*	*Butomus umbellatus*	(*Phalaris arundinacea*
Sp. erectum	some small hilly)	*Glyceria maxima*	hilly)
Enteromorpha sp.			

Table 6.4. Species tolerant to some other pollutions

(a) Tolerant to fish farm pollution, Denmark (incomplete)

Tolerant	**Sensitive**
(*Callitriche* spp.)	*Glyceria fluitans*
Potamogeton crispus	*Lemna trisulca*
P. pectinatus	*Ranunculus flammula*
Sparganium emersum	*Sparganium erectum*

Table 6.4 (cont.)

(b) Tolerant to rice paddy, and to domestic, etc. pollution; Po plain, Italy. With the rice paddy pollution the community is reduced, with the other, it is skewed. Typical downstream patterns after pollution are:

	Rice paddy	Domestic/industrial
Near discharge, pollution severe	*Carex* sp.	Nil
Downstream, moderate pollution	*Carex* sp., *Phragmites communis*	*Phragmites communis*
Downstream, mild pollution	4 spp., e.g. *Carex* sp., *Phragmites australis*, *Callitriche* sp., *Ranunculus* sp.	4 spp., e.g. *Phragmites australis*, *Polygonum hydropiper* agg., *Rorippa austriaca*, blanket weed

	Both the same
Downstream, near clean	6 or more spp., including *Callitriche* sp., *Ranunculus* sp.

(c) Tolerant to wash-house pollution, France, A typical downstream pattern after mild pollution (extending over 25 m):

1	Near discharge, worst pollution (10 m length)	Nil
2	Downstream, improving	Unhealthy *Callitriche* sp.
3	Downstream, where small effluent enters	Very unhealthy *Callitriche* sp.
4	Downstream	Healthy *Berula erecta, Callitriche* sp.
5	Downstream and upstream, near clean	*Apium nodiflorum* (much), *Berula erecta* (much) *Callitriche* sp., *Myosotis scorpioides, Phalaris arundinacea, Nasturtium officinale* agg.

Calculating the damage rating

- First write down the appropriate reference vegetation (from Chapter 4), the minimum expected diversity and cover, and the Colour Band, then the same information for the site in question, plus the pollution-tolerant species.
- **Diversity.** Do not use negative numbers.
- **Cover.** Use *percentage* decrease in *percentage* cover, not decrease in absolute cover. Ignore, if over 10%, cover of land species, or of *Lemna* spp. or *Azolla* spp.
- **Colour Band.** A change of ONE band is from, e.g., *Blue* to *Purple*. A change of a half band is from, e.g. *Blue–Purple* to *Purple*. A change to an UNCERTAIN band is a change from e.g., *Blue* to a community of *Phalaris arundinacea, Agrostis stolonifera* and *Lemna minor* agg. A change to NIL band is a change to nil vegetation. When more than one Colour Band is given for the reference community type, the Colour moves towards *Yellow* in swifter flow and coarser substrates, and towards *Red* with slower, siltier and downstream conditions. A one-point error by beginners is of little moment.
- **Pollution tolerance.** Determine, from Table 6.5, which species present are tolerant, semi-tolerant and which are neither. Calculate the proportion of tolerants present, scoring ONE for each tolerant species (including the pollution-favoured *Potamogeton pectinatus* and blanket weed), and HALF for each semi-tolerant species, and determine the percentage tolerance (e.g. six species; two tolerant, score TWO; two semi-tolerant; score two halves, ONE; two sensitive species, score NIL. Total score, THREE, species present six in all, 50% tolerant). Table 6.5 is used for ordinary British STW pollutions. It is usually adequate for general surveys. For detailed work, or different pollutions use a locally created list, such as those presented in Table 6.8.
- **Special species.** This is a weighting for the two pollution-favoured species, *P. pectinatus* and blanket weed. When these are dominant, high cover means a dirty, not a clean stream, so a correction is needed to the weighting.

Categories coming from this rating are broad, e.g. a mildly polluted stream just into size (iv) may be classed as *b*, while if it were a trifle smaller and put into size (iii), which has the lower diversity requirement, the rating may come out as *a*.

Beginners should use a minimum of THREE similar (or progressively-changing) sites for monitoring and are recommended to record one site in the catchment for each kilometre of the main river length, to gain experience. There are too many damage factors not obvious to beginners for single sites to be reliable (e.g. a dog's swimming place, last week's canoe race, a gardener ornamenting a stream).

NEVER, whatever method is used to assess pollution (whether chemical, invertebrate, fish, diatom or vegetation) make a formal report of newly discovered bad pollution while getting used to a method, during the first week or two. The finding may be true (and a week's delay on a chronic pollution is unlikely to matter much), but vegetation damage could also be due to e.g. swans or boats. A false report of bad pollution does much more harm than good. A sudden accidental (non-chronic) pollution, causing many animal and plant deaths is, of course, a different matter and should be reported immediately.

If there is no physical damage great enough to influence vegetation, the damage rating IS the pollution index. If physical damage is severe enough to remove all vegetation, pollution cannot be assessed. In between, the pollution index is appropriately lowered from the damage rating.

Table 6.5. The effects of different types of damage on the components of the stream damage rating. The typical, not the sole type of response is shown

Type of damage	Diversity	Cover	Colour Band	% tolerant spp.[1]	Blanket Weed	*Potamogeton pectinatus*	Notes
Dredging	++	++	?	?	++	—	
Cutting	+	++	?	?	+	—	
Shade	+	++	—	—	—	—	
Herbicides, on emergents	—	?	?	—	?	—	
Herbicides, on channel	++	++	++	++	++	—	
Boats	+	++	?	++	—	+	Delicate spp. lost first
Trampling, etc.	+	++	?	—	??	—	
Unstable bed	+	++	—	+	?	—	Channel spp. lost first
Drought	++	+	+	+	++	—	Submergents lost first; land spp. scored in % tolerant
Storm flow, etc.	+	++	?	—	?	—	
Eutrophication	—	—	++	?	?	—	
Turbidity	+	+	—	+	—	—	Submergents lost first
Salt	++	+	—	—	?	++	
Town effluent	++	++	?	++	++	++	Blanket weed and *P. pectinatus* irregularly affected

[1] These criteria have provisions for scoring even if all vegetation is lost. Such scores are not included in this table.

Symbols: ++, strong effect; +, mild effect; ?, doubtful effect; —, negligible effect.

A good pollution index means the stream is necessarily satisfactory. It does not follow that it is also completely satisfactory, either chemically or structurally (see Chapters 3, 7).

If the banks are unduly gentle compared with the reference cross-section in Chapter 4, damage ratings and pollution indices will be unduly good (Fig. 6.11(a)), and should be corrected accordingly (with a written explanation, of course). If banks are the reverse, unduly high and concave, the rating and index should be correspondingly raised (Fig. 6.11(b)). In a natural-type stream both will occur, and the average will be as in the reference section, so no correction need be made. In a moderately polluted lowland pool-and-riffle system, cover is typically lowered in the riffle, and diversity, in the pool.

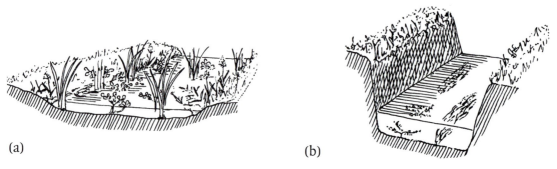

(a)   (b)

Fig. 6.11 *Effect of unduly gentle, (a), and unduly steep, (b), bank slopes on edge vegetation.*

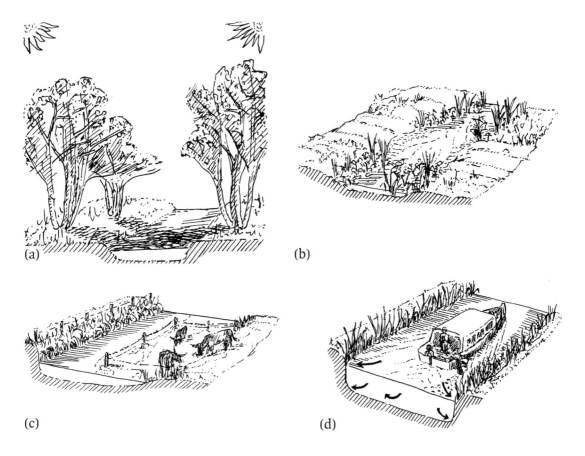

(a)   (b)

(c)   (d)

Fig. 6.12. *Some sources of damage other than pollution (Haslam & Wolseley, 1981). (a) Substantial at sides or over whole channel. (b) Visitor trampling, paddling or swimming.(c) Cattle disturbance, trampling or grazing. (d) Boats.*

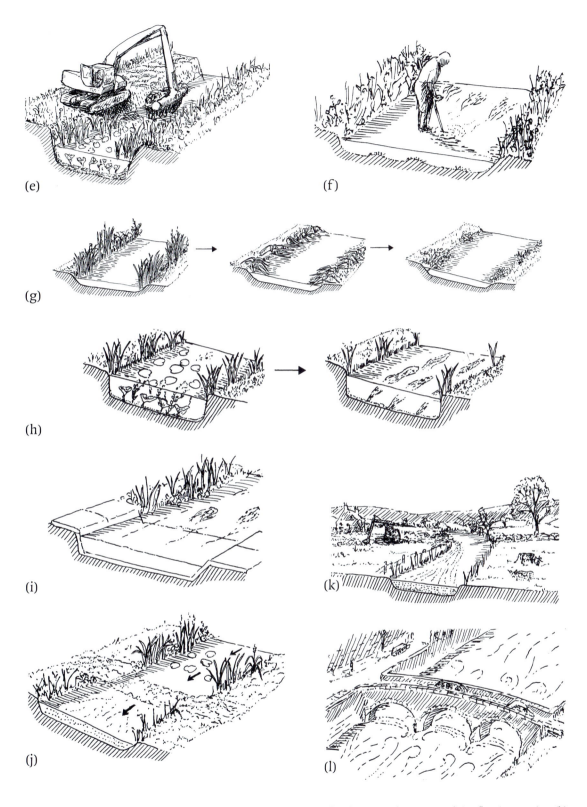

Fig 6.12 (cont.) (e) Recent dredging. (f) Recent cutting. (g) Herbicides sprayed on emerged (or floating species. (h) Aquatic herbicides used in the water of the channel. (i) Bed made of concrete, boulders or other coarse substrates. (j) Bed of man-made unstable substrate. (k) Construction temporarily causing extra mud, etc., to wash into channel. (l) Undue turbulence or deep water caused by bridge piers or other structures.

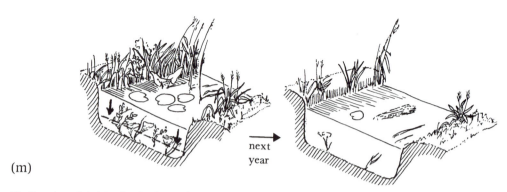

(m)

Fig 6.12 (cont.) (m) *Drying in the previous year, in channels not long-adapted to this (i.e. not winterbournes, not shal-low).*

To those who find this method too fearsome, a rough guide can be given. Be able to iden-tify *Potamogeton pectinatus* and blanket weed. Note that a common site diversity of streams of size (ii) is 6 species; of size (iii), 7; and of size (iv), 8. Count the species present. If there are at least this number, the cover in water up to 1 m deep is at least 60% and if neither *P. pecti-natus* nor blanket weed are prominent, there is not much wrong (probably *a* or *b*, perhaps *c*, rarely *d*). The lower the diversity and cover, excluding *P. pectinatus*, blanket weed, and the more the pollution-favoured species, the worse the rating – except, of course, that no vegeta-tion is the worst of all. (Remember that water force reduces vegetation in the hills!) It is important to remember that damage does not necessarily mean pollution. The sewage works must not be blamed for vegetation harmed by boats!

Nitrate assessment

The legislators who settled on nitrates as 'bad' and as bad for human health had never allo-cated funds to analyse the entire contents of water, clean or polluted. There are numerous pol-lutants (some twenty thousand organic ones are known so far) and an unknown number are, like nitrate, causing eutrophication (indeed many breaking down to nitrates) and another and overlapping unknown number will be harmful to human health in concentrations occurring in rivers. Nitrate is not necessarily a good measure of nitrogen-eutrophication, or of health haz-ards. It comes from many sources, including STWs, fields, septic tanks, farm spills and vari-ous run-offs.

Nitrate assessment, though, is obviously valuable as a measure of fertiliser run-off to streams. Since nitrate fertilisers are used particularly widely (e.g. on permanent grass), mea-suring nitrate is the best choice. Nitrate levels above background level, with no other incom-ing source, mean agrochemical pollution.

For health, it would be better to concentrate on that which, on river values, can be proved to harm living things: a pollution index of *b* or worse on the basis of the vegetation. Vegetation may well be a better monitor here than within-water animals, as the animals are, in non-severe pollution, harmed primarily by oxygen deficiency in the water – which is of no moment to domestic supply. Poisons rank second. Vegetation, however, is primarily harmed by poisonous substances in the water. The sensitivity can be judged by the fact that water down to at least grade *c* is abstracted as 'clean' for drinking water. There is, therefore, a case for using vegeta-tion as a *preliminary* assessment of 'clean' water. Zoologists, of course, prefer invertebrates.

Plants take up chemicals (nutrients, pollutants) mainly from substrates though to a minor extent from water. Substrates, though interacting with water, are likely to be chemically more stable, integrating the fluctuating values of the water. Of the substrate types, silt contains the most nutrients – and pollutants. Spills, and surges of damaging levels of fertiliser (run-off), of course act through the water.

In Britain, clay streams are the richest in major ions. Sandstone and chalk streams are both mesotrophic, but differ in chemistry and in vegetation type. Chalkstream flora, in particular *Ranunculus calcareus*, the dominant of the typical river, do not suffer from lack of nitrate and phosphate above 1 ppm nitrate-nitrogen and c. 30 μg of phosphate-phosphorus in the water. Even in a chalkstream which is only nutrient-medium, water values are well above these, and (see above) water may have less than 10% of the total available nitrogen (the rest being in the substrate, or in non-available forms in water). Vegetation growth and decay had little influence on water values of nitrate, phosphate and potassium. Therefore, it seems more the general nutrient environment and balance that influences vegetation: nitrate and other nutrients are not likely to be limiting in ordinary British streams of middle (mesotrophic) and high (eutrophic) nutrient status, perhaps not even in low (oligotrophic) ones.

Different species, naturally enough, respond differently to different chemicals. Small sandstone brooks bear dominant *Callitriche* spp., small equally mesotrophic limestone ones bear *Ranunculus* spp; *Oenanthe fluviatilis* is more tolerant to septic tank effluent than to STW effluent. On the continent, a *Potamogeton coloratus* community (low-nutrient, lime-influenced) was correlated with nitrate-nitrogen levels of under 0.003 mg/l, but nevertheless occurred with over 500 mg/l. Is the latter perhaps tolerable only temporarily, or is the causal relationship with another factor? Another study showed that some of the highest nitrate values occurred in the (overall) nutrient-poor *Berula erecta–Mentha aquatica* community. Ammonium-nitrogen values correlate better with species and communities than nitrate ones – because ammonium is also found in organic effluents?

Overall, domestic, urban and industrial pollution pervades European streams, even small lowland ones; this is FAR more damaging to river life than is fertiliser pollution (and the better correlations of vegetation with ammonium than with nitrate reflect this). There are, therefore, difficulties in using animals or plants to assess, not stream nutrient status, not stream eutrophication, not stream nitrogen, but stream nitrates. Change of nutrient status band indicates inorganic eutrophication, therefore more nutrients. For example, fertilised cress-bed effluent brought more nutrient-rich species into a mesotrophic chalk stream. An increase in the percentage of the flora tolerant to organic pollution indicates, of course, the presence of that pollution, which also raises nutrient levels.

THEREFORE, CHANGE IN NUTRIENT STATUS BAND WITHOUT CHANGE IN (SITE DIVERSITY, COVER OR) PERCENTAGE POLLUTION TOLERANTS IS A GOOD WARNING OF INORGANIC EUTROPHICATION (i.e. eutrophication not due to organic pollution).

Such eutrophication may be from nitrates. Obviously, most streams are polluted with STW, etc. effluents as well as agrochemicals, and agrochemicals include biocides as well as fertilisers. The pollution index assesses the total effect.

Research is needed to find the individual species most sensitive to nitrate, and to other fertiliser poisoning. Nitrate assessment is currently inexact, but there is no reason why it could not be made exact. (For buffer strips see Chapters 3, 5, 8.)

Dykes and drains

These are scored differently. Table 6.6 gives an architecture index, which can also be used on (lowland) streams. Table 6.7 is a damage rating. Table 6.8 lists effects of some damage factors on the dyke damage rating.

Wetland water-channels have different names around the country, dykes being the smaller, drains the larger Fenland watercourses (reens or rhynes are in the west, sewers in the south). Those up to c. 0.5 m deep, and most of those to c. 1 m deep will be covered with tall monocotyledons if unmanaged for a few years, and those drier may bear land vegetation.

Phragmites australis is the most abundant dominant; *Glyceria maxima* is the most common in shallow dykes and outside eastern England; *Carex acutiformis* is mainly southern; *C. riparia* is mainly on fen peat; *Phalaris arundinacea* is most often in summer-dry dykes, especially on clay;

Scirpus maritimus is found near the coast; and *Sparganium erectum*, not in drier channels. In channels where scour is low, tall monocotyledons may dominate even in considerable pollution, so their presence merely shows pollution is not gross. They should be encouraged wherever possible, as they are so very effective at cleaning polluted water.

A species-rich community of water-supported species usually occurs in water at least 50 cm deep for much of the year, though a particularly stable depth of 25 cm is a possible habitat. It is in channels potentially with such communities that damage ratings can be used. In deeper drains vegetation may be restricted to side bands, but the reference (optimal) site diversity is at least nine species. Drains are more often arterial waterways, needing clear through-flow, but even so they should have good architecture (Table 6.6) and high site diversities. Without these, a drain can become damaged beyond what is necessary. Table 4.6 (p. 130) summarises communities and species of different habitat, and should be consulted here. (For detail on community changes with habitat changes, see Chapter 3 Appendix.)

Table 6.6. The de Lange and van Zon dyke architecture index. Calculation of the structural evaluation number (SEN)

(a) Structural index

% cover of higher plants	Emergent score	Floating score	Submergent score
76–100	1	1	2
46(51)[1]–75	2	3	4
25–45(50)[1]	3	5	6
5(10)–25[1]	4	6	5
1–4(9)[1]	5	5	4
<1	3	3	3
0	1	1	1

[1] Depending whether cover measured to nearest 5% or 10%.

(b) Diversity index

No. of species	Score
<4	1
4–5	2
6–7	3
8–9	4
10–11	5
12–15	6
16–20	7
<20	8

(c) Index of filamentous algae

% cover	Score
76–100	-4
51–75	-3
26–50	-2
5–25	-1
<5	0

Structural index = emergent + floating + submergent scores
SEN = structural index + diversity index + index of filamentous algae, all divided by 2.5, and then rounded to one decimal place.

Table 6.7. Damage rating for British dykes and drains. Site length: view from raised point site, see Appendix

1. Score for species present:
1	for each tolerant sp. (Table 4.6)
2	for each semi-tolerant sp. ('Frequent' spp. in Table 4.6)
3	for each other sp.

2. Score for species diversity allowance:
0	for 0–3 spp. present
1	for 4–6 spp. present
3	for 7–9 spp. present
5	for 10+ spp. present

3. Score for cover allowance (not including tall edge plants):
0	for up to 50% cover
1	for 50–70% cover
2	for 75–100% cover

Add the numbers for criteria 1–3. The damage rating is then:

Total	damage rating
27+	a_1
20–26	a_2
11–19	b
6–10	d
2–5	f
0–1	h

NB If the water is shallow or the dyke is covered with tall emergents, the rating cannot be used.

Table 6.8. The effects of different types of damage on the components of the dyke damage rating. The typical, not the sole type of response is shown

Type of damage	Diversity	Cover	Tolerant spp. important	Sensitive spp. important	Notes
Dredging	+	++	—	++	
Cutting	+	++	—	++	
Herbicides	++	++	++	—	Discoloration
Boats	++	?	—	—	Submergents lost first
Trampling, etc.	++	+	—	—	
Drought	++	++	—	++	Water-supported species lost first, particularly if slow growing
Flooding	++	++	+	—	

Symbols: ++, strong effect; +, mild effect; ?, doubtful effect; — negligible effect.

Canals

(also see Chapter 3)

This discussion does not include: 1 disused and silted-up canals, which are seldom or never flooded, and are usually dominated by *Glyceria maxima*, less often by *Phragmites australis* or land vegetation; 2 ship canals, which are large, turbid, carry large ships and have negligible vegetation; and 3 the Caledonian canal, which has a stony bed, deep water and negligible vegetation.

Used canals have their potential vegetation lessened (damaged) by boats. Management is, of course, needed to keep this man-made aquatic habitat in being. The 'optimal' reference vegetation is in consequence, that of sites where diversity, cover and quality of vegetation are not obviously harmed.

Most English canals are on (eutrophic) clay with *Red–Purple* Colour Bands. On alluvial silt and sandstone *Turquoise–Purple* to *Purple* is usual, on peat, *Turquoise*, and on resistant rock and chalk, *Turquoise–Purple*. (As in streams, the rock type at the source of the water as well as that of the site, is important.) Canals with *Redder* vegetation than this may be eutrophicated, but as several Red species are also semi-tolerant to damage, if they alone are present, eutrophication may be absent.

As boat movements increase, vegetation is lost in the following pattern:

1 water-supported species in the channel centre;

2 the more sensitive water-supported species at the channel sides;

3 most water-supported species at the sides, leaving scattered plants;

4 most of the fringing emergents, leaving occasional clumps of emergents, and rare clumps of water-supported species;

5 the remaining vegetation.

Table 6.9 gives a damage rating, and Table 6.10, a Colour Band scheme for canals.

Table 6.9. Damage rating for British (i.e. small) canals.
Site length: view from raised point site (see Appendix)

1. Score for species present:

   1   for each tolerant sp.[1]

   2   for each semi-tolerant sp.[2]

   3   for each other sp.

2. Score for species diversity allowance:

   0   for 0–2 spp. present

   1   for 3–5 spp. present

   2   for 6–8 spp. present

   5   for 9+ spp. present

3. Score for cover allowance:

   -1   for less than 5% cover

   1   for 10–25% cover

   3   for over 30% cover

Add the numbers for criteria 1–3. The
damage rating is then:

Total	Damage rating
30+, cover 60+%	a_1
20–29 and/or cover less than 60%	a_2
10–19	b
6–9	d
3–5	f
0–2 (including negative numbers)	h

NB If the water is shallow or the canal is covered with tall emergents, the rating cannot be used.

[1] Tolerant species: *Acorus calamus*, *Glyceria maxima*, *Lemna minor* agg., *Potamogeton pectinatus*, *Sparganium erectum*, small grasses, blanket weed.

[2] Semi-tolerant species: *Butomus umbellatus*, *Carex acutiformis* agg., *Nuphar lutea*, *Phragmites australis*, *Rumex hydrolapathum*, *Sparganium emersum*, *Enteromorpha* sp.

Table 6.10. Canal Colour (nutrient status) Banding (Britain)

Species listed from nutrient-low to nutrient-high. If additional species are present, the stream Colour Band usually applies (Table 4.3)

Utricularia vulgaris	*Grass-leaved Potamogeton* spp.	*Sagittaria sagittifolia*
Hydrocotyle vulgaris	*Elodea canadensis*	*Enteromorpha* sp.
Hydrocharis morsus-ranae	*Iris pseudacorus*	*Butomus umbellatus*
Berula erecta	*Potamogeton perfoliatus*	*Sparganium emersum*
Lemna trisulca	*Ceratophyllum demersum*	(*Scirpus lacustris*)
Mentha aquatica	*Potamogeton lucens* and hybrids	*Nuphar lutea*
Lemna polyrhiza	*Juncus effusus*	Red
Ranunculus spp. (short-leaved)	*Phalaris arundinacea*	
Callitriche spp.	*Myosotis scorpioides*	
Potamogeton natans	*Typha* spp.	
Mosses	*Polygonum amphibium*	
Blue	*Alisma plantago-aquatica*	
	Myriophyllum spicatum	
	Potamogeton crispus	
	Epilobium hirsutum	
	Purple	

Cover–diversity number (too much human impact)

This is a much simpler tool than the damage rating, and has a partly overlapping sphere of usefulness. No plant names are needed.

Rivers are surveyed as usual, from a bridge or other vantage point. Each species seen counts as ONE, each 10% of cover also counts as ONE, and the total, diversity plus cover percentage, is the cover–diversity, or CoDi number. (As in the damage rating, some species are aggregated and together count as ONE, e.g. all mosses, *Callitriche* spp., Batrachian *Ranunculus* spp. The cover is that in water up to 1 m deep, or, if all is deeper, then the cover at the sides. If floating duckweed, etc. (*Lemna* spp. or *Azolla* spp.) cover more than 10% of the channel, they still score only ONE.)

The CoDi number is an absolute value, unlike the damage rating, which is comparative (the site being compared against a reference community). CoDi values measure reduction in vegetation, but not changes in its quality, skewing. Some typical British CoDi values are shown in Table 6.11.

CoDi numbers of under 10 indicate poor vegetation, those of 20+, good vegetation (though not necessarily vegetation pleasing to flood controllers or anglers!). From a conservation viewpoint, a brook with 20 is excellent, while 15 is all right. High diversities mean good physical structures. Many different species present means a variety of microhabitats – and a reasonably clean stream.

This tool, at first sight, is too simple to be useful, and trying it out is therefore recommended! Walking along a hill river shows CoDi is linked to water force: e.g. whitewater, CoDi 1; a sheltered bar, CoDi 6; neither, CoDi 3; a low-scour sheltered tributary, CoDi 15; the hill river into which it flows, CoDi 5; CoDi values raised above weirs, lowered with trampling. Walking along a lowland river, where water force varies little, shows more variation with other factors, e.g. concave banks, CoDi 7; next reach with normal banks, CoDi 12 (the concave banks excluded emerged aquatics). Once noticed, the fact that concave banks are poor for emerged aquatics is obvious, but these 'obvious' things are easy for beginners (and indeed experts) to miss, and using CoDi numbers ensures they are not missed.

Table 6.11. Typical British cover–diversity values

Stream type	Stream size[1]		
	(ii)	**(iii)**	**(iv)**
Clay			
Lowland	4,11[2]	13	15
Upland[3]	6	6	—
Sandstone			
Lowland neutral	6	12	—
Acid	8,2	11,13	—
Moor, Caithness	5	6	9
Upland	8	8	7
Mountain	0	0,2	0,7
Alpine[3]	0	0,1	—
Limestone			
Lowland (soft, chalk, etc.)	13	14	17
Upland	7	9	9
Mountain and alpine	0	0	1
Resistant			
Lowland bog	8	9	6
Lowland moor	6	10	8
Lowland farmland	2	5	4
Upland, usual	5	3	1+
Upland, more fertile	7	8	9
Mountain	1	1,5	0,6
Alpine	0	0	0

[1] see Chapter 4, Fig. 4.1; [2] different types; [3] for landscape types, see Chapter 4, start.

Table 6.12.
Cover–diversity values varying with
total impact; streams paired for size, flow, etc.

	Habitat	CoDi No.
Better	In pasture	12
Worse	In intensive farming	8
Better	Mountain Corsica (very low impact)	14
Worse	Mountain Britain	1
Better	Frontier river, Denmark (needs two-country agreement, so impact low)	18
Worse	Other branch same river, entirely in Denmark (more impact)	11
Better	lowland Corsica (very low impact)	14
Worse	Lowland Britain	2–8
Better	Hilly south Norway (low impact)	13
Worse	Hilly Britain	5–7

CoDi values are also useful for assessing total human impact. A stream may not be seriously polluted, its channelling could be worse, the land beside is not entirely arable, the picnic places are empty mid-week, and so on. Each separate impact is low, the total is great, and a CoDi of 8 in a lowland river demonstrates this. Table 6.12 shows how CoDi values can vary due to human impact in otherwise-comparable streams.

Straightening lowers CoDi number, e.g. CoDi 14 in a winding part, CoDi 8–10 in a straightened part of the same stream. In extremes, channelling can lower CoDi values from e.g. 11 (which already shows considerable impact) to 3.

CoDi values can be used to compare vegetation on different rock types (i.e. comparing between reference community types in Chapter 4). Hilly clay has lower values than hilly limestone or sandstone, because bed and flow are more unstable. Sandstone is easily eroded, its mountain streams have unstable beds, and very low CoDi numbers. In some lowland sandstone streams vegetation becomes very sparse with what is really only a mild impact. The sands are soft and erode easily, and once the vegetation cover is damaged, the unstable bed makes recovery very difficult.

7 RIVER STRUCTURE
for larger animals

(no special expertise required for habitat identification, but no identification of species given here)

SUMMARY

Larger animals need satisfactory habitats for feeding, resting and breeding. Any one animal may therefore need several habitats, and, of course, different animals usually differ in habitat. No one habitat houses all. All streams, though, should support good populations of larger animals, and management plans should take their needs into account. Disturbance and pollution, as well as structure, must be suitable. For the more characteristic river birds and mammals, as well as some lower animals, typical habitats are described and depicted. Although the animals will not occur without suitable habitat, they may not in fact occur with satisfactory ones, and further advice may be necessary.

Introduction

A river animal's structural habitat is the relevant part of the inorganic bed, bank and riverside, PLUS that of the living structure, vegetation, growing on these. Vegetation provides cover, shelter, breeding places, etc. It provides food, for herbivores, for those living on detritus, and for those eating animals growing within the vegetation habitat. It also provides for more specialised needs, as when invertebrate nymphs climb to the air for their adult stage.

Suitable structure for animals is that suitable both for the shelter of the animal (e.g. holes, nesting sites) and for the good development of the food supply of that animal. The food needs of each species are therefore listed below. Without the appropriate food (appropriate in kind and quantity), the site will be without the larger animals. Animal welfare depends on plant welfare. Major changes in vegetation mean major changes in animals. Channelling, by removing fringe vegetation, can also remove perhaps three-quarters of the duck population. Slight changes in vegetation may also be significant. By altering invertebrate populations, for instance, they may change the fish or bird populations feeding on those invertebrates.

Vegetation stays put. Most larger animals move. The animals may therefore be temporarily in places they could not survive permanently.

THE STRUCTURAL NEEDS OF DIFFERENT ANIMALS VARY. There is no one 'good' structure for animals, there is structure good for trout or for crayfish, or for kingfishers or for mayflies. There is, more or less, a 'bad' structure. A channel whose bed and banks are bare concrete supports few satisfactory animal populations. Otherwise, the habitat should be scored on what it could support, as

- Structure suitability;

- Pollution suitability;

- Disturbance suitability.

Pollution

Animals, like plants, are affected by harmful pollution reaching their bodies (via the skin or outer cell layer, or by breathing and feeding). Unlike plants, animals are affected by pollutants in the food they eat. Polluted fish mean polluted herons. Since many pollutants (including heavy metals, polychlorine biphenyls (PCBs) and organochlorine biocides) are difficult to remove, they become more concentrated in plant-eating animals than in the plants, and more so again in animal-eating animals than in plant-eating ones. The higher the position in the food chain, the more concentrated the pollutants. Concentrations too low to kill plants may, up the food chain, be enough to kill birds of prey, or reduce their breeding success.

Pollution alters animal communities as well as the plant ones described in Chapter 6, and bed invertebrates in shallow sides and riffles are commonly used to assess pollution. Animals may be weakened rather than eliminated, and breed less, have shorter lives and have more diseases. Many river fish populations are now diseased.

Pollution may also decrease numbers of larger animals by affecting their food supply. If small fish are absent, waterfowl eating these will also be sparse. If water is made turbid, animals hunting in water by sight (e.g. cormorant, otter) catch less prey.

Disturbance

If structure is good, food may well be abundant, but if disturbance is great, larger animals will be absent. Tolerance varies with species, of course: mallard will tolerate disturbance impossible to redshank, for instance. A Environment Agency (EA) officer kick-sampling will disturb a small area of invertebrates, but will scare away sandpipers from a much larger area. Further, there may be thousands of *Gammarus* (freshwater shrimp) in just 10 m of river, but only one otter in 20 km. If one, or indeed one thousand *Gammarus* are lost by disturbance, the community is hardly changed. If the one otter is lost, the whole otter population is gone. The larger and more mobile the animal, the greater, generally, the susceptibility.

The type of disturbance is also important. Someone walking along a footpath will not affect bed invertebrates, nor fish unless an occasional unexpected shadow is thrown (when movement may occur), but the walker will send most birds and mammals into hiding or flight. Habitual disturbance irrelevant to the animal will often be ignored, however. Birds are more tolerant to regular than to irregular disturbance. For instance, a major disturbance at mid-day will disperse birds, but they are likely to return (less so if nesting), while constant lesser disturbances randomly distributed are more likely to lead to departure.

Structural suitability

With the wide variety of requirements of different animals, it should always be possible to make a habitat good for some of them, and assessments can be made, for this. The ideal is a wide variety of fauna, with good populations, **the fauna being appropriate to the river type and the locality.**

Many animals also use the land beside the river. Ponds of course increase aquatic habitat, and give still water. Marsh, pasture, tall herbs, shrub and woodland all have their typical fauna – and so do arable fields. Management should make rivers more animal-friendly (except for moles and rats, which can be a disaster, undermining banks). Increasing aquatic animals should be an aim of the EA, and not be solely left to the Royal Society for the Protection of Birds (RSPB). Even a small percentage return of what has been lost would mean thousands more birds and fish, and hundreds more mammals.

The ancient trades of wetlands included the hunting of fish and fowl. The early seventeenth century Surveyor of Manors (Norden) lists birds for the table, including waterfowl, as expected economic assets from the manor. The eighteenth century, with its improved communications, over-exploited the crops, and the nineteenth- and twentieth-century pollution and drainage have culminated in what, compared with earlier centuries, are near-sterile rivers.

Table 7.1 summarises the structural requirements for a variety of animals. It shows the diversity of needs (other species can be gauged by the nearest one in the table). Lack of disturbance is the most consistent requirement: as few people and human happenings as possible (and also few predators – bearing in mind that predators as well as prey require conservation!). Shallow water is the next most generally important requirement. Wading birds wade, i.e. in shallow water, to feed.

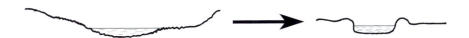

Fig. 7.1. *Wading habitat lost by channelling in mountains.*

Table 7.1. Major habitat requirements for some animals

Species	Shallow water	submerged plants	Emergent plants	Tall herbs	Trees & shrubs	Sun	Wind shelter	Shorelines	Marsh	Ponds	Lack of disturbance	Other
Dragonflies	★	★	★	★	★	★	★			★		
Fish	★	★										Deep water
Amphibians	★	★	★	★		★		★	★	★		
Dabchick	★	★	★								★	Fish
Great crested grebe	★	★	★								★	Fish
Grey heron	★								★		★	Fish and amphibians
Mute swan	★	★									★ (for wild ones)	Grazed grassland
Mallard	★	★		★				★	★	★	(★)	
Other dabbling ducks	★	★		★				★	★	★	★	
Tufted duck and pochard	★	★	★	★				★			★	
Redshank	★			★				★	★	★	★	
Lapwing								★			★	Short grass or bare ground
Ringed and little ringed plover and common tern	★							★			★	Bare shingle
Migrant and wintering waders	★							★	★	★	★	
Kingfisher	★						★				★	Nest banks
Sand martin											★	Nest banks
Sedge and reed warblers			★	★	★						★	
Water vole	★	★	★	★				★				
Otter	★	★	★	★	★			★	★		★	Fish and amphibians

Modified from Andrews & Kinsman (1990).

Dabbling ducks are those which up-end and feed in the top of the water, where their beaks can reach, with or without shallow dives. They therefore need their food, whether plant or animal, to be in the top of the water. Food, therefore, is more likely to be abundant in shallow water. Diving duck can go deeper, but diving consumes much energy so short distances – shallowish water – are advisable. The only birds in Table 7.1 not requiring shallow water are those using not the river, but the riverside. (Swimming birds of course swim over water of any depth; the shallow water is needed for feeding.)

Birds and mammals must also have places for getting in and out of the water. Waders need a nice gentle shelf, so placed to remain a nice gentle shelf when water level changes. Swimmers need scramble-access; if necessary, steps. Consequently, the typical dredged edge is highly unsuitable (see Figs. 7.1 and 7.2).

(a)   (b)   (c)

Fig. 7.2. (a) Wader's edge, (b) scramble-access, (c) typical dredged edge.

Some animals live on the riverbank, some also make holes and burrows in it, above or below water level. For these, the type of earth must be suitable, and the holes be permitted by the engineer.

Shelter from wind is the next factor in general importance. Wind brings cold (the wind-chill factor), increases stress and may disrupt nesting. In small streams shelter may be given by high banks, in larger streams by very high banks, trees or other tall vegetation. Permeable tree belts provide good shelter (for a distance of sixteen times their heights). Shade, of course, is a factor in weed control (see Chapters 3, 6), and for this, trees are typically planted on the south bank. Woods, copses, shrub patches, pollards, etc., also shade, and reduce wind, and planning is recommended. Both siting and permeability should also be considered in relation to bird habitat, especially since sunny shores are an important habitat too, important for butterflies as well as birds. For this, there must be a shore (a beach, gentle slope) and access to sun. It is quite satisfactory to have scattered sunny shores, giving intermittent shading for weed control.

The productivity of rivers, the plants and the animals supported by those plants, varies. High productivity, assessed by the quantity of fish, of duck, and of the otter and herons, etc. at the top of the food chain, should be planned for. Good structure, good vegetation, low pollution, shallow sunny water, etc. make for this high productivity. The invertebrate population, as a food source, is much increased by those falling into the stream from trees and other plants, especially in autumn. (However, chemically to increase productivity, by fertiliser, effluent, etc., is to alter stream type, and is therefore incorrect.)

There are, regrettably, conflicts. Duck and some fish (bream, carp, tench, perch, roach particularly) compete for food. Gadwall and swan compete for plant food with bream. (Removing bream may increase the birds.) Pike eat ducklings and fish. Here:

1 increase total productivity, to support more river life – this is the best choice;

2 choose the wanted species, remove the unwanted – the wanted being those traditionally proper to the stream type;

3 do nothing and hope for the best – the commonest choice, with the hope too often unfulfilled.

WITHOUT THE PROPER HABITAT, BIRDS WILL NOT USE RIVER BANKS. What the proper habitat is, differs with different birds, and no one river habitat can harbour all aquatic birds.

The presence of a bird species cannot, however, be deduced from the presence of its habitat. This is a general principle: that a *community* can be predicted from habitat (Chapter 4), but *one species* cannot.

Food varies not just with bird species, but with their developmental stage. Various ducklings, for instance, eat chironomids while the adults have larger fare. If the habitat is suitable for nesting but not for chironomids (due to human impact), ducklings will die. Food also varies with availability. Mallard and dabchick, for example, eat mostly invertebrates when these are plentiful in summer, but when they become scarce, mallard eat much vegetation, dabchick much fish. WITHOUT ENOUGH OF THE PROPER FOOD, BIRDS WILL NOT SURVIVE.

When not feeding or courting, birds seek undisturbed and sheltered places, safe from predators, where they can rest, preen and sleep. All wildfowl become flightless in late summer, and gather where there is much food and little disturbance. It is therefore most important to preserve and encourage such places. Islands can be used to increase birds (when suitably maintained), as people, foxes, cats, etc. are discouraged. Nestboxes can also be used to increase some species (see Andrews & Kinsman, 1990).

Exotics

Alien species may have been introduced, or may have escaped, and may have altered the balance of the native community, e.g. coypu in the 1960s in east England. This also applies to alien strains: far too many strains of brown trout, other than those native to the particular stream, have been introduced to streams.

Information presented

HABITAT PHOTOGRAPHS ARE PROVIDED FOR THE SPECIES DESCRIBED. HOWEVER, SPECIES CAN OCCUR IN MORE THAN ONE HABITAT, SO THESE PICTURES SHOULD BE TAKEN AS GUIDES ONLY. THE SAME APPLIES TO HABITAT DESCRIPTIONS, ETC.

Finally, **EA surveyors should always survey small tributaries which are not Main River, since many populations depend on good habitats there for their survival.**

Information is listed, where possible, as: 1 habitat and distribution, 2 residence, 3 feeding, 4,5 nesting, young, 6 other.

Invertebrate: Crayfish

Crayfish (*Austropotamobius pallipes* **(native), and introduced species)**

1 Throughout England, north-west Scotland. (Introduced *A. leptodactylus*, in east and south east; *Pacifastacus leniruscullus*, signal crayfish, scattered.)

2 Holes and crevices in bed or bank, tree roots, overhanging banks: dark places for crayfish to creep into by day. They move at night. Also riffles, for feeding. Calcium in the water for their shells. Crayfish do not occur in calcium-deficient waters. Well-oxygenated water.

Clean water. Some alien species are more tolerant to pollution, but the native species demands clean water, so is THE HEALTH INSPECTOR OF THE WATERS.

3 Plentiful plants and small animals for food. A good population substantially reduces vegetation, and so reduces weed control costs. (They are themselves eaten by swans and eels; swans also decrease vegetation.)

6 Crayfish plague (*Aphanomyles astaci*), introduced in 1981, has wiped out crayfish from many streams. Crayfish are susceptible to disease (especially from fungi and yeasts). Diseases presumably increase where populations are weakened by non-lethal pollution.

Signal crayfish are less good clean-water indicators, as they have a wider habitat range. They are aggressive and invasive. They carry crayfish plague, are already too common, and are spreading rapidly. Legislation has been introduced to stop the spread, including banning new farming over much of the country.

PLENTIFUL native CRAYFISH = CLEAN RIVER OF GOOD STRUCTURE (the reverse does not apply in calcium-low rivers or those subject to crayfish plague). Crayfish are large enough to be easily identified and found, so are useful for this purpose.

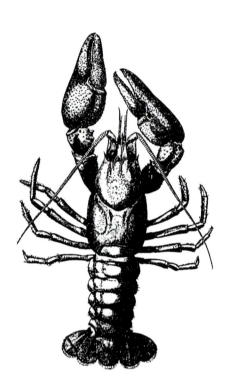

Fig. 7.3. Crayfish habitat.

Amphibians

Frogs, toads, newts

1 Slow or still watercourses, ditches, pools in buffer strips. Temporary pools are valuable for breeding (fewer predators). Warm and shallow waters, shallow margins (sloping to e.g. not over 2 m, 5 m from the edge), or stepped edges, with ledges (berms) and embayments, etc. These shallow margins should be unshaded, for warmth. They need not be continuous, so in many watercourses suitable profiles could be provided intermittently.

Fig. 7.4. Amphibian habitat.

2/3 Food and shelter should be available within 200 m of the water, preferably slightly damp ground, with thick vegetation, rough grass, trees, scrub, tall herbs, hedges, etc. or e.g. rocks, piles of logs, dead leaves, compost heaps. Bands of emergent aquatics are helpful. Adult newts spend more time in the water, and feed more there, than do frogs. Toads, outside the breeding season, are found largely on dry land.

3 Adults eat invertebrates.

3 Vegetation is required as food for tadpoles, and as cover for spawning. Tadpoles also eat dead animals and micro-organisms. Tadpoles are eaten by fish, especially stickleback, perch and pike.

6 Disruption of the habitat (e.g. dredging) should be minimised, especially between February and September.

It may take ten years for a new population to become fully established. Recovery programmes are trying to replace lost populations.

- **Smooth newt**. Widespread and common. Prefers still, hard waters.
- **Great crested or warty newt**. Rare. Hard waters, breeds in still or slow waters over pH 5.5.
- **Palmate newt**. Widespread, more in north and west. Soft still water, sometimes breeds in flow.
- **Common frog**. Widespread and declining. Breeds usually in warm shallow edges. (There are also two alien frog species.)
- **Common toad**. Widespread. The commonest in rivers.

Birds

Mallard (*Anas platyrhynchos*)

1 Fairly quiet waters in lowlands and hills. Common throughout Britain. Good riparian vegetation is crucial (see photographs). Wintering tends to be on larger, more open sites than small rivers.

2 Resident in Britain, a winter visitor from the north (so numbers are higher in winter) and a passage migrant (passing through).

3 Water feeding, mostly dabbling in the top of the water, preferring areas less than 1 m deep, but occasionally diving to 2 m. Abundant food is therefore wanted in this depth range. Omnivorous feeders, more vegetarian in winter when fewer invertebrates are available. May feed in adjacent fields, particularly in winter. Good diverse tall emergents, with tall herbs, bramble, trees or scrub behind is preferred for land feeding and cover. Sheltered bare ground or short grass, close to the water for escape, are wanted for preening, etc. Access areas to water are needed.

4 Nesting is in tall vegetation, including edges of woods (pollard crowns, etc.), and as nesting is early, **last year's dead vegetation should not be cut**.

5 Ducklings eat chironomids and other small invertebrates for their first three weeks (so nesting is unsuccessful if these are sparse).

6 Mallard are unusually tolerant to disturbance, so are the most common duck seen on rivers. Many, however, remain sensitive to disturbance.

Fig. 7.5. Mallard, moorhen, coot, dabchick, habitat.

Moorhen (*Gallinda chloropis*)

1 Common, especially in slow rivers with fringing emergent or bankside vegetation. Good riparian vegetation (including trees) is crucial (see photographs). In summer, common everywhere except west and north Scotland; in winter, avoiding higher ground.

2 Resident in Britain. In winter moving off higher ground, remaining territorial or forming flocks. Some passage migrants.

3 Feeding on aquatic vegetation and seeds (and insects). Adults also feed on plants in the open, some distance from water.

4 Nests usually anchored in emergent aquatics or occasionally just above water surface in overhanging or fallen trees or bushes. Susceptible to flooding (though platforms may be built-up to avoid this). May be away from river.

5 Young eat insect matter from the water surface in their first few days.

6 Breeding birds generally remain in the same habitat all year.

Coot (*Fulica acra*)

1 Slow rivers (rather than brooks) in lowlands, with fringing emergent or bankside vegetation. Good riparian vegetation is crucial (see photographs). Common during the breeding season.

2 Resident in Britain, densest in the English lowlands, sparsest above 250 m altitude, and in the far north and west. Small-scale movements, e.g. towards tidal waters in severe weather, some come from north and west.

3 Largely vegetarian, often diving up to 2 m to collect plants and their invertebrates. May graze fields. In winter, gather in large flocks in good feeding areas, usually on reservoirs and gravel pits.

4 Nests usually on floating structures anchored in emergent vegetation susceptible to flooding. Typically require 0.5+ ha of open water as well as the emergents negotiation for nesting (dammed streams are good).

Dabchick, Little grebe (*Tachybaptus ruficollis*)

1 Slow lowland streams, with fringing emergents, etc. Frequent (tends to avoid higher ground).

Muddy bottoms are preferred in rivers, to help invertebrate development. Marginal trees are tolerated (provided the emergent fringe remains), and dead trees help nesting and cover.

2 Resident in Britain, mostly in the lowlands. In winter many move to tidal waters (e.g. when fish fry grow too big). Winter visitors come to the east coast.

3 Shallow (75–125 cm), productive, nutrient-rich waters are wanted, to provide plentiful invertebrates for food. Fish (up to 7 cm long) are also eaten in winter when invertebrates are scarcer.

4 Nests as for coot.

Great crested grebe (*Podiceps cristatus*)

1 Mostly lowlands, slow rivers. Throughout England, less in Wales and south Scotland.

2 Resident in Britain and winter visitor. The higher winter population (enough to be termed 'frequent') is affected by a general winter movement to tidal waters.

3 Feeds on fish, molluscs, newts, insects and other invertebrates, and water plants.

4 Nesting is mostly in still waters. The nests are mounds of vegetation.

Fig. 7.6. *Great crested grebe habitat.*

Swan, mute swan (*Cygnus olor*)

1 Mostly lowlands, slow to moderately flowing streams, avoiding land over c. 300 m, and that without fertile fresh water. Frequent.

2 Resident in Britain. Occasional winter visitor from continent. In winter remaining territorial or gathering into flocks. In summer, non-breeding birds may flock.

3 Water shallow enough to give abundant vegetation in the upper 1 m of water. Swans eat up to 4 kg/day of (wet) plant, plus the animals in this. Swans also graze on land beyond the river, eating, e.g. wetland herbs, grasses. SWANS CONTROL VEGETATION. Slopes of less than 40° should be present intermittently, for access. Islands, backwaters, spits, etc., are valuable.

4 Nests are at the margins; they are huge mats of dead and fresh plant material.

5 Lead fishing weights left in rivers by anglers are eaten by and kill swans (by the thousand), and are now banned. This was one of the more dramatic examples of heavy metal poisoning by man.

Fig. 7.7. Swan (mute swan) habitat.

Teal (*Anas crecca*)

1 In summer, concentrated in the north, in winter in the south. Winter habitat includes marshy river valleys. Lowland, wet grassland. Very shallow (up to 20 cm) slow or still water, with short fringing emergents for feeding: therefore infrequent in rivers (though common in Britain).

2 Resident in Britain, winter visitor (with fewer leaving) and passage migrant.

3 Mud flats and sand bars with little water for roosting and loafing with thickly

fringed water for escape. Teal eat plant seeds (e.g. *Potamogeton* spp.) plants, and, especially in summer, invertebrates. They may feed in fields, e.g. on stubble.

4 Teal nest in quiet, shallow marshy places with tussocky grass or tall ground cover, mostly under trees. Cattle may trample and destroy nests, so avoid grazing in April–June.

5 Ducklings eat invertebrates for their first three weeks.

Shoveler (*Anas clypeata*)

1 Mostly lowlands. Only occasional on rivers, though some hundreds may occur (infrequent in Britain as a whole).

2 Resident in Britain, though breeding birds go south in winter. Winter visitors come from the north east, and passage migrants pass through.

3 Productive water, of variable depth. Shoveler eat zooplankton and small insects (they filter-feed), and in winter, water-plant seeds. Mud flats and sand bars with little water for roosting and loafing, with thickly fringed water for escape.

4 Nests in short cover, often almost in the open, usually near the water. Grazed land is good (as long as it is not grazed between April and June). Wetland dykes may be used.

Fig. 7.8. Shoveler and gadwall habitat.

Gadwall (*Anas strepaca*)

1 Mainly south, central and east, mostly on lakes, very scarce on rivers, though occurring on lowland ones such as the Suffolk Lark.

2 Resident in Britain, though winter visitors are greater in number. Passage migrant.

3 Clear shallow water, with ample water-supported vegetation, and its invertebrates, for food. Occasionally eat land plants.

4 Nests are in well-concealed places in thick grass, scrub, etc. near water.

5 Ducklings eat invertebrates (mainly flies) in their first three weeks.

6 Gadwall share wintering habitat with mallard (above).

Wigeon (*Anas penelope*)

1 Not really riverine. Breeding populations are mainly highland. Winter populations occur on the Ouse washes, the Trent flood plain and similar habitats.

2 Resident in Britain, winter visitor and passage migrant. Common in winter, sparse in summer.

3 Places with good all-round views, with roosting, loafing and feeding areas close together. Wigeon feed on plants (water and land), particularly on fine, short grasses, so short pasture near the water (with no tall plants between) is preferred. In winter, wigeon mainly gather in flocks, feeding on short pastures, reservoir margins, etc., often in estuaries.

4 Nests are by water, or up to 150+ m from it. Moorland streams, cut-off meanders, etc.

Fig. 7.9. Wigeon habitat.

Tufted duck (*Aythya fuligula*)

1 Lowlands. Sparse in sluggish rivers. Avoids acid waters, concentrated in the Thames, Ouse and Trent valleys, and central Scotland.

2 Resident in Britain, winter visitor and passage migrant. Frequent in winter, infrequent in summer. Many breeders go south for the winter.

3 Water 0.5–5 m deep, with enough water-supported vegetation to provide plenty of invertebrates for food, also eats plant seeds, berries, etc., and feeds from sediment.

4 Nests are close to the water, in tall herbs, brambles, etc.

5 Shallow water (< 1 m deep) is wanted for ducklings, which eat vast amounts of chironomids (*c.* 1 000/day of large chironomids).

6 Tufted duck gather in flocks in winter, generally on flooded gravel pits.

Fig. 7.10. *Tufted duck habitat.*

Pochard (*Aythya ferina*)

1 Mostly lowlands. Not really riverine (more in marshes), occurring in some slow streams and dykes.

2 Resident in Britain (except the Outer Isles). Sparse. Winter visitor, usually on flooded gravel pits and other fresh water, including large rivers.

3 Water up to 2.5 m deep. Pochard eat vegetation, many seeds and, to a lesser extent, invertebrates.

4 Nests are in tall vegetation; fringing reedswamp over water or up to 10 m from water. Breed in wetland dykes.

Goosander (*Mergus merganser*)

1 River habitat, mostly on large clear rivers in Scotland, northern England and Wales; spreading south. One to two pairs per 16 km of river. Locally common, mostly in summer. In winter, goosander often move to lowland rivers, reservoirs and gravel pits.

2 Resident in Britain, a quarter of the breeders move south in winter, and many more winter visitors arrive (giving about four times the summer numbers). Passage migrant also.

3 Dives for fish up to 4 m deep. Conflict with fisheries is claimed but not currently substantiated. May feed in rivers by day and roost in larger waters.

4 Nests on wooded shores, islands, among boulders, etc. Goosander will use nestboxes placed on trees close to suitable rivers.

5 Susceptible to disturbance.

Fig. 7.11. Goosander habitat.

Goldeneye (*Bucephala clangula*)

1 Not really riverine, though on large rivers in winter. In summer, rare in the north, in winter most at sea, in Scotland, also on lowland rivers, reservoirs and gravel pits.

2 Winter visitor and passage migrant. Frequent. Rare in summer.

3 Dives up to 4 m deep, catching fish and invertebrates from the water and bed. Also feeds on grain and vegetable waste, and at sewer outfalls.

4 Breeds along highland rivers, particularly the River Spey, using tree holes and nestboxes.

Cormorant (*Phalacrocorax carbo*)

1 Slow rivers or large open waters with suitable fish stocks. Flocks occur on rivers. Inland in all but the more mountainous parts; more birds in winter, also on lowland rivers, lakes and (especially) reservoirs. Frequent but mostly coastal.

2 Resident in Britain and winter visitor.

3 Dives and swims for medium-sized fish (many species, e.g. trout, salmon, eel, perch). Conflict with fisheries is claimed but currently not substantiated.

4 Breeding commonly around rocky areas, also nesting in trees.

Fig. 7.12. Cormorant habitat.

Grey Heron (*Ardea cinerea*)

1 Easily accessible shallow water with a good food supply. 'Accessible' is gently sloping shores or vertical banks less than 60 cm above the water, with open view (not obscured by tall emergents). Wades to 50 cm deep.

2 Resident in Britain, also passage migrant. Throughout the country, but sparse at high altitudes and in north Scotland. Frequent.

3 Herons eat 330–500 g/day of fish (up to, usually, 16 cm long), invertebrates, amphibians, reptiles, small mammals and birds.

4 Nests are in heronries, in open woods or groups of mixed-size trees. These may be near a river, or up to 30 km from the feeding grounds.

6 Avoids much disturbance.

Fig. 7.13. Grey heron habitat.

Dipper (*Cinclus cinclus*)

1 Rocky/stony rivers of highland Britain, locally into the lowlands, especially with turbulence.

2 Resident in Britain. Mostly in the north and west.

3 Feeds on invertebrates taken from under stones in the river bed. Wades, swims and dives. Particularly sensitive to water quality: if invertebrates are reduced, as by acidification, dipper also are reduced.

4 Nests in holes in stony banks, in tree roots and under bridges, but can be encouraged to use nestboxes in bridges or other river structures. Always over or close to water.

Fig. 7.14. Dipper habitat.

Redshank (*Tringa tringa*)

1 River habitat restricted, as redshank need very shallow water, preferably on mud, for foraging, and no emergents on the margins.

2 Resident in Britain, wintering mainly on the coasts; winter visitor and passage migrant.

3 Feed on small insects and aquatic invertebrates.

4 Nests are hidden in tussocky grass or sedge in wet or damp ground (*c.* 20 cm high: taller than for lapwing, shorter than for snipe). Cattle grazing gives a better tussocky structure than does sheep grazing. Two-stage channels may be suitable. Nests may be up to 1.5 km from the feeding sites.

6 No grazing, mowing or other disturbance from April to June (during nesting).

Fig. 7.15. *Redshank habitat.*

Lapwing (*Vanellus vanellus*)

1 The most abundant and widespread British breeding wader. Not riverine, though may use adjacent land. Less closely associated with water than redshank.

2 Resident in Britain, winter visitor and passage migrant. Chiefly summer resident in north Scotland. Some summer here and winter south.

3 Feeds mostly on land, also on bars (particularly mud ones) with little vegetation (as in mountain rivers); feeds on earthworms and other surface-living invertebrates.

4 Nests are often in short, damp grassland or in arable land (less than 15 cm high in mid-May).

5 Young feed on small surface invertebrates.

6 No disturbance from mid-March to mid-June (nesting).

Fig. 7.16. Lapwing habitat.

Oyster catcher (*Haematopus ostralegus*)

Fig. 7.17. Oyster catcher habitat.

1 Scattered particularly on shingle rivers, mainly in north England and Scotland. Very common in winter, frequent in summer, but mostly coastal.

2 Resident in Britain, winter visitor and passage migrant.

3 Feeds on insects, crustacea, molluscs and other invertebrates, and plants and seeds, on shores; also on fields.

4 Nest-hollows in sand, shingle, rock and turf near water, and on fields (arable, pasture) and moorland, etc.

Ringed plover (*Charadrius hiaticula*)**, Little ringed plover** (*C. dubius*)**, Tern (Common tern,** *Sterna hirundo*)

Fig. 7.18. (a) Tern feeding habitat, (b) Plover habitat.

1,2 Ringed plover: resident in Britain, winter visitor and passage migrant. Infrequent, mostly northern and East Anglia in summer, East Anglia in winter. Little ringed plover: scarce, summer resident and passage migrant, rare riverine. Tern: summer resident, infrequent inland.

3 Plovers feed on invertebrates from water and land, terns only on fish (up to 10 cm long).

4 Bare shingle (or sparse vegetation) or, for terns, steep mounds are preferred for nests. Nests on shingle can be swept away in spates. Trees and shrubs, which harbour predators, should be at least 100 m from the breeding area.

5 Chicks need access to shallow shoreline feeding grounds, with no tall vegetation between this and the nests.

Sandpiper (Common sandpiper, *Actilis hypoleucas*)

1 Frequent in highland rivers with shingle and/or sand banks, and little or no vegetation. Shores productive for invertebrates. Rare on low-land river banks.

2 Resident in Britain. Summer resident and passage migrant, sparse in winter. Mostly in highland Britain in summer, lowland in winter.

3 Feeds on invertebrates.

4 Nests on the ground on shingle banks.

6 Susceptible to disturbance from fishermen and others.

Fig. 7.19. Sandpiper habitat.

Other (barely riverine) waders

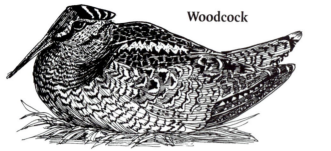

Woodcock

Green
Sandpiper

Fig. 7.20. Green sandpiper habitat.

1 All want shores productive for invertebrates, with little or no vegetation. Few use steep banks. Wet carr (e.g. willow) benefits **woodcock** (*Scolopax rusticola*) in winter. Woodcock often go to springs or ditches at night. Ditches and brooks should have shelves (at spring and autumn water level) for waders. Cress beds and small flushes are good for **green sandpiper** (*Tringa ochropus*).

2 Woodcock is largely resident in Britain, green sandpiper is mainly a passage bird, and summer resident.

Kingfisher (*Alcedo atthis*)

1 Slow-flowing or still clear waters, rarely fast ones in highlands. Infrequent: densest in England (except north) and Wales. In winter, highland kingfishers may move to the lowlands.

2 Resident in Britain.

3 Perches above water, so needs trees, shrubs, overhanging tall herbs (or fences or river structures) for these. Dives for food, from perch or hovering, up to 1 m deep, but prefers shallower water. Catches small fish, e.g. minnow, stickleback, fry, and other small animals.

Fig. 7.21. Kingfisher habitat

4 Nests are in earth cliffs, usually in the upper 50 cm, and 0.75–2 m above normal water level. The earth must allow tunnelling, but not be soft enough to fall into the hole. Suitable cliffs occur with natural winding in many river types, and cliffs up to 250 m from the river are also used. May also nest by drying ditches.

Sand martin (*Riparia riparioides*)

1 Not aquatic (except they will eat airborne insects, over water and marsh).

2 Summer resident, some passage migration. Common.

3 Feeds on invertebrates.

4 Nest in colonies in sandy cliffs, which may be riverside cliffs, 1–5+ m high, and may be unstable, when the colony must move frequently. May nest in pipes deliberately placed into bank sides. The cliff must be unobstructed.

Fig. 7.22. Sand martin habitat.

Sedge warbler (*Acrocephalus schoenobaenus*)

1 Lowland rivers, with good waterside vegetation, usually on drier margins than reed warbler. Uses bushes as song posts. Common, least so in the south west, Wales, Pennines, central and west Scotland.

2 Summer resident and passage migrant.

3 Feeds on invertebrates by and near the river edge, usually small, slow-moving prey. Aphids in *Phragmites* reedbeds along the south coast are an important pre-migratory food source.

4 Nests in marshy river edges or behind in marshes, scrub (up to 3 m high), brambles, tall herbs or even arable. **Rough vegetation should not be cut in autumn** as it is needed in the spring until the new growth is up.

Fig. 7.23. Sedge warbler habitat.

Reed warbler (*Acrocephalus scirpaceus*)

1 Lowland rivers, mainly south and east. More localised than sedge warbler. Reedbeds backed by wet woodland are most preferred.

2 Resident in Britain.

3 Feeds on insect larvae, etc. in willows, scrub and reedbeds.

4 Nests in damp places (wetter than sedge warbler), riverside reeds, tall emerged aquatics, willow herb, etc. The nests are often 1 m (20 cm–2.5 m) above water. Young often are still in the nest in August.

5 Vulnerable to habitat destruction.

Fig.7.24. *Reed warbler habitat.*

Reed bunting (*Emberiza schoeniculus*)

1 Common on river banks, in the drier margins. Formerly mostly in reedbeds, etc., now often in drier habitats, even hedgerows. Needs high song post, e.g. reeds. Common, less in the far west; wintering more in the lowlands.

2 Resident in Britain, winter visitor and passage migrant.

3 Feeds on grass, seeds and herbs, and insects in the breeding season.

4 Usually nesting on the ground in tall grasses and herbs or short scrub, preferably damp and near water.

6 In winter, flocks feed on the land by day and roost in marshes.

Fig. 7.25. *Reed bunting habitat.*

Grey Wagtail (*Motacilla cinerea*)

1 Widespread, more in fast-flowing rocky hill streams in summer and lowland rivers (canals, cress beds, etc.) in winter. Moves to the south of the country in winter.

2 Resident in Britain, winter visitor. Frequent.

3 Feeds on Diptera, other insects and other river invertebrates; also off farms, gardens, etc. In streams commoner in base-rich (more fertile) types, and with deciduous trees (more invertebrates).

4 Breeds more in the north, in the south usually by broken water. Nests are in rocky ledges, holes of cliffs, walls, bridges, steep banks, tree roots, etc., usually over or close to running water.

Pied wagtail (*Motacilla alba*)

1 Not particularly riverine, but often by rivers, particularly lowland rivers in winter. Widespread, and common, particularly in winter. May roost and feed in flocks in winter.

2 Resident in Britain. Most from south Britain are winter resident, most from the north move south (to or beyond England).

3 Feeds on Diptera, chironomids, other insects, other invertebrates and seeds. Young mostly eat clock beetles, flies and caterpillars.

4 Nests in holes of walls, banks, pollarded willows, thatch, etc.

Yellow wagtail (*Motacilla flava*)

1 Wet grassland, of the river corridor. May occur in tall grassland on lowland two-stage channels (see Chapter 3). Frequent.

2 Summer resident, and passage migrant.

3 Feeds on flies, aphids, beetles, etc. Young eat small flies, etc.

4 Nesting is usually near water or in wetland, in tufts of, e.g., grass.

Birds on large banks, on flood banks

Land birds may occur here on natural or created wide banks (two- or multi-stage channels), and a typical pattern in grassland and wood is shown in Table 7.2.

1 A patchwork of vegetation structure is desirable, if consistent with good maintenance (scrub can be at non-vulnerable points).

2 Short grass favours meadow pipit, skylark and linnet.

3 Longer grass favours yellow wagtail, reed bunting, and hunting owls.

4 Low-intensity management favours predators, e.g. barn owl, kestrel, wintering short-eared owls.

Fig. 7.26. Yellow wagtail habitat.

Table 7.2. Birds of large banks

	Grass Open	Bushes, hedges Open	Bushes, hedges Dense	Tree canopy Open	Tree canopy Closed
Skylark					
Meadow pipit					
Yellowhammer					
Linnet					
Willow warbler					
Dunnock					
Blackbird					
Chaffinch					

Fig. 7.27. Mixed habitats on wide banks.

5 More (but not over-) intensive management, discouraging predators, favours the prey of the former, e.g. voles, shrews, mice.

6 Seed-eating birds like linnet, greenfinch, goldfinch and siskin need to find seeds: seeding should not be prevented by mowing or spraying during flowering and fruiting.

7 Nesting birds should not be disturbed.

Mammals

Water vole, Water rat (*Arvicola terrestris,* not the same species as the true, brown or sewer rat)

Fig. 7.28. *Water vole habitat.*

1 Although widespread in, especially lowland, England, Wales and much of Scotland, in decline because of loss of habitat and pollution

2 Structure should be good and diverse, preferably with thick (non-scrub) vegetation spreading into the water, in which the water rats can move unseen. Extensive tunnels are burrowed for resting and breeding, these may be in the riverbank (giving direct access to water) or in other banks a little further from the river. Vertical banks about 50 cm high are recommended when creating habitat. The soil consistency must be such that the tunnels do not collapse.

3 Water rats feed on vegetation, mostly grasses and tall monocotyledons, so grazing fringes are desirable.

4 Water rats are territorial, males needing up to 130 m of river, females perhaps 80 m. (If a colony is suspected, it should be checked, as it is likely to be of brown rats.) Long lengths of good habitat are therefore desirable.

5 In decline, due to loss of habitat. Predators, including mink, can take them easily when vegetation is short or absent. Fragmentation and other damage aid loss.

Water shrew (*Neomis fudiens*)

1 Widespread, but scarce in north Scotland.

2 Like the water rat, lives in burrows in the bank, but is less common.

3 Hunts in water, feeds on animals: caddis larvae, snails, other bottom-living invertebrates, occasionally fish fry, etc. Most often by clear, clean, swift streams.

4 Nests are at the ends of long burrows. There may be up to three families per season, each with six to eight young.

Otter (*Lutra lutra*)

1 Abundant in north-west Highlands and Islands, formerly abundant, now sparse, absent, or local elsewhere.

2 Otters are territorial, males needing up to 40 km of river, females less, often up to 10 km.

3 They roam the riverbank and the land beside, and swim in the river.

4 They can travel through open land, but need safe secure places for resting and making their burrows or holts. Otters often rest by day. Males need safe places at least every 5–6 km.

5 Safe places are made in tall bankside vegetation, brambles, woods, scrub, carr and marshes, especially in trees overhanging the water or with good spreading roots (e.g. ash, sycamore). An otter may use more than 20 safe places. Planting trees and allowing tall vegetation to develop increases otter habitat.

6 Otters will travel 1 km or more along ditches and small brooks to reach good habitat, whether for hunting, breeding or lying up. It is important to keep numerous small watercourses, suitably protected by vegetation.

7 The greater the human disturbance, the more the cover needed, though excessive disturbance eliminates otters.

Highlands usually have lower disturbance, and should have at least 10% of the territorial river length made up of thick (little-disturbed) wood, tall vegetation, peat banks or rocky outcrops (the two latter if they can be excavated for holts), and all extending at least 10 m back from the river.

Lowland rivers are usually more disturbed, and the cover should extend further from the river, to at least 50 m. There should again be at least 10% of damp woodland, brambles, tall herbs, etc., but much of the remaining 90% should have a varied bank structure, allowing access for otters, and the good development of prey. There should be patches of low disturbance and of good cover. Damp woodland is particularly good as it is rarely disturbed: but it must be riverside, or accessible by tributaries.

Upstream reaches, where the EA does not come, may therefore be the best for otters – if other managers have left trees or tall vegetation.

The Norfolk Broads, with extreme daytime disturbance, have also large undisturbed alder and sallow carrs, and marshes, so otters can lie up safely by day and move at night. Otters vary, though, in their individual response to disturbance, and not all can tolerate this much. Disturbance by day is preferable to that by night. Day-time anglers are usually tolerated. Power-boats are often not tolerated.

Fencing to protect the river bank and damp woodland, etc. from people (to lessen disturbance) and livestock (to lessen disturbance and allow tall vegetation and woody plants to grow) much improves habitat (in areas of dense people or livestock).

Breeding can occur at any time of year (in the most secure holt in the home range). It is essential that there is no disturbance while the cubs are young.

8 Otters also need a clean habitat. Being at the top of the food chain, otters are particularly sensitive to accumulating poisons such as biocide and PCBs in their food.

9 They are carnivorous, and need plenty of fish, eels and other small animals: and therefore need productive rivers of good structure. Otters hunt by sight, so water must be clear (though they can use their whiskers in turbid rivers).

10 Otters can be, and are being, successfully re-introduced into rivers, and are increasing (including in south Wales).

11 These are general guidelines, and will not fit all habitats, or all otters.

Fig. 7.29. Otter habitat.

Mink (*Mustela lutreola*)

Mink have escaped from mink farms and are living wild along rivers, being particularly widespread in the north. They are smaller than otters (well under 1 m long). They are carnivorous, and are a significant nuisance on some rivers, eating fish, birds, eggs and small other animals.

8 DEVELOPMENT: enhancement, improvement and geomorphology

(further expertise needed to carry out most improvements; this book is not a handbook on restoration and for practical directions one of those from e.g. English Nature or the Royal Society for the Protection of Birds should be consulted)

SUMMARY

There is now – at last – a demand for rivers to stop being featureless open drains. The call is for 'restoration' (without, usually, specifying exactly what type of river in what past period is to be restored!). This has led to a new field of study, with geomorphology, the science of river movements, to the fore, since if bends, riffles, deep water, etc. are to be inserted successfully into uniform watercourses, river processes, the inherent mobility and stability of river systems, must be worked with, not against. Chapter 3 describes and assesses river structure. This chapter looks at, in effect, the same material, but primarily considers how bad structure can be improved. This needs some understanding of geomorphology and hydraulics: putting good structure in place is useless unless it remains as such for years and preferably decades ('improvements' that are dynamically wrong may be washed away and lost, or even worse, may lead to unwanted erosion, bank-fall or floods).

Introduction

Rivers change. They change because it is in their nature to do so: flowing water is changing water, and flowing water changes the land (and bed) through which it flows. As importantly in Britain, rivers change because human influences on them, human demands upon them, change. They change with the years, and have changed over the centuries. Alterations for flood prevention, waste disposal, land drainage, prevention of channel movement, and ensuring that rivers take the least possible space, are among present human aims. Navigation, power from watermills and fisheries, vital in the past, are now merely local uses, mainly for leisure activities. For river quality, the best management is usually the least management, the least interference. However, when past management has severely damaged a river (as in Fig. 8.1) then active measures of enhancement (improvement) are necessary: presuming a wait of maybe centuries for natural recovery is not acceptable. These enhancement measures may be to decrease pollution or to improve structure. Except for physical measures designed to increase self-purification, this chapter is not concerned with pollution (for which, see Chapters 5 and 6).

Restoration can be defined as returning the system to a close approximation of the traditional ecosystem that is persistent and self-sustaining. So 'restoration' means bringing back to an earlier state. Restoration techniques are therefore directed to a specific aim, an earlier state of the river. What earlier state? What river? Natural lowland rivers, in the sense of being without human interference, are unknown not just in Britain, they are unknown in Europe as a whole. The most nearly natural occur in the least-managed parts, like Sardinia, Corsica, parts of Ireland and Norway. Highland rivers generally have less interference, but even so the contrast between the more managed Alpine rivers of say the Pyrenees and the less managed ones of Corsica is great, and shows the degree of interference even in high mountains.

Fig. 8.1. *Rural and urban rivers in need of re-creation (and see pp. 3,5) (Haslam, 1991). (a), (b) Banks vertical, of stone or metal, (c), (d) banks are stone, etc., but offer no useful habitat even though they are sloping.*

Consequently, enhancement (the raising in quality) does not seek, in Britain, to create natural-type (pristine) rivers, since what these were like is unknown. Until the second half of the nineteenth century the lack of drainage in the lowlands, particularly in clay and clay-mix valleys, meant that these were dangerous and unhealthy places to live, with not just flood, but malaria-like and other fevers, rheumatism, and liver, digestive and scrofulous complaints. Restoring river valleys to such a state would be unsuitable. The aim is probably to reproduce the state of (clean, relatively undamaged) rivers from between about 1865 and 1945, as far as is practicable. (Practicable means not just considering cost, but also liability to flood, since waterlogging of soil is less acceptable than it used to be, and there is more development near the river.) What were these rivers like? One way to find out is to look at landscape paintings and old photographs (bearing in mind that scenes with boats were picturesque, and much navigation in maintained rivers results in smooth banks and little vegetation!). The other is to examine the area for rivers in the best available state (those rating high in Chapters 2–5 and 7). Fig. 8.2 gives a selection of such rivers. Appearance and structure vary with stream type and size: please note THE APPROPRIATE RIVER TYPE FOR THE ROCK TYPE, TOPOGRAPHY AND SIZE MUST BE AIMED AT, NOT AN OFFICE-CREATED IDEA OF AN ALL-PURPOSE GOOD RIVER.

Fig. 8.2. *Exemplars for river re-creation (and see Chapter 1 pp. 2,4) ((a) from Haslam, 1991).*

(c)

Fig. 8.2 (cont.)

River enhancement may be passive, where the river is left alone and natural recovery takes place. The end result will be good, but may take decades or centuries to achieve. Rehabilitation may also be active, with direct intervention into channel pattern or shape. Pollution, if chronic (rather than accidental) will need to be actively improved. A stream returned to excellent physical structure and architecture will still be impoverished or worse if the water quality is poor.

Development is the working out or new form of that which is already there – whether 'there' is in the river or in the mind of the developer!

Before doing other than trivial (active) improvements, a site should be examined for historical (Chapter 10) and archaeological (Chapter 11) heritage. To destroy these unbeknownst while improving river structure or landscaping is WRONG.

Rivers developed in this way should also maintain or recover their unique 'sense of place' so important for amenity as well as for habitat. Amenity planning, however, should come second. A river correct for its physical and vegetation structure will also be aesthetically pleasing, and footpaths, etc. can be added (see Chapter 12). A river 'restored' just for amenity, though, may be lacking in ecology (e.g. with clumps of alien trees, bad bank structure and so bad flora and fauna). Good game fisheries, in contrast, imply good birds, mammals, invertebrates, plants, etc.

Before rehabilitation, or, come to that, when seeking to lessen the impact of a damaging change, the stream should be studied, upstream (for at least 1 km) as well as downstream, to assess its mobility and stability. Aerial photographs can help, unstable rivers being more likely to have slumped banks, fallen trees and wide bars on convex bends. Vertical instability can be seen at e.g. bridges. The success of enhancement measures depends on this.

At present (1994) the demand for restored and improved rivers has exceeded the knowledge and expertise available. Two points follow:

1 Follow-up studies should ALWAYS be commissioned and arranged, with a minimum of yearly checks for five, preferably ten, years. Alterations, however good, which have lasted for three years in one river type will not necessarily last for three in another, or for twenty years in either. The results of (remember, costly) alterations must be discovered and made generally available so that others can know what to do and what not to do.

2 Habitats reasonably good in themselves should not be 'improved' until more knowledge is available. The first rule is to do no harm. Concentrate at present on the bad rivers, where almost any change will be an improvement, and do not try to enhance the good.

In addition:

3 Environmentalists should always be present when the engineering works are carried out. This is partly to ensure that they are carried out as intended. It is the ecologist, not the construction worker, who is at fault if the willow wands are washed out because they were placed 25 cm too low or 5 cm too far to the left on the bank. It is not the latter's business to know such things – which are difficult to convey on plans, anyway. The second reason for environmentalist presence is to record detail, for later assessment of the success (or failure) of the scheme.

(Alterations done solely for leisure pursuits, e.g. footpaths, car parks, angling areas, are considered in Chapter 12.)

Flood and waterlogging

The main reason for the river works which in the past have caused so much river damage is to stop floods where they endanger people, buildings and farming. It is, of course, unnecessary to build new developments in land liable to flood: it is far better (cheaper, and giving cleaner water) to keep these as wetland or wet (or flood) grassland, and build further up. It is also unnecessary, in these days of 'Set Aside', etc., to convert more damp (or wet) grassland to other crops – and wet grassland is an endangered British habitat which should be preserved. In fact, some riverside grain land could with advantage revert to grassland, lessening the need for drainage. In order to protect the national water resources, it would, in theory, be possible to raise the water level to get more water back in the land, breed crop strains more resistant to waterlogging (the main cause of crop harm from too much water), and convert to machinery suitable for waterlogged land.

Too much vegetation is the bugbear of the drainage engineer, vegetation which would cause water to pond, and flood or waterlogging to occur. The danger is much less than it was even a few decades ago, since the vast amount of bed lowering and channelling means water levels can often rise the 30–50 cm typically caused by ponding without damage. In flood, certainly the river rises more, but it may well flow over the channel vegetation, thus having no further effect. That conclusion is tentative, and awaits the results of studies currently (1994) under way.

Typically, bed vegetation, when abundant, is cut once each summer. Dominant *Ranunculus* (in chalk streams, etc.) may need more, but early summer cutting should be avoided as it encourages vigorous regrowth. Rivers formerly had a vast population of herbivorous fish and fowl, not to speak of herbivorous invertebrates and, earlier, herbivorous beaver. River plants were, therefore, as much grazed as is grassland, and it is not surprising that some of the water plants that became river plants are species that (in summer) grow more and faster if cut.

Calculations on the effect of bed vegetation on flow are difficult. Traditionally, flow resistance is measured by using Mannings 'n', but a logarithmic equation that can take better account of vegetation shape, flexibility, flow and season is better – and may show less flow resistance than does the Mannings 'n'. Different species show different flow resistance, plant shape and size being important (Fig. 8.3, Table 8.1). Comparing very slow flow channels (flexible stems near-vertical) with slow–moderate flow ones (flexible stems at least 30° from vertical) shows that some fine-leaved species, such as fine-leaved *Potamogeton* and *Ranunculus*, have more resistance in swifter flow, while firm emergents like *Phragmites*, *Nuphar lutea* and *Potamogeton perfoliatus* (both large-leaved) have less resistance in swifter flow, when the leaves bend sideways and offer a narrower surface to the flow. Similar examples can be cited for other factors.

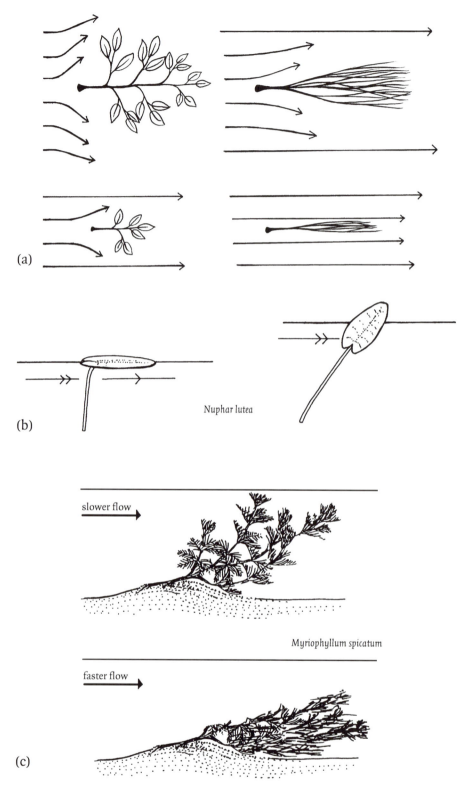

Fig. 8.3. *Variation in plant size and shape with force of flow. (a) Smaller size causes less resistance to flow, and more streamlined shape causes less resistance to flow, (b) shape more streamlined in very slow flow, (c) shape more streamlined in faster flow. (Haslam, 1978).*

Table 8.1. Resistance to flow offered by different species
(for similar sizes of shoot: larger shoots offer more resistance)

Variation in resistance in different species in moderate–fast flow (tested shoots c. 30 cm long)

High resistance

Apium nodiflorum, Berula erecta, Elodea canadensis (when much branched), *Epilobium hirsutum, Myriophyllum spicatum, Nasturtium officinale* agg., *Nuphar lutea, Ranunculus peltatus* (when much branched)

Medium resistance

Elodea canadensis (when less branched), *Mentha aquatica, Myosotis scorpioides, Myriophyllum spicatum* (when less branched) *Polygonum amphibium, Potamogeton pectinatus* (when much branched), *P. perfoliatus* (when branched), *Ranunculus peltatus* (when less branched), *Sparganium erectum*

Low resistance

Callitriche spp., *Potamogeton crispus, P. pectinatus* (when less branched), *P. perfoliatus* (when unbranched), *Ranunculus penicillatus, Scirpus lacustris, Sparganium emersum, Zannichellia palustris*

Variation in resistance with flow type

Species offering less resistance when erect than when in flows bending shoots at least 30° from the vertical (note 'soft' species can be packed more thickly when bent by flow)

Carex spp. (large), *Phalaris arundinacea, Phragmites australis, Potamogeton pectinatus, P.* spp. (grass-leaved), *Ranunculus* spp., *Sagittaria sagittifolia, Sparganium emersum, Sp. erectum, Typha* spp., *Zannichellia palustris, Enteromorpha* sp, blanket weed

Species offering less resistance when bent at least 30° from the vertical

Nuphar lutea (unless twisted), *Nymphaea alba, Potamogeton lucens, P. natans, P. perfoliatus*

Species differing little in resistance in the two shapes

Butomus umbellatus, Callitriche spp., *Ceratophyllum demersum, Glyceria maxima, Lemna* spp. (unless piled in heaps), *Myriophyllum spicatum, Polygonum amphibium, Scirpus lacustris*, fringing herbs (bushy short emergents)

Resistance to flow is also given by rough bank vegetation (often cut in winter, when needed), by rough banks, trees in the water cross-section (or at least in the higher level of flood cross-section), and by obstructions in the channel, whether this is deposited silt, fallen trees, or dumped fridges. In the natural river, when clogging occurs, the next floods may clear it, or may force a way through a new channel. In (particularly lowland) Britain, where unrestrained floods are unwelcome, obstruction is kept low.

It now (1996) seems – subject to current research results – that too much emphasis may have been placed on the post-drainage dangers of vegetation in flowing waters. More care has to be taken in wetland dykes, unless these are in wet grassland, etc. Certainly in channels without liability to flood flows, and where either ponding does not cause waterlogging or waterlogging is irrelevant, vegetation may safely dominate. Cutting (mechanically or manually) is the main form of control in flowing waters, and this or herbicide in wetland dykes. (It must be remembered that herbicides are a form of pollution.) Integrated control regimes are being researched. Dredging of accumulated silt, and clearance of other obstructions, is routinely undertaken by the Environment Agency. Wetland dykes, which are man-made and have no intrinsic flow, will silt up and be lost without dredging.

Rehabilitation and enhancement

Introduction

In a rehabilitated river, the hydraulic properties and the morphological features should be as close as possible to those of a traditional river of the same type.

Flowing water has power, stream power. The water's energy moves sediment, erodes and deposits material, etc. The flatter the stream, the more lowland, indeed the more wetland, the lower the power, and the steeper, the more alpine, the greater the power, the greater the energy available for changing channels (Fig. 8.4). Making a channel straight and uniform, therefore, increases its slope, and its speed of flow, and so its stream power. Alterations to power can then start off changes in sediment transport and channel shape (Fig. 8.5 and Table 8.2). Lowland improvement schemes are most likely to be successful in streams of moderate power and flow.

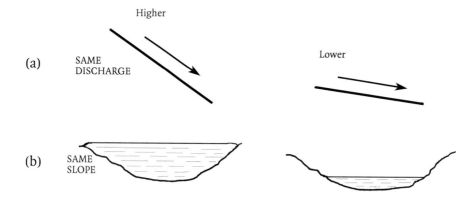

Fig. 8.4. *Stream power (re-drawn from Gordon et al., 1992).*

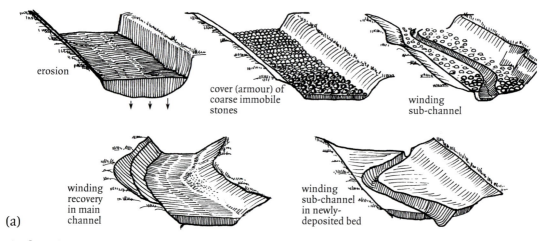

Fig. 8.5. *Changes in shape of channels after channelisation (re-drawn from Brookes, 1988). (a) Different ways that straightened streams adjust, (b) adjustment over time in an American stream.*

Streams with the power of the Severn may well restore their pattern naturally, over a century or so. Small lowland streams are a different matter. Their power is low, and their bending may be inherited from early post-glacial times when, presumably, the streams were more active. Consequently, active intervention is often necessary for enhancement. The simplest enhancement measure is to leave alone (without disturbance).

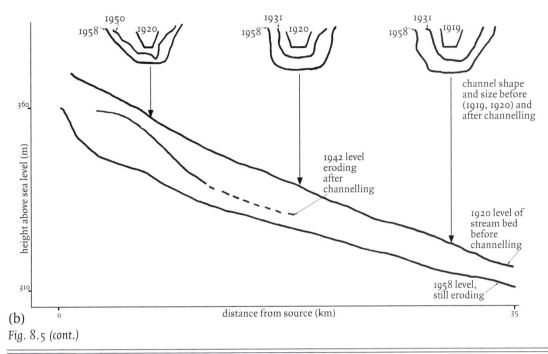

(b)

Fig. 8.5 (cont.)

Table 8.2.

Behaviour of high- and low-energy streams after channelling

Type of stream	Energy	
	High	Low
Much sediment available	If channel over-wide, deposition Banks slump Sediment trapped, may re-form pool	Over-wide trapezoids will narrow May become sinuous Shelves stabilise Limited pool development Deflectors and new substrate could be buried by sediment
Little sediment available	No recovery if over-wide Severe bank slump New substrate or deflectors are likely to wash out if the channel is self-adjusting	Little or no recovery Intervention needed for good morphology to develop Good designs are successful
Erodible if bends have been removed	Nickpoint usually moves upstream (rarely, bends may form), bed may become armoured with cobbles or gravels, and erode laterally	Limited adjustment Bends restorable at low risk
Non-erodible once bends are removed	Limited recovery, restoration may fail unless the design is exceptionally good	No natural recovery, may be silting Silting may cover new substrate, or block restored bends

After Brookes in Boon et al. (1992).

Intervention, as indicated in Table 8.2, if successful, must be in accordance with the geomorphological and hydraulic properties of the stream, and expert advice is needed here. The basic tools of enhancement, restoring pool–riffle sequences, planting brambles and wild flowers, etc., are described here: their successful application needs further expertise. This is needed both for the overall pattern, the expectation of, say, deposition or slumping in given circumstances, and for the exact placing of a recommended enhancement feature, such as a groyne or willow. A groyne on the wrong part of the bend may be lost within a few months. Changes made without proper ecological knowledge may greatly damage the communities of insects and other invertebrates. Expert advice on catchment planning may also be desirable – advice on the linkage and effect of any one feature on the downstream (and indeed, for mobile nickpoints, upstream) pattern of the whole, and on how best to design each part to give the best overall result.

No river should be sterile or be without larger plants and animals, or even approach this state. Given that, however, the degree of enhancement possible depends on the site and the type of stream. London must not flood, its rivers must stay in place. A bog stream may both flood and be mobile, cutting more bends and, eventually, cutting off meanders into ox-bows. The degree of enhancement also depends on the riparian owners, since an enhanced stream may have a different course (one like that it had before channelisation) and may be wider, so taking up more space. If a buffer strip is created, yet more space is used.

Some of the techniques described below involve lowering the river bed yet further from its traditional level. This is an Elastoplast-like treatment, in that it creates deeper water now, which may be a good thing if the stream has in the past been left too shallow (see Chapter 12). However, considering the land as a whole, lowering bed level is at least potentially lowering water level, and so causing yet more water loss. It is a technique to be considered with care.

Many enhancement projects end up less satisfactory than they might be because of too much bank protection, too little space for stream and trees to develop or too much civil and landscape engineering (imposing a fixed artificial pattern on the stream and its environs).

Some of the possible techniques for stream enhancement follow. Before carrying any out, Dr P Kirby's book, *Habitat Management for Invertebrates* (Royal Society for the Protection of Birds, 1992) should be consulted.

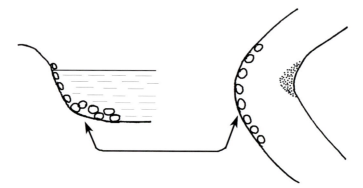

Fig. 8.6. *Protection of concave (eroding) bends, to stabilise stream pattern.*

Re-inserting bends

The position of the original channel may be discovered by looking on the ground (e.g. Fig. 3.65), at similar rivers in a more natural state, at old maps, and perhaps at old pictures. If this is not possible, an artificial course must be designed. The length of the channel should be at least 1.5 times the distance straight down the valley. This, obviously, provides much more aquatic habitat in total (at least half as much again) than would be in a straight course. A natural course has more than one wave pattern (see Fig. 3.67).

If the stream is geomorphologically mobile, but is wanted immobile, it may be necessary artificially to protect the concave bends (Fig. 8.6) so that the natural erosion there cannot occur. This protection may be by rough stone (rip-rap) or other artificial material, or may be woven willow mats (willow spiling, from which rooting willows will grow, stabilising the bank when the original weave rots), or other plant material. It is best to have a mobile stream, but far better to have one with appropriate but secured bends than to have a straight channel. Preventing erosion on the concave bend will not prevent deposition on the convex one, so maintenance must be planned in accordance with channel geomorphology.

Re-inserting pool–riffle sequences

A pool and riffle should be roughly every (3–) 5–7 (–10) times the river width (i.e. a stream 1m wide with a pool and riffle pair every 5–7 m, and a stream 10 m wide with them every 50–70 m), the riffle being a little longer than the pool. With this, a stream ought, in floods, to adjust itself to the stable or natural mobility pattern. Success is when the pair can be maintained by the size of storm flow (flood) which can be expected once every one to two years. Pools that are too wide, long or deep may trap over-much silt. The minimum depth is around 30 cm below low-flow level.

Pool–riffle sequences increase habitat diversity, and oxygenation (and so self-purification). They decrease scouring (so are valuable in over-straightened over-channellised streams with excessive scouring and whose bends cannot currently be put back). They provide resting places for salmon and other fish, so may be inserted by anglers.

Where the river carries excess silt (e.g. from over-intensive farming), pools can be inserted where silt will accumulate, in places from where it can easily be excavated. These pools are called silt traps.

Altering substrate

Badly damaged lowland channels may have little hard bed and much silt, giving a habitat not only uniform, but smothering, which is bad for many plants and animals. This can be cured by altering flow, and increasing scour. (Incoming silt can be collected in silt traps (pools) from which it can easily be excavated.) Much more silt enters rivers than in the past, due to more intensive farming and development. Small streams can have river-gravel (taken from gravel-pits) put in, in barrowloads, to create a new (to be) consolidated bed. This raises the bed. Both raising and lowering may alter stream development (geomorphology). The particles must be of sizes that stay put, and the amount must be that which creates a staying substrate, unless natural redistribution of particles is desired, when material that is hydraulically chosen for this must be added.

Channels may be lined (with stone, concrete or plastic, etc.) and so be impervious to water. For rehabilitation, this is another Elastoplast-on-a-road-accident situation. If water level has been lowered by abstraction and drainage, and the river is in danger of being lost, by its water sinking down through the bed, the water resources should be amended, not the channel bed altered by lining. However, lining is occasionally acceptable over short lengths, for instance when the bed is cracked and water is led to deep underground waterways, or when a quarry has been excavated too close to the stream, and the stream water is seeping and flowing into the quarry instead. Lined rural streams are more likely to flood, since no water can escape downwards through the bed.

Channels lined in the past, and where site and design allow no other cheap solution (usually in towns), may be cobbled, or have sediment deposited on them. A layer of cobbles stuck to the bed looks better, and if the substrate is irregular (i.e. cobble sticking up, not sunk in concrete), a fair invertebrate habitat results (which aids fish). Mosses may be able to grow. If riffles are created by the cobbling, oxygenation increases. Gravel may be added. Alternatively, it may be possible to have flow such that a natural-type bed is deposited and developed, with plant and animal communities indistinguishable from those of unlined channels. If all else fails, at least shelves can be added.

Whether the method is adding gravel, cobbling or lining, the added material should be compatible with the original. Limestone, for instance, should be added only to limestone streams: elsewhere it would add an improper limestone influence to, say, a granite stream. Particle size and shape must also be specified. Added bed material should be river gravel, which is angular, not beach shingle, which is rounded.

Several techniques can be combined, e.g. restoring a salmonid spawning area by removing the unsuitable fine substrate, replacing it with an appropriate rubble mixture, placing boulders downstream of the riffles to stop new substrate moving out, inserting groynes to ensure riffle survival, inserting scattered boulders to help flow patterns, and stabilising banks.

Opening closed channels

All watercourses should be open to the sky, unless their water is dirty enough to be a health hazard, cannot be cleaned, and runs to the sewage treatment works. Otherwise, channels in pipes or culverts should be open, for self-purification and for habitat. (There will, of course, be places where this action, however desirable, is not practical). Even small watercourses can be a focus for the view, and can convert a dull landscape, to a pleasing one (Fig. 8.7).

Fig. 8.7. A small, relatively dull stream can yet be a focus in the landscape (Haslam, 1978).

Underdrains can be opened up within the buffer strip – if there is one (Figs. 3.65, 5.6). These may be termed 'horseshoe wetlands'. Underdrains can also be stopped at the start of the buffer strips, with their contents passing through, and being partly cleaned by, the soil before reaching the river.

Inserting or raising weirs and dams, including debris dams

The upper permissible water level above weirs, dams and other fixed controls is fixed formally by flood requirements. Here, there is often surplus capacity and weirs can be installed or be raised without exceeding the permissible level. There is also an ecological requirement, that weirs should not prevent the passage of fish and other mobile animals and plants. Fish passes, etc., can be built if needed.

Weirs alter flow. They pond it upstream of the structure, creating deep, slow habitats, with water running free downstream, creating swift, oxygenating, coarse-substrate habitats. Weirs also keep water in the river, slowing it up and hindering it on its way to the sea.

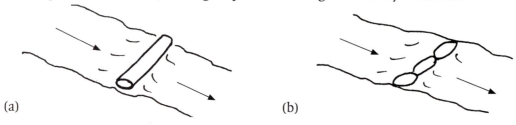

(a)   (b)

Fig. 8.8. *Weirs and gates of various types ((c)-(g) Haslam, 1991). (a) Tree trunk or equivalent, (b) sand bags or equivalent, (c) control gate on right, overspill weir on left, (d) entrance to mill stream (near left), exit from similar (far), (e) control gate (f) control gate, (g) hydroelectric power station, with control gates on right, overspill on left.*

Weirs, necessarily, are man-made (except for debris ones, see below). Since they were abundant in the eleventh century (*Domesday book*: mills), and no doubt earlier, they do form the traditional habitat of many British rivers. In the hills, with steep slopes and high-force flows, the traditional weirs tended just to create pool–riffle sequences, which were more accented than the natural ones. In, particularly, lowland clay rivers, though, the weirs often keep much of the river ponded, deep and slow-flowing. River rehabilitation here includes restoring this ponded habitat.

Weirs (Fig. 8.8) can be small or large, can be made of old rubble or bricks moved in free, they may be sandbags, or built of stone or concrete, to a proper civil engineering standard, costing maybe a five-figure sum. Weirs for catchment-planned flow must be well built and long lasting. Weirs for conservation, however, with levels within those of the latter, can be cheap and temporary. It is better to have cheap little weirs for ten years than to do without, and it may be better to have a dozen sandbag weirs than a single built one. Sandbag weirs may reduce the natural pool riffle pattern, but as the usual reason for installing them is too little water, this is seldom a problem.

Debris dams are little dams within a river which collect drifting organic matter (debris), fallen tree-leaves, twigs, etc. Most often these are created by fallen trees (Fig. 8.9). Fallen trees (aggregated) may obstruct channels and cause floods, and therefore they are rightly regarded with suspicion by engineers. However, not each and every standing or fallen tree is a danger. Again, expert advice is needed, on what size, type and frequency of logs, etc., are safe in a given river. The largest possible should be aimed for.

Forested catchments contribute the most organic debris to a stream, concrete ones the least. The debris accumulation affects the potential energy, and therefore the erosion–deposition pattern, the pool–riffle sequence, roughness, routeing of flow, routeing and storage of sediment, sites of channel change, and bank stability. This has major effects on the habitat for flora and fauna and so in the flora and fauna themselves. Perhaps the extreme is in streams in acid, nutrient-poor sands, where the debris dams form the predominant source of organic substances, and of a non-shifting habitat. Dams can be 'active', forming a complete barrier across the channel, and if the stream is seen in long-section, with a step in the (long) profile. They can be 'complete', forming a complete barrier but without a step in the long profile, or they may be partial, extending over only part of the channel. In light and moderate flows, debris dams decrease light and moderate flood peaks. Removing debris increases overall sediment transport and erosion, and decreases macroinvertebrates.

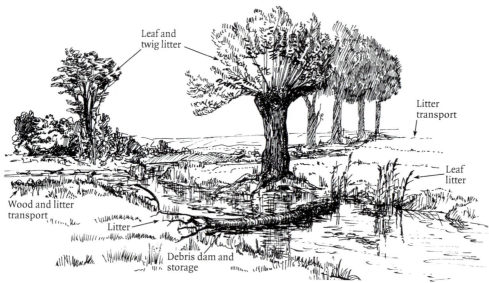

Fig. 8.9. *A debris dam.*

Debris dams vary in longevity, from maybe a few months, to decades (one in the Aberdeen River Don is still a good habitat for macrophytes after ten years). Longevities of up to two centuries are recorded. It is thought that a dam retains maybe two-thirds of the annual input for long enough to be biologically useful. The importance of the organic carbon to stream metabolism and community has been stressed elsewhere (Chapters 3 and 5). Debris dams are an integral part of the stream system, important in its dynamics and in its habitat. They should be encouraged wherever possible, and, ideally, it should be the removal, not the retention of one which needs careful justification.

Creating buffer strips (buffer zones, riparian protection strips)
(see Chapters 3 and 6 for discussion)

The importance of strips alongside the river, bearing vegetation and without poisoning (no agrochemicals, etc.), has been described in Chapter 3, pp. 54–6 and Chapter 5, pp. 148–50. Such buffer zones provide much water cleansing as well as habitat. It is important to protect little brooks in this way as well as big rivers, as the water from the little brooks makes up that of the big river.

For purification, the buffer strip is best if it is waterlogged in winter or is wetland. If not wetland, trees and shrubs with a good diverse flora are the most efficient, followed by shorter plants with good diversity. Monodominant grassland has had the most research, and is very effective, but it may well be the least effective of vegetation types (non-vegetated soil or built-up land is less useful again). (For conservation preferences see Chapters 3–5.) Buffer strips aid bank stability, in that the land is not ploughed.

Banks

For good architecture and habitat for animals and plants, there should be, over a length of river, a variety of bank patterns and slopes: gentle, steep and cliff-like, low and high, with vegetation everything from tall trees to short grasses. Islands are advantageous, particularly for birds (non-bird predators finding it difficult to reach islands). A stream with active meanders and pool and riffle sequences, and without too much active engineering, will develop satisfactory banks.

Bank stability depends on slope, material, vegetation and stress (stresses include cattle, trampling, footpaths, roads, tractors, etc.)

Low slopes are more stable; cohesive soil is more stable; vegetated banks are more stable; banks with low stress are more stable; banks of streams with little-varying flow are more stable; banks of meandering streams are more stable; and banks of streams geomorphologically engineered are more stable.

Unstable banks may slump if steep. 'Steep' here may include the 1.5:1 slope so typical of channelised watercourses. Making the bank more gentle (e.g. 2:1) (like e.g. Fig. 3.52) takes up more space, but stops the slumping, and in Sweden has proved cost-effective on maintenance. Allowing bank-holding woody plants in the channel (Fig. 8.10) has proved effective in parts of France, where again this is cheaper than trying to maintain a smooth channel – and is clearly better for habitat.

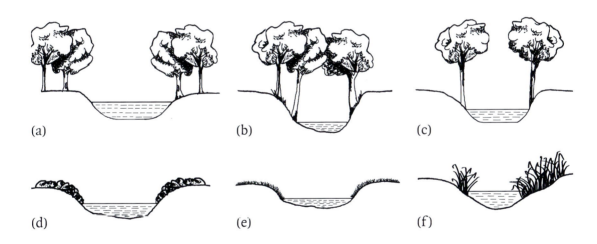

Fig. 8.10. *Some types of bank vegetation. (a) Trees above channel, (b) trees within channel, (c) trees binding base of bank, (d) brambles, (e) fescue sward, (f) reedswamp fringe.*

Slumping slopes shored up by stone or concrete (e.g. rip-rap) are expensive. If of bare stone, they are bad for bank habitat (though necessary in some continental places, where bank plants are a valued resource, traditional controls have decayed, and all vegetation has been removed). Putting soil on top and re-vegetating is better.

Stoned banks below water level may be very bad for habitat, removing the diverse shallow-water natural homes for small fish and fish fry, many invertebrates and macrophytes.

Gentle banks may also be put in for watering livestock – short lengths in special drinkers, or longer lengths for more widespread access. Non-maintained banks may be made gentle by livestock.

Smooth uniform banks pass water on faster, have a lower resistance to flow (less roughness), and less plant and animal habitat (though a good, diverse bank structure includes some of this, along the river length, for the sake of those animals and plants able to grow best there). Smooth banks are expensive to maintain. Appropriate vegetation stabilises banks, and it may be much cheaper to have stabilising vegetation than to have smooth banks.

What vegetation? First, why vegetation? Vegetation may be increased to return it to normal after damage or destruction, for plant and animal survival and development. Vegetation may be altered to be more acceptable to ecologists, land-owners, anglers, and for other leisure purposes. For high-quality habitat and high-quality invertebrates, there should be diversity of architecture and community (see Chapter 3). Vegetation may be brought in, or increased, to clean entering run-off water. Here, purification is improved with more vegetation, and with more diverse vegetation (see Chapter 5 for further details). And, of course, vegetation may be wanted to stabilise banks.

Second, which source of the vegetation? As far as possible all should be local – local strains of willows or brambles, self-regeneration of grassland, marsh, etc.; if not possible, local wildflower seed, whenever practicable. Only this is restoration. Alien trees or 'wildflower grassland' commercial seed, even alien strains of local species, are creating alien communities. Self-generation may be possible over years, even if not over the first months, and is the best.

Third, which vegetation type (Figs 8.11, 8.12; Table 8.3)?

Fig. 8.11. (a), (b) Watercourse enhancement using trees. (a) different rooting types; bank is better stabilised by type on left; (b) inserting wooden piles; (c) new woody growth from such piles, increasing protection (and see Fig. 3.22, p. 33) (Lachat, 1988).

(c)

Fig. 8.11 (cont.)

Table 8.3.
Suitable grasses, herbs and trees for banks

(a) Grass

Species	Qualities
Crested dog's-tail (*Cynosures cristatus*)	Short, tufted, likes poor conditions, low productivity
Common bent-grass (*Agrostis capillaris* synonym: *A. tenuis)*	Likes poor conditions, rhizomes, good binding quality
Highland bent-grass (*Agrostis castellana*) (foreign)	Is cheaper and is usually sold instead of *A. capillaris* in mixes. It is relatively productive and hence very invasive, with vigorous rhizomes and stolons. In contrast with the native species, it is taller, more productive, has poor summer colour but is very green in winter
Flattened meadow-grass (*Poa compressa*)	Stress tolerant, rhizomes, low productivity
Golden hair-grass (*Trisetum flavescens)*	Stress tolerant, tufted, low productivity, attractive
Slender creeping red fescue (*Festuca rubra)*	Good binding quality, low productivity
Chewings fescue (*Festuca rubra* ssp. *commutata)*	Stress tolerant, tufted, low productivity
	Ordinary creeping red fescue (ssp. *rubra*) has good binding ability but will swamp herbs if sown in any quantity. The use of slender creeping red fescue such as ssp. *pruinosa* or ssp. *litoralis* and/or Chewings fescue (ssp. *commutata*) gives good binding properties with lower productivity
Sheep's-fescue (*Festuca ovina*)	Tufted, drought resistant, low productivity, wide adaptability to pH
Sweet vernal-grass (*Anthoxanthum odoratum)*	Short, tufted, likes poor conditions, low productivity, attractive to livestock

From Newbold *et al.* (1989).

(b) Herbs

Species	Qualities	Flowering
Bird's-foot-trefoil (*Lotus corniculatus*)	Food plant of common blue butterfly and six-spot burnet; a tufted legume; it has little enriching effect, unlike white and suckling clovers, which should be avoided	May–Sept.
Common cat's-ear[1] (*Hypochoeris radicata*)	Good nectar/pollen source, bright yellow flowers, rosette	June–Sept.
Cowslip (*Primula veris*)	Early pollen source, spreads readily once established, rosette	April–May
Selfheal (*Prunella vulgaris*)	Generally short, pollen and nectar source	June–Sept.
Oxeye daisy (*Leucanthemum vulgare*)	Nectar source, aesthetically pleasing, readily established on neutral to basic soils	June–Aug.
Upright hedge-parsley[2] (*Torilis japonica*)	Annual, but seeds readily. Medium height, attractive	June–Aug.
Wild carrot (*Daucus carota*)	Does well on neutral to basic soils; good nectar/pollen source, biennial, deep rooted, medium height	June–Aug.
Yarrow (*Achilles millefolium*)	Medium height, nectar source, deep rooted	June–Aug.

[1] Autumn hawkbit (*Leontodon autumnalis*) and rough hawkbit (*Leontodon hispidus*) are good alternatives when seed is in short supply.

[2] Native form preferred but agricultural form acceptable.

(c) Woody plants

	Acid	Type of soil Neutral	Alkaline	No. of associated invertebrate species
<5 metres in height				
Alder[1]		★	★	141
Birch	★		★	334
Blackthorn		★	★	151
Crab apple		★	★	116
Dogwood		★	★	
Field maple		★	★	51
Guelder rose		★	★	
Hawthorn	★	★	★	205
Hazel		★	★	106
Holly	★	★	★	96
Rowan	★	★		58
> 5 metres				
Ash		★	★	68
Oak	★	★	★	423
Willows	★	★	★	

[1] *Phytophthera* disease is (1995) killing riverside alders patchily but increasingly. New alder plants should not be brought in from possibly-infected areas.

(d) Plants for encouraging butterflies and moths

By encouraging the appropriate food plants for caterpillars, nectar plants for adults and in some cases scrub for sheltered flight, conditions for the following can be created.

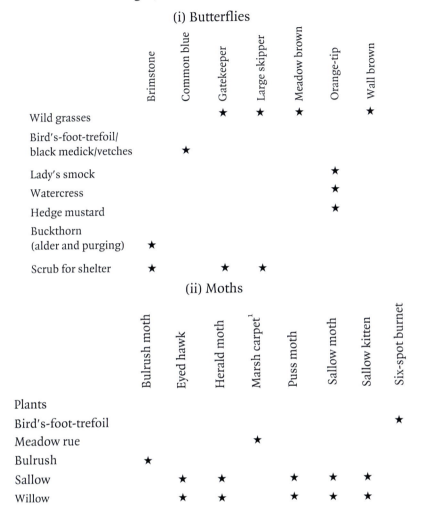

(i) Butterflies

	Brimstone	Common blue	Gatekeeper	Large skipper	Meadow brown	Orange-tip	Wall brown
Wild grasses			★	★	★		★
Bird's-foot-trefoil/ black medick/vetches		★					
Lady's smock						★	
Watercress						★	
Hedge mustard						★	
Buckthorn (alder and purging)	★						
Scrub for shelter	★		★	★			

(ii) Moths

	Bulrush moth	Eyed hawk	Herald moth	Marsh carpet[1]	Puss moth	Sallow moth	Sallow kitten	Six-spot burnet
Plants								
Bird's-foot-trefoil								★
Meadow rue				★				
Bulrush	★							
Sallow		★	★		★	★	★	
Willow		★	★		★	★	★	

[1] Unlike the other moths listed, this moth is very local in its occurrence. It is found with its food plant on drain banks on the Nottinghamshire/Lincolnshire border. Its continued survival is largely dependent on the sympathetic management of these banks.

Roots of trees are very efficient for stabilising banks, for cleaning water, for providing organic carbon to the river, and for providing animal habitat. Their effect in holding banks is seen in the wider channels occurring after tree removal. New trees may be planted separately, or grow from protective willow-weave spiling, which is fixed in place as protection for the lower parts of vulnerable banks (on concave bends, straightened channels, or where there is other cause for slumping). New shoots often need to be protected from grazing (fenced). The more the erosion, the wider the tree belt should be: with several rows (above water level) with potentially severe erosion. Woody growth may be within the channel, above it, or only well away from it. The patterns seem to be determined by local tradition. Trees within the channel are effective and cheap bank-protectors, but there must be adequate free space for floodwater to fill despite the trees. The current tradition in lowland England, though, is that trees must be over 8 m from the bank except with special permission from the Environment Agency. Trees collapse only if they are high on the bank, and soil below and within the roots is washed away. Pollards are important habitat and important heritage. They should be maintained (pollarding can be combined with, e.g., dredging, although for invertebrate habitat to be maintained, only short lengths should be cut at any one time) and, as necessary, replaced. Brambles are efficient bank stabilisers, and so are fescue swards. Fescue (*Festuca ovina, F. rubra*) roots are narrow, tolerate drought, are unlikely to crack the bank, and the even sward makes erosion difficult. Fescue growth is fairly slow, especially where nutrients are, or have been made to be, low, so maintenance is cheap. Tall fast-growing grasses contrast with this, and should be avoided. (NB, keeping nutrients low, for cheap maintenance and a more diverse flora, is important.)

Tall monocotyledons (reedswamp species) are very effective by the water's edge, and bank erosion often follows their removal. Because reed (*Phragmites*) is used in constructed wetland pollution purification in northern Europe, there is a tendency to import it, for cleansing, into rivers where it is not native. This is a mistake: it (or other tall monocots) may by all means be planted in constructed ditches for run-off, but it is not so much better than other species (in fact, for degrading some pollutants, it is worse) to justify creating improper communities.

Working *with* the vegetation native and traditional to the river will give cheaper and effective bank maintenance. It is better, almost always, to retain (and encourage) existing satisfactory vegetation than to remove it and start afresh.

Three invasive aliens may be troublesome and need treatment: giant hogweed (*Heracleum montegazzianum*), which has poisonous sap, Japanese knotweed (*Fallopia japonica*) and Himalayan balsam (*Impatiens glandulifera*), which last, in suitable quantities, fits in best with the native flora. All three, though, leave banks open to erosion when they die back.

Channel alterations, other

Channels may be widened (Fig. 8.12) either just for conservation or to take more water during storm flows. This gives more space for aquatic communities, and makes flow shallower (in small streams maybe too shallow for water-supported vegetation), swifter and so perhaps more scouring. Patterns of emergents separated by deeper channels carrying most of the flow may develop in smaller streams.

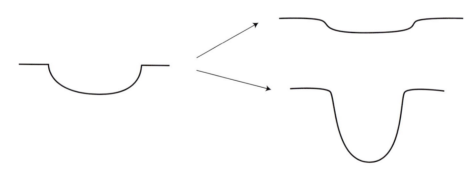

Fig. 8.12. *Changing channel width.*

Channels may be deepened and so narrowed (Fig. 8.12), either just for conservation or for anglers or to make it look as though water had not been taken by abstraction or land drainage. Because of this last reason, narrowing to under 4 m is not to be recommended. Indeed, a further narrowing when even less stream water is available may make the stream hard to see, and once the public is accustomed to not seeing a river, that river can be quietly disposed of – rather than having its water restored.

However, groynes and deflectors may be put in a bed to direct flow and narrow the flow path (not the bed) in shallower streams (Fig. 8.13) Groynes may be logs, hurdles, boulders or stone, etc. They may be permeable or impermeable. Impermeable groynes trap transported sediment. Permeable ones let water through and the deposit is above the groyne. Vegetation may invade and anchor the new bar. Flow may be directed from potentially slumping banks, or to where it may cause increased erosion, or increased circulation in ponds, fish shelters, etc. Height, distance into the flow, shape and angle are all important in determining the effect. Scattered boulders may be effective – but should only be used in stream types where they occur naturally.

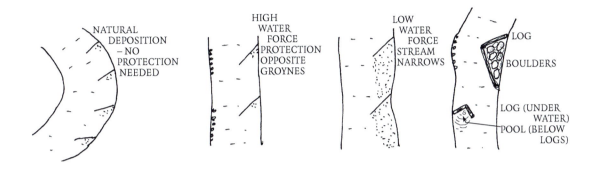

Fig. 8.13. *Groynes (deflectors) for directing flow and, in some habitats, narrowing channels.*

Bars (berms) may be inserted (on convex, or to-become-convex bends), and may either be colonised by vegetation naturally, or be planted (Fig. 8.14). These grade into specific 'planters', which when inserted are already bearing vegetation. The material may be degradable, if the plants are likely to remain in the stream, or be for example stone, in a stream with less satisfactory (e.g. more scouring) habitat. In urban streams, or by rural buildings, planters can be used to break up harsh concrete outlines (as can shrubs, where appropriate, above water).

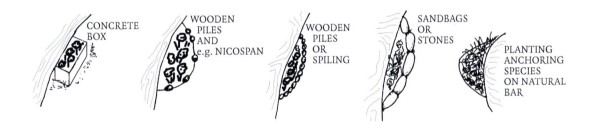

Fig. 8.14. *Berms, planters, etc.*

Widened bays can be inserted into streams (Fig. 8.15), giving shallow-water habitat for plants and animals. Conversely, if livestock trampling makes shallowed areas too large and too wide, the stream can be fenced off.

Vegetation within the channel, as that on the banks, is wanted as the 'proper' state of the traditional river (for communities and quantities see Chapter 4). It provides habitat and cover for mammals, birds, fish and lower animals, food for the herbivores among them, cleans the water passing through it, and may help stabilise substrate. Vegetation protects bed and lower bank from physical stresses like storm flows and boats. Two- or multi-stage channels can bear a variety of communities (Fig. 8.16).

Species planted in streams should be those proper to the river type (Chapter 4). Species should NOT be introduced to look pretty (e.g. iris, pink water lily) or even to purify (e.g. reed). The native local species should be used, and if at all possible, the local variants of those species. The species used must be those that can anchor and root in the substrate and bank provided (unless they are put in planters), and they must be appropriate for the water quality.

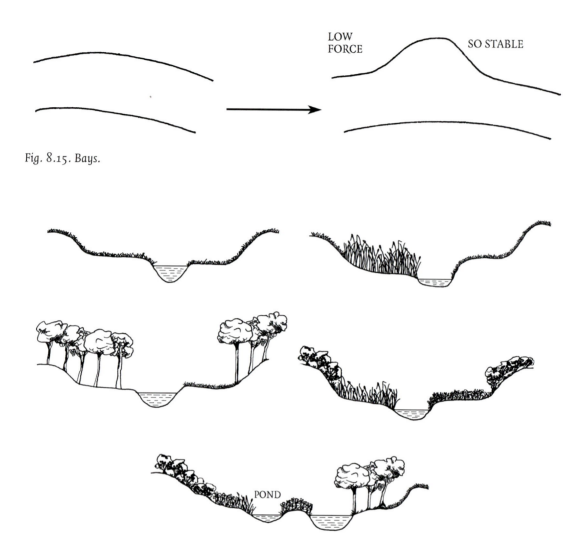

Fig. 8.15. *Bays.*

Fig. 8.16. *Multi-stage channels and variations in vegetation.*

It is not sensible to plant *Ranunculus* or other pollution-sensitive species in a badly polluted chalk stream. *Potamogeton crispus* or equivalent (see Chapters 4, 6) should be used instead.

Watching over river plant communities is nothing new. Lately, it has been done mainly for conservation, but for a long time it was practised to improve the vegetation for salmonids, in rivers of high angling quality. It is unproven whether *Elodea canadensis* really is 'that evil weed' for angling, but it could be and was removed annually, and *Ranunculus* substituted, even in slow, deep, silted places where *Ranunculus* transplants were unlikely to live for long.

Dredging to remove deposited silt is done intermittently in clay rivers (usually every 4–10 years), usually less in lowland sandstone rivers, and less again in other river types. Routine maintenance dredging of this type should never break the hard bed of the river. Recovery can then be very quick, often within a few months and – even with rather less care – seldom in over two years.

9 LAW and PLANNING

(little specialist expertise required)

SUMMARY

The Environment Agency (EA) (from 1989 to 1996 the National Rivers Authority) and, as appropriate, the Internal Drainage Boards have control over every river and ditch in England and Wales. This power is granted under (currently) 1995 and 1991 Acts and a 1988 Statutory Instrument. With this control goes a duty of conservation and enhancement, of both the natural and the cultural heritage. Consent must be sought for enhancement (development) works by landowners, and the EA may be able to supply free advice, and, sometimes, even meet the cost of a scheme. In Scotland, the Scottish Environment Protection Agency (SEPA) is responsible (from 1989 to 1996 various organisations, all reporting to the Scottish Office, catered for different functions of rivers). Environmental Statements are legally required for many types of scheme in or near rivers. These discuss alternative ways of securing a given aim (e.g. to increase flood protection for a village); their environmental impacts; the option chosen, and why; and the expected environmental effects and the measures to be taken to reduce damage and enhance habitat.

Introduction

All rivers, streams, ditches, drains, cuts, culverts, dykes, sluices and sewers in England and Wales, through which water flows, come under the Water Acts, currently the Water Resources Act 1991, the Land Drainage Act 1991 and the Water Industry Act 1991, brought into the Environment Act, 1995. (These will no doubt be superseded in due course.) No English or Welsh watercourse is outside the provisions of the law. The brook in the garden, the ditch in the field are in theory as under the laws as are the Thames or Severn, though in practice more attention (per mile) is given to the larger rivers. Scottish law differs, and in some respects (e.g. duty over little rills on mountain and moorland) is less rigorous.

The Environment and Water Acts

The Environment Agency, the body with the most power over rivers, was established under the **Environment Act 1995**, taking powers from the 1991 Water Resources Act. The authority itself, contrary to popular belief, is neither the buildings nor the officials in them. It is 8–15 people, three appointed by the Minister of Agriculture, the rest by the Secretary of State for the Environment. Its functions include:

- water resources;
- pollution control;
- flood defence and land drainage;
- fisheries;
- navigation;
- and any other subject allocated to it.

The Internal Drainage Boards (IDBs) cover the lower-lying parts of the country (under the **Land Drainage Act**). The Environment Agency, may become, or cease to be, an IDB in any given area. The IDBs are the senior bodies, but now are supervised by the EA, need to apply to the EA in various circumstances, and may even be directed by the EA. An IDB exercises general supervision over all matters relating to the drainage of land within its district, and has various other powers, and various obligations (it may not, for instance, obstruct navigation without the consent of the appropriate Navigation Authority).

The third 1991 Water Act, the **Water Industry Act**, deals with water supply and sewerage, impinging on the rivers as:

1 Abstraction for supply, which may lower levels in aquifer and river, and may alter flow regime (e.g. by inserting flow gates, reservoirs).

2 Discharge of polluting effluent from sewage treatment works (STWs). These pollute. They also enhance flow, though having a stabilising effect on discharges, since they run perpetually. In the natural river (unless it is spring-fed) flow is more dependent on rainfall.

Pollution of waters is an offence under this Water Industry Act; this includes pollution from STW effluents. There are two important exceptions, farming pollution if the farmer is practising 'good husbandry' as laid down by the Ministry of Agriculture, and re-surfacing roads (constructing new roads, however, is not excepted). This act is not concerned with the limits of abstraction, i.e., how low river levels may fall. Specified minimum flows come under the Water Resources Act and the EA.

The Environment Act 1995 makes minor amendments to the earlier Acts, such as the 1991 Water Acts, the 1990 Environment Protection Act, the 1989 and 1974 Control of Pollution Acts, but in general incorporates these into current legislation. Over the years, the environmental component has been strengthened. Even pollution must now be considered in relation to conservation.

The Environmental Protection Act 1990

Under the Environmental Protection Act 1990, under powers from the Secretary of State, Her Majesty's Inspectorate of Pollution (for England and Wales, and River Purification Boards, etc. in Scotland) controls emissions of substances into the environment: not to clean up rivers, but to control input. It prescribes what substances are to be subject to control (of concentration, period of release, etc.), to prevent or minimise their release, and to render these and other pollutants harmless (using the best available techniques not entailing excessive cost).

Conservation duties

The EA and the IDBs, under their respective acts, have a duty to such extent as they consider generally desirable to promote the conservation and enhancement of natural beauty and amenity of inland waters and their associated land (so including banks, flood plains, etc.), to conserve the flora and fauna which depend on the aquatic environment, and (less for IDBs) to promote the use of these places for recreation.

Under the acts, flora, fauna and geological and physiographic features of special interest are to be conserved and enhanced. Regard shall be taken to the desirability of protecting and conserving buildings, and sites and objects of archaeological, architectural or historic interest. Any effect which the EA or IDB proposals would have on the beauty or amenity of any rural or urban area, or on the flora, fauna, features, buildings, sites or objects is also to be considered. Research is to be carried out in respect of this, as well as the other functions of the EA and IDBs. When works may affect Sites of Special Scientific Interest, the relevant conservation organisations must first be consulted (except in an emergency).

These acts, therefore, give wide powers to the EA and to the IDBs. It is they who decide what is generally desirable: featureless channels, or good-quality rivers like those shown in Fig. 9.1. It is the EA and the IDBs who decide whether considering conservation interests means considering them ridiculous, or means deciding these are in principle essential and in practise should always be applied to some degree. For the first time it is open to the EA to carry out schemes for restoring rivers solely to improve the quality of the river. Previously such enhancement was allowed only as part of a wider scheme involving for example land drainage.

The EA generally allocates up to 5% of the cost of new schemes (for flood control, drainage, etc.) for conservation, sometimes averaging 5%, with some schemes gaining even 10%. This funding is not laid down in the act, so is optional, and the EA can choose whether to provide it. Enhancement schemes depend on the goodwill of the Authorities; such goodwill is partly a

response to public opinion and the views of conservation organisations. That goodwill does exist is a tribute to the EA (and its predecessor the National Rivers Authority), and its sense of public responsibility.

All features praised in this book, whether bank architecture, dippers or earthen wharves, are permitted to exist under the acts, but that existence is not prescribed or guaranteed. It depends on the goodwill of the EA and the IDBs, and their ability to combine a high-quality river with appropriate flood defence, land drainage, etc. The most appropriate flood defence is obtained by whole catchment planning. Major intrusive schemes at individual and multiple trouble spots are less satisfactory. Unfortunately, water shortage is insufficiently considered in the acts, so the wisdom of draining water from the land (where it acts as a buffer source for capacity) when water resources are becoming short, is not addressed.

Water protection areas and nitrate-sensitive areas are in the acts; these are intended to protect the quality of drinking water. Buffer strips are not in the acts; these are intended to protect the quality of the river water and the river. When river water is used for supply, the two overlap.

Fig. 9.1. Desirable rivers: (a) excellent pristine structure and diversity, (b) hillfort and minor river fort guarding river village – historic value, (c) old bridge leading to Water Street and town – historic value.

THE MAFF (Ministry of Agriculture, Fisheries and Food) Habitat Scheme.
Water fringe areas, 1994

> 'The fields alongside England's rivers and lakes are among the country's most important wildlife habitats. They can be managed to support a wide range of waterside flora and fauna. Of equal importance, the management of this land also has a great effect on the plant and animal life within the adjoining rivers and lakes.'

MAFF's excellent scheme offers money for riverside land in the following ways:

1A *Permanent grassland withdrawn from production:* No agricultural production. Mow in August or develop scrub. No chemicals or manure (except specified herbicides for specified pest species, e.g. giant hogweed). Maintain existing trees and hedges, and obtain advice on planting more (of local species). Maintain aquatic habitats. No new land drainage. No damage to buildings, stone walls or features of archaeological or historical interest. Increased public access needs agreement.

1B *Arable land withdrawn from production:* Establish permanent mixed grass sward of approved British species. Otherwise as 1A above.

2A *Managing extensive grassland on existing permanent grass:* Maintain grassland. Graze (but not solely with horses) and avoid poaching (trampled and disturbed soil). No cutting before 1 July. No extra feed for stock. Otherwise as 1A above, starting at 'No chemicals'.

2B *Managing extensive grassland on currently arable land:* Establish permanent mixed grass sward of approved British species and maintain it, as described above.

3 *Supplement for raising the water level.*

This scheme shows a clear grasp of riverside principles, since plant and animal habitat, cultural heritage, and the cleaning of incoming run-off water are all enhanced or preserved. Wet riverside grassland is traditional, species-rich, valuable for waterfowl and other animals, and its restoration is much wanted. Intermittent woodland, especially wet woodland, is also desirable, and this scheme fosters both, without permitting cultural damage. It is greatly to be hoped that much land will be brought into this scheme.

Legal powers and duties of the Environment Agency and the internal drainage boards

The EA has to classify the quality of waters, and to specify that quality (though licences may be given to pollute anywhere). Water protection, or nitrate-sensitive areas, may be designated, and the EA then specifies the management intended to achieve these ends. The EA has to protect against pollution the surface and underground waters from which it takes, or is authorised to take, water.

For resources, the EA is to conserve, redistribute or otherwise augment water resources, secure their proper use, and develop them. The EA may decide the minimum acceptable flows in rivers, and then specify that these will pertain. The flow will not be less than that needed for public health and other lawful uses including agriculture, industry, water supply, navigation, fisheries and land drainage. This last, regrettably, does NOT include conservation, river quality or river water quality. Minimum standards for those do not come under the act.

The EA is in control of abstraction. Only small amounts of water (less than 5 cubic metres at a time, or less than 20 cubic metres in 24 hours) may be taken from a watercourse without applying to the EA. Regrettably, this section excepts the huge amounts lost in land drainage (when water is taken from the land and hustled through lowered-flow channels to the sea), and the further amounts lost through irrigation (when water is taken back to the land from the river – spray irrigation needs EA consent, though). Existing mining, quarrying, engineering, building, etc. may also abstract water without EA consent.

For flood defence, the EA has a general function to carry out, and oversee, river works.

The EA has general control of fisheries, with a duty to maintain, improve and develop salmon, trout, other freshwater fish and eel fisheries. The duty to improve river habitat for fish, i.e. to have suitable flows, substrates, depths, water quality, vegetation, etc., is usually seen as less important than other functions. If it had been overriding, channelisation would be rare.

Various other powers are given to the EA by the act, of which the most relevant here are the power to raise money (as general drainage charges, and special drainage charges for agriculture, which should not be charged solely because the power exists!), acquire fisheries, lay pipes, apply measures for the control of pollution, and, significantly, make by-laws (see below).

The IDBs have similar but lesser powers, exercising general supervision over all matters relating to the drainage of land within their districts, subject to their supervision by the EA. IDBs can maintain existing works, improve them or construct new works for drainage, flood prevention and flood minimising. Within their districts, IDBs alone may touch the watercourses. It is irrelevant who owns or has rights over the land, it is for IDBs to carry out, consent to, or prohibit works in watercourses, and the erection or alteration of weirs, mill dams, etc., or culverts likely to affect flow, except those under a Navigation Authority or another act. (Similar powers are taken by the EA under by-laws.) IDBs may require works for maintaining the flow of a watercourse, and may order the cleaning (clearing: not pollution control), protection or construction of ditches, and, like the EA, may raise drainage rates.

The EA has much power: power to prohibit, power to do. Much of what the EA does is permissive, not mandatory, e.g. the duty to maintain lies with the landowner – except that the EA prohibits such maintenance without its consent.

Basically, anyone wanting to do anything in, beside or by a river, whether this is planting a willow wand, providing habitat for moorhen nests or discharging effluent from a new factory, must obtain the consent of the EA (or IDB, as relevant), and must pay £50 for each alteration requested: though in practice telephone advice from the EA on enhancement does not cost £50 for each plant planted! The EA (or IDB) has to give consent if the proposal will not endanger river or flood flow.

Statutory Instrument 1217

The Land Drainage Improvement Works (Assessment of Environmental Effects) Regulations 1988, Statutory Instrument 1988 No. 1217 specifies that drainage organisations may not carry out improvement (improved outwards movement of water) works until environmental investigations have been done, if the works, by their nature, size or location, are likely to have significant effects on the environment:

1 an Environmental Statement must be available for the public to inspect, and to buy; and

2 advertisements shall be placed in at least two local newspapers, describing the works and the legal rights of the public.

This is a safeguard against river mutilation: but only if the drainage body values river quality.

Scottish law

The Scottish Environment Protection Agency has similar but not the same duties and powers as the EA. It also has a duty to have regard to the desirability of conservation and enhancement in similar terms, but also to include natural heritage, and the promotion of water cleanliness. Before 1996, river functions were divided between several organisations (including the River Purification Boards, Rural Affairs and Civil Engineering and Water Services). Unlike in England and Wales, farming pollution may (not must) be considered an offence even if the farmer is following approved practices.

By-laws

By-laws are made by each EA region (Anglia, Severn-Trent, Thames, Yorkshire, etc.). They are as comprehensive as the acts, and more detailed.

There is an old English and Welsh separation between the 'Main River', the main water-course channels, and the minor brooks and rills. Control by local and national organisations came first over the main rivers, and these still have the most control, but power to control lesser channels has recently been shifting from individuals to authorities. Main Rivers are shown on maps in EA offices. (Roughly, any channel over 8 m wide is probably a Main River and any over 4 m wide may be so.) Outside Main Rivers, the EA may prohibit anything that might affect flow (dams, weirs, water mills, culverts (pipes), etc.). Within the Main River, doing (virtually) anything within 8 m of the river is prohibited, even repairing an existing building of historic value is prohibited unless EA consent is given (and the £50 paid). Equally prohibited are diverting rivers or floods, any work to river banks (including repairs) and any structures or earthworks on the area marked on EA maps as flood plain. Low fences, etc., for agriculture are, however, excepted. In addition, local government may have by-laws prohibiting other things near rivers, so they also must be contacted.

This is comprehensive, and indeed brutal for its effect on river quality. However, the EA, with its duty of river enhancement, may not just grant permission, but just possibly may pay for, or even carry out, proposed enhancement works.

By-laws may cover all detailed aspects of river works, with the EA prohibiting, for example:
- cutting or removing turf, etc. from banks;
- tunnelling or draining in or under river or bank;
- dredging or removing soil or shingle from or near the river;
- endangering bank stability or interfering with banks (except for EA-approved livestock drinking);
- endangering or interfering with (including dumping rubbish or taking vehicles on) any EA property, bridge, drainage works, etc.;
- putting or permitting obstructions which may impede flow, such as fallen trees, debris, soil or rubbish ('obstruct' is not defined); the debris dams so important for river quality should keep within permissible 'obstruction';
- planting trees or shrubs close to the river;
- altering the level or direction of flow in, into or out of rivers (except for lawful navigation, e.g. at locks) or interfering with river control works (see note on fallen trees, above – restoration of flow may require alteration, here).

Statutory quality objectives

The legislation permitting objectives was set in the 1991 Water Resources Act and the 1990 Environment Protection Act, and the parameters for each objective have been set by EU and national decisions. Various statutory and non-statutory river classes and standards are in operation. The EA has a general duty to achieve and maintain the set objectives, which came into practice in 1993. The Secretary of State defines stretches of water, specifying their use-related and EU class and the target date by which the set standards should be achieved. These use-related (non-statutory) classes are:

- Basic amenity
- General ecosystem
- Special ecosystem
- Salmonid fishery
- Cyprinid fishery (coarse fish)
- Migratory fishery
- Commercial marine fishery
- Commercial harvesting of shellfish

The two statutory objectives to be started first are Fisheries Ecosystems, and the Surface Water Directive (on drinking water standards).

While it is good that attention should be paid, in law, to river quality, it is much to be hoped that this legislation will be very slow to come in. The law's idea of a good river is all too plainly not the traditional clean-water river with much plant and animal life. Considering the very low standard of fisheries now thought acceptable (compared with those of the past), the general river habitat, if based on these, is hardly likely to improve. The proposed use of 1990 river parameters as a base-line below which no river should deteriorate shows the thinking. 1990 was a drought year, so there was less water in the rivers, less dilution of pollution, and therefore higher concentrations of pollutants.

The chemical standards dissolved oxygen, biological oxygen demand and ammonia (total and ionised) and pH, plus zinc and copper, modified by EU directives on nitrates, etc., with less reliance on other substances. Ecologically, only invertebrates may override this, i.e. only pollution picked up by invertebrates is considered to be pollution, not that picked up by mammals, birds, vegetation, or diatoms, etc.

In this area, therefore, reliance must instead be placed (a) on the conservation sections of the EA, conservation organisations, and individuals, whose standards may far surpass those of the law; and (b) future EU directives, which, it may be hoped, will raise standards.

Environmentally Sensitive Areas (ESAs)

The Agriculture Act 1986 permitted the designation and management of environmentally sensitive areas (ESAs). This can be done if it appears to the Minister desirable, in any area, to conserve or enhance natural beauty, to conserve flora, fauna, or geological or physiographical features, or to protect buildings or other man-made structures, and if this conservation can be effected by maintaining or changing the agricultural methods used on the land.

The act provides for agreements with the landowners, etc., by which they are paid to manage the land in order to conserve or enhance these features. The pioneer of such legislation is in the Wildlife and Countryside Act 1981, for the protection of habitat and species. Environmentally Sensitive Areas have money available for specifically conservation work in the first years of an agreement.

Environmentally Sensitive Areas are therefore to do with land management for agriculture. However, rivers flow across agricultural land, and once it is recognised that rivers also are part of our heritage and need protection or enhancement, Environmentally Sensitive Area agreements may also specify river management. Environmentally Sensitive Area agreements are specific to each site (the protection of e.g. chalk grassland containing archaeological sites requiring different procedures to the protection of e.g. the Norfolk Broads.) BUFFER STRIPS, in the form of open grassland margins on the edges of arable fields where they adjoin watercourses or ditches, MAY BE SPECIFIED, which is excellent. It is to be hoped more diverse and effective buffer strips will enter Environmentally Sensitive Area agreements later, and that such things as winding channels will also come in.

Planning

Rivers receive their water from the land, and flow over the land, so hydrologically the two are connected and planning and management must cover both.

Floodwater exists and will continue to exist. As development continues , leading to swifter and swifter run-off, so flash floods (and their waters) will increase. There are two (overlapping) courses of action: planning the water movements in the catchment as a whole, or curing the trouble at the site of the trouble.

Rivers have been so altered by people in the last century, that, generally speaking, it is these interferences and not the natural functions of the river which should be blamed for unwelcome floods.

Floods increase with:

1 more intensive farming, water running more easily from large smooth surfaces and from bare soil;

2 more roads and settled areas, where water cannot sink into the soil;

3 straighter, smoother and lower-lying rivers, hurtling water down;

4 loss of flood plains to development;

5 raising land level (e.g. by waste disposal, hastening run-off).

It is better to stop floods getting worse by control of land use (particularly by stopping new housing in flood plains) than by ever-increasing traditional engineering, causing ever-increasing damage to the rivers. The former is usually better socially as well as environmentally; and is usually cheaper in both capital works (new major works) and for channel maintenance (which, not surprisingly, becomes more expensive the more the channels are forced out of their natural pattern (see e.g. Fig. 3.65, p. 51).

Flood defence may be:

1 barriers to floodwater moving to the protected part, the most ancient means;

2 deepening the river so the floodwater remains within the channel;

3 managing the channel so that the flood is slow and low and any excess water is stored where it is, in itself, of value.

By proper planning of the whole river, floodwater should move to places, and at speeds, calculated to give, at most a situation with water sitting quietly below house level, and definitely not the situation shown in Fig. 10.58(a), p. 284.

Surface water, ground water, and land use are all influenced and changed by humans, and their interaction must be understood so that the river corridor can be planned for appropriate land use, development, and control of urban run-off – and for the use of vegetation in the river, and the vegetation and appropriate soil conditions in the buffer strip, to clean the water.

It is important to maintain both the natural and the cultural features that give a locality its 'sense of place', its heritage value. The components of the riverscape vary from topography to waterlilies, from dragonflies to tow-paths. This applies equally to all living components, the appropriate plants and animals finding their 'home' there and the people finding the distinctive habitat. To people, the riverscape conveying that sense of place may be wide, as on the Scottish moors, where the river may be a focus, but is only a small part of the view, or it may be small, as within an alder carr, where all that can be seen is the stream and the trees within maybe 10 m of the stream. There is, therefore, no one recommendable width of river corridor to plan for, as being the optimum for sense of place. Nor is there one that is the optimum for habitat, legal or financial considerations. In downstream reaches, 100 m can be a convenient width for habitat, but since the corridor is for water purification as well as habitat, it is just as important to have a protected corridor round brooks and rills, even if it has to be narrower.

River corridors should receive formal protection for functions varying from storage of flood water to improving water quality, preserving historic and archaeological sites and conserving natural habitat and 'sense of place'. The natural capacity of aquatic ecosystems is not without limit. Whether to retain otters or to transport water, schemes must keep within the most sensitive of those limits.

If the aim is not reached exactly, the result will more often be worse than better for river quality. In order to achieve good-quality rivers, therefore, excellent ones should be aimed at. This means expert knowledge of rivers. A planner who has never seen a river better than that in Fig. 9.2(a) may well end with one like that in Fig. 9.2(b). One who has studied a good alluvial wetlands stream (see Fig. 9.3(a)) may still be at a loss as to how to restore a good moorland stream, which should look like that shown in Fig. 9.3(b). No British rivers look like that in Fig. 9.1(a), but it is as well to remember that such do exist.

Environmental planning has greatly improved in Britain in the past decade, but it is still flawed. Firstly, demand for river 'restoration' has exceeded knowledge of the result aimed for, and secondly, the 5(–10)-year monitoring of schemes to check how far that which was planned has come to be, is inadequate or indeed absent. Only with such checks can effective plans be made.

Fig. 9.2. (a) A third-class river, (b) an attempt to copy it leading to a fourth-class one ((a), from Haslam, 1990).

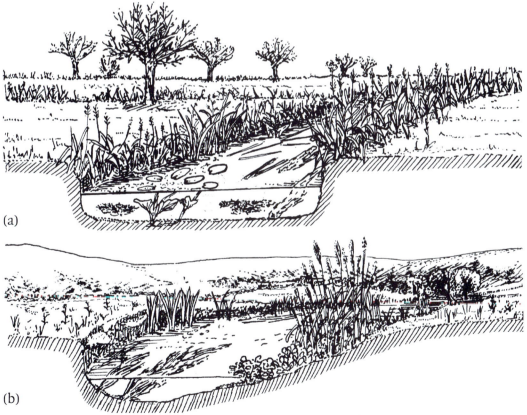

Fig. 9.3. (a) Satisfactory alluvial stream, (b) moorland stream (Haslam, 1987).

Expertise will accumulate at ever-increasing speed over the next decade, and planners will do well to practise on places of low habitat value, and leave those of higher habitat value to be rehabilitated later. In other words, DO NOT INTERFERE WITH NOW-GOOD HABITAT, merely enhance the bad rivers with the available expertise (unless, of course, major works destroying good habitat are being demanded, in which case the best option is to aim to reproduce the same habitat).

Environmental statements must be prepared by the EA or IDB before major, and often minor, works are undertaken (see Statutory Instrument 1217, above), and some environmental assessment is usually made for the remainder. Before carrying out the works, the environmental position must be considered – by the EA (or IDB) and by those members of the public who so wish. In some EA areas environmental agreement and signatures are needed before work starts, though of course cost as well as habitat has to be a consideration.

The Statutory Instrument 1217 (requiring Environmental Statements) covers:

- Bank protection for drainage/flood defence
- Channel renewal, piling, walls, etc.
- Sluices and flow-control structures
- Weed cutting that alters water level
- Major flood alleviation where works can be individually isolated
- Major flood alleviation with new flood or diversion channels
- New flood embankments in flood plain at a distance from watercourse
- Culverts
- Dredging
- Flood alleviation
- Weirs and weir alterations
- Flood storage reservoirs
- New locks with impounding

It does not cover:

- Bridges
- Navigation lay-bys or marinas
- Modifications where water levels are not affected
- Minor works in flood plain at a distance from watercourse
- Low-flow amelioration works
- Channel access ramps.
- Aqueducts
- Existing locks
- Lock houses
- Sanitary stations
- Flow gauging stations

However, some of these need local authority planning permission, and this in turn, though mainly for larger works, may require an environmental statement. Others need permission from the appropriate navigation authority.

The statutory instrument requires the environmental statements to be made, but does not require these to be implemented, nor follow-up monitoring to be done. The Statements describe the purpose and site of the works proposed, the alternative schemes considered, their expected environmental effects, and the reasons for choosing the selected schemes. The existing environment is considered, with (in full) the expected environmental effects of the chosen option.

The remedial measures to be taken in planning, design and construction are outlined, including explaining why some measures will not be taken (e.g. too expensive). The remaining predicted adverse effects are given, and any follow-up monitoring is mentioned.

The following features should be considered, and discussed if relevant. For each, it should be queried whether the site is appropriate for the proposed works, what effect they will have on the feature, and on human use and resources, and what measures should be taken to conserve, improve or enhance the river.

- Land
- Water
- Land use and landscape characters
- Habitats
- Transport
- Amenity
- Recreation and fishing
- Sewerage
- Water supplies
- Telecommunications
- Air pollution
- Water pollution
- Noise and vibration
- Waste disposal
- Risk and hazard

The agreed environmental measures should be described in fair detail in environmental statements, and in great detail to the construction company (who should also have an environmental officer – from the EA or elsewhere – on site much of the time, as the construction workers cannot be expected to tell exactly where a tree, groyne, etc. should be placed, and inexact placing may mean failure).

It is most important that ECOLOGY be considered, not just amenity. A group of alien trees can look nice, and superficially resemble a nineteenth-century painting, but the habitat, flora and fauna remain incorrect.

10 HISTORIC and RECENT CULTURAL HERITAGE

(no specialist expertise required)

SUMMARY

The cultural heritage of rivers (their human ecology) should rank near-equal in value with their natural heritage. People have used and been dependent on the river from time immemorial, and many river-linked features of the last few hundred years remain today. They, and their present counterparts, should be found, identified and preserved. This conservation may be as 'monuments' but may also be by maintaining ancient patterns in modern uses (e.g. mill field to Millfield Industrial Estate). Evolving landscapes maintain the past, razed and re-developed ones do not. Examples of the principal river uses are depicted.

Introduction

Rivers have been used by people since time immemorial. Much still remains, above ground, from at least the past few centuries. This past use is often unrecognised, so the features are liable to destruction not just by the careless and indifferent, but by careful, conservation-minded people doing their best to enhance riverscapes – and destroy the irreplaceable. To replace a chalk stream may be difficult and expensive but, in the 1990s, is possible. To replace a Middle Ages earthen village wharf is impossible. It is gone, and has probably gone without even being photographed.

Human dependence on rivers has changed, over the past two centuries, from being direct and immediate to being indirect and distant; consequently, the present dependence is often forgotten. Water is not fetched from a spring or stream, but taken from a tap leading from water far away, and quite likely from several sources, at that. The tap is not thought of as an extension of the river. Instead of supplying fish and fowl for the table, the river's main rôle in food production is to drain (and irrigate) farmland. Few think of this as a dependence on the river. Few people travel on the river for business. There are innumerable leisure craft, but leisure is not considered to be in the mainstream of life, so again the work of the river is distanced from 'real life'. Mill wheels rarely turn for water power. That more water than ever before is used in power production is known to only few. This distancing of people and river has led to ignorance and lack of appreciation.

Rivers show how people used to live and work. Much of our present is rooted in the past, and only by understanding that past can the present environment be understood – here, boats arrived with meal and malt, there, stands the holy well which helped sore eyes, that was the village supply channel, there, the fish ponds, the flood-protection works, and over yonder, the water mill, in whose field, now the Millfield Industrial Estate, the present industrialists still daily go to work. The riverside is not static, but dynamic. Gradual change, from path to lane, from mill to factory, maintains the ancient pattern. Wholesale change destroys this living pattern and heritage for ever.

All British lowland rivers, and most highland ones, are in their present forms because of specific types of management.

There is no current organisation concerned with this field, though several (including English Heritage, the Countryside Commission, the National Trust and the Environment Agency) are concerned with small parts, e.g. fish ponds, locks.

Place names

These are heritage! They should be checked – English ones in *The Concise English Dictionary of English Place Names* (Ekwall, 1960). The following Tables 10.1 to 10.6 give some examples:

Table 10.1. Some English place names connected with streams

OE = Old English; ON = Old Norse; ME = Middle English

aewelm.: OE 'river source', e.g. Ewen (Glos.).

a: ON 'river', e.g. Aby (Lincs.) Ambleside (Cumbria).

baece, bece: OE 'stream', 'valley', e.g. Beachampton (Bucks.), Evesbatch (Herefordshire).

baeth, bathum: OE 'bath', e.g. Bath (Avon), from at least 796 AD, Moorbath Dorset).

bekks: ON 'stream', 'beck', e.g. Coldbeck, Beckermet ('stream junction') (Cumbria).

broc: OE, 'brook', 'stream', in place names after 730 AD, in river and field names only, earlier, e.g. Begbroke (Oxon).

burna: OE 'stream' pre-730 AD, (earlier, brunna), e.g. Burnham (Essex), Bourne (Cambs.), Washbourne (Glos.).

celde: OE 'spring', e.g. Bapchild (Kent).

ea: OE 'river', e.g. Eton (Bucks.), Pevensey (Sussex), Eamont (river junction) (Cumbria).

fleot fleote: OE 'estuary', 'small stream', e.g. Fleet (Dorset), Swinefleet (Yorks.).

flode: OE 'channel of water', e.g. Cheselade (Somerset).

funta: OE 'spring', from Latin *fons, fontis* and apparently used for a spring with Roman building-work, differing to those to which OE *well* was applied, e.g. Chalfont (Bucks.).

gemythe: OE 'river junction', e.g. Eamont (Cumbria).

hyth: OE 'landing place on a river', 'inland port', e.g. Lambeth, Chelsea (London), Earith (Cambs.).

kelda: ON 'spring', northern counties and Scotland, e.g. Keldhome (Yorks.), Threlkeld (Cumbria).

lad: OE, *lode:* ME one meaning is 'watercourse', 'aqueduct', open drain in fenny districts, e.g. Whaplode (Lincs.).

laecc, laece: OE 'stream', 'bog', e.g. Lache (Cheshire).

loekr: ON 'brook', e.g. Leake (Notts.)

pol, pull: OE 'pool'; *pyll:* OE 'tidal creek', ?'small stream', e.g. Pool (Cheshire), Walpole (pool, oxbow, by stream during flood) (Suffolk).

rith, rithig: OE 'small stream', e.g. Ryde (Isle of Wight), Sawtry (Hyde), Reed (Yorks.).

sic: OE 'small stream', tiny watercourses, common in fields, but too small to be more than rare in minor settlement names, e.g. Sitch, Seech (as names of fields).

sik: ON as last, e.g. Sykehouse (Yorks.).

staeth: OE 'landing place', e.g. Stathe (Somerset), Statham (Cheshire).

waeter: OE 'water', 'river', 'lake', e.g. Bourton-on-the-Water (on R.Windrush, Glos.).

well, wella, welle: OE 'spring', 'stream', e.g. Well-under-Heywood (Salop), Upwell (Cambs).

Table 10.2. Some English place names connected with crossings

Brycg: OE 'bridge', e.g. Bridge (Kent), Breighton (Yorks.), Handbridge (Cheshire). Also 'causeway', e.g. Bridgend (Lincs.), Ricebridge (probably 'brushwood causeway') (Durham).

faer: OE 'passage', probably 'difficult passage', e.g. Denver (of Danes) (Norfolk), Laver (at a place a Roman road was lost for 2 miles, perhaps in marsh) (Essex).

ferja: ON, ferrye, ME, 'ferry' e.g. Ferriby (Lincs.), Ferry bridge (Yorks.).

ford: OE 'ford'. Probably the second most frequent topographical term. Some have become major towns, e.g. Bradford, Hereford, Guildford, Oxford. Most were crossing of only local significance, e.g. Fordham (Cambs.).

cont.

Many compound names describe the ford, e.g.:
'bright', e.g. Shereford (Norfolk)
'broad', e.g. Bradford (Avon, etc.)
'deep', e.g. Defford (Worcs.)
'double', e.g. Twyford (Bucks. etc.)
'foul', e.g. Fulford (Devon, etc.)
'hidden', e.g. Durnford (Suffolk)
'long', e.g. Longford (Beds. etc.)
'red', e.g. Radford (Devon, etc.)
'rough', e.g. Rufford (Lincs., Notts.)
'shallow', e.g. Scalford (Leics.)

Other names describe the ground, e.g.:
'gravel', e.g. Gutford (Beds.)
'mud', e.g. Mudford (Somerset)
'sand', e.g. Sampford (Devon, etc.)
'stone', e.g. Stafford (Dorset)

Parts added by people are in e.g.:
'flagstone', e.g. Flawforth (Notts.)
'planks', e.g. Bretford (Warks.)
'posts', e.g. Stapleford (Cambs. etc.)
'tree-trunk', e.g. Bamford (Derbys.)

Goods carried over are shown in, e.g.:
'barley', e.g. Barford (Beds. etc.)
'chalk', e.g. Chalford (Glos.) (probably)
'charcoal', e.g. Coleford (Glos.) (probably)
'hay', e.g. Heyford (Oxon)

There are many other elements, including personal names, animals, and topographical features.

gelad: OE 'difficult river crossing', e.g. Evenlode (Oxon).

gewaed: OE 'ford' (out of use early), e.g. Wadebridge (Cornwall), Iwade ('yewtree') (Kent), Lenwade ('lane') (Norfolk).

vath: ON 'ford', e.g. Wath (Yorks.), Waithe (Lincs.). The commonest first element describes the ford, e.g. 'long', Langwathby (Cumbria), 'stone', Stenwith (Lincs.).

Table 10.3. *Some English place names indicating clean water*

NB *since clean water was the norm, the absence of mention does not mean dirty.*

Arkendale (Yorks.): 'pure, clear stream'.
Brightwell, Britwell (Berks.): 'Bright spring'.
Errington (Northumberland): 'enclosure on a bright stream'.
Fairford (Glos.): 'clear ford'.
Farewell (Staffs.): 'beautiful stream'.
Harwell (Notts.): 'pleasant stream'.
Limebrook, Lingen (Herefordshire): 'clear, beautiful stream'.
Rother (river, Sussex): 'bright river'.
Sherborne (Dorset, Glos. Hants. Yorks.): 'bright stream'.
Sherford (Norfolk, Devon): 'clear ford'.

Shirebrook (Derbys.): 'bright stream'.
Shirwell (Devon): 'clear spring'.
Skerne (river, Yorks.): 'bright, clear'.
Skinfare (river, Yorks.): 'bright stream'.
Skirbeck (Lincs.): 'bright brook'.
Tanat (river, Salop): 'brilliant river'.
Wendover (Berks.): 'white river'.
Whimple (Devon): 'white stream'.
Whitford (Devon): 'white ford'.
Winford (Somerset): 'white (holy, happy)' with 'stream torrent'.
Worf (river, Salop): 'turbid' (possibly 'winding').

Table 10.4. *Some English place names indicating coloured water*

NB *coloured water is not necessarily dirty, but polluted waters will be included in the list.*

Blackburn (Lancs.): 'dark stream'.
Blackford (Somerset): 'black ford'.
Blackfordby (Leics.): 'homestead at black ford'.
Blackwater (Dorset, Hants.): 'dark stream'.
Coldrey (Hants.): 'coal (black) brook'.
Doulting (Somerset): 'dirty river'.
Drybeck (Westmorland): 'dirty stream'.
Fortherley (Staffs.): 'slope by the dirty stream'.
Fulbeck (Lincs.), Fulbrook (Berks.): 'foul/dirty brook'.
Fulford (Somerset, etc.): 'dirty ford'.
Fulready (Warks.): 'foul/dirty brook'.
Fulwell (Durham): 'foul/dirty stream'.
Glazebrook (Lancs.): 'blue, green, grey brook'.
Harborne (Staffs.): 'dirty stream'.

Radford (Beds.): 'red-soil ford' (usually).
Radwell (Beds.): 'red spring/stream'.
Retford (Northants.): 'red ford'.
Shambrook (Beds.), Shamford (Leics.): 'muddy brook/ford'.
Shernborne (Norfolk): 'muddy brook and tun (settlement)'.
Skeckburn (Northumbria): 'muddy stream'.
Slimbridge (Glos.): 'bridge in a muddy place'.
Surfleet (Lincs.): 'sour stream'.
Tame, Thames, Teme (Oxon, etc.), Taff (Wales): 'dark river'.
Wennington (Lancs.): 'dark river'.

Table 10.5. Some English place names to do with river use

Watercress

Bilbrook (Somerset), Carlswall (Glos.), Carshalton (Surrey), Carswell (Berks.), Caswell (Northants.), Craiseland (Lincs.), Cresswall (Herefordshire), Cresswell (Derbys.), Kearsley (Lancs.), Kearnsey (Kent), Kerswell (Devon), Rib (river, Herts.), Ribbesford (Worcs.).

Waterfowl

Ducks: Andwell (Hants.), Emborne (Berks.), Enford (Wilts.), Entwhistle (Lancs.), Hendred (Berks.)

Goose: Gosbed (Suffolk), Gosford (Derbys., etc.), Gosforth (Cumbria, etc.).

Fish

Crayfish: Crabwell (Cheshire).

Eel: Ely (Cambs.), Whaplode (Lincs.)

Fish, general: Fangdale (Yorks.), Fishbourne (Sussex), Fishburn (Durham), Fishlake (Yorks.), Wembdon (Somerset)(?), Structure for catching, Yarpole (Herefordshire), Yarm (Yorks), Yarwell (Northants.).

Gudgeon: Blandford (Dorset).

Trout: Farnham (Suffolk), Rawtrey (Yorks. etc.). (?) Shottersbrook (Berks), Troutbeck (Cumbria), Trouts Dale (Yorks.).

Watering of stock

Bulls: Bulwell (Notts.)

Cows: Cole (Wilts.)

Goats: Gateford (Notts.), Gateforth (Notts.)

Horse: Bayswater (Middx)

Oxen: Oxford (Oxen).

Mill

Curborough (Staffs.), Melbourne (Derbys.), Meldreth (Cambs.), Melford (Suffolk), Melplash (Dorset), Meltham (Yorks.), Millbeck (Cumbria), Millbrook (Beds., etc.)

Weir, dam (and see fish, general, above).

Weare (Derbys.), Ware, (Herts.), Wareham (Dorset), Warford (Cheshire), Wargrave (Berks.), Warehorne (Kent), Warleigh (Somerset, etc.), Edgeware (London).

Fulling

Washburn (Yorks.).

Sheepwash

Washbourne (Glos.), Washbrooke (Suffolk) (or washing clothes).

Criminals, felons, and where they were executed (drowned)

Weybourne (Surrey), Wreigh Burn (Northants., etc.), Warnborough (Hants.), (?) Wheldrake (Yorks.).

Supernatural

Wishing-well: Elwell (Dorset), Frithwell (Oxon), Holywell (Lincs.).

Troll, goblin, water-sprite: Flawith (Yorks.), Puckeridge (Herts.), Purbrook (Hants.), Shobrooke (Devon), Shocklach (Cheshire).

Holy: Holiwell (Middx), Hakwell, Halwill (Derbys.), Holwell (Dorset), Holybourne (Hants.), Holywell (Hunts., etc.), Winford (Somerset) (or 'white', 'happy').

Prophetic: Ladbrook (Warks.).

Miscellaneous

Thralls (Slaves): Threlkeld (Cumbria).

Nuns: Nunwells Park (Isle of Wight).

Bathing: Bath (Avon).

Table 10.6. Some English place names to do with land use by water

Aldreth (Cambs.): 'landing place by the alders'.

Barnwell (Cambs.): 'spring (stream) of the warriors'.

Birdforth (Yorks.), Bridford (Devon): 'ford of the brides'.

Chillwall (Lancs.), Chilwell (Notts.): 'stream of the children'.

Chopwell (Durham): 'stream where commerce took place'.

Coleford (Glos.): 'charcoal ford'.

Creekson (Essex): 'landing place at the creek'.

Glandford (Norfolk): 'ford where sports were held'.

Harford (Devon), Hereford (Herefordshire): 'army ford'.

Harpswell (Lincs.): 'harpers' spring'.

Honeybourne (Glos.): 'stream in whose banks honey was gathered'.

Hungerford (Berks.): 'stream where there was starvation'.

Huntingford (Dorset): 'huntsmen's ford'.

Kilburn (Yorks.): 'stream by a kiln'.

Langwathby (Cumbria): 'homestead at long ford'.

Lathford (Somerset): 'beggars ford'.

Leconfield (Yorks.): 'people at the brook'.

Lotherton (Yorks.): 'people at a clean spring'.

Matlask (Norfolk): 'ash where a moot was held'.

Matlock (Derbys.): 'oak where a moot (official gathering) was held'.

cont.

Melverly (Salop): 'land by the mill ford'.

Montford (Salop): 'men's ford'.

Mottisfont (Hants.): 'spring where moots were held'.

Mutford (Suffolk): 'ford where moots were held'.

Oxford (Oxon): 'ford for oxen'.

Playford (Staffs): 'ford where sports were held'.

Quarnford (Staffs.): 'ford by a mill'.

Rotherhithe (Surrey): 'landing place where cattle were shipped'.

Salford (Oxon): 'ford over which salt was carried'.

Salterford (Northants.), Salterforth (Yorks.): 'salt-sellers ford'.

Salterhebble (Yorks.): 'salt-seller's footbridge'.

Sawtry (Hunts.): 'landing place at the salt-sellers'.

Sheepy Magna and Parva (Leics.): 'sheep river and sheep island'.

Shefford (Beds.): 'sheep ford'.

Shipbourne (Kent), Shiplake (Oxon), Shiplate (Somerset): 'sheep wash'.

Shipston on Stour (Warks.): 'tun (settlement) at a sheep wash'.

Stafford (Staffs.): 'ford by a landing place'.

Stathe (Somerset), Toxteth (Lancs.): 'landing place'.

Sykehouse (Yorks.): 'house on a stream'.

Treville (Herefordshire): 'mill, (query with a hamlet)'.

Walbrook (London), Walburn (Yorks.): 'Welsh or serf's brook'.

Walkerith (Lincs.): 'landing place of the fullers'.

Walkern (Herts.): 'fulling mill or fuller's house'.

Wansford (Yorks.): 'ford of the mobs'.

Washingborough (Lincs.): 'burg (settlement) of the people at the whirlpool'.

Westmill (Herts.): 'west mill'.

Whorlton (Durham): 'tun by the mill stream'.

Windsor (Berks.) (with): 'bank with landing-place'.

Structures and features

The rest of this chapter is concerned with physical structures, which are mainly shown in pictures. These types of structure should be looked for. Their appearance should be recorded, usually by photographs, and, if relevant, their history and historic value should be checked. They are divided according to their purpose.

The drawings come from Haslam (1991) unless otherwise acknowledged.

Water supply

Wells

Fig. 10.1

Fountains

Fig. 10.2. Simple. Also see Ornament below.

Pumps

pump-
house

Fig. 10.3.

Drinking troughs

Fig. 10.4.

Cattle-drinkers

Fig. 10.5.

Laundry

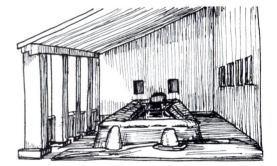

Fig. 10.6. All non-British examples.

Diversion of streams to supply settlements

(a)

Fig. 10.7. (a) Natural course base of valley to left, diversion for houses to right

Fig. 10.7 (cont.)(b) natural course to right, diversion channel left, (c) natural course on left.

Reservoirs

Fig. 10.8.

Aqueducts

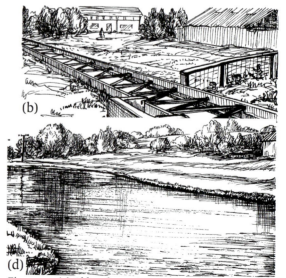

Fig. 10.9. (a) Old and massive structure, (b) modern light and small aqueduct, (c), (d) Lea Valley waterworks and New River from it to London.

Waterworks

Fig. 10.10.

Water towers

Fig. 10.11.

Abstraction

Fig. 10.12. Boreholes (and see Figs. 10.9, 10.10).

Irrigation

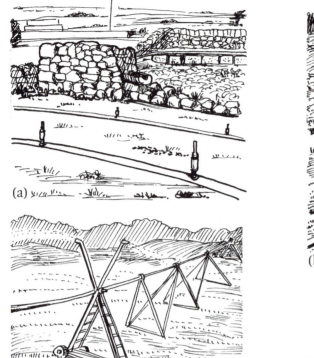

(a)

(b)

(c)

Fig. 10.13. Irrigation. (d) Traditional watering
system.

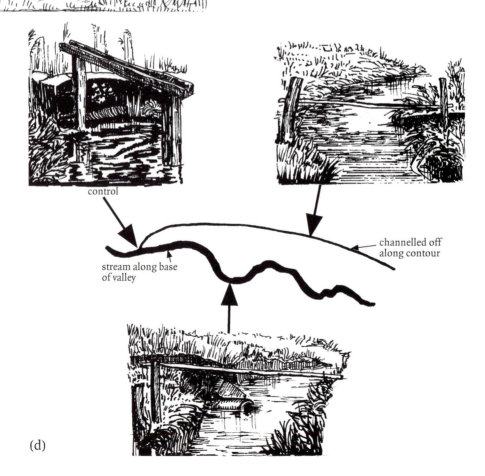

control

stream along base
of valley

channelled off
along contour

(d)

Food and materials

Fishing

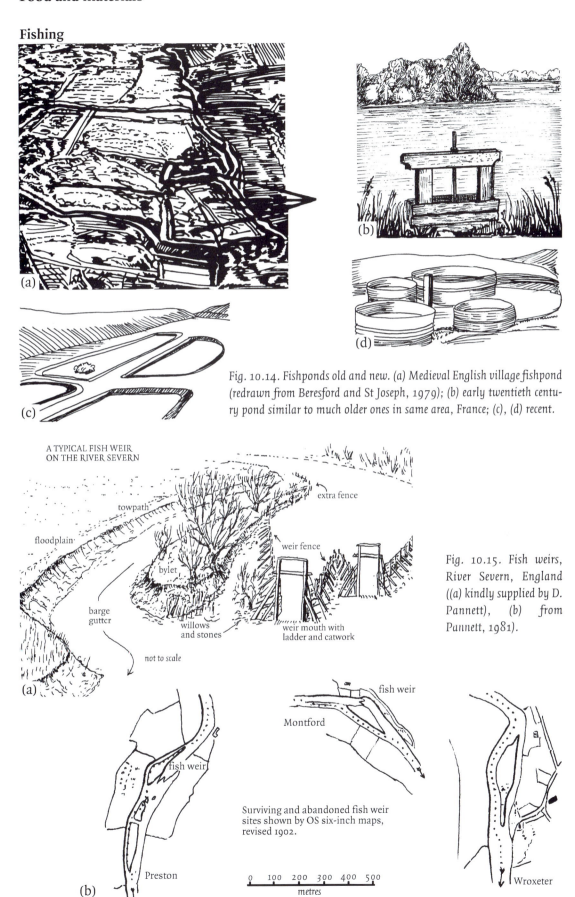

Fig. 10.14. Fishponds old and new. (a) Medieval English village fishpond (redrawn from Beresford and St Joseph, 1979); (b) early twentieth century pond similar to much older ones in same area, France; (c), (d) recent.

A TYPICAL FISH WEIR ON THE RIVER SEVERN

floodplain

towpath

extra fence

weir fence

bylet

barge gutter

willows and stones

weir mouth with ladder and catwork

not to scale

(a)

Fig. 10.15. Fish weirs, River Severn, England ((a) kindly supplied by D. Pannett), (b) from Pannett, 1981).

fish weir

Montford

fish weir

Preston

(b)

Wroxeter

Surviving and abandoned fish weir sites shown by OS six-inch maps, revised 1902.

0 100 200 300 400 500
metres

Fig. 10.16. River fishing, net and line (Haslam, 1990).

Waterfowl

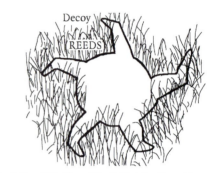

Fig. 10.17.

Sheep wash

Fig. 10.18. Sheep wash in the foreground.

Willows   Fig. 10.19.

(a) Pollards tracing line of dried stream

(c) withy bed.

(b) pollards beside brook,

Old Pollards can be used to trace the line of an extinct brook. Polls can be re-planted for new willows, or used commercially. Willows are used for baskets, cricket bats, fences, hurdles, ladders, binding and tying, various farm uses and crafts.

Reeds

(a)

Fig. 10.20. Reedbed: (a), (b) reed-ditch, (c) reed thatch.

(b)

(c)

Watercress

Rushes

Fig. 10.21.

Fig. 10.22

Table 10.7. Medicinal plants – some medicinal plants growing in or by water

The information here is inadequate for self-medication, for which see, e.g. Stuart (1982) from which most is extracted.

Acorus calamus (dried rhizome): for colic, dyspepsia; as a vernifuge, diaphoretic, slight sedative. (Probably introduced to Europe in the eleventh century: to England by 1660).

Alnus glutinosa (bark, leaves): as a tonic and astringent. Once used as gargle and for external inflammation.

Apium graveolens (fresh or dried plants, seed): as tonic, appetisers, diuretic; for nervousness, once used for rheumatism, obesity.

Filipendula ulmaria (dried flowers, rootstock): for diarrhoea, influenza, peptic ulcers, gastritis, etc.

Mentha aquatica (usually fresh herb): for diarrhoea, etc., colds.

Menyanthes trifoliata (dried leaves, usually): as gastro-intestinal tonic, liver and skin complaints.

Nasturtium aquaticum (leafy stems): as stimulant, diuretic, antipyretic, stomachic; coughs.

Nymphaea alba (usually rhizome): for sore throats, external ulcers.

Petasites hybridus (dried rhizome, usually): for skin conditions; once as antispasmodic.

Salix alba partial source of (pre-synthetic) aspirin (with meadow sweet) (for fever, sore throats, arthritis).

Scrophularia nodosa (dried rootstock, flowering tops): as poultice; for skin diseases, once for glandular and tumerous conditions.

Symphytum officinalis (fresh or dried rootstock, leaves): for gastric and duodenal ulcers, and diarrhoea, for pleurisy and bronchitis, for wounds and skin complaints, for neuralgia and rheumatism, once for fractures.

Valeriana officinalis (dried rootstock): for nervous disorders, colic, hypertension, insomnia.

Veronica beccabunga (fresh or dried plant, leaves): once for liver and gastro-intestinal complaints, externally for ulcers.

Grazing of banks

Fig. 10.23

Gravel extraction

Fig. 10.24.

In Britain, extraction is from the flood plain, not the riverbed. The abandoned pits have much potential for conservation and recreation.

Drainage
(also see Chapters 2, 3, 6)

Fig. 10.25. Drainage: (a), (b), (c) for recognition, not necessarily for emulation! (d) New 'Cut' around Fenland, to catch and divert incoming floodwater.

Power

Water mills

Fig. 10.26(a)–(n) is a series showing the development of water-based industry – watermill, water developed to steam and electrical power and mills in various stages of development to factory, farm or dwelling.

Fig. 10.26. Water-based industry: (a) water power; (b) water power developed to steam power; (c) electric power, still by, and using, the river; (d) to (n) mills. ((a), (b) Haslam, 1990; (d), sixteenth century German woodcut.)

Water power

Water power developed to steam power

Electric power, still by, and using, the river

(c)

Small 1500s mill

(d)

mill→farm

(e)

mill→farm

(f)

mill→1800s factory

(g)

mill house (dwelling separate)

(h)

mill→1980s battery chicken complex

(i)

mill→steam

(j)

mill→ factory

(k)

mill→home

(l)

mill field→industrial estate

(m)

mill-owner's house, separate from mill

(n)

River-linked industry

(a)

(b)

(c)

(d)

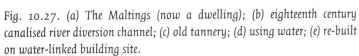

(e)

Fig. 10.27. (a) The Maltings (now a dwelling); (b) eighteenth century canalised river diversion channel; (c) old tannery; (d) using water; (e) re-built on water-linked building site.

Cooling Towers

Fig. 10.28.

Hydroelectricity

Fig. 10.29.

Transport

Water lanes

Fig. 10.30. Traffic and streams use the same Way, now tarmacced.

Wharfs, various ages

Fig. 10.31.

Fig. 10.31 (cont.)

old
woodcut

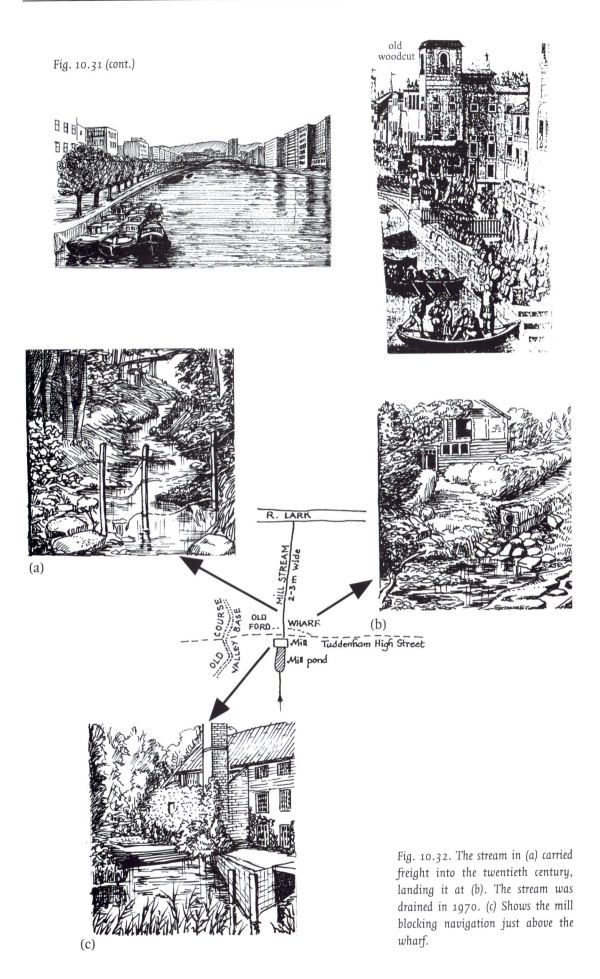

(a)

(b)

R. LARK

MILL STREAM
2–3 m wide

OLD COURSE
VALLEY BASE

OLD
FORD

WHARF

Mill

Tuddenham High Street

Mill pond

(c)

Fig. 10.32. The stream in (a) carried freight into the twentieth century, landing it at (b). The stream was drained in 1970. (c) Shows the mill blocking navigation just above the wharf.

Positions of mill and ford

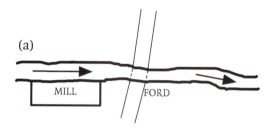

(a)

(b)

Fig. 10.33. (a) Diagrammatic, (b) a long and deep ford, picture taken from footbridge; far, road to right, mill (and river) to left.

Canalised rivers, canals

(a)

(b)

Fig. 10.34. Canals.

Fig. 10.34 (cont.)

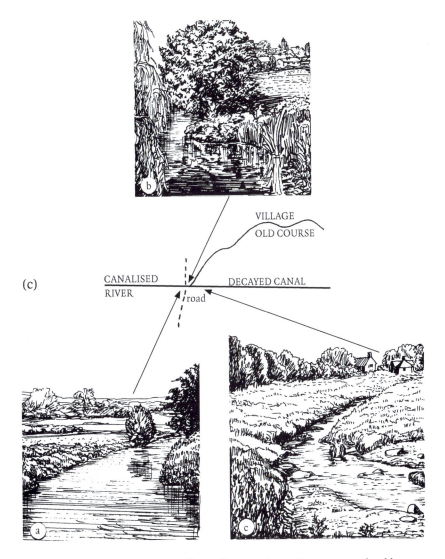

(c) (Essex River Stour) the river is still canalised to point a. Downstream, the old course of the river curves off by a river village point b, while the canal, now decayed, has been re-channelled, point c. The canal by-passed the village, as motorways do nowadays.

Tow path

(a)

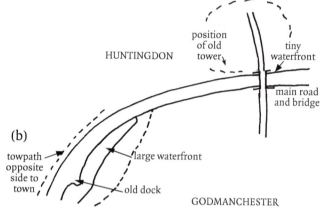

(b)

towpath
opposite
side to
town

large waterfront

old dock

GODMANCHESTER

HUNTINGDON

position
of old
tower

tiny
waterfront

main road
and bridge

Fig. 10.35. (a) From the
Cambridgeshire Collection; (b)
Towpaths are usually on the
opposite bank to the river port, to
separate traffic.

Crossings

Fords

Fig. 10.36.

Ferries

old ferry point

Fig. 10.37.

Bridges

Fig. 10.38

Settlements: cities, villages and farms

European City development

Fig. 10.39. Views of cities in different stages of development.

(a) Roman

(b) Dark Ages

(c) Late Mediaeval

(d) 1493 (Nüremburg Chronicle).

Fig. 10.40. *Maps of cities in different stages of development.*

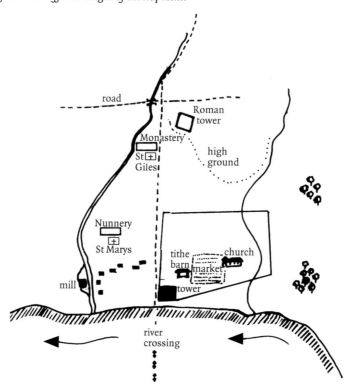

(a) *Early Mediaeval*

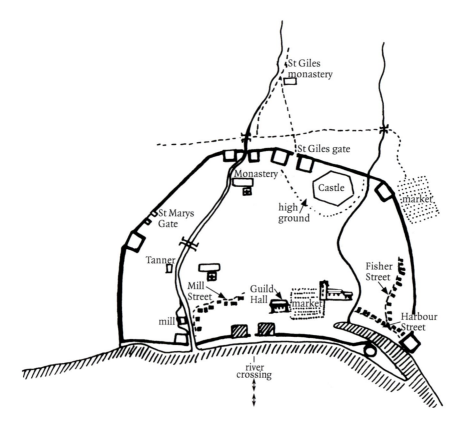

(b) *Middle Mediaeval*

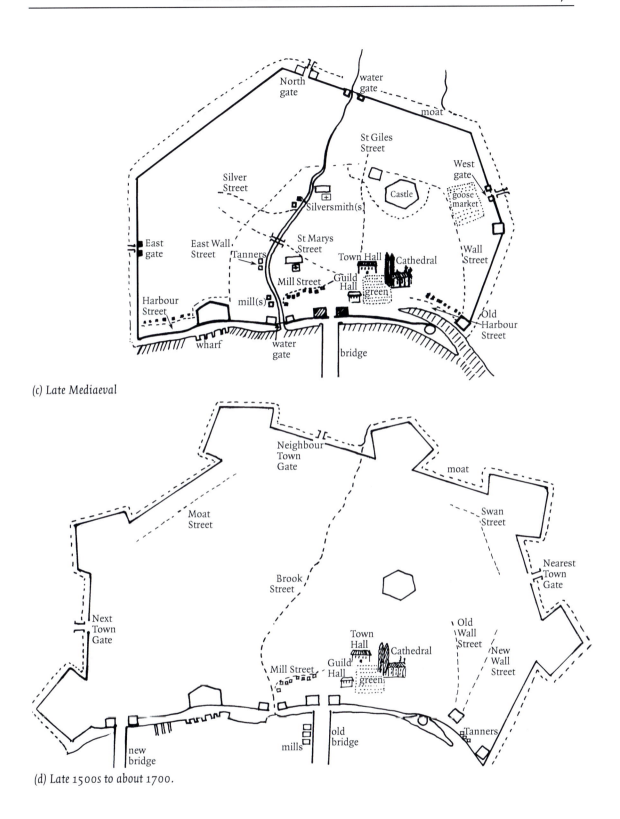

(c) Late Mediaeval

(d) Late 1500s to about 1700.

By the Middle Mediaeval period the basic 'furniture' consisted of guard towers, castle, harbour, monasteries, garrison, mill, tannery, church, market, ice cellar, smithy (silversmith). The harbour–church–market place–tithe (=town) hall complex behaves as one unit. Walls are usually named after the bastion or church nearby. The stone tower is sometimes, not always, associated with the harbour. The crossing can be ford, ferry or bridge, with little or nothing on the far bank. The market place was for the town. Trading fairs were held outside the walls (perhaps being later incorporated, e.g. as the poultry market).

Building grows, town walls are pushed out, often leaving the original harbour defences intact. The tithe barn becomes a town hall, the market place church, a cathedral. The nunnery and monastery have new churches, other religious foundations develop outside the wall. A ditch is added to the fortifications. One wall is likely to be called Swan's Wall, often associated with a goose or swan market, later with Swan Lane (swans, being valuable, could be kept on any spare water). There may be a gate here. There is no obvious waterfront development, the harbour is doing well, and there may be a citadel or other fort on the river. Water-intensive craft shops congregate down the tributary or mill stream (Fig. 10.41 shows re-development).

Fig. 10.41. Craft on stream.

Similar occupations also congregate together, e.g. Silver Street, Copper Street. The outer fields for smiths, foundries are incorporated later, as are the markets for hay, swans, cattle, etc.

Next, some towns are re-fortified in the stellate form. The harbour often moves downstream, and the old one may have been eroded into enough for the City Island to form. If the harbour moves, the market place moves with it, often with a new town hall. Increased industry may cause pollution – in Köln, Tanner Beck becomes Blue Beck. The market place may even move away from the river, when there may be a 'hay market' by the harbour. The original keep will probably be re-built as a dwelling-castle. There is usually a moat, if space and terrain allow. Gates and walls are named after compass points.

The seventeenth century introduces town planning, a grid pattern of streets being characteristic. (This had been found earlier, in towns designed as a whole, but in the west these were sparse.) Villages expanded, developing their own, barely fortified harbours. Much fishing is still done locally, but it is declining towards the end of the century. (By then in Germany the watermills on small streams have declined.) City gates are often named after the town the road leads to.

The eighteenth century still has the grid pattern, and has extensive private buildings on the outskirts. The Big House is typical. If the town wants water above ground, there will be a canal network. If not, it starts putting streams underground. There is an industrial waterfront, with warehouses with living accommodation above. The mill moves to the main river, and tributaries may be covered over as sewers. Building increases outside the city walls (where these were left), castles are re-built and re-furbished, and parks created round palaces. The moat may be turned into an ornamental lake. Fishing and fish-harbours decline. Streets on the periphery are often named after the town they go to.

The nineteenth century has a definite town plan, perhaps with a fan of boulevards. Much peripheral building may obscure remaining fortifications. Ornamental lakes replace moats – if this has not happened earlier. The railway appears, quite often following the line of a straightened river or a tributary. The new town hall may be built anywhere. The waterfront moves outwards both up- and downstream and on both banks (where space and bridges allow). It may have smart development or, and in Britain far more often, slums. New bridges are common. Street names often commemorate kings, writers, battles, etc. Cultural buildings (opera, theatre) appear, mostly within the old town.

In the twentieth century new ground is acquired beside the river (channelling, drainage), often used as park land, and the leisure use of water is now distinct from commercial. Leisure buildings (sport, parks, etc.) increase, and so do tower blocks and industry on the peripheries. Water fronts are neglected or recreational.

Fig. 10.42. Town Plans.

(a) Town fossilised in mediaeval form (Cardigan).

(b) Grid-type seventeenth century town (Valletta).

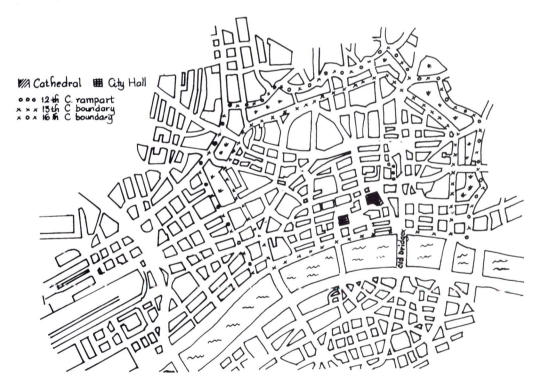

(c) Typical European growth (Frankfurt).

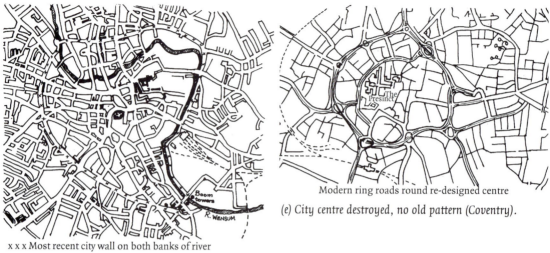

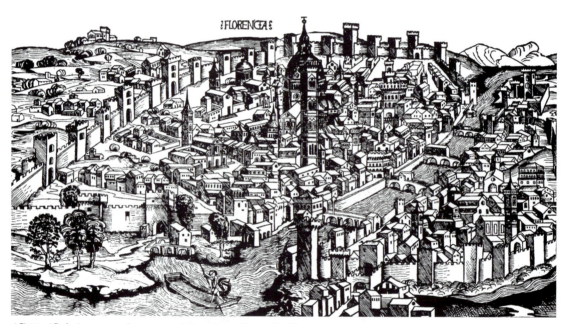

x x x Most recent city wall on both banks of river

(d) Fortified river type, old on both sides (Norwich).

(e) City centre destroyed, no old pattern (Coventry).

(f) Fortified-river town, late 1400s (Nüremburg Chronicle) (Florence). Compare with Figs. 10.39(d), 10.40(c).

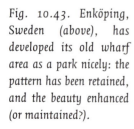

Fig. 10.43. Enköping, Sweden (above), has developed its old wharf area as a park nicely: the pattern has been retained, and the beauty enhanced (or maintained?).

Variable patterns

Variants on the typical pattern in-clude those based both sides of the river, because of early settlements on both banks (e.g. York, Cambridge) or, like other east-facing towns such as Norwich, be fortified rivers (see Fig. 10.42(d) and (f)). THE RIVER PATTERNS OF TOWNS SHOULD BE INTERPRETED, AND NEW PLANNING SHOULD RETAIN THESE FEATURES.

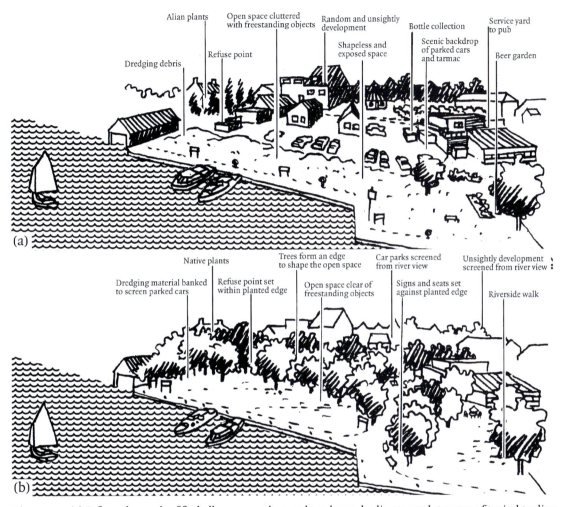

Fig. 10.44. (a) Before – large wharf for bulky cargo such as reeds and peat, leading to market square of typical trading village (not town). Positions of buildings used by overseer of market (centre) and overseer of wharf (left) visible. History missed – only superficial ugliness noted; (b) after landscape treatment for public amenity.

Coventry (Fig. 10.42(e)) has lost its old pattern – and should remain unique in this respect! One is fine, to show what happens, but all like this, no!

The before-and-after figure (Fig. 10.44(a), (b)) shows how easy it is, in the name of beauty, to destroy heritage. To destroy is easier than, by taking more thought, enhancing the old to make a place of beauty – as in Enköping.

The City Island

The town plan in Fig. 10.40(c) shows how this island develops by incutting of wharfs. Fig. 10.45(a) shows one in picture form. Use varied from being part of the city, to grazing, ship-building, etc. The presence of this island may be the only sign of an old port, as at Torksey on the Trent, a busy and prosperous port until the fourteenth century, now a remote village. In Fig. 10.45(b), Newark, the City Island – much smaller than it was three centuries ago – has been used as the structure always needed on now-navigable rivers: that separating lock and weir.

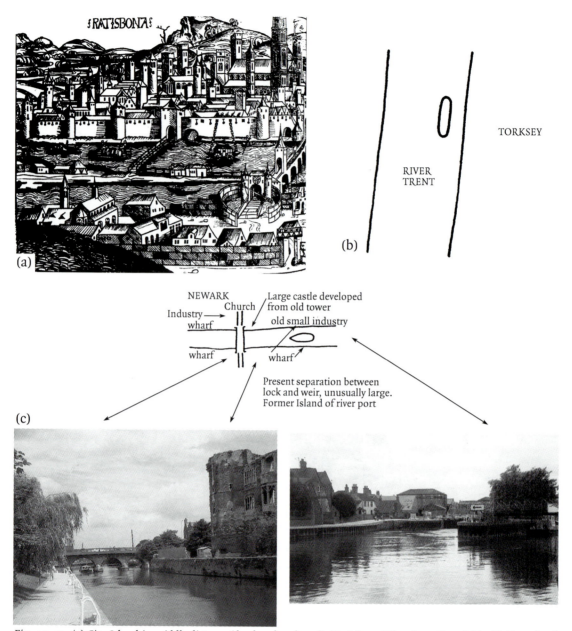

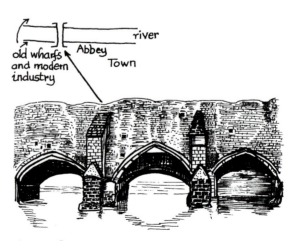

Fig. 10.45. (a) City Island in middle distance (developed and used) (Ratisbon, Nüremberg Chronicle); (b) City Island on right (developed and disused); (c) City Island re-used as support between lock and weir (Newark).

Some town examples

Bury St Edmunds

Here is a fairly standard old abbey town, the old town within the walls – and the fortified entrance bridge. Downstream, where there was more space, the larger later wharves developed, then redeveloped as modern industry.

Fig. 10.46.

Lincoln

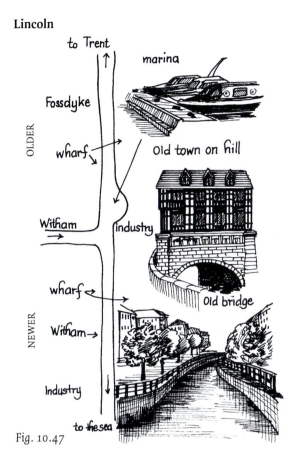

Fig. 10.47

This is a city with two waterway patterns. The main early route (from Roman times) was from the north, down the Trent, across the Fossdyke, to Lincoln, and the main harbour, now the marina, is still here. Later, the direct route up the Witham from the sea, by Boston, developed, and the lesser but longer waterfront is along that part.

Godmanchester and Huntingdon

(a)

Fig. 10.48. (a) Godmanchester: part of large (secondary) wharf. City Island is at the far left.

Both of this pair were chartered in the thirteenth century, and both were good towns in the eighteenth. Godmanchester, the river trading town, decayed to a village when it lost the river trade which made it prosperous. Huntingdon, a county capital on the Old North Road (Ermine Street) has never depended on river trade, and remained prosperous.

Fig. 10.48 (cont.)

(b) Huntingdon: all of a small
wharf (see also Fig. 10.35(b)).

Cambridge

Unusually, a quarter of the old town was removed in the fifteenth century, to make way for University Colleges. Note the City Island, the site of the Old Harbour, persisting for centuries after the loss of the harbour.

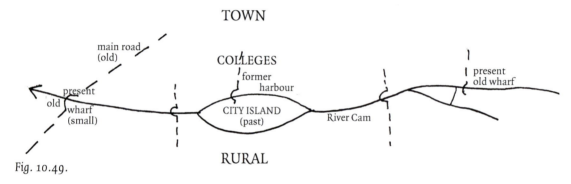

Fig. 10.49.

Dorchester

This is an ancient but now busy and modern county capital. Yet, in the middle, is the old canalised access by boat. Which should be preserved!

Fig. 10.50.

Some village patterns

Fig. 10.51. Village patterns in relation to water include:

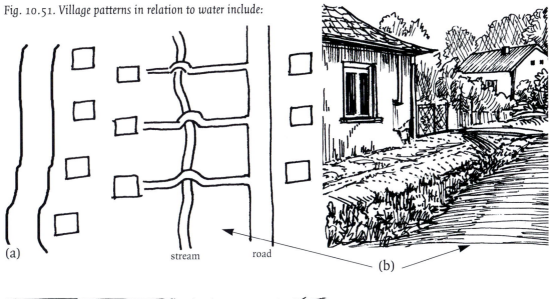

(a) stream road (b)

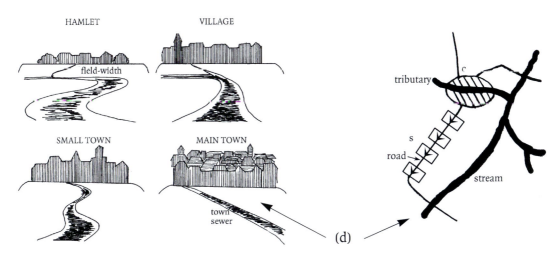

(c)

(a) A line of houses on one side, usually lost in later development.(b) Houses on both sides. (c) Bridgehead.

(d)

(d) A very common type, the village developing on a minor tributary enough to supply water in normal circumstances but not large enough to flood. The main stream is at the bottom of the valley, a field's width downstream. Here water is always present, though inconveniently far, and floods were frequent. These may develop into main towns. (c= old Centre, s = houses along old Street.)

Some less frequent types include:

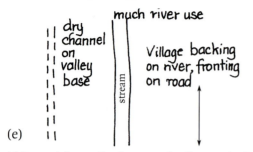

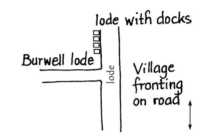

(e) Stream left on valley base, non-flooding supply channel diverted up the valley, where village built.

(f) River trading village, with many individual merchant's docks.

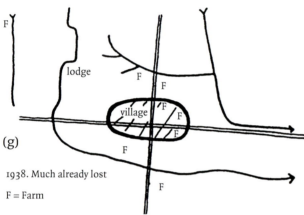

1938. Much already lost

F = Farm

(g) Stream diversions for farms and village. Villages pre-dating mains supplies had to have a local water source. These should be found and preserved.

(h) Little evidence of former water supply in village — but old bridge over dry channel downstream.

(i), (j) Same village, (i) old, water-related; (j) new, not water-dependent.

Some farm patterns

Fig. 10.52. (a)-(l) Some farm patterns.

Various patterns are shown in Fig. 10.52. Older farms tend to be closer to streams, newer ones tend to be closer to roads (e.g. Fig. 10.52(h), and to be above flood level. In Fig. 10.52(g), the stream is drained and sunk. There are hens. In the past, with easy access to water, surely there were ducks!

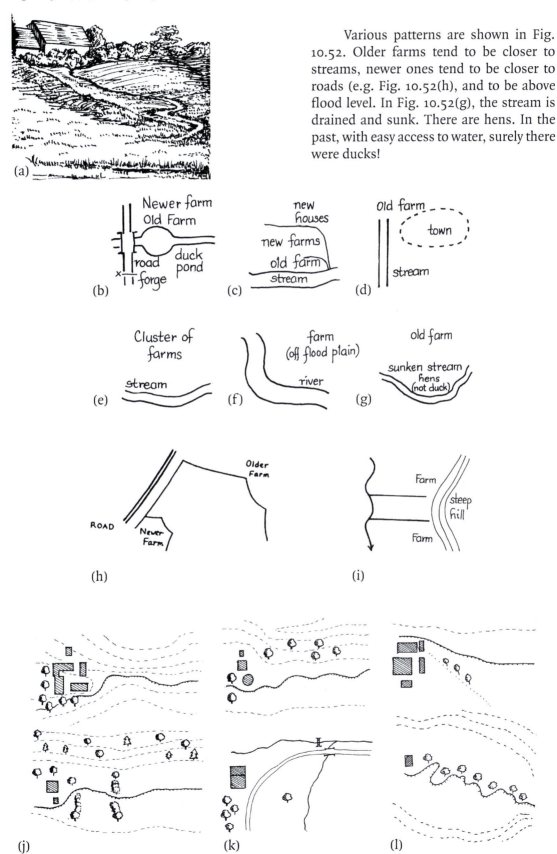

Duckponds (farm and village)

Fig. 10.53.

Waste removal
(*for* POLLUTION *see Chapters* 5 *and* 6)

Road run-off channels

The diversity is worth observing and retaining

Fig. 10.54.

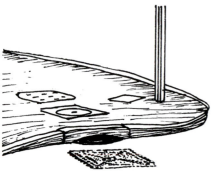

Fig. 10.54 (cont.)

Rubbish dumps

Fig. 10.55.

Rubbish attracts rubbish. Low places attract rubbish. Less is dumped if sites are regularly cleaned.

Flood
(also see Chapters 3, 8 and 9, and Drainage, above)

Undesirable works have been shown in plenty, but here are two more:

Fig. 10.56.

Too often, flood protection is over-done. It is rare to find a presumptively unsafe house like that shown in Fig. 10.57.

The object of flood protection works is, of course, to ensure that scenes of mass destruction, as shown in Fig. 10.58(a), do not happen, and that floods occurring are as shown in Fig. 10.58(b), with water quietly sitting on grassland below house level.

Flood relief channels may be cut around plains, catching and diverting incoming hill water, to prevent floods in those plains.

Fig. 10.57.

(a) Sixteenth century woodcut

(b)

Fig. 10.58.

Fig. 10.59. A flood relief channel.

Washland means rivers may flood near the river, storing surplus water, while an embankment prevents the water going further, where it is unwanted.

Fig. 10.60.
Washland.

Fig. 10.61.
The Thames
Barrage.

Reservoirs may control discharge to prevent flooding below.

The Thames barrage (Fig. 10.61) can be raised to stop incoming high tide water flooding London, upstream.

Defence

The Hill Fort

Fig. 10.62. (a) Typical position of a hill fort, now replaced by a church.

(b) Fort ruined.

Fig. 10.62 (cont.) (c) Windsor Castle (Girls Own Paper, 1887), re-developed hill fort brooding over the river Thames.

The River Fort

Newark (Fig. 10.45(c)) shows re-development of fort to Castle.

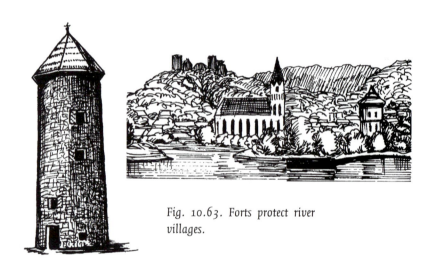

Fig. 10.63. Forts protect river villages.

Other fortifications

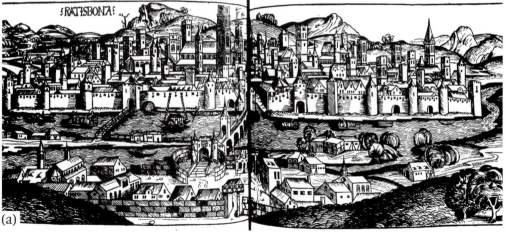

Fig. 10.64. (a) (Nüremburg Chronicle) fortified walls, bridges, etc. (and see figures of city development (Figs. 10.39, 10.40, 10.42) for other fortified walls, bridges, river chains, etc.).

Fig. 10.64 (cont.) (b) Old town fortifications marked by inner and outer walls. Old access wharf and way in shown.

Ornament

Fountains

The older fountains were constructed for water supply, but if in city centres, palaces, etc., were also beautiful. Today's ornamental fountains were not designed for use.

Fig. 10.65.

Fig. 10.65 (cont.)

Water-enhancing beauty

Fig. 10.66.(photograph, R.M. Haslam)

Fig. 10.66 (cont.)

Bad improved by water

Fig. 10.67.

Ornamented rivers

Fig. 10.68.

Recreation

Fig. 10.69(a) shows decorous behaviour AND few people mean negligible damage, but (b) is the reverse and means the river falling apart: the bank is eroding, trees are falling, vegetation of bank and channel is near-absent, birds and mammals are unwelcome. The picture is worth studying in detail, for the various damages and the instability of the whole.

(a)

Fig. 10.69. (a) Negligible Damage (from Girls Own Paper, 1887). (b) Much damage. (c) Swimming place. (d) Paddling place.

Fig. 10.69 (cont.)

(b)

(c)

(d)

Holy and healing waters

Holy, healing and wishing wells

Fig. 10.70. Wells. ((a), (b) redrawn from Trubshaw, 1990.)

(a)

(b)

Fig. 10.70
(cont.)

(c)

In Fig. 10.70, (a) and (b) are enclosed, simple wells; (c) is an open well in a churchyard. The church is dedicated – as expected with a holy spring – to a lady, here St Mary-the-Virgin. The present spring dedication to the Baptism is new; (d) is in an ancient chapel. St Winifrid's well; (e) are wishing wells, presumably ancient holy wells (surely deserving a better fate!); and (f) shows well-dressing in Derbyshire.

Many wells had local reputations for sanctity, healing or both. The 'Wells and Springs', 'Water Supply', County Series of Memoirs of the Geological Society, HMSO, London are a useful source. In Herefordshire in the 1920s, for instance, 55 named wells were recorded with names to do with sanctity, saints, the Lady, and including 12 healing wells.

Important wells occurred at now-unexpected places, e.g. at WELLingborough, Northants. It is some centuries since that town was a significant watering place.

Spa wells and structures are scattered. They may be tiny, their only remains a pump or (single) bath, or they may be major, as at Bath itself. The spas are healing places, though many (including Bath and Malvern) are on earlier holy well sites. The basics are a pump (developing as the Pump Room), when waters were drunk, and the baths, when they were used for bathing). Different types of water – naturally enough – healed different ailments, and the cures tended to take weeks or months, in contrast to current medicines. Spas on the continent are still much used.

(d)

(e)

Fig. 10.70
(cont.)

(f)

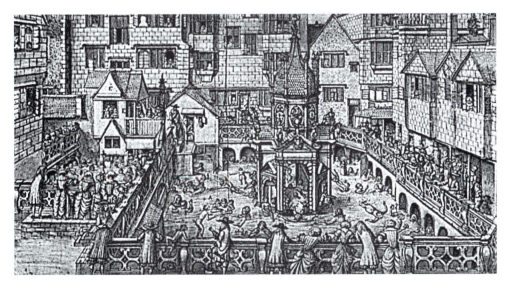

Fig. 10.71. *A spa (Bath, old picture).*

Table 10.8. English Spas in the mid-nineteenth century

Chemical composition can be inferred from cures reported, and vice versa. Originally cold springs were primarily used for drinking, hot for bathing, but by 1840 most were used for both, cold water sometimes being heated. Granville approves of bottled water only if the spring is cold, and without sulphur or other substances lost on storage. Earth-heat is, he considers, far more beneficial than ordinarily heated water. This list is restricted to large springs (not just wells) and is entirely secular.

Spa	Temp.(°C)	Water type	Recommended for	Comments
Buxton	28	Close to pure[1]	Rheumatic, gout, paralytic affections and weakness after; faulty internal organs; debility; not for inflammation	May be heated to 36 °C; effect due to heat.
Matlock	20;15.5; 10.5	Slightly calcareous, close to pure	Dyspeptic and nephritic affections?	Patients drink at spring-head; iron 'untraceable' after first day; cold baths.
Monkswell, Lincoln	4.5	Chalybeate[2]	Dyspepsia with acidity, green sickness, female debility, glandular disorders, muscle torpor	
	11.5	No iron		
Woodhall Spa, Lincoln	16.5	Iodine, bromine, brine, some CO_2 (champagne-like)	Scrofula, glandular affections, disordered digestion, some rheumatism, gout	
Ashby-de-la-Zouch	9	(Uncertain)	Internal diseases, rheumatic and paralytic affections	Water brought to town from colliery for bathing
Willoughby Spa, Rugby	10	Sulphurated saline?	Female complaints, (?) certain children's maladies	Water is for drinking
Salt Wells, Dudley	9	Salt, muriates[3] of lime, magnesium, iron	Weakness of limbs, palsy (if non-inflammatory), glandular and scrofula affections	Probably better than Cheltenham
Tenbury	9	Salt, muriate of lime, trace iodine, bromine; water is sparkly	Glandular swellings, internal trouble, scrofula, scurvy, gout, rheumatic gout, paralytic affections, worms, skin troubles	Can be bottled and sent away
Leamington Spa	10	Saline, sulphuretted	Several moderate virtues for drinking	
Malvern	10	Pure		Pure water, healthy site on hill
Cheltenham	9.5	Muriates, sulphate of soda, etc. Proportions vary with depth.	Chronic derangements of stomach and liver	Declined as Spa, grown as town; water is for drinking
Gloucester		Saline, iodine		Water is for drinking
Clifton	23	Slightly saline	Irritative fever, phthisical complaints; various; not for lungs	Benefit is from heat; in the past patients were too often sent who could not recover
Bath	up to 46.5	High mineral, iron, some CO_2	Stimulates skin, strengthens muscles, joints, limbs, quickens circulation; wide range; paralysis, rheumatism, gout; female complaints; as drink, diuretic, diaphoretic, not purgative; only for some	Temperature lowered for bathing; cannot be bottled
Tunbridge Wells	10	Poor chalybeate		Undeserved fame; now a social town only; if water was sparkly, would be excellent; as good chalybeate can be found at any turnpike in Yorks
Harrogate	11.5–15.5	Pure chalybeate, saline chalybeate, saline, sulphur; vary in strength	Wide variety; glandular, scrofulous and digestive complaints; especially slow-acting skin diseases (not fever or inflammation)	Different wells have different effects; water is for bathing in (and drinking); should be heated before drinking

Spa	Temp. (°C)	Water type	Recommended for	Comments
Knaresborough	11	Sulphuretted hydrogen, less saline, more muriates and carbonate than the last (there is another well, which is chalybeate)	Better than Harrogate for many irritable skin diseases	Water is for drinking and bathing in
Aldfield Spa	11	Sulphur, in between the last two		
Thorpe Arch	9.5	Saline	Diuretic, like Harrogate	
Malton	–	Saline chalybeate	Many chronic diseases, liver, digestion, debility	
Scarborough	10.5	Saline chalybeate, lime, etc.	Digestive and varied complaints (debility, skin disorders, etc.)	Water is for drinking; there is also marine bathing
Croft	10.5	Saponaceous alkaline Strong sulphur	Diuretic drink Sulphur baths (not for drinking), refreshing various complaints	
Dinsdale	10.5	Sulphuretted	As other sulphur ones	Water is for bathing in and drinking; sulphur remains after heating
Guisborough	10	Slightly sulphuretted, low mineral	Not much use (too dilute)	Water is for bathing
Butterby	10	Near-pure (lime carbonate); sulphur and muriates; iron and saline (in middle of Wear: unusable unless enclosed)	Alterative [improving the metabolism]	
Shotley Bridge	9	(Alterative) chaly-beate, muriates, CO_2 etc.	Weakness and obstruction in circulation, indigestion, skin diseases and, in warm bath, rheumatism	Differs from other British waters; water is for drinking (and bathing in)
Gilsend Spa	10.5	Sulphuretted, strongly	As other sulphur waters	
Skipton Spa	10.5	Alkaline sulphuretted	Warms stomach, intestines, muscle joints; improves vitality; relieves female complaints	
Horley Green Spa	10.5	Chalybeate, strong (sulphate of iron)	As other chalybeate	Water is for bathing and drinking
Ilkley Spa	8.5	Muriates of lime and magnesia (2:1), CO_2	Scrofula, eye inflammation, atrophy, mesenteric diseases, stiff joints, muscles, stomach irritability, chronic weakness, some female complaints	After bath, rub, exercise or have a hot drink until the skin feels warm

[1] Pure = solute low;   [2] Chalybeate = iron;   [3] muriate = chloride.

Spa remains should be located, the tiny as well as the famous. A variety of sources and types of water is interesting and health-giving! And well and spring water, in the past, emerged clean and pure from the ground. It would be nice to again have rivers clean enough for river baptisms to be recommended.

Fig. 10.72. *Nineteenth century river baptism (M. Bower).*

11 ARCHAEOLOGICAL HERITAGE

(specialist expertise should be sought)

SUMMARY

The archaeological component of a river may be of great potential value. Many traces of settlements along riverbanks and the use of rivers are preserved underground, and such remains should be recognised and conserved. This may mean preservation in the form of buildings and earthworks, or as greenfield sites, or preserving a record of the remains by excavation. In general, the best policy is preservation in place, followed by excavation.

Introduction

People have been resident in Britain for over a quarter of a million years. With such an immense time-depth of occupation, it cannot be surprising that archaeological remains are ubiquitous in Britain. Rivers have throughout time served as transportation corridors and as foci for settlement. It therefore follows that riverine areas have some of the country's best and most important sites, out of all proportion to the small percentage of the country's land area that they cover.

Archaeological sites occurring within riverine areas include, among others, sites of communication and travel (e.g. ports, harbours, wharves and quays, boats, boatyards, locks and many more), religious sites (witness the huge collection of late Bronze Age and Early Iron Age swords from the lower Thames River), and thousands of farming and industrial sites of all periods of prehistory and history, all reflecting the use of the rivers for water, power, transport, etc. This extremely wide coverage makes this collection of sites a balanced and very valuable sample of the full national range of cultural heritage sites.

Why are riverine sites so valuable? One of the most important aspects of riverine or coastal archaeological sites is the degree of preservation that the presence of the water affords. Most objects made and used by people in the past were of perishable materials – cloth, wood, and leather. Such items rarely survive on 'dry-land' sites. However, these materials and much environmental evidence (seeds, insects, wood) for both the immediate site environs and the wider site catchment zone may be preserved in waterlogged conditions on sites near rivers or meres. The presence of such objects, available nowhere else, makes these sites valuable. The concomitant is vulnerability – if the sites dry out due to changes in land use or water management, then the archaeological remains are destroyed.

A second reason that such sites are important is the presence of stratigraphy and built structures preserved by land reclamation or alluviation. This is best illustrated by the famous Roman waterfronts excavated along the River Thames in London, where succeeding generations built new waterfronts over and above earlier phases.

By a similar process, either by human make-up or river flooding, soil is built up over riverside settlements, resulting in the preservation of walls and floors. These would ordinarily be damaged or destroyed by later activity such as ploughing or construction.

Even when sites are not wholly waterlogged or buried by layers of soil, parts of the site such as in-filled ditches, wells, and pits may have localised waterlogged preservation and thus still be very valuable.

Identifying sites

Most archaeological sites are invisible to the layman, simply because they are buried below ground or hidden by later settlements and structures. There are, however, many clues as to their presence.

Built-up areas, e.g. existing farms, mills, and villages, are hints that other remains may be present. Many of these will hide earlier sites. There is a strong tendency for good riverside sites to be more or less continuously occupied. Look for Mediaeval and earlier settlements below or adjacent to historic villages and towns. Also make use of place names (as in Chapter 10), which may provide clues to earlier (Mediaeval or Anglo-Saxon) settlements, and by extension still earlier settlements too. Ordnance Survey maps will occasionally mark towns and settlements with early origins with names in Gothic script. The present waterfront of Godmanchester (Cambs) was established during the Danish occupation of the ninth century, but in turn is built over part of the older Roman town and fort established at this important river crossing point in the first century AD.

Earthworks are commonly preserved in riverside fields used for pasture. These are often the surviving remains of Mediaeval mills or villages, but may be much older.

Fig. 11.1. Excavation of the Iron Age and Roman Settlement at Gravelly Guy, Stanton Harcourt, Oxon, on river gravel terraces of the Thames (Oxford Archaeological Unit photograph).

Sites below ground level make up the vast majority of sites alongside rivers, and there may be little or no above-ground clues to their presence. Locating these sites can be difficult, and professional archaeological advice will be necessary. The first place to begin the search is in the County Archaeology Office, which will maintain a Sites and Monuments Record (SMR – usually a map- and text-based record) which is a database of all known archaeological remains within the county. Another source of information is English Heritage, which, as adviser to the Department of the Environment, is responsible for some 13 000 *Scheduled Ancient Monuments*. A third source is the Royal Commissions on Historical Monuments, especially for industrial archaeological sites such as mills, pumping stations, and so on. Please note that the SMRs and lists of monuments are records of all *known* sites. Realise that this is not definitive. New sites are continually being discovered.

The best way to understand the diversity and value of archaeological sites is to consider a number of representative examples. Urban waterfront sites, such as the spectacular Roman waterfront in London, Roman, Saxon and Viking York, or Mediaeval Bristol and Exeter, have received international attention (see e.g. Good *et al.*, 1991). While most of these excavations were prompted by land development proposals during the economic boom of the 1980s, river management schemes in historic towns and cities may be expected to have similar archaeological implications. Somewhat more difficult to anticipate are rural riverine sites such as those discussed below.

Flag Fen

The site of Flag Fen is located near the edge of the Cambridgeshire fens, immediately south-east of Peterborough. Excavations of the site, which was threatened by de-watering, began in 1982 assisted by the (then) Anglian Water Authority, and have continued annually under the direction of Francis Pryor of the Fenland Archaeological Trust (Pryor, 1991). Initial interpretations of the site as an artificial inhabited 'island' were overturned by the 1989 discovery of a post alignment, 10 m wide and more than 850 m long, linking the 'island' to the contemporary fen edge previously excavated by Pryor.

Fig. 11.2. Flag fen. Causeway from the air (Oxford Archaeology Unit photograph).

The post alignment leads directly into a complex Bronze Age field and settlement system – the two are clearly intimately interrelated. Both the 'island' and the alignment are characterised by thousands of pieces of wood preserved in the anaerobic water-logged conditions – by 1986 over 10000 timbers had been excavated.

One of the most striking features of the post alignment (and possibly the 'island' too) is the deliberate destruction and deposition of fine metalwork items either in, or beside, the timber structures. To date over 300 such items have been recovered, ranging from complete ceramic pots, shale bracelets, bronze pins and inlaid jewellery to knives, swords, daggers and parade armour. The final interpretation, following from many more years of excavation, is keenly awaited, but the destruction and deposition of symbols of rank and prestige indicate that at least one facet of the site is a religious monument.

Fig. 11.3. Flag fen (G. Wait photograph).

Redlands Farm, Stanwick, Northants

Archaeological investigations by the Oxford Archaeological Unit from 1989 to 1992 in advance of gravel quarrying operations have in many ways typified the value of riverine landscapes. The Redlands Farm area, adjacent to palaeochannels of the river Nene, was initially cleared of woodland in the late Mesolithic/early Neolithic period (c. 4500–2500 BC). Subsequently, a Neolithic long barrow was built, housing a number of burials. Indications are that the immediate surrounding area was set aside for this purpose. If so, this partition of the riverside meadows continued, for during the following Bronze Age a series of round barrows was built aligned on the still surviving mound of the earlier long barrow. The round barrows were similarly built of gravel and turf, covering burials. The riverside meadows remained relatively dry and were subsequently turned over to arable use, during the course of which the ploughing regime largely destroyed the Neolithic and Bronze Age ritual burial mounds. The water table was sufficiently high throughout this period that the deeper archaeological contexts contained preserved wood and other organic remains. During the early Roman period two of the palaeochannels were canalised and used as leets to power a stone-built watermill. In the middle of the Roman period this was converted into a villa establishment, although the infilled leets rendered the villa walls unstable.

Ultimately, the villa walls collapsed and occupation was shifted into sunken-feature buildings, often associated with early Anglo-Saxon settlement. Simultaneously, changes in land-use patterns meant that the Nene was locally beginning to flood, and the collapsed walls of the villa, associated barns and sunken-feature buildings began to be buried by waterborne silts. The Roman site was therefore sealed and protected by the alluvial covering. The rapidly rising water table and the overlying alluvium meant that preservation of organic artefacts was excellent. Throughout later history the riverside fields remained as pasture and water meadows. The value of the Roman period site was such that quarrying plans were redesigned in order to leave much of the area preserved. This sequence illustrates both the development and preservation of sites along rivers, and the great value that waterlogged preservation can offer.

Somerset Levels

The Somerset Levels Project ran from 1973 to 1989 under the direction of Professor John Coles (see the annual Somerset Levels Papers and Coles & Coles, 1986). Over 130 reports have appeared, marking the extraordinary diversity and value of the archaeological sites preserved in the peats of the levels. The archaeology was threatened by desiccation and destruction through the activities of peat extraction companies, who generously supported the project. The Neolithic raised trackway, called the 'Sweet Track', must stand as representative of the many sites investigated.

The Sweet Track was built around 3900 BC (possibly the earliest wooden trackway in western Europe) linking two small islands – Westhay and Shapwick Heath – to each other and to the higher hills to the south. The trees used were all felled in a single year. Planks were of oak, ash, and lime – 4000 m of planking were used. Some 500 trees provided foundation rails, and 6000 pegs (over 1.0 m long) of hazel, alder, willow, ash and oak were also used. The scale of the project, and the prodigious use of long straight poles, indicate a complex and well-managed woodland. Environmental evidence from both peat and insect remains documents arable farming activities on the islands and the 'mainland'.

The track was constructed by laying a line of large timber rails on the surface of the peat marsh. Long poles or pegs were then driven into the marsh beside the rails at an oblique angle. Planks were then laid in the 'X' created, so that the surface of the plank was maintained at about 30–50 cm above the marsh. The planks formed the walkway surface, usually only 30 cm. Along the 1800 m long track was the debris of use – lost and dropped objects, and some deliberately (ritually?) placed objects as well. Wear is evident along the track but repairs are relatively rare – tree-ring data suggests repair at one point some seven years after initial construction – so the track may have had a relatively short life-span.

Essex coastal survey

The Essex coastal survey, or Hullbridge Project, was initiated in 1982 to find and record archaeological sites within the intertidal zone of the Crouch, Blackwater, and Thames estuaries, and to place them in their stratigraphic and environmental context. The main threats were from marine erosion and coastal sea-wall construction – the project was funded by the Department of the Environment, English Heritage, and the British Museum (Wilkinson et al., 1988). Most sites occur between the high and low water marks, with peripheral structures like jetties built below low water level. The complicating factor is the steady rise in sea levels in the last 10000 years, as a consequence of which earlier prehistoric sites located on the contemporary sea-shore are now below low water level and so remain inaccessible. Sites discovered belong to every period of British prehistory and history – Mesolithic and Neolithic occupation sites located above the then high water mark, and later prehistoric and historic sites more directly linked to exploitation of the marine resources, such as fishing and salt production. Most or all of these sites were originally 'dry-land' sites, subsequently flooded by the sea, so that many organic artefacts disappeared before inundation could preserve them. These sites do, however, have well-preserved environmental evidence, and because of their inundation, they have never suffered plough damage. While not classic 'wet' sites, they are nonetheless very valuable.

Fig. 11.4. Farmoor. Artists reconstruction of the Middle Iron Age settlement alongside R. Thames, near Farmoor, Oxon. The settlement was occupied seasonally to exploit the riverside meadows as pasture (Oxford Archaeological Unit photograph).

Fig. 11.5. The Mediaeval settlement and fishery at Rushey Weir, Oxon, showing the effects of river bank erosion (see Chapter 10, Fig. 10.16) (Oxford Archaeological Unit photograph).

Addresses of archaeological organisations

Institute of Field Archaeologists
Minerals Engineering Building
University of Birmingham
PO Box 363
Birmingham B15 2TT

English Heritage
Fortress House
23 Savile Row
London W1X 1AB
Tel: 0171 973 3000

Royal Commission on the Historical Monuments of England
Fortress House, 23 Savile Row
London W1X 1AB
Tel: 0171 973 3500

References

Good, G.L., Jones, R.H. & Ponsford, M.W. (eds), 1991. *Waterfront Archaeology*. CBA Research, Report 74.

Pryor, F., 1991. *Flag Fen: prehistoric Fenland centre*. Batsford, London.

Coles, B.J. & Coles, J.M., 1986. *Sweet Track to Glastonbury: The Somerset Levels in Prehistory*. Thames & Hudson, London.

Wilkinson, T.J., Murphy, P., Juggins, S. & Manson, K., 1988. Wetland development and human activity in the Essex estuaries during the Holocene transgression. In *The Exploitation of Wetlands*.

12 RECREATION

SUMMARY

To foster recreation is a duty required of the Environment Agency and similar bodies. Recreation, though very desirable, if uncontrolled is most damaging. Balancing access, beauty and conservation is an art, but an attainable art. Ecological principles applied to car parks, footpaths, disturbance, etc., are described.

Introduction

Under the Water and Environment Acts, described in Chapter 9, the Environment Agency (formerly the National Rivers Authority) and similar bodies have a duty to foster recreation in the areas under their jurisdiction. Recreation is coupled with conservation in the acts. Indeed, if too few see rivers – if recreation is discouraged – conservation, which depends on the public will (not the will of a few academic ecologists), will go. Likewise, if too few people see good-quality rivers, the public view will be that rivers as a whole are a nuisance and should go.

RECREATIONAL ACCESS IS THEREFORE VITAL FOR THE PRESERVATION OF RIVERS.

Uncontrolled and inconsiderate recreational access, on the other hand, can lead to complete degradation. In addition, recreational uses can conflict. They conflict between themselves (e.g. birdwatching is likely to be poor if boats, paddlers and mountain bikes swarm over the site; those walking on a riverside footpath just behind anglers do not appreciate being caught in back-casting), and they conflict with other uses (footpath users disturbing and harming stock, boat users destroying vegetation and eroding banks, vandalism).

Fig. 12.1. This is not calculated to enhance public will to retain rivers (Haslam, 1991).

Much thought and creativity are therefore needed in this almost new field of developing riverside and river access for leisure activities, while enhancing (overall) the conservation value of the rivers for both natural and cultural ecology – and preventing quarrels or lawsuits with other riparian users, of course!

Objectives

When people visit and enjoy rivers they need:

1. Easy and safe access to the river and riverside.

2. Beauty. The natural beauty of the countryside and the man-made beauty of the towns.

3. Interest. People must be able to do what they have come for. This varies from looking at flowing water or birdwatching to driving or whitewater rafting. (Activities causing more habitat disturbance and damage will be in restricted sites.) They must also find more than they expect: they should be able to see, with understanding, some of the ecology and cultural heritage around them.

4. A sustainable environment. Visitor damage should be kept low, so that next year and in ten years' time a returning visitor can find a site of at least the same quality.

These objectives need not conflict with conservation and enhancement. True, excessive and uncontrolled use can lead to the situations depicted in Fig. 12.2. There is, though, no need to have such degradation.

(a)

(b)

Fig. 12.2. Sites of recreation impact, worn by visitors. (Haslam, 1991)

Conflict there is, and always has been. By *Domesday Book* times (1086) it was mostly between, on the one hand, millers and (commercial) fishers, and, on the other, the trading and passenger boats and trading centres. Magna Carta (1215) is one of many documents attempting to regulate these conflicts. Groups that cannot all, and simultaneously, use the same site, but often wish to, include:

- Birdwatchers
- Anglers
- Riders
- Cars
- Picnickers
- Power-craft users
- Researchers
- School education groups
- Walkers
- Cyclists
- Artists

and:

- Abstraction for domestic supply
- Abstraction for irrigation
- Abstraction for power supply
- Road construction
- Vandalism
- Rubbish dumping

- Swimmers
- Paddlers
- Craftsmen (and commercial)
- Canoers
- Other boat users
- Wildfowlers
- Conservers of fragile species and habitats (special conservation measures)
- Conservers of 'ordinary' species and habitats
- And others

- Waste disposal (run-off, effluents)
- Drainage for farming
- Drainage and defences against flood
- Domestic, commercial and industrial building
- Complete private use on all riverside land (no public access)

Creative thought and a sense of balance are needed. Some activities are compatible, e.g. artists and anglers. Others are not, e.g. power-craft and fragile habitats. Access (and damage) can usually be controlled both simply and pleasantly. Recreation may be instream (paddle, boat) or riverside (walk, picnic).

Activities

Car parks

If more than a handful of people visit a rural site, there must be a car park. This should be sited discreetly, not obtrusively. It is best in trees. It should have a more rural surface than the road (e.g. crushed gravel), have bays marked by vegetation rather than metal and paint. If it can be slightly excavated, even by as little as 30 cm, cars are better hidden, and bays are clear but unobtrusive. Local trees, shrubs and other vegetation can be fostered in the area, to make it both beautiful and proper to the locality. Depending on the numbers and type of visitors and the nature of the site, wooden picnic furniture and litter bins can be added, so can toilets and a children's play area. ('Sanitary woodland' or 'sanitary riversides' must not be allowed to develop.) If properly designed and screened, these can enhance rather than damage a site. Maintenance is necessary. It is, of course, agreed that no car park should be made on land of conservation value, only on ex-arable, much-disturbed or equivalent places. It should also be placed where it will not detract from the interest and beauty of the riverside.

There is another important design feature to a car park, and indeed to a busy access road: ensuring that run-off will be cleaned before it reaches the river. Adding pollution to a river is not a proper or a necessary consequence of adding visitors (see Chapters 5 and 8).

Footpaths

A pleasant, well-made and well-maintained footpath is, for most people, more attractive to walk on than rough grass, let alone rank vegetation. Therefore, by making the footpath, visitors are pleased and the site is protected from excessive trampling. Dykes provide beauty and interest, and effectively deter visitors from crossing the water of the dyke. Tall thick vegetation does the same: hawthorn hedges, blackthorn hedges, brambles, even nettlebeds (which are good moth habitat). Where, for some reason (e.g. the start of private land), no visitors at all may pass, a fence can be concealed by a hedge or equivalent. Paths can wind, and can cross rivers by ornamental wooden footbridges (either by initial choice, or as wished by certain riparian owners). Footpaths should be in themselves pleasing, and have good views of pleasing structures. Cattle-proof swing-gates (better) or easy stiles should be used. These are but a few of the many ways of enhancing riversides for visitors while keeping them sustainable.

Those who object (on aesthetic or conservation grounds) to people walking by should remember that until this century the countryside was well populated, with barges on rivers down to 2 m wide, with watermen, etc., commercial as well as leisure fishers, millers, shepherds, cowmen, dairy maids, hedgers and ditchers, collectors of e.g. rushes for chair seats, pollard and withy cutters, and many others making their living by or in the river. A depopulated countryside is new. What is also new of course is the complete poverty of the river, its lack of water, vegetation, fish and fowl. It therefore cannot sustain the degree of impact it used to, but, with care, the riverside can be re-populated.

The public has lawful access to riverside footpaths wherever they were towpaths on legally constituted navigations (not the same thing as navigated rivers), or are public rights of way. Many councils and the Environment Agency are, fortunately, extending the range, though this needs separate agreements with each riparian owner. Public (though not legally required) access has decreased in many villages where settlement has extended along the river, and private householder withhold what was previously given freely by landowners and farmers.

Networks or long lengths of footpaths are being constructed – completed in e.g. Derby; proposed in e.g. Gainsborough. Town footpaths may run along old wharf or towpath areas, be constructed on or by the riverside trading buildings, or be set back on banks not previously built on. Country banks may again be towpaths, whether on navigations or on other streams. They may be constructed on the top of flood banks. These, not being built for the purpose, may repeat the eighteenth-century conflicts between the watermen and the engineer in the fenland.

The impact of the footpath may erode the bank. Footpaths can also be put behind flood banks, or behind hedges. Variety adds interest: though the river should be in view over much of the length. Paths can be made or restored under bridges, so there is no need to cross busy roads.

Trails, clearly posted and with attractive notices, add much to well-visited sites (including unobtrusive control of visitors). Where there is an attendant, booklets can be written, and sold.

Birdwatchers can be filtered off from other visitors, and go to those areas designated for waterfowl and other birds, where good design and proper behaviour by the watchers ensure both groups do well. Access to hides can be screened, and hides placed at edges of tall vegetation, on floodbank walls, raised up, etc.

effects of disturbance

Public access has only local effects on river and riverbank vegetation (paddling areas, coarse angling sitting-places, etc.). The same applies to the within-water animals (disturbed substrate, perhaps shadows for fish). For birds and mammals, public access is of greater importance.

Table 12.1. Factors influencing the amount of disturbance to birds

Cause of disturbance	Worse	Better
People	On foot, on skyline	In vehicle Against background
Dogs	Off leads	On leads
Cars	Stopping	Going past
Boats	Rapid, erratic movement	Slow, straight movement
Aircraft	Low, helicopter	High Fixed wing
Noise	Loud, sudden	Soft Continuous
Colour	Bright	Dull
Any activity	Irregular	Consistent

Birds can keep a 'safe distance', which varies with species (goldeneye more wary than wigeon), experience (mallards tame where fed, not where shot), weather (hungry birds come closer), cover (for security) and disturbance type (Table 12.1). As usual, multiple impacts combine, e.g. ducks on water swim away from people on land, ducks on banks ignore a few boats; but have the two, and the ducks fly. Disturbance may stop birds feeding, over-use their energy in flight (perhaps leading to death), or cause them to desert the site. There is also obvious conflict with walking here: birdwatching is better from that polluting, noisy, vehicle so objectionable for conservation, the car.

Surrounding and enhancements

Particularly, but not solely in and near towns, the surroundings of a path may be deplorable: ugly fences, ugly bridges, ugly modern river protection. Who will be interested in the river shown in Fig. 12.3? Who will instead – and with fair reason – consider it is a council tip? Frequently, once a riverside is improved and enhanced, waste is dumped less, or indeed not at all. It can actually save money for authorities to substitute pleasantness for ugliness!

Why are ugly fences put up? Often through lack of thought! All fencing is not ugly, and that which is can often be screened with, e.g., blackthorn. Fences or walls are often on both sides of a riverside path, on one side protecting private property (school fences are often particularly ugly), on the other preventing access to the river. Why? On tow paths, etc. there is no question of fencing off the canal. Why are urban and suburban rivers so much more hazardous – or private? More private they are not. More hazardous they often are: because the river authority has

Fig. 12.3. Ugly and unsafe (Haslam, 1991).

created steep or vertical lined banks up which no child alone can safely climb (Fig. 12.3). Instead of giving safe child access, and pleasure to both children and those who look after them, the river structure is destroyed, access made dangerous, and the ugliness compounded by fencing. This may not keep people out, anyway. A river is no more – in fact far less – dangerous than a busy road. We do not fence our pavements; we try to teach road safety. Gentle and firm slopes into streams, so people can walk to and into the water's edge safely, are what is needed – even after channelling, even by flood banks. (Fig. 12.4). The same principle applies in other habitats. It is better to have safe access, whether to a bridge, bank or weir, than to try to prevent it and let injury occur because prevention is often incomplete (other than outside, e.g. Ministry of Defence installations) quite apart from the fact that safe access gives much pleasure, prevention, none.

Fig. 12.4. Access permitted (Haslam, 1990).

Riverside land may be enhanced for pleasantness. In towns, dreary urban corners can be integrated into the river. New riverside defences can resemble the old rather than the recent, variety can be added, shapes can be made to fit with riverside buildings, etc. (Fig. 12.5).

Fig. 12.5. Re-building retaining the character of the eighteenth/nineteenth-century river. The bridges are not so designed.

Modern, ugly linings can be given intermittent facings on which either emerged aquatics can grow from below, or land plants in the middle. It should always be remembered that the costs of creating pleasantness and beauty are ordinarily (if done properly) more than recouped by lessened vandalism and increased visitors.

In the country and village, much also can be done. Trees, shrubs and other vegetation (local species; see Chapter 7) can be planted to give variety, screen constructions and roads, provide habitats, etc. This can be in corners that are difficult to farm, on public land, on land available through, e.g., the Water Fringe Scheme (see Chapter 9), etc. Ugly fencing can be replaced, screened or removed, concrete facades can have timber fronting or habitats inserted for emerged aquatic plants to grow into from below. Ugly, modern footbridges can be replaced with traditional designs when replacement is needed. Pollarding can be maintained, or re-introduced (into areas where it is traditional). Flood banks can be positioned for access and landscaping. A little thought can turn a stone or concrete ugly lump on the bank into an attractive sitting area, with benches. Looking at rivers with the aim of making riversides both pretty and valuable to visitors will suggest many enhancements. Enhancements for people, though, should not cause destruction to other groups of plants and animals. (Invertebrates are particularly sensitive, needing continuity as well as particular structure, vegetation and lack of disturbance and pollution.) Ecological advice should be sought.

Riverside access may also be by lanes, whether by walking or by driving, etc. in both town and country. Lanes so used should be kept small and rural: turning them into 'A' roads destroys their recreational function.

Within the river much also can be done for enhancements, and money may be available for amenity use, if not for conservation. If the enhancement is done wisely, it will fulfil both functions. Uniform flow can be broken up by sandbag weirs, bays and pools can be inserted, structure on which vegetation can grow can be created or artificially inserted, stepping stones, etc., can be put in (see Chapter 8).

Fig. 12.6. Riverside used for recreation. The eroding, vertical bank 'drop edge' is typical of worn edges not otherwise interfered with (see Figs. 3.7, 3.8, p. 26). Note riverside made path; seat and picnic table (the latter with stone surrounds to prevent wearing of grass by feet); good river vegetation in the centre, little at the side, where children paddle; and trees for habitat variety and bird life.

Fishing and boating

Fishing and boating are not considered here in detail, as there are ample clubs, magazines and books catering for each interest group.

Fishing is the largest participant sport in Britain. Rights (or, rather, the rights, in England, to be somewhere in order to fish) to fish are vested in the riparian owner or government authority. Angling clubs buy these rights, and they cover much of the lowlands. Game fishers (salmonids: trout and salmon) are usually very good for the environment, since conditions favourable for the fish are favourable also for river structure and quality. An exception though, is when non-local strains or species of fish are stocked, contaminating gene pools. Coarse fish grow well in poor-quality rivers, and their anglers carve out 'homes' on banks, so their sport is less environment-friendly. (However, if fish depart from loss of water, pollution, etc., anglers' pressure may result in bringing the habitat back.)

Boating brings legal complications for access. Some rivers are covered by (mostly eighteenth-century) Navigation Acts, under which a company could improve boat passage and then charge for such passage. In these, there is right of passage. Elsewhere, boats may have always passed, streams only 2 m wide being used for freight barges even into the twentieth century. They can, though, be stopped, by the Environment Agency, etc., without the individual Acts of Parliament required to cancel Navigation Acts.

Fig. 10.32(a) shows that boat damage to vegetation is nothing new. Banks erode at launching and mooring sites, and where total impact is high (it takes many canoes to do the same damage as a few power-craft). Boats damage vegetation directly, and through turbulence disturbing the substrate, washing out plants and creating unstable, soft substrates and turbid silty water. Some precautions can be taken, regulating numbers, speeds, and waste disposal, and using 'soft' engineering to protect banks by tall monocots, etc. While it is important for people to travel by water, it is also important that this be regulated, and restricted to some rivers. The ultimate river for navigation is shown in Fig. 12.7.

Fig. 12.7. The navigation river (Haslam, 1990).

Erosion

Erosion is the primary hazard from visitors both on riverbanks and on the riverside. It is caused by high impact of people and that which they bring with them (boats, cars), without proper design. Good footpaths and, if necessary, other guidance devices (dykes, scrub) prevent wearing from trampling. Nicely designed small gates prevent cars reaching footpaths. Launching sites of firm (yet pleasant-looking) material prevent erosion from main canoe sites – if sited where canoers wish. Advice to anglers catching coarse fish lessens damage to bank vegetation. Places having very dense use, e.g. traditional family-outing and paddling sites, can be worn, as they are only local, but if impact gets too great, 'soft' engineering should be used (e.g. using the techniques described in Chapter 8).

Conclusions

The changes and enhancements described can all be enhancements for river structure and river and riverside vegetation, if done with a proper sense of the characteristics of the appropriate river type (see Chapters 3 and 4). They can also be degradations and lead to the approach of the designer uniform 'recreation river', if done without this sense (Fig. 12.8). IT IS VITAL TO MAINTAIN TRADITIONAL PATTERNS AND SENSE OF PLACE.

Fig. 12.8. Environmentally managed, no character, natural or cultural heritage (Haslam, 1990).

It is also vital to maintain cultural heritage. Fig. 10.44 shows how a well-intentioned landscaper can ruin the heritage of centuries – through ignorance of its meaning. No one should plan to alter any solid features without understanding of the content of Chapters 10 and 11. Old earthen wharfs, village supply channels, stone fish-traps, holy wells and water-collecting access steps should all be preserved (or repaired). It is appallingly easy to destroy in the name of 'restoration' as well as in the name of 'progress' and 'planning'. Anthony Trollope referred to 'that form of destruction which is called restoration'. So much of our rivers is now in a deplorable state. 'That form of restoration' we can do without!

With proper design, many activities, much wildlife and good vegetation can all co-exist. The town council of Melton Mowbray made a new balancing lake. Then they added sailing, fishing, footpaths, birdwatchers, etc. – the birds (including great crested grebe) duly arriving into suitable habitat. This provides excellent recreation for new residential development. There is a skilled warden, which is important, indeed essential, for such a habitat. This ensures good management (mowing, etc.) and minimises conflicts between activities, and between these and habitat.

Recreation and leisure activities are already large, rapidly expanding sectors of British life. It is for those now planning such activities – whether for the Environment Agency or for the garden – to choose whether the activities destroy or enhance natural and historic heritage. Enormous numbers of people can visit riverside sites safely (with proper safeguards for animals), or they may destroy those sites (see p. 3).

New developments should be considered in relation to the environment. New golf courses: all nice grass, what could be better? Well, arable would be better, as that is likely to take less water from river or borehole and use less biocide. Golf courses can very well do without both (as in good coastal turf), but many recent ones use them excessively. Also, too much is just grass. There should be more trees, shrubs and tall vegetation. All the vegetation types should contain appropriate, including rare, species.

IF RIVERS AND RIVERSIDES ARE (CONTROLLABLY) ACCESSIBLE AND PLEASANT TO LARGE NUMBERS OF THE PUBLIC, THEY WILL BE CONSERVED at least to some extent. The might of farmers, gravel extractors, and developers of roads, houses, factories and leisure centres far exceeds that of the conservation organisations, and without public will, commercial and 'national' considerations will destroy the river environment.

APPENDIX
Survey methods and recording

SUMMARY

This appendix describes survey and recording. The necessary equipment is listed, and the assessment is given as a questionnaire.

Introduction

There is no substitute for field work. Site photographs or videos come closest, but can never show everything relevant, and a surveyor has to visit to photograph anyway, so can also take other records. Aerial photographs can enhance and extend field records, but cannot substitute, as detail may not show or may be only recognisable if the feature has been seen on the ground (e.g. plant communities). It is also important that the person responsible for the final report and recommendations has done most of the field work. Understanding is built up only by experience. (It is not the business of the junior to visit the river and the senior to write about it, but for both to do both.)

Field visits without method, without a system of recording, however, do not accomplish much, a memory of trees, a bridge, perhaps iris and kingfisher and a vague idea of 'that is good': inadequate to evaluate the site, let alone compare it with others and build a picture of the whole river. Therefore, there are survey methods, plenty of them. Their object is to record relevant information in a systematic, reasonably simple, and safe way. There is no single perfect method: any method achieving these aims will do. Therefore it is satisfactory for anyone using this book to use either the methods listed here, or others which record at least the same amount of data. Those who can interpret them should obtain and use the current National and EU methods.

Recording using the method given here may be done either by reproducing the sheets here, or by recording in a notebook. After recording comes storage. The data must be available for consultation and analysis both at the time and, for comparative work, decades later. The records must therefore be legible, durable, and be presented in a systematic order either in a file or drawer, or on a disk with a label which can be traced years later. This may sound obvious, but it is by no means always kept to!

Computer, paper or both? Here, facilities, purpose and personal preference all play their part. Paper is more bulky but less likely to vanish during storage. Putting data into a computer is very time-consuming, but once in, information can be retrieved much quicker than from papers. ALL records must be entered, e.g. not just '4–8 m wide', but also 'wider with grazing, narrower with trees'.

Analyses and reports form the final part of an evaluation scheme. It is no good having excellent records if no one knows where they are and what they say about a river. Methods of analysis vary from simple diagrams through statistical programs like regression analysis, twinspan, or principal components analysis to integrated systems like the EA River Habitat Survey or SERCON. Publication is part of evaluation, the audience for that publication being, for example, a school class, the readership of a learned journal, or the members of a wildlife trust. The river should be evaluated in the appropriate terms for the chapters of this scheme. Diagrams often convey more information more clearly than an equal area of text.

At this point, please re-read the legal and safety note in Chapter 1, pp. 7-8.

Equipment

For all sections:

1. Relevant Ordnance Survey Maps.
2. Notebook or score card, ball-point pen or pencil, polybag large enough to hold these while writing in the rain, or lap-top computer.
3. Camera (and spare film or tape).
4. Towel.
5. Field glasses (if found of use).
6. First Aid kit.
7. (Aerial photographs will often prove helpful, particularly in catchment study.)

If entering or measuring streams (Chapters 2, 3, 4, 6):

1   Gumboots or thighboots (depending on water depth and personal preference).
2   Spade or stick to help when on slippery slopes, in swift water, etc.
3   Either depth markers on this spade or stick, or a measuring pole.

If naming river plants (Chapters 4, 6):

In the field:

1   Identification books, such as: Spencer-Jones, D. & Wade, P.M. 1986. *Aquatic Plants: A Guide to Recognition* (common species, colour photographs). Haslam, S.M. *et al.*, 1982. *British Water Plants* (complete, fully illustrated in black and white). Clapham, A.R. *et al.*, 1987. *Flora of the British Isles* (total and definitive flora, no illustrations). Chapter 4 of this book for brief key and illustrations of common species.
2   Plant grapnel or heavily weighted hook on a long rope. Polybag to keep it in when wet.
3   Polybags in which to put unknown, or odd forms of plants in. Containers for these in the car (buckets, sandwich boxes, etc.); in sunny or warm weather a thick rug or equivalent to cover these. Scrap paper to label them. *Note: The provisions of the Wildlife and Countryside Act prohibit collection of rooted plants without a permit (though weed control personnel need no permit for so doing). Rare species, or species suspected of being rare, should NEVER be picked. Photographs and notes are usually adequate.*
4   Plant press (or keep in lab). This can be made from two wire-net oven trays and strong straps. A thickness of 2–5 cm of newspaper should be put in the press, and wet specimens should be well separated. Plants will dry well if the press is kept in a car in summer. In winter, or if the specimens are needed in a hurry, put in a warm place.

In the lab:

1   10× lens.
2   White dish in which living plants can be examined under water for identification when identification was not possible in the field.
3   Thick white paper or thin card on which to mount pressed specimens. Plants may be attached by transparent tape or gum. Each should be labelled with the plant's name (send to an expert if necessary), site, habitat and the date of collection.
     A REFERENCE COLLECTION OF PRESSED (NON-RARE) SPECIES WILL BE FOUND TO BE VERY USEFUL.

For identifying community types:

Rock type maps, e.g. Geological Survey 1:250,000, solid and drift. Haslam, S.M. & Wolseley, P.A. (1981), *River Vegetation*, Cambridge University Press.

If studying catchment pollution (Chapter 5):

It is improbable that all the information requested in the questions here will be available, or indeed be necessary. That which is needed for the particular survey should be sought for that survey. As wanted:

1   Rock type maps (for nutrient-poor and nutrient-rich rocks in the catchment), see above.
2   Land use and soil type maps as available.
3   The Environment Agency or Scottish Environment Protection Agency (earlier, National Rivers Authority and River Purification Board), giving positions, type and severity of major discharges, and of some minor pollutions.
     These should include:
     (a) entries of main sewage treatment works effluent;
     (b) town areas whose run-off goes to sewage treatment works, and areas with untreated run-off;
     (c) streams carrying dirty run-off from settlements or main roads, and whether there is any purification;
     (d) smaller pollution sources, factories not discharging to STWs, mines, etc.; spills, etc., in the recent past.
4   Up-to-date map showing roads, plus observations on which are busy.
5   Farm pollutions (silage, slurry, etc.). (Theoretically, none.)
6   Distribution of septic tanks, cesspits, etc., draining into watercourses, small and large. (This may be difficult to determine, but perseverance with field observations, village enquiries, water and local authorities usually produces results.)
7   Whether unusual substances likely to reach streams, e.g. sewage sludge, are applied to fields.
8   Treatment applied, if any, to unimproved grassland, moor, woodland and similar.
9   Whether fertiliser and biocide use is as standard for the land and crop concerned.
10   Positions of weirs, cascades, bridge piers with swirling water, and other oxygenating structures in the streams.

If naming larger animals (Chapter 7):

1   Identification books, available from public libraries and educational institutions. *The New Rivers and Wildlife Handbook*, Royal Society for the Protection of Birds (etc.) is a good introduction.

2   Recent records on populations, if available (e.g. from the British Trust for Ornithology, County Trusts, Royal Society for the Protection of Birds, Environment Agency, Otter Trust, Royal Society for the Conservation of Nature).

3   Severity of pollution in the site area (if available: from using Chapter 6, or from the records of the EA and SEPA).

If studying cultural heritage (Chapter 10):

1   Relevant street maps of town centres, if available. 1:60,000 (or larger-scale) Ordnance Survey maps usually show the position of the old centres.

2   As available, local history books, pamphlets, Victoria County History, etc.

If studying archaeological heritage (Chapter 11):

No equipment, as only preliminary observations can be made (see below).

If studying Recreation (Chapter 12):

No equipment.

Recording and assessment

First decide – and mark – which parts are going to be recorded! Beginners, please do not be put off by the seemingly fearsome list of attributes that can be recorded: stick to the sections in which you have an interest and which do not appear fearsome. **Study the section before recording,** as many of the questions require text knowledge to answer.

The records here are a guide and minimum. Anyone wishing to evaluate and interpret in detail should, after recording the site data here, re-read the relevant chapters and make further notes from that, and, indeed, then go further into the patterns seen in the field and the literature and make further comments.

In recording, there may be only one answer to a question, e.g. a brook 0.5 m wide, on stream width, will score only the first of 'up to 1 m/1–3 m/4–8 m/10–25 m/over 25 m'. There may also be multiple answers, though, as when a stream, over the visible reach, varies 6 m–3 m–2 m–5 m, and both 1–3 m and 4–8 m are scored. Some questions are not applicable to all sites, and so are sometimes left unanswered.

PHOTOGRAPHS show many features better than do words or figures, and show features other than those being studied currently, which may be essential to later projects. A photographic collection is most valuable – provided it is easily accessible. A4 notebooks, with six photographs on a double-page spread, are good for both study and storage. Each photograph MUST BE LABELLED with full identifying data, whether or not this is also written in the notebook. If the photographs are stuck down with Bluetak, they remain in place and are easily removed for other studies.

When variations in rivers are due solely to the presence of bridges, etc., they should be ignored in the recording unless of direct relevance. For instance, that a bridge shades and therefore reduces vegetation below it, is of no ecological relevance to river type unless for example the degree of shade necessary to produce a given vegetation loss is being studied. Channels narrowing or widening under bridges are equally irrelevant – unless for example the water depth for each width of that river is under study. The turbulence caused by bridge piers is relevant to river oxygenation, but not to the vegetation patterns of the main course of the river (unless vegetation is being studied in relation to flow variables).

When constructing a computer program to store the data, the site data (locality, grid reference) MUST be entered for each site. Information without this is worthless. All other information is optional, and the program should allow entry or no entry. The 'comment' for each question comes under the 'free text' domain heading.

For example, for ORACLE, using the attribute of stream width, the program would read:

Name of attribute	Stream width
Domain	Width code, for any or several of: up to 1 m, 1–3 m, 4–8 m, 10–25 m, 25+ m
	Free text
Optional	Yes (not being site data)[1]
Format	Code for width
Unique	No, repeatable on other visits
Definition	Explaining width (if necessary)

[1] Sub-programs can of course be devised for particular purposes, which specify which attributes are to be entered. These should always be for minimum entries so that the observer must enter the specified data, but may enter all else that seems relevant.

Summary sheet

The summary sheet can be used alone, or to summarise part or all of the later sheets. It is probable that many observers will be wanting to study a smaller number of aspects, and construct their own summary sheets.

1. Site data

Site, locality (including grid reference) and date of record should all be noted.

Site [   ]   Grid reference [   ]   Date [   ]   Site No [   ]

AFFIX PHOTOGRAPH — 15 cm × 10 cm

1. Water adequate for stream type and width   Yes/No   Comment:
2. Architecture of bed and bank satisfactory   Yes/No   Comment:
3. Architecture of vegetation satisfactory   Yes/No   Comment:
4. Structure in settlements satisfactory   Yes/No   Comment:
5. Buffer strip present and satisfactory   Yes/No   Comment:
6. Stream type (vegetation) [   ]   Comment:
7. Purifying power of river satisfactory   Yes/No
8. Pollutants entering.   Agrochemicals   Much/Little/No   Run-off   Much/Little/No
    Small effluents   Much/Little/No   Large effluents   Much/Little/No
9. Land use of catchment: [   ]   [   ]
10. Fragile watercourse present   Yes/No   Type [   ]   Comment:
11. Damage Rating [   ]   Pollution Index [   ]   Comment:
12. Comment:

    Geomorphological features [   ]
    Recreational features [   ]
13. Evidence of larger animals seen [   ]   Comment:
14. Features of historic or cultural interest present [   ]

    Comment:

15. Site is in an excellent state for: [   ]

    Good state for: [   ]

    Fair state for: [   ]

    Poor state for: [   ]

Comment:

16. Recommendations: [   ]

For water (Chapter 2)

Surveys can be done at any time of year, but as streams are usually shallowest in late summer, records then are the most valuable for assessing damaging levels (in the present state of British streams).

Surveying can be from any site beside or above the river which gives a clear view of the water and bed (looking down rather than sideways decreases reflection and improves visibility. Polaroid lenses also help some people here). Bridges are useful sites with legal access.

Storm water levels should be noted as such. Looking for tributaries needs good vantage points or access along river banks.

For large-scale patterns, open views, large-scale maps or aerial photographs are needed.

Where water-gauges are in operation their records (if obtainable) are of course invaluable: but the relationship between the water at the uppermost gauged site, and of the tributaries and Main River above that site should be established.

2. Width

With a little practice on marked lengths, width can be estimated by eye to the nearest metre up to *c.* 5 m, to the nearest 2 m up to *c.* 10 m, and equivalently thereafter. Those accustomed to jumping brooks will already be able to judge their maximum jumping width, and be able to use this as a standard.

0–3 m (i and ii) [Yes/No]   4–8 m (iii) [Yes/No]   10–25 m (iv) [Yes/No]

25+ m (v) [Yes/No] | Comment: |

3. Depth

With practice using a marked pole or spade, this can be estimated by eye to the nearest 10 cm up to 30 cm, to the nearest 25 cm, up to 1 m, and equivalently thereafter (excluding any very clear springs, which must be measured individually). Those accustomed to walking in streams will already be able to judge 'gumboot depth' or 'thighboot depth' and be able to use these as standards. Turbid waters need a pole or a weighted rope, but for this survey a depth of 'at least 1 m', ordinarily estimable by eye, is commonly all that is wanted.

The depth recorded is that of most of the bed, not that of deep holes, shoals, etc. – unless these also are wanted.

Dry [Yes/No]   Up to 15 cm [Yes/No]   20–30 cm [Yes/No]

30–75 cm [Yes/No]   75–120 cm [Yes/No]   Deeper [Yes/No]

Is depth appropriate for width (see Table 2.1) [Yes/No] | Comment: |

4. Flow type

Negligible flow: water hardly moving. *Slow flow*: water obviously moving, water surface calm, trailing plant parts still. *Moderate flow*: water surface somewhat disturbed, trailing plants moving. *Fast flow*: water surface disturbed, trailing plant parts moving vigorously. *Rapid/whitewater*: water surface broken, much swirling and disturbance.

Negligible [Yes/No]   Slow [Yes/No]   Moderate [Yes/No]   Fast [Yes/No]

Rapid/whitewater [Yes/No] | Comment: |

5. Water loss

Dry bed [Yes/No]

Depth under 75 cm, little or no vegetation (and few species) across the 3+ m wide bed, but a well-developed emergent fringe (generally with more species present than in the reference community) usually recent drying | Yes/No |

Sunk channels, land drainage | Yes/No |

If relevant, and aided by large-scale recent and old maps:

Tributaries being lost? | Yes/No | What percentage of tributaries lost? | Yes/No |

When? | _____ | Tributaries piped underground: | Yes/No |

| Comment: |

6. Stream pattern (and see Chapter 3) (if relevant)

Stream order | 1 | 2 | 3 | 4 | 5 |

Density of tributaries | High/Middle/Low |

Pattern typical of | _____ | | Comment: |

7. Flow regime (from gauge results) (if relevant)

| Comment: |

8. Water quantity (see Table 2.1)

Satisfactory | Yes/No | Doubtful | Yes/No | Endangered | Yes/No |

| Comment (including action recommended to restore water): |

9. Water quality (if relevant)

Pollution index from Chapter 6 | Yes/No | Pollution indices from EA chemical surveys (e.g. NWC) | Yes/No |

Pollution indices from EA invertebrate surveys(e.g. BMWP) | Yes/No |

For River Structure (Chapter 3)

The purpose of the survey should be clearly determined before recording. It is rare for full field data to be needed on all points.

Surveys for banks and beds can be done at any time of year, but as they are usefully combined with those of vegetation structure and architecture, are best done between mid-June and mid-September.

Surveying can be from any site above or beside the river which gives a clear view of both below- and above-water features and vegetation, or by walking river banks, equally if there is a clear view. Bridges are useful sites with legal access. Looking down rather than sideways (and, for some people, using polaroid glasses) decreases reflections and improves visibility.

For some features (such as trees, channel position, banks grazed or recently dredged) adequate information may be obtained from scattered single sites, such as bridges, providing these have clear views. For other features, such as the suitability of reaches as legacy areas, overall shading and, especially, potential for management for enhancement, much of the relevant river length must be seen. Aerial photographs may be valuable.

In the field, brief notes can be made of features which need enhancement (poor vegetation, over-smooth banks, etc.) and those that are particularly satisfactory. Later, the records of river management, etc., can be matched with the results as surveyed. Then, with due regard to flood, hydraulic, geomorphological and other (e.g. money) constraints, plans can be made for the enhancement of poor areas and the conservation of good ones (see Chapter 8).

10. River architecture

See the figures in Chapter 3 for guidelines on what constitutes good, and bad structure, and those in Chapter 4 for whether the architecture seen is proper to the stream type.

Bank: height, slope and diversity; and whether stoning or other constructions are present.

Bed: substrate type, diversity, degree of shoaling or accumulation of other unconsolidated material, any obvious organic carbon (peat, fallen leaves, fallen wood, etc.); and whether stoning or other constructions are present.

Vegetation: complexity and quantity of that on the upper bank, lower bank plus waters edge, and bed. Complexity is the more important – and a choked channel has little complexity of vegetation. For trees, record their presence and the proportion of length covered. If relevant, note in 'comment' how much of the channel is shaded; whether the trees contribute to the habitat diversity beside the water or on the bank; whether they contribute, through falling material, to organic carbon, invertebrates' food, and falling invertebrates as food, to supplies in the river; the tree grouping: scattered, in lines, patches, woods, etc.

The table gives only minimum data.

	Exceptional diverse	Good	Fair	uniform /none	Stream type	Proper to stream	metres (length/)
Bank							
Indigenous materials							
Constructions, e.g. fence, wall, lined channel							
Bed							
Indigenous material							
Features e.g. pool–riffle sequence							
Trees on bank							
Vegetation in bank							
Excluding trees							
Upper bank							
Lower bank							
Vegetation in bed							

Comment:

11. Channel position and pattern

Is the channel at the base of the valley? If not, note the presumed cause (e.g. mill stream, watering channel, motorway or buildings necessitating diversion). Is the channel straight or winding? If winding, how much and whether showing one, or more than one, wave pattern (see text). Observe whether the shape appears to have been determined by topography or by human impacts.

Channel in valley base   Yes/No   If No, why? [   ]

Channel straightened   Yes/No   If Yes, what %? [   ]

Importance of topography in positioning channel Much/Little/No   Winding Much/Little/No

Wave pattern   [1 | 2 | 3] Comment:

12. Bank stability (architecture, not geomorphology)

Banks slumping   Yes/No   Erosion at bends   Yes/No

Other (specify)   Yes/No   [   ]

How is stability maintained (or lost?):

Banks low and firm   Yes/No   Held by trees   Yes/No   Held by brambles or other tall vegetation   Yes/No

Held by grasses   Yes/No   Held by tall monocots at water's edge   Yes/No

Held by concrete, piles, etc.   Yes/No   Comment (including causes, e.g. trampling, anglers, incorrect channelling):

13. Organic carbon

Plenty of dead leaves, twigs, other debris visible (not choking or 100% cover, but well obvious)   Yes/No

Comment:

14. Sediment deposition

Are silt-banks (or other sediment) accumulating ☐ Yes/No

If yes, is this likely to be due to anything other than excessive erosion? ☐ Yes/No

Comment:

15. (Buffer strips, see 30)

16. Legacy areas

Are there any stretches which are, or could be made, suitable?

Present ☐ Yes/No   Enough ☐ Yes/No   Potential for more ☐ Yes/No

Legacy areas need clean water as well as good structures

Suitable ☐ Yes/No | Comment:

17. Management to reduce vegetation

Shading efficiently reduces vegetation below.

Recent dredging: bare banks, often 1.5:1 slope, spoil obvious, *Juncus effusus* on lowland banks, etc.

Recent cutting: cut banks or beds, piles of cut bed vegetation, no trees on ungrazed bank, no woody plants on ungrazed bank (the latter indicate regular, not necessarily recent management).

Grazing or trampling: short grass swards indicate grazing, or frequent mowing, growth retardant sprays – but slow-growing grass species need but infrequent mowing.

Biocides: herbicides may be used to control bank or bed vegetation, and the long-term results are rather similar to those of cutting.

	Major	Minor	Absent (probably)	Ecologically satisfactory	Comments:
Shading					
Dredging					
Cutting					
Grazing					
Biocides					
Boats					
Trampling					
Picnic, walk by					
Anglers					
Other (specify)					

Comment:

18. Rivers in settlements

	Exceptional	Good	Fair	Bad	Comments:
For conservation value					
For ornamental value					

Comment:

19. Wetland dykes (see Appendix to Chapter 3)

	Exceptional	Good	Fair	Bad	Comments:
Status					

Comment:

20. Features needing improvement

Comment:

For river types: vegetation (Chapter 4)

Surveys should usually be done between mid-June and mid-September. They can start two weeks earlier in the south, particularly in a warm year, and may have to start up to two weeks later in the north in a cold year. The first severe autumn storms (or frosts) usually disrupt vegetation, and it is too late for re-growth. These storms are usually in late September, but may be earlier or later. Storm flows should be avoided (unless both vegetation and 'normal' depth can be seen). If storm flows remove much vegetation, a recovery period should be allowed (unless, of course, it is storm damage which is being measured).

Sites are what can be seen and recorded from bridges or other vantage points. Looking down, and, for some people, using polaroid glasses, decreases reflections on, and improves visibility through the water. Where necessary or relevant, grapnel or wading should be used. (Short browny species in deep water are under-recorded by this method, so are not used in classification. Other errors are corrected for by using the one method consistently. See Haslam, 1987 for justification of using point sites.)

Species to be recorded are those plants within the water, on bed and bank; on the bank, only plants rooted in the water (or, if summer water levels are abnormal, only those in the normal summer channel). This method leads to pollution assessment, so scores only those species regularly affected by polluted water. Count all mosses as one species. Count the common (non-oligotrophic) *Callitriche* spp., *C. obtusangula*, *C. platycarpa* and *C. stagnalis* as one species. Count *Lemna minor* and *L. gibba* as one species. Count Batrachian *Ranunculus* spp. as one species, except where easily distinguished (so species complexes are not present). Fig. 4.5 helps assessment of cover.

> **If relevant for the purpose in hand, then also record any or all of:**
> - Width.
> - Water clarity. With Secchi disc or just the depth to which objects can be seen.
> - Flow type, see 4 above.
> - Pattern of width and depth, if present.
> - Types of substrate, their pattern and distribution.

The numbers of sites to be recorded varies with the purpose of the survey and the variability of the river. For a general survey of a whole river on a single rock type and representative topography, as a general guide estimate the length from source to mouth (say 50 miles, 80 km) and record this number of sites in miles (i.e. in this instance, 50 miles, 50 sites), or rather over half the number of the length in km (i.e. in this instance 80 km, 50 sites). The sites should be SPREAD OVER BOTH THE MAIN STREAM AND ITS TRIBUTARIES, whether or not these are Main River.

Such a survey may of course miss sewage treatment works, reservoirs, recent drainage, etc., and their effects. It is a general survey only. When surveying for special purposes, e.g. for STW effluent effects, vegetation outside the affected reach should be recorded (beginners using at least three sites, and if variable, more), and then the affected reach, recording each stage and change in the pollution pattern (unless only the length of the affected reach is wanted). Depending on habitat, records may be needed every 25 m, or every 2 km may suffice.

The records gained from the above surveys will enable damage ratings and pollution indices to be calculated, see Chapter 6. Some of the optional records may then be advantageous or necessary in the interpretation of the damage rating.

21. List of species present at site (note if 'much' or 'little')

22. Community characters

Site diversity, number of species [   ]   cover % [   ]

Colour Band [   ]   Pollution-tolerant or semi-tolerant species present, % [   ]

Diversity and complexity of plant habit in channel [Much/Medium/Little]

[Comment:]

23. Stream type:

Rock type [Limestone/Sandstone/Clay/Resistant/Acid peat/Fen peat/Alluvium] Other (specify) [   ]

Landscape type [Plain/Lowland/Upland/Mountain/Alpine] Size category [(i) / (ii) / (iii) / (iv)]

(i): 0–3 m, no water-supported species. (ii): 0–3 m with water-supported species, (iii): 4–8 m. (iv): 10+ m. Check whether depth of site corresponds with width, and correct if not – see text).

[Comment:]

24. Comparison with reference community in Chapter 4

Are (21) and (22) in agreement with the reference vegetation in Chapter 4? [Yes/No]
If 'No', site is damaged. For assessment see Chapter 6, nos. 32, 33 below.
Is the bank at the site in agreement with the reference vegetation in Chapter 4? [Yes/No]
If 'Yes', it is appropriate to the river type.
If 'No', does it have less complexity, more steep banks, more smoothness, more short dull uniformity? [Yes/No]
If 'Yes' bank is damaged.
Or does bank have more complexity, or more variation in architecture or diversity or lower banks? [Yes/No]
If 'Yes', bank is, in the absolute, better architecturally and structurally. However, study of Chapter 4 is needed to show whether this is a 'better' bank for the particular river type, or whether management has been inappropriate.

[Comment:]

25. Vegetation pattern and distribution

Detail is essential for the intensive study of vegetation, and for monitoring long-term patterns! (e.g. 5 × 3 m *Sparganium erectum* clump downstream from left pier). Photographs are advisable. The general pattern is necessary for assessing habitat for larger fauna (Chapter 7, see 40–42 below).

[Comment:]

26. Fragile watercourses: those dependent on the continuance of traditional management for their existence

Moorland, heath, chalk-spring and acid sands, etc. streams are very easily destroyed. It would be valuable to monitor those remaining every five years, recording also the land use. More intensive land use may well destroy the habitats, e.g. more intensive farming (fields and livestock units), more roads, more built-up areas, supermarkets, factories, etc. (See text for more details.)

Fragile watercourse present? [Yes/No]   Type [   ]

Is protection adequate at this time? [Yes/No]

If 'No', what further protection could be given? [   ]

If 'Yes', describe. [   ]

[Comment:]

For Pollution (Chapter 5)

Surveys are best done between mid-June and mid-September when vegetation is up, but can be done at any time for non-vegetation features.

For a full survey, banks must be walked along the whole river system, large rivers and brooks, and the full use of all the catchment should be known. However, preliminary surveys from point sites (e.g. bridges or other vantage points) and short lengths of easily-accessible banks, together with notes made while driving between these, can be revealing and can determine whether a more detailed study is needed for the purpose in hand. This is particularly true for observers using vegetation to assess pollution (32, 33 below), who can quickly infer whether there are effluents, etc. entering between two recorded sites and influencing the downstream one.

27. Area assessed for this survey

Is the area being assessed:

| That seen from point site? | Yes/No | Along what length (in km or m)? | Yes/No |
| All upstream of site seen? | Yes/No | The whole catchment of the stream? | Yes/No |

Comment:

28. Purifying power of river

Light. Is channel well-lit? If small, is water above-ground, and channel wide enough not to be bank-shaded? Is there shade from trees or buildings?

Is light Exceptional/Good/Fair/Poor/None

Oxygen. Is water well-oxygenated by the flow? Is the water surface disturbed by the moving water? Are there intermittent weirs, bridge-piers, cascades?

Is incoming oxygen Exceptional/Good/Fair/Poor/None

Vegetation. Is vegetation adequate? Is total cover at least 20%? Is architecture complex? Is there a good source of organic carbon, either from leaf, etc. fall from above or from within-river vegetation? Very thick vegetation in still or slow water can be oxygen-deficient.

Is vegetation Exceptional/Good/Fair/Poor/None

Purifying ability. Since good vegetation can compensate for lack of turbulence, and vice versa,

Is purifying power Exceptional/Good/Fair/Poor/None

Comment:

29. Pollutants entering, chronic pollutions, and non-catastrophic spills

Agrochemicals. In the near catchment, how much receives intensive, few and no agrochemicals? (Gardens may produce more poisonous run-off per unit area than fields.)

Along the stream is there a buffer-strip of at least 10 m wide? (5 m if peaty, 50 m if not, both do a better cleaning job). Is a buffer strip only along the Main River or also along the feeder streams whose entering chemicals are even less diluted?

Run-off. What are the sources of damaging run-off? Include busy roads, garages, rural industrial premises, village housing estates, etc. – and town ones if not connected to sewage treatment works. Walking the banks is essential to trace the (many) unrecorded inputs.

Is there any amelioration: settling ponds, flow through vegetated ditches, etc.?

Small effluents. Known effluents can be checked at their points of entry. The previously unrecorded ones must be found by walking the banks. They can be spotted by their unpleasing water, or by their harmful effects on stream vegetation (Chapter 6) or by invertebrate, etc. study. Important finds should be further investigated (source, and as relevant, chemical analyses, invertebrate indices, fish ecology, etc.). Effluents too minor to cause further damage to a river may yet be harmful enough to prevent recovery from pollutions entered upstream.

Is there any amelioration: settling ponds, flow through vegetated ditches, etc.?

Sewage treatment works and other large effluents. Are there any?

Rubbish. Is this dumped in rivers? at bridges?

Note: *the combined effect of many small sources of run-off and small effluents is often, in the 1990s, more damaging than effluents from STWs.*

	Extreme	Much	Moderate	Low	Nil
Agrochemicals					
Run-off from built-up areas, busy roads, car park, etc.					
Small effluents individually the sum of all					
Large effluents, STW etc.					

Comment:

30. Protection from pollution

(a) **Buffer strips.**

Strips of unpoisoned land beside the stream

One side (specify) [　　　] Width [　　] (m) (including [　] m of wide bank) % channel [　　]

Other side [　　　] Width [　　] (m) (including [　] m of wide bank) % channel [　　]

Length or % of strip upstream [　　　] On Main River only [Yes/No] On feeder streams also [Yes/No]

Vegetation: Species diversity [High/Middle/Low]   Complexity [High/Middle/Low]

Community type:

Tree	[Yes/No]	Shrub	[Yes/No]	Grass	[Yes/No]
Tall land herbs	[Yes/No]	Tall wetland herb	[Yes/No]	Grass (land)	[Yes/No]
Grass (Wetland)	[Yes/No]	Short wetland mix	[Yes/No]	No vegetation	[Yes/No]
Concrete or the like	[Yes/No]	Roads	[Yes/No]	Other (specify)	[Yes/No]
				[　　　]	

(b) **Unpoisoned land by river** (wider, so more effective than buffer strips).

Traditional grassland [Yes/No]   Marsh, fen [Yes/No]

% length or km [　　　]   % length or km [　　　]

Moorland, heath, bog, etc. [Yes/No]   Traditional woodland [Yes/No]

% length or km [　　　]   % length or km [　　　]

Total, length or % of all these upstream [　　　　　]

on Main River any [Yes/No]   On feeder streams also [Yes/No]

(c) **Vegetated ditches** and **settling ponds** for small pollutions.

Ditches: present [Yes/No]   Long enough/(water clean at end) [Yes/No]   Enough of them [Yes/No]

Settling ponds: present [Yes/No]   Large enough/(exit water clean) [Yes/No]   Enough of them [Yes/No]

(d) **Underdrain water cleaned.**

Underdrains run direct into streams [Yes/No]   If 'No': open and seep into buffer strip [Yes/No]

Dug to form horseshoe wetlands [Yes/No]   Other (specify) [Yes/No]

[　　　]

Comment:

31. Land use

The land use near the stream has a greater effect than that further off.

(a) **Nutrient-poor influences** (e.g. bog, moor, heath, birch- or conifer-wood).

Present [Yes/No]   Specify [   ]   Influence [Major/Minor/Negligible]

Note: influences are relative as well as absolute, a bog stream flowing through grassland will be raised in nutrient status, 'eutrophicated'.

(b) **Nutrient-rich influences** (e.g. well-farmed, ploughed, fertilised land, gardens).

Present [Yes/No]   Specify [   ]   Influence [Major/Minor/Negligible]

(c) **Nutrient-neutral influence** (e.g. marshes, unfertilised woods, traditional grassland).

Present [Yes/No]   Specify [   ]   Influence [Major/Minor/Negligible]

(d) **Lakes** (cleaning influences).

Present on the studied river [Yes/No]   Influence [Major/Minor/Negligible]

Present elsewhere in vicinity (less use to the river) [Yes/No]

(e) **Built-up major roads car parks, etc.** (dirty and nutrient-rich influence).

Present [Yes/No]   Specify [   ]   Influence [Major/Minor/Negligible]

(f) **Set-aside** or other EU/Government scheme land left unpoisoned (check: golf courses are treated).

Present [Yes/No]   Specify [   ]   Influence [Major/Minor/Negligible]

Entered under neutral influence above? [Yes/No]

(g) **Silting and flash floods.** These are increased by having much bare soil, large fields, few cross-ditches and bare soil on hills; flash floods also by tarmacced and built-up land. The features can be seen, their effect usually needs enquiries, or repeated visits, not just a single visit.

Condition present [Yes/No]   Specify [   ]   Influence [Major/Minor/Negligible]

[Comment:]

For assessing pollution and other damage using vegetation (Chapter 6)

32. Simple stream pollution assessment

From point sites, use the method described in Chapter 6, p. 174 (at the same season, etc. as described in **33** here).

Pollution [Severe/Moderate/Mild/Perhaps none]

This method is inaccurate, and is intended for beginners wishing to understand the effects of pollution on vegetation. For this, it is invaluable. With more experience, the proper method can be used, and only these latter results should appear in official reports.

[Comment:]

33. Stream damage rating

Determine the reference stream type and size category from Chapter 4, and list its minimum diversity, minimum cover and its Colour Band.

For lowlands and lower hills, calculate damage rating and pollution index as described in text. When doing intensive work in any region, and when experienced in the principles involved, determine both the reference communities and the pollution-tolerant, etc. species for this local region, and use these. Greater accuracy and a more detailed grading will then be obtained.

For highlands, after experience has been gained in the lowlands, and if enough vegetation is intermittently present, determine and then calculate a damage rating (three-, five- or even eight-point, depending on the habitat) for the rivers concerned.

Reference river community, name [   ]

Minimum site diversity [   ]   Minimum site cover [   ]   Colour Band [   ]

Investigated site [   ]

Diversity [   ]   Cover [   ]   Colour Band [   ]

Pollution-tolerant species present: [   ]

Semi-tolerant species present: [   ]

Use Table 6.7.

Species diversity allowance [   ]   Decrease in diversity [   ]

% decrease in % cover [   ]   change in Colour Band [   ]

% pollution tolerance [   ]   Weighting for special spp. [   ]

Weighting for clay [   ]   **Total no.** [   ]

DAMAGE RATING [   ]   Estimate of non-pollution damage [   ]

Estimated POLLUTION INDEX [   ]   Comment: [   ]

34. Sewage fungus, 'sewage algae'

Sewage fungus [Present/Frequent/Abundant]   typical length (m) [   ]

Sewage algae [Present/Frequent/Abundant]   Comment: [   ]

35. Nitrate assessment

Is nitrate the only pollutant to the stream? [Yes/No]

(Sewage, factory and farm effluents, urban, road and car park run-off contain numerous chemicals, often including nitrate or substances degrading to nitrate, and most arable fields are given a mix of fertilisers.)

Is there (eutrophic) change in Colour Band with no change in total cross-section diversity, cover [Yes/No] or pollution tolerance?

If 'Yes', fertiliser pollution is probable.

Is self-purification of other pollutions quicker in otherwise-similar reaches with wide buffer strips [Yes/No] or unpoisoned land by the river than in arable, etc.?

If 'Yes', agrochemical pollution is present.

36. Comments on pollution damage

[   ]

37. Comments on non-pollution damage

[   ]

38. Wetland dyke and British canal damage rating

de Lange and van Zon architecture index (dykes)

Damage rating (Britain) (dykes and canals)

Comment on pollution and other damage:

39. CoDi, cover-diversity numbers

Surveys are best done from mid-June to mid-September, but from early June to early October will usually be adequate. Point sites such as bridges and other vantage points should be used (for reasons, see above). After storms, wait until swirling brown water has subsided and visibility is normal. If much vegetation has been removed, wait a few weeks unless the purpose is to assess storm damage.

When recording,

- For each species, score one, except that aggregates e.g. *Callitriche* spp., Batrachian *Ranunculus* spp. and all mosses each score as one.
- For each 10% cover, score one, except that over 20% of *Lemna* spp. or *Azolla* spp. scores only one.
- Add the cover and diversity scores.

CoDi numbers along stretch

Causes of variation

Surroundings influence vegetation. These may be simple, e.g. pool–riffle sequences, or complex, e.g. land use. When working only with CoDi numbers, therefore, it may be easier to record on preliminary survey those factors which are having an obvious effect (see text). Afterwards, diagrams and maps can be drawn, and the CoDi numbers matched to the known habitat factors. A repeat survey can then, if necessary, identify factors responsible for discrepancies.

If the habitat factors reducing CoDi numbers in a region are predominantly man-made, the CoDi number from more detailed surveys can be used alone, without accompanying habitat data, as a general index of degree of human interference.

Comment:

For structural habitat for larger animals (Chapter 7)

Surveys may be done at any place or part of the river, or along the whole (Main River plus smaller streams) depending on the information wanted.

Where herbaceous vegetation is relevant, surveys should be done between May and October. Where vegetation height and type are irrelevant, surveys may be done at any time. However, in all places avoid, if at all possible, disturbing potential hiding places, and in remote parts, avoid disturbance during the breeding season.

Assessing potential habitat is only the first step, particularly for birds and otters. Advice should next be sought from experts to find out whether the site is a haunt of the particular species, or whether (geographically) it could be made so. Available habitat should be checked along the length, watching also for non-obvious hazards (e.g. birds nesters, intermittent visitors leaving tins and polybags). It may be possible to introduce otters or common waterfowl.

40. Larger animal species seen

List the species seen, also evidence of recent presence (e.g. otter spraints, fallen egg shells).

List separately the non-riverine species seen (e.g. Barn Owl, Woodpecker)

If full data are wanted, ten visits is the standard adopted by the International Bird Census Committee between mid-March and mid-June in southern England, later further north; and preferably in the early morning.

Crayfish Yes/No

Amphibians: no. of species seen: as adult

tadpoles

spawn (March to May)

Species names, if known

Birds: no. of species: [　　] Species names, if known [　　　　　　　]

[　　　　　　　　　　　　　　　　　　]

If not known:

No. of species on water (swimming: duck, grebe, etc.) [　　]   No. of species wading at edge   [　　]

No. of species otherwise water-associated (e.g. kingfisher) [　　]

No. of species on bushes, trees, etc. by river [　　]

How many breeding pairs of each bird species (if relevant) [　　]

Mammals: no. of species: [　　]   Species names, if known [　　　　　　]

[　　　　　　　　　　　　　　　　　　]

If not known:

About 0.75–1.25 m long (otter, mink, coypu) [Yes/No]   About 0.5 m long (water vole, etc.) [Yes/No]

Smaller, mouse-sized [Yes/No]   How many riverine species per unit length (say, 1 km) [　　]

How many of each species (approximate, if relevant) for the same length [　　]

Comment: [　　　　　　　　　　　　　　　　　]

41. Pollution

If a species is resident in a habitat, obviously it can tolerate the water quality of that habitat. However, adult animals may tolerate pollution severe enough to prohibit the food of the young (e.g. mallard), and animals passing through and stopping for a few hours or days may be unable to tolerate a given river's pollution long term.

Pollution status [　　　　　　　　　]

Animals tolerating this as resident adults (if known) [　　　　　　　　]

Animals breeding satisfactorily in this (if known) [　　　　　　　　]

Improving pollution can only seldom be done by individuals: it is the business of the Environment Agency.

42. Disturbance

If a species is resident in a habitat, obviously it can tolerate the disturbance of that habitat. However, adults may tolerate disturbance severe enough to prohibit the rearing of young (e.g. otters), and animals passing through and stopping for a few hours or days may be unable to tolerate a given river's disturbance long-term.

Disturbance affects species unequally, e.g. crayfish will be unaffected by movements sufficient to disperse oyster catcher or otter.

Disturbance status of reach (e.g. little; weekend visitors; busy road but no pedestrians). [　　　]

If basing this on only one visit, put a large question mark! [　　　　]

Animals tolerating this as resident adults (if known) [　　　　]

Animals breeding satisfactorily in this (if known) [　　　　]

Does disturbance appear to be too much for any of the animals seen [Yes/No]

Should something be done to lessen disturbance?   [Yes/No]

If 'Yes', what? [　　　　　　　　　　　　　]

Chapters 8, 9, and 12 have no specific assessments, but general comments concluded from a study of the site and the text (or from relevant books) can be listed here

[　　　　　　　　　　　　　　　　　　　　　
　
　
　　　　　　　　　　　　　　　　　　　　　]

For historic and recent cultural heritage (Chapter 10)

Cultural heritage may be surveyed at any time of year. Buildings and other structures may be seen from beside the river, from bridges, from the river itself or, for larger structures and groups of structures, from more distant vantage points. Access to private land will be wanted sometimes.

In towns, the old centre should be visited. This can most easily be found using a street map. The old centre is (usually) a cluster of close-packed (often curved or irregular) streets near the river, typically with more spaced-out streets around. The original crossing point of the river was here. All (pre-mains) villages, farms, etc. had local supplies of water, usually streams. Even in some chalk areas where houses relied on wells there was usually a sizeable stream within 2 km, accessible for large quantities of water, or in time of drought. Most villages had a small stream, which may now be extant, or dried, or underground, but whose existence may be inferred from development patterns (see text). These should be located. Full developmental patterns should be worked out wherever relevant. Local history books often help with individual features, but seldom do so with river-related patterns over space or time.

Conjunctions of streams and roads (or paths), particularly old crossways, often show good patterns for villages, isolated water mills, farms, etc. Most isolated farms were built after the Enclosure Acts. Isolated watermills are often ancient (many are recorded in *Domesday Book*). Watering, drainage, irrigation and some navigation patterns are seen in open countryside, as are sites of various river crops, some holy wells, decayed small spas, etc.

Place names should be listed.

Structural features (related to the features in 45) should be listed, and as appropriate, photographs could be taken or drawings made. These can be attached to extra pages. **It is important that visual records are made in this section.**

43. Photographs

Make a reference collection. Repeat every 5–10 years.

44. Place names

List place names of river-related interest, together with their meanings

45. Structural features

Related to:

| Water supply |
| Food and materials |
| Drainage |
| Power |
| Transport |
| Crossings |
| Town, village and farm patterns |
| Road run-off pattern |
| Flood protection |
| Defence |
| Ornament |
| Recreation |
| Holy and healing waters |
| Comment: |

46. Undesirable features (best guess), and, if possible, show on photograph for later comparative assessment)

Water level (too dry/too wet)	Yes/No	Recreation (too much damage)	Yes/No
Traffic (too much)	Yes/No	Buildings (too many/too inappropriate)	Yes/No
Rubbish (too much)	Yes/No	Anglers (too much damage)	Yes/No
Disturbance, other (too much) (specify)	Yes/No	Other (specify)	Yes/No

If desired, further information on rubbish, e.g. on 50 m of bank, the number of small (less than 30 cm) and large pieces, the number of biodegradable and non-biodegradable, the number of, say, bicycles.

Comment:

47. Overall assessment of site

Is the site, for the features present (excluding their present condition): Excellent→/Good/Fair/Poor/None

Is the condition of the features: Excellent→/Good/Fair/Poor/None

Comment:

Should the site be reported to the relevant authorities for its conservation value? Yes/No

Comment:

Should the site be reported to the relevant authorities for repair of features? Yes/No

Comment:

For archaeology (Chapter 11)

Archaeological sites are valuable and fragile, and are frequently protected by national and local statutes. They should not be excavated or metal-detected by amateurs – seek professional advice in the County Archaeology Office.

First, identify the more obvious places for sites, such as villages and towns. Next, walk the area, looking for earthworks and isolated Mediaeval or early Post-Mediaeval buildings such as mills, any of which may hint at earlier remains. Most information will be gained from visiting the County Archaeological office with a map of appropriate scale, and note down *scheduled ancient monuments*, *listed buildings*, and other known sites and areas with highest potential. A necessary prerequisite for effective consideration and management of archaeological remains is knowledge of the remains, specifically their character, date, condition, vulnerability and relative importance. This cannot be undertaken by the layman – a professional should be consulted. Archaeological consultancy and fieldwork is undertaken by many organisations operating within local authorities (counties and districts) and by independent groups (companies or trusts) based in universities or museums. A County Archaeology Office will provide a list of companies working in the area, and the Institute of Field Archaeologists maintains a list of recognised archaeological consultants. A step-by-step procedure for rescue archaeology has been published by English Heritage in the form of *The Management of Archaeological Projects*, second edition (1991). This suggests a sequence of phases of work with reviews of each phase, intended to make archaeological projects question oriented and cost effective. This management procedure is now standard in the archaeology profession.

Finally, the educational and public awareness opportunities of the heritage should be recognised and exploited. Much land and many buildings are of archaeological, historic and architectural interest, and that interest should be presented to the public.

For recreation (Chapter 12)

48. Leisure activities present (and proposed):

49. Facilities, enhancement, modifications and restrictions present:

50. Recommendations, for present (and if relevant, proposed future) numbers of visitors:

River plans

River plans (on paper or GIS on computer) are often helpful, or indeed essential, when discussing conservation interest with those intending to change rivers, whether riparian owners, the Environment Agency, Internal Drainage Boards, County Councils, Wildlife Trusts, or Consultants, etc. They may also be very valuable for research. These are working maps, large-scale plans showing features of interest. Tracing from 6″ OS maps gives a reasonably large-scale plan, which can be enlarged further on a photocopier. Smaller-scale maps can be used for less detailed mapping.

For any stretch of river, several different plans can be constructed, depending on the purpose of the survey.

These might include:
1   Land use (also including fences, roads, buildings).
2   Plant communities including trees. With relevance for birds, etc. (including stability, substrate, inflows, etc.).
3   Bank features.
4   Channel features (including cross-section, islets, weirs, substrate, water, etc.).
5   Historic environment.
6   Recreational features.
7   Habitats for larger animals (otters, duck, newts, etc.) plus signs of their presence.
8   Damage factors, including pollution and recreation, etc.
9   Most crucial or fragile river features.
10 Most deplorable river features.
11 Proposed changes and their expected effects.

Photographs should be used to explain markings on the plans.

Working maps should not be overcrowded. It is far better to have several clear ones (on transparencies if required) than to have one difficult to understand. Those planning river changes will be using River Corridor Survey maps of this type, so it is useful to be able to both construct and interpret them. (Standard symbols are given in RSPB's *The New Rivers and Wildlife Handbook*.)

Glossary

Abstraction drawing off water (e.g. from below the ground in soft limestone or sandstone, from a river, from a spring).

Acid poor in nutrients, of low pH (see dystrophic, oligotrophic).

Agg. (aggregate) used after a plant name to denote an aggregate of species which are difficult to identify separately.

Agrochemical chemical used in agriculture, e.g. fertiliser, herbicide, pesticide.

Agriculture cultivation (tillage) of the land.

Algae small green plants, not composed of stems, roots and leaves. Strictly, chlorophyll-containing thallophytes, which usually grow immersed in water (fresh or marine).

Alien belonging to somewhere else, to another country or continent. Believed on reasonable evidence to have been introduced.

Alkaline with relatively high amounts of bases, such as lime; with pH above 7.

Alluvial plain flat tract of country composed of alluvium.

Alluvium deposits of silt (sand, etc.) left by water flowing over land which is not permanently submerged; especially those deposits left in river valleys and deltas.

Alpine in river types, used in a technical sense for the most steep hill landscapes, with falls from hill top to upper stream channel of 305 m and more (or rainfall very high), upper stream channels sloping steeper than 1:40, hill height usually over 610 m and great liability to spate.

Alternate arrangement of leaves, etc. placed singly at different heights on the axis or stem, not opposite or whorled.

Amenity pleasantness of feature, view, etc., pleasantness for human life.

Angular with corners, as of stems, leaf outlines, etc.

Anion electronegative substance such as nitrate, phosphate, sulphate and chloride (see cation).

Aquatic (1) living or growing in or near water. (2) A water plant or animal.

Aquifer rock which yields water.

Arable land fit for ploughing and tillage; not grassland, woodland or built-up land; bearing crops.

Archaeology scientific study of human antiquities.

Architecture structure; patterns and style built up; the art or science of building (including of vegetation, river banks, etc.).

Bank margin of a watercourse, in this scheme used for that part above normal water level, unless otherwise stated.

Basic rich in lime or similar alkaline mineral, and probably in other nutrients also.

Bed (of river) bottom or floor of watercourse.

Benthic of the bottom, the river bed.

Berm ledge, within or just above stream water-level.

Biocide killing life – herbicides, insecticides, pesticides, rodenticides, etc.

Biological of the structure and functioning of plants and animals.

Blanket bog nearly flat tract of country composed of wet bog, wet acid peat.

Blanket weed filamentous algae (chiefly *Cladophora*) large enough to trail from the watercourse bed.

Bog wet spongy ground, consisting chiefly of decayed moss (especially *Sphagnum*) and other plants, nutrient-poor and acid.

Boulder clay clayey deposit of the Ice Age, affecting watercourses like clay.

Brook small stream.

Buffer able to neutralise extremes.

Buffer strip (zone) strip beside a watercourse, capable of cleaning (neutralising poisons in) water passing through to the stream.

Canal artificial watercourse uniting rivers, lakes or seas for the purpose of inland navigation (in various other countries, artificial channels used for irrigation or drainage).

Carbon essential element in organic compounds and hence life.

Carnivore flesh (meat-) eating.

Carr wet or damp woodland, especially in East Anglia.

Catchment natural drainage area or basin, wherein rainfall is caught and channelled to a single exit point (= American watershed).

Cation electropositive substance, such as calcium, sodium, copper or manganese (see Anion).

Channel (1) bed and below-water sides of a watercourse (sometimes extended to include above-water banks). (2) Groove or furrow in leaf, etc.

Channellised   watercourse deepened, straightened, made uniform.

Colour Band   nutrient status band.

Community, plant   the plants present in a site and their social ordering.

Conserve   to keep entire, to manage in such a way as to keep entire, to preserve and care for.

Constructed wetland water purification works using an artificial marsh, usually of reed (*Phragmites*).

Control of flow   restraint or regulation of flow, as a weir, dam, sluice, lock, etc.

Course   channel for water and its direction.

Cover   area occupied by, e.g. vegetation.

Covert   shelter (covered-over part) for mammals and birds.

Culture   type of civilisation.

Culvert   arched channel for carrying water beneath a road, railway, etc.

Dam   structure to keep water back.

Debris dam   small dam, often of tree trunk or branch, retaining debris.

Debris   remains of plants, etc., broken down or destroyed.

Deflector   groyne, a structure inserted to divert (or break-) water and drifting bed material.

Detritus   debris and other broken-down material (e.g. from river beds) usually broken down more than that referred to as debris (plant or animal).

Development   working out, unfolding or new form of that which is already there. Used both for what is there in the river and for what is there in the mind of the developer.

Discharge   total volume of water per unit time flowing through the channel.

Ditch   a long narrow channel (hollow) dug to receive or conduct water, usually 0.5–2 m wide. In North America used synonymously with British dyke, drain, etc.

Diversity   range of features or habitats, number of species present. *Site diversity*, number of species present in a given site area.

Drain   drainage channel, the larger channels of the Fenland, etc., drainage system, usually 6–20 m wide.

Drainage   drawing off water from the land.

Drainage Order   stream order, analysis of the pattern of tributaries of a river.

Dyke   an artificial watercourse for draining marshy land and moving surface water, usually 2–4 m wide. Derives from Anglo Saxon term meaning a large defensive ditch with hollow facing the enemy, bank facing the defenders.

Dystrophic   of negligible nutrient content, acid and usually composed of or stained with, bog peat. For simplicity, used instead of *dystraphent* to describe species characteristic of such a habitat.

Ecology   study of plants and animals in their habitats; mutual relations between plants and animals and their environment.

Ecosystem   the land and water, the plants and animals in these and the functioning of all these together.

Effluent   outflow from sewage treatment works, factories, farms, etc.

Emerged   (of plant parts) above water.

Emergent   a plant mainly or entirely above water.

Enhance   to rise in value, to add to.

Entire   (leaf) without toothing or division, with even margin.

Erosion   scour, the removement of material from the channel of a stream.

Eutrophic   of high nutrient status. For simplicity, used instead of *eutraphent* to describe species characteristic of such a habitat.

Eutrophication   raising of nutrient status.

Evaluate   to determine the value of.

Evapotranspiration the water lost to the air (in gas form) from the land or water plus that lost from the vegetation thereon.

Exotic   introduced from a foreign country, alien.

Fen   lowland, now or formerly covered with shallow water, or intermittently so covered. Any peat developed is alkaline (contrast bog peat) because of the high base status of the water derived from the land around.

Fen peat   peat developed in a fen.

Fertile   nutrient-rich.

Fertiliser   that which makes fertile, usually now meaning nutrients added as powders or sprays.

Flaccid   limp, lax.

Flash flood   storm flow in which water rises very rapidly, due to a combination of heavy rainfall and quick run-off in the catchment.

Flood	(1) an overflowing of water over land. (2) A storm flow.
Flood gate	contrivance for stopping or regulating the passage of water.
Flood hazard	that which, by obstructing water movement, may or will cause flooding.
Flow	water movement, quantity of water moving.
Flow type	type or kind of flow, here negligible, slow, moderate, fast and rapid or white water.
Fragile watercourses	watercourses whose habitat or ecology can be harmed or destroyed by a small change in land use or other aspect of human activity.
Fringing herbs	group of semi-aquatic, rather bushy short emergents (dicotyledons), commonly fringing the edges of certain stream types, occurring more sparsely in a wider range of types.
Gauge, water gauge	an apparatus to measure stream flow.
Geology	geologic features (rock types, etc.) of a district, science relating to the history of the earth's surface.
Geomorphology	morphology of the earth's surface.
Ground water level	plane below which the rock or soil is saturated with water.
Groyne	deflector, a structure inserted to divert (or break-) water and drifting bed material.
Habit	characteristic mode of growth and appearance of a plant or animal.
Habitat	kind of locality in which a plant or animal characteristically lives and grows.
Hardness ratio	chemical parameter devised by Dr B. Seddon, calculated as the calcium-plus-magnesium content divided by the sodium-plus-potassium content (here, usually of silt-water).
Hatch	flow-control with a half-gate that can be opened or shut.
Herb	plant of which the aerial stem does not become woody or persistent.
Herbaceous	plants not forming wood, but dying down every year.
Herbicide	substance, usually synthetic, used to kill herbs, used for weed control.
Herbivore	animal feeding on plants.
Heritage	that transmitted from ancestors or past ages.
Highland	high or elevated land. Used here in a general sense for hilly ground, and with the capital H, for the Scottish Highlands.
Hill	natural elevation of the earth's surface. Used here in a general sense.
Horseshoe wetland	small pond or wetland dug in a buffer strip at the end of an under drain, so that the drain water is (partly) purified before entering the river.
Humus	vegetable mould, brown or black substance resulting from the slow decomposition of organic matter.
Hydraulic	pertaining to water as conveyed through channels.
Hydrology	the study of water, water resources, in land areas.
Impoundment	(American) a pond caused by a dam across a stream, used for supply, water power, etc.
Improvement	change for the better: 'better' being a value judgement. Hence *improved drainage*, more water removed from the land, *improved farmland*, higher crops, *improved rivers*, improved for conservation, drainage, etc., as relevant to context.
Infertile	nutrient-poor.
Inorganic	not formed from plant or animal parts (except when these have been completely broken down); mineral.
Invertebrate	animals without backbone: insects, spiders, molluscs, worms, crustacea, etc.
Irrigation	supplying land with water.
Land Drainage	drawing off water from the land.
Leaflet	a single division of a compound leaf.
Leat	watercourse bringing water to a watermill wheel.
Legacy area	part of river managed for plant and animal populations which can act as a source to colonise other areas.
Ley	now describing temporary grassland.
Ligule	thin projection from the leaf sheath, at the base of the leaf blade.
Loafing	(birds) passing the time idly.
Lock	(of canal, etc.) portion of the channel shut off above and below by gates and provided with sluices, etc. to let the water out and in; used to raise or lower boats from one level to another.
Lowland	low-lying land. In river types, used in a technical sense for land with not over 60 m fall from hilltop to stream channel in upper reaches, slopes of channels of upper streams flatter than 1:100, hills not over 245 m, with no liability to spate flows.
Lush	luxuriant in unhealthy manner.

Macrophyte	large plant, the higher plants (angiosperms), horsetails, water ferns, mosses, liverworts and the large algae (e.g. *Chara*, *Enteromorpha*).
Main River	watercourses designated as such, in law, by the Environment Agency.
Marsh	a tract of wet land, not bearing crops.
Meadow	grassland mown (harvested) for hay (may be grazed at a different season of the year).
Meander	bend in a winding course.
Median	middle, of a line, etc.
Mesotrophic	of moderate nutrient regime. For simplicity, used instead of *mesotraphent* to describe species characteristic of such a habitat.
Metabolism	the process by which nutritive material is built up into living matter, or by which the complex substances of protoplasm are broken down to perform special functions.
Microhabitat	subdivision of a habitat, in which one or more environmental influences differ somewhat to those of other parts of the same habitat, as stony and silty patches on a stream bed.
Micro-organism	bacteria, viruses, smaller algae and fungi. *Microbial* to describe functions of these.
Migrant	of birds, etc., one changing its abode from one country or region to another.
Mineral	natural substance of neither animal nor vegetable origin.
Mobile	able to move; of stream moving rapidly, not fixed.
Monocotyledon	one of the two main groups of angiosperms (seed plants) having one seed leaf. Most often with narrow leaves and parallel veins. *Tall monocot(yledon)* term used to describe reeds, rushes and sedges.
Moorland	uncultivated land with some (dry) acid peat or humus and much heather or similar vegetation.
Morphology	study of form, of plants, animals, landscapes, etc., and the structures, etc. which influence that form.
Mountain	large hill. In river types used in a specialised sense for land with the fall from hill top to the upper reaches of the stream channel of at least 185 m, the slopes of the channels of upper streams greater than 1:40, hill heights of at least 610 m, and rivers of much liability to spate.
Multi-stage channel	watercourse which is on three or more levels in cross-section.
Navigable	of a watercourse along which boats may pass.
Navigation	(1) a navigable route. (2) A watercourse which (often in the eighteenth century) was developed for improved boat passage, on which tolls were paid, and whose rights could be bought and sold.
Neutral	belonging to neither of two opposites, as acid and alkaline.
Niche	ecological. Place or position suited to a particular plant species or community.
Nutrient	serving as nourishment, normally used of inorganic substances necessary for plant growth, such as calcium, phosphate, etc.
Oligotrophic	low in nutrients. For simplicity, used instead of *oligotraphent* to describe species characteristic of such habitat.
Omnivore	animal feeding on animal and vegetable matter.
Opposite	leaves. On both sides of the stem at the same level.
Organic	of, or pertaining to, or composing plants or animals. *Organic carbon* the carbon in living or decomposing matter.
Ovate	shaped like the longitudinal section of a hens egg, the broader end basal.
Oxygenation	supplying with oxygen.
Passage	of birds passing through.
Pasture	grazed grassland.
Peat	plant material stored and partly decomposed under water. Found in fens (alkaline peat), bogs (acid peat), moors (acid peat), etc.
Perennial	of flow running throughout the year.
Pesticide	chemical which kills pests. Usually used for synthetic chemicals killing small animals harmful for crop production or human health.
Physiography	physical geography, description of nature.
Pinnate	feather formed, as with the leaflets of a compound leaf placed on either side of an axis.
Plain	flat tract of country.
Pollard	tree, usually willow (*Salix* spp) harvested regularly by cutting above the level at which livestock can graze.
Pollutant	substance causing pollution.
Pollution	the alteration of chemical status by human interference causing alteration to plant or animal communities.

Pond	a small (usually) man-made waterbody or lake.
Ponding	rising of water level because of obstruction.
Pool	a small body of water, usually of natural origin, with slow or no water movement. As in pool and riffle sequence in streams. Also used for created deeper slower areas in streams.
Predator	one that devours other animals.
Prey	animals eaten by predators.
Productivity	rate at which new organic matter is formed.
Propagule	plant part used for propagation, such as fruit, seed, bulb, rhizome, winter bud, fragment.
Reach	portion of watercourse which can be seen in one view, hence 'lower reaches' for the lower or downstream end of a river, and 'upper reaches' for the part near the source.
Reedswamp	marsh dominated by reeds, sedges, rushes (tall monocots).
Regulation	control and order imposed on the flow of a river.
Rehabilitation	enhancement of the river towards its traditional habitat, flora and fauna.
Reservoir	receptacle constructed, usually in a river course, to contain and store a large supply of water for ordinary uses.
Resident	(bird), dwelling all year in the specified country or region, or, as summer resident, breeding there.
Restoration	bringing back to a supposed former state. Returning to a close approximation of the traditional state that is persistent and self-sustaining. (To be used with care, River Restoration usually meaning enhancement.)
Rhizome	perennial, horizontal root-like stem, usually underground but sometimes floating.
Rhyne, reen	system of dykes and drains, South Wales, south west England.
Ribbed	of leaf, longitudinal veins prominent.
Riffle	shallow section in a river where the water flows swiftly.
Rill	small brook, rivulet.
Riparian	of (or inhabiting) a river bank.
River	large stream of water flowing in a channel towards the sea, a lake or another stream.
Robust	stream type not easily changed by minor interferences, strong.
Rock	(1) material composing the hard surface of the earth, e.g. clay, limestone, resistant rock, sandstone. (2) bedrock exposed in the channel or particles the size of boulders.
Run-off	water flowing from, on and through land into watercourses, etc.
Salmonid	fish of the family salmonidae, salmon, brown trout, sea trout, etc.
Secchi disc	disk of specified type for measuring turbidity of water
Sediment	particles which fall by gravity in water: mud, silt, sand, gravel, stones and boulders.
Seepage	small water source oozing up through the ground.
Sewage	human waste, detergents and other house chemicals, etc. More widely, and originally, all wastes carried by sewers, so including industrial effluent and urban run-off.
Sewage sludge	solid wastes separated out in Sewage Treatment Works.
Sewage Treatment Works	works constructed for the purification of sewage.
Sheath	of leaf. Lower tubular part, usually enclosing stem.
Shingle	coarse gravel, bed or bank of large stones.
Shoal	submerged bank or bar.
Shrub	a low woody plant, a bush.
Silting	depositing silt.
Sinuous	winding.
Skewed	distorted, awry.
Sluice	structure for ponding the water of a watercourse, provided with an adjustable gate or gates by which the volume of water is regulated or controlled.
Soil	earth, substrate.
Solid rock	all rock types except glacial drift and recent alluvial deposits.
Solute	a dissolved substance.
Spate	large discharge or storm flow caused by heavy rains, etc., in hill streams where the water force is great.
Species	group of plants or animals having certain common and permanent characteristics distinguishing it from other groups.
Spiling	weave of willow (or other) branches used to protect watercourse banks (plug holes, plug erosion sites).

Spring	flow of water rising or issuing naturally out of the ground.
Sterile	barren, without life.
Stolon	a creeping stem produced by a plant which has a central rosette or erect stem, when used without qualification, is above ground.
Storm flow	the large water discharge that follows heavy rain.
Stream	course of water flowing along a bed on the earth, forming a river or brook.
Stream Order	drainage order, analysis of the pattern of tributaries of a river.
Stress	pressure of some adverse force or influence.
Structure	(1) constructions altering flow in streams, e.g. lock, weir, sluice. (2) manners of organisation, arrangement of parts in and by rivers.
Submerged	(of plant parts) within the water.
Submergent	a plant within the water.
Subsoil	stratum of soil lying immediately under the surface soil.
Substrate	material near the surface of the bed of the watercourse, the rooting medium, the soil.
Summer-resident	(bird). Dwelling and breeding in summer in a country or region.
Suspended solids	particles diffused throughout the water.
Synergistic	combined action greater than the sum of the component individual actions.
Tall monocotyledons	group of tall emerged aquatics with long narrow leaves, potentially forming dense stands.
Topography	morphological features of a region or locality.
Toxic	poisonous, strictly a poison derived from a plant or animal.
Transfer	water transfer. Movement of water, usually for domestic supply, from one river to another.
Translucent	imperfectly transparent.
Trapezoid	describing a channel with straight sloping banks and a flat bed, a quadrilateral with no sides parallel.
Tributary	stream that runs into another.
Trophic	of or pertaining to nutrition.
Turbid	thick or opaque with suspended matter, cloudy, opaque.
Two-stage channel	watercourse which is on two levels in cross-section.
Under-drain	small drain under field, to keep field soil dry for crops.
Unstable	apt to change or alter.
Upland	hilly country. In river types used in a specialised sense for land with falls from hill top to upper stream channels of 90-150 m, slope of channels of upper streams 1:40 to 1:80, hill heights of 245-365 m, and rivers with some liability to spate.
Vegetarian	animal eating plants.
Vegetation	plants in general, the plant life at a site.
Vein	(leaf) strand of vascular tissue.
Watercourse	stream of water, a river or brook; an artificial channel for the movement of water. The general term for water channels, including all other types defined here.
Water force	integrated physical effect of water (on plants, beds and other objects) in aggregate.
Water-supported	of plants supported by the water, floating and submerged species.
Water table	plane below which the rock or soil is saturated with water.
Water transfer	movement of water, usually for domestic supply, from one river to another.
Weir	barrier and dam to restrain water.
Well	spring, now usually a lined shaft sunk into the earth from which water is drawn.
Wetland	low-lying flat land, damp or wet when without drainage.
Wetland dyke	dyke in wetland, usually for drainage.
Wetland horseshoe	small pond or wetland dug in a buffer strip at the end of an under drain, so that the drain water is (partly) purified before entering the river.
White water	foaming water in rapids, etc.
Whorled	(leaves) cyclic arrangement of leaves on a stem.
Winterbourne	brook on soft limestone which has water flowing in a well-defined channel in winter, but dries in summer.
Wintering	(bird) present in winter.

List of principal Latin and English plant names used in the book

Contractions are those used in the river maps in Chapters 4 and 6.
An illustrated key to, and pictures of, common river plants are given in Chapter 4.

Latin name	Contraction	English name
Acorus calamus		sweet flag
Agrostis stolonifera	(Grass-a)	Fiorin, creeping bent
Alisma plantago-aquatica	(Alis)	water-plantain
Alnus glutinosa		alder
Apium nodiflorum	(Ap)	water celery, fools water-cress
Azolla filiculoides		water fern
(Benthic algae)	(B. alg)	(green patches on bed)
Berula erecta	(Ber)	water celery, lesser water-parsnip
(blanket weed)	(Bl wd)	(long trailing green algae)
Butomus umbellatus	(But)	flowering rush
Calamagrostis		
Callitriche spp.	(Call)	(term includes: C. obtusangula, C. platycarpa, C. stagnalis water starwort)
C. hamulata	(C. ham)	intermediate water starwort
Caltha palustris	(Caltha)	kingcup, marsh marigold
Carex acuta		tufted sedge
Carex acutiformis	(C. acut)	plus C. riparia, pond-sedge
Carex pendula	(C. pend)	pendulous sedge
Carex rostrata		bottle sedge
Catabrosa aquatica	(Catab, Grass-c)	whorl-grass
Ceratophyllum demersum	(Cerat)	rigid hornwort
Chara hispida		chara
Chara spp.		chara
Crassula helmsii		
Drosera anglica		great sundew
Drosera rotundifolia		sundew
Eleocharis acicularis		slender spikerush
Eleocharis palustris	(El. pal)	common spikerush
Elodea canadensis	(Elod)	Canadian pondweed
Elodea nuttallii		
Enteromorpha	(Enter)	
Epilobium hirsutum	(Epil)	great hairy willow-herb, codlins and cream
Equisetum palustre	(Eq. pal)	marsh horsetail
Eriophorum angustifolium		common cottongrass
Filipendula ulmaria		meadow-sweet
Glyceria declinata	(Grass-g)	
Glyceria fluitans	(G. fl) long-leaved, (Grass-g) short-leaved	float (flote)-grass, floating sweet grass
Glyceria maxima	(G. max)	reedgrass, reed sweet grass
Glyceria pedicularis	(Grass-g)	
Groenlandia densa	(Groenl)	opposite-leaved pondweed
Heraclium montegazzianum		giant hogweed (POISONOUS)
Hippuris vulgaris		mare's-tail
Hottonia palustris		water violet
Hydrilla verticillata		hydrilla
Hydrocharis morsus-ranae		frogbit
Hydrocotyle vulgaris		pennywort
Impatiens glandulifera		policeman's helmet
Impatiens capensis		
Iris pseudacorus	(Iris)	yellow flag, yellow iris
Juncus articulatus		jointed rush
Juncus bulbosus	(J. bulb)	bulbous rush
Juncus effusus	(J. eff)	soft rush
Juncus inflexus	(J. infl)	hard rush
Juncus subnodulosus		blunt-flowered rush
Lemna minor agg. (L. minor plus L. gibba)	(L. mi)	common duckweed
Lemna minuta		
Lemna polyrhiza		greater duckweed
Lemna trisulca		ivy-leaved duckweed
Littorella uniflora		shoreweed
Mentha aquatica	(Ment)	water mint
Menyanthes trifoliata		bog bean
Mimulus guttatus	(Mim)	monkey-flower
(mosses)	(Moss)	mosses

Latin name	Abbrev.	English name
Myosotis scorpioides	(Myos)	water forget-me-not
Myriophyllum alterniflorum		alternate-leaved water milfoil
Myriophyllum spicatum	(Myr. sp)	spiked water milfoil
Najas flexilis		slender naiad
N. marina		holly-leaved naiad
Narthecium ossifragum		bog asphodel
Nasturtium officinale agg.	(Ror. n)	water cress (formerly *Rorippa nasturtium-aquaticum*)
Nuphar lutea	(Nuph)	yellow water-lily
Nymphaea alba	(N. alb)	white water-lily
Nymphoides peltata		fringed water-lily
Oenanthe crocata	(Oen. cr)	hemlock water-dropwort (POISONOUS)
Oenanthe fluviatilis	(Oen. fl)	river water-dropwort
Osmunda regalis	(Osm)	royal fern
Parnassia palustris		grass of Parnassus
Petasites hybridus	(Pet)	butter bur
Phalaris arundinacea	(Phal)	reed-grass, reed canary-grass
Phragmites australis	(Phrag)	reed, common reed
Pinguicula vulgaris		butterwort
Polygonum amphibium	(Polyg. a)	amphibious bistort
Potamogeton alpinus		red pondweed
Potamogeton coloratus		fen pondweed
Potamogeton crispus	(Pot. crisp)	curled pondweed
Potamogeton friesii		flat-stalked pondweed
Potamogeton gramineus	(Pot. gram)	various-leaved pondweed
Potamogeton lucens	(Pot. luc)	shining pondweed
Potamogeton natans	(Pot. nat)	broad-leaved pondweed
Potamogeton nodosus	(Pot. nod)	loddon pondweed
Potamogeton pectinatus	(Pot. pect)	fennel pondweed
Potamogeton perfoliatus	(Pot. perf)	perfoliate pondweed
Potamogeton polygonifolius		bog pondweed
Potamogeton × sparganifolius		
Ranunculus spp.	(Ran)	(Batrachian) water crowfoots, short-leaved, including *R. aquatilis, R. circinatus, R. peltatus, R. trichophyllus*; mediumum-leaved, including *R. aquatilis, R. calcareus, R. penicillatus*; long-leaved, *R. fluitans*
Ranunculus flammula		lesser spearwort
Ranunculus hederaceus		ivy-leaved crowfoot
Ranunculus omiophyllus		round-leaved crowfoot
Ranunculus sceleratus		celery-leaved crowfoot
Rorippa amphibia	(Ror. a)	great yellow-cress
Rorippa austriaca		
(*Rorippa nasturtium-aquaticum*)		(see *Nasturtium officinale* above)
Rumex hydrolapathum		great water dock
Sagittaria sagittifolia	(Sag)	arrowhead
Salix alba		white willow
(*Schoenoplectus lacustris*)		(see *Scirpus lacustris*)
Scirpus fluitans		floating clubrush
Scirpus lacustris	(S. lac)	common clubrush, greater rush, bulrush
Scirpus maritimus	(S. mar)	sea clubrush
Scirpus sylvaticus	(S. sylv)	wood clubrush
Scrophularia nodosa		figwort
Solanum dulcamara	(Sol)	bittersweet, woody nightshade
Sparganium angustifolium		floating bur-reed
Sparganium emersum	(Sp. em)	strapweed, unbranched bur-reed
Sparganium erectum	(Sp. er)	bur-reed
Sphagnum spp.		bog moss
Stratiotes aloides		water soldier
Symphytum officinale		comfrey
Teucrium scordium		water germander
Typha angustifolia		lesser bulrush, lesser reedmace
Typha latifolia	(T. lat)	bulrush, greater reedmace, cat's-tail
Urtica dioica		stinging nettle
Utricularia vulgaris		greater bladderwort
Valeriana officinalis		valerian
Vallisneria spiralis		
Veronica anagallis-aquatica agg. (*V. anagallis aquatica* plus *V. catenata*)	(Ver. a)	water speedwell
Veronica beccabunga	(Ver. b)	brooklime
Zannichellia palustris	(Zann)	horned pondweed

Sources of information

References

The (not-new) information, figures and tables in this book come from the following publications. For further information, a convenient way into the voluminous literature is via the reference lists at the end of the books here.

Acts and By-laws: The Agriculture Act 1986; The Environment Act 1995; The Environment Protection Act 1990; The Water Acts 1991; The Wildlife and Countryside Act 1981; The Ministry of Agriculture, Fisheries and Food (MAFF) habitat scheme: water fringe areas, 1994; Statutory Instrument No. 1217, 1988; By-laws of the National Rivers Authority.

Andrews, J. & Kinsman, D. 1990. *Gravel Pit Restoration for Wildlife.* Royal Society for the Protection of Birds, Sandy, Bedfordshire.

Archaeology and Planning. 1990. Planning Policy Guidance Note 16, Department of the Environment.

Boon, P.J., Calow, P. & Petts, G.P. 1992. *River Conservation and Management.* John Wiley and Sons, Chichester.

Brookes, A. 1988. *Channelized Rivers: Perspectives for Environmental Management.* John Wiley and Sons, Chichester.

Carbiener, R. & Ortscheit, A. 1987. Wasserpflan zengesellschafen als Hilfe zur Qualität süberwachung eines der grössen Grundwasser – Vorkammens Europas (Oberrheinabene). In A. Miyawaki (ed.), *Vegetation Ecology and Creation of New Environments. Proc. Intern. Symp. Tokyo.* Tokai University Press, Tokyo, pp. 283–312.

Clapham, A.R., Tutin, T.G., & Moore, D.M. 1987. *Flora of the British Isles.* 3rd edn. Cambridge University Press, Cambridge. (*Total flora, definitive, no illustrations.*)

Darvill, T.C. 1987. *Ancient Monuments in the Countryside.* English Heritage.

Ekwall, E. 1960. *The Concise English Dictionary of English Place Names.* Oxford University Press, Oxford.

Gordon, N.D., McMahon, T.A. & Finlayson, B.O. 1992. *Stream Hydrology: An Introduction for Ecologists.* John Wiley and Sons, Chichester.

Granville, A.B. 1971. *Spas of England.* 2nd edn. Adams & Dart, Bath.

Haslam, S.M. 1978. *River Plants.* Cambridge University Press, Cambridge.

Haslam, S.M. 1987. *River Plants of Western Europe.* Cambridge University Press, Cambridge.

Haslam, S.M. 1990. *River Pollution: An Ecological Perspective.* Belhaven Press, London.

Haslam, S.M. 1991. *The Historic River,* Cobden of Cambridge Press, Cambridge.

Haslam, S.M., Harding, J.C. & Spence, J.H.N. 1987. (Authors not listed on title page.) Methods for the use of aquatic macrophytes for assessing water quality 1985-86. *Methods for the Examination of Waters and Associated Materials.* HMSO, London.

Haslam, S.M., Sinker, C.A. & Wolseley, P.A. 1982. *British Water Plants.* Field Studies Council.

Haslam, S.M. & Wolseley, P.A. 1981. *River Vegetation.* Cambridge University Press, Cambridge.

Hellawell, J.M. 1986. *Biological Indicators of Freshwater Pollution and Environmental Management.* Elsevier Applied Science, London.

Holmes, N.T.H. 1983. *Typing British Rivers According to their Flora.* Nature Conservancy Council, Attingham Park, Shrewsbury.

Holmes, N.T.H. 1993. *British Rivers According to their Flora – Update.* Report, Scottish Natural Heritage.

Klrby, P. 1992. *Habitat Management for Invertebrates· A Practical Hand Book.* Royal Society for the Protection of Birds, Sandy, Bedfordshire.

Köhler, A., Abt, K. & Zdesny, H. 1989. Das grünland gebiet des württembergischen Allgäu aus der sicht der Landschaftsökologie. *Information für der Landwirtsch-aftsberatung in Baden Württemberg.* Baden, Würtemburg, pp. 335–47.

Lachat, B. 1991. *Le cours d'eau, entretion et aménagemant.* Serie aménagement et gestion, **2.** Council of Europe, Strasbourg.

Lack, P. (ed.) 1986. *The Atlas of Wintering Birds in Britain and Ireland.* British Trust for Ornithology, Irish Wildbird Conservancy, Tring.

Murphy, K.J. & Eaton, I.W. 1983. The effects of pleasure boat traffic on macrophyte growth in canals. *J. Appl. Ecol.,* **20,** 713–29.

Newbold, C., Honnor, J. & Buckley, K. 1989. *Nature Conservation and the Management of Drainage Channels.* Nature Conservancy Council and ADAS, Peterborough.

Purseglove, J. 1989. *Taming the Flood.* Oxford University Press and Channel Four Television Co., Oxford.

Schedel, H. *Liber cronicarum.* Nüremburg (*The Nüremburg Chronicle*).

Sharrock, J.T.R. (ed.) 1976. *The Atlas of Breeding Birds in Britain and Ireland*. British Trust for Ornithology, Irish Wildbird Conservancy, Tring.

Spencer-Jones, D. & Wade, M. 1986. *Aquatic Plants: A Guide to Recognition*. ICI Professional Products, Woolmead House East, Farnham, Surrey. (*Common species, colour photographs*.)

Stuart, M. (ed.). 1982. *The Colour Dictionary of Herbs and Herbalism*. Orbis, London.

The Management of Archaeological Projects. 1991. (Second Edition) English Heritage.

The Otter Trust, Earsham, Bungay, Suffolk.

The Royal Society for the Protection of Birds.

Trubshaw, R.N. 1990. *Holy Wells and Springs of Leicestershire and Rutland*. Heart of Albion Press, Loughborough.

Ward, D. 1991. River Banks and their bird communities. *River Bank Conservation*. Hatfield Polytechnic Occasional papers in Environmental Studies, 11, 9–20.

Wolseley, P.A., Palmer, M.A., & Williams, R. 1984. *The Aquatic Flora of the Somerset Levels and Moors. S.W. Region.* Nature Conservancy Council (Dyke Management).

Organisations

There are many organisations with relevant knowledge on rivers, and these may have literature or experts available for consultation. These include:

ADAS, Agriculture and Drainage Advisory Service.

Aerial photograph collections (universities, research organisations, ecological consultants)

Angling societies, periodicals, books, etc.

British Trust for Ornithology.

BSBI, Botanical Society of the British Isles.

Canoe Club.

Conservation organisations, statutory and voluntary.

Countryside Commission.

Countryside Council for Wales.

County Trusts for nature conservation/wildlife.

EA, Environment Agency (formerly National Rivers Authority)

Ecological consultants, various.

Electricity companies (much water used in power development).

English Heritage.

English Nature.

Field Studies Council.

Forestry Commission.

Freshwater Biological Association.

IDBs, Internal Drainage Boards.

Institute of Field Archaeologists.

Institute of Freshwater Ecology.

Institute of Terrestrial Ecology.

Institute of water and environmental management.

Local history experts and books on towns, monuments, shrines, wells, etc.

Long Ashton Research Station (Sonning station), Aquatic Weeds Unit.

MAFF, Ministry of Agriculture, Fisheries and Food.

Maps, old and new, large and small scale, geological, solid and drift.

National Water Council, maps, etc.

NCC Flood Studies Reports.

NCC Nature Conservancy Council (now English Nature and Scottish Natural Heritage and Countryside Council for Wales).

(NRA, The National Rivers Authority.)

Otter Trust.

Red Data Books.

River Purification Boards.

Royal Commission on the Historic Monuments of England.

Royal Commission on the Historic Monuments of Wales.Royal Society for Nature Conservation (and its component organisations).

Royal Society for the Protection of Birds (also see *The New River and Wildlife Handbook*, 1994. Ed. D. Ward, N. Holmes, P. Jose).

Scottish Agricultural College.

Scottish Environment Protection Agency

Scottish Natural Heritage.

Scottish Office.

Surface Water Year Books (old).

Victoria County History.

Vincent Trust.

Water companies.

Water Space Amenity Commission.

Wildlife Trusts.

Index

Some index entries give only the main references for the topic. These are indicated by the word 'main'.